DUMBARTON OAKS TEXTS

XI

THE CORRESPONDENCE OF IGNATIOS THE DEACON

CORPUS FONTIUM
HISTORIAE BYZANTINAE

CONSILIO SOCIETATIS INTERNATIONALIS
STUDIIS BYZANTINIS
PROVEHENDIS DESTINATAE EDITUM

VOLUMEN XXXIX

IGNATII DIACONI EPISTOLAE

EDIDIT, ANGLICE VERTIT, ADNOTAVIT
CYRILLUS MANGO

ADIUVANTE STEPHANO EUTHYMIADI

SERIES WASHINGTONIENSIS,
EDIDIT IHOR ŠEVČENKO

In aedibus Dumbarton Oaks
Washingtoniae, D.C.
MCMXCVII

THE CORRESPONDENCE OF IGNATIOS THE DEACON

TEXT, TRANSLATION, AND COMMENTARY

by

CYRIL MANGO

WITH THE COLLABORATION OF STEPHANOS EFTHYMIADIS

Dumbarton Oaks
Research Library and Collection
Washington, D.C.
1997

Manufactured in the United States of America by
Sheridan Books, Inc., 450 Fame Avenue, Hanover, PA 17331 | (717) 632-3535

LIBRARY OF CONGRESS CATALOGING IN PUBLICATION DATA
Ignatios, the Deacon, ca. 775–ca. 848.
[Correspondence. English]
The correspondence of Ignatios, the Deacon
text, translation, and commentary by Cyril Mango ;
with the collaboration of Stephanos Efthymiadis.
(Dumbarton Oaks texts ; 11) (Corpus Fontium Historiae Byzantinae ; 39)

Includes bibliographical references and indexes.

ISBN 978-0-88402-243-5 (hardcover: alk. paper)
ISBN 978-0-88402-451-4 (paperbound: alk. paper)
LCCN permalink: https://lccn.loc.gov/96033247

1. Ignatios, the Deacon, ca. 775–ca. 848—Correspondence.
I. Mango, Cyril A. II. Efthymiadis, Stephanos.
III. Title. IV. Series. V. Series: Dumbarton Oaks texts ; 11.
BX395.I45A4 1997
270.3'092–DC20 96-33247

In accordance with the rules adopted by the
International Commission
for the Edition of Sources of Byzantine History,
the text and translation of this volume have been verified
by Ihor Ševčenko

EU GPSR Authorised Representative
LOGOS EUROPE, 9 rue Nicolas Poussin, 17000, La Rochelle, France
E-mail: Contact@logoseurope.eu

CONTENTS

PREFACE

This slender book has been long in the making; so long, in fact, that I must offer an apology for its unduly tardy appearance. I was first introduced to the Letters of Ignatios by the late P. J. Alexander, who kindly passed on to me a set of photographs of Gedeon's very scarce *editio princeps* of 1903. The existence at Dumbarton Oaks of a microfilm of the *codex unicus,* Vatopedi 588 (procured for the purpose of editing the Letters of Patriarch Photios), enabled me to collate the text. In 1972–73 I organized a seminar on Ignatios at Dumbarton Oaks, in which R. Cormack, J. Duffy, E. and M. Jeffreys, D. O'Meara, and L. Rydén took part and offered many valuable observations. I can only apologize to the above scholars if, after the passage of so many years, I have not always attributed correctly some of the conjectures recorded in the apparatus. The text was subsequently read by I. Ševčenko, who, with his usual acuity, made further emendations, as well as by N. G. Wilson and P. Odorico. I am indebted to K. Alpers for the elucidation of certain difficulties relating to Greek grammarians and to the late Cynthia Stallman for having typed the text on the computer.

In spite of the contribution made by so many eminent scholars, the text remained in parts unsatisfactory and of doubtful interpretation. Further work, I felt, was needed before it could be presented to the public. And so Ignatios was consigned, *τὸ δὴ λεγόμενον*, to the back burner. Finally, in 1990 I went through the text once again with my then students (now doctors) A. Alexakis, S. Efthymiadis, and I. D. Polemis, who provided further suggestions and improvements. So many years having elapsed, it became clear to me that I would not be able to make any significant advance in the resolution of several remaining cruces. So here is the text, warts and all.

The final editing was carried out by Dr. Efthymiadis with the help of a grant made jointly by the British Academy and Oxford University. He is also responsible for the description of the manuscript, which he inspected in the monastery of Vatopedi, and for many substantive additions. Finally, I am grateful to the two anonymous readers, whose detailed comments have been taken into account.

It remains for me to crave the indulgence of the learned public for a piece of work that is far from perfect in spite of all the effort that has gone into it. As Ignatios might have said, quoting Gregory of Nazianzus, *φίλον θεῷ τὸ κατὰ δύναμιν*.

Oxford, August 1995 C.M.

LIST OF ABBREVIATIONS

AASS	*Acta Sanctorum* (Brussels, 1643–)
AJA	*American Journal of Archaeology*
AnalBoll	*Analecta Bollandiana*
BHG[3]	F. Halkin, *Bibliotheca Hagiographica Graeca,* 3rd ed., 3 vols. (Brussels, 1957)
Bonn	*Corpus Scriptorum Historiae Byzantinae,* ed. B. G. Niebuhr et al. (Bonn, 1828–97)
BSl	*Byzantinoslavica*
Bury, *System*	J. B. Bury, *The Imperial Administrative System in the Ninth Century* (London, 1911)
Byz	*Byzantion*
BZ	*Byzantinische Zeitschrift*
CahArch	*Cahiers archéologiques*
CFHB	Corpus Fontium Historiae Byzantinae
Chron. Pasch.	*Chronicon Paschale,* ed. L. Dindorf, I (Bonn, 1832)
Darrouzès, *Épistoliers*	J. Darrouzès, *Épistoliers byzantins du X*[e] *siècle* (Paris, 1960)
Darrouzès, *Notitiae*	J. Darrouzès, *Notitiae episcopatuum Ecclesiae Constantinopolitanae* (Paris, 1981)
Darrouzès, *Offikia*	J. Darrouzès, *Recherches sur les ὀφφίκια de l'Église byzantine* (Paris, 1970)
DHGE	*Dictionnaire d'histoire et de géographie ecclésiastiques* (Paris, 1912–)
Dölger, *Regesten*	F. Dölger, *Regesten der Kaiserurkunden des oströmischen Reiches von 565–1453,* 5 vols., (Munich-Berlin, 1924–65)
DOP	*Dumbarton Oaks Papers*
ΕΕΒΣ	*Ἐπετηρὶς Ἑταιρείας Βυζαντινῶν Σπουδῶν*
EO	*Échos d'Orient*
Fedalto, *Hierarchia*	G. Fedalto, *Hierarchia Ecclesiastica Orientalis,* 2 vols. (Padua, 1988)
Georg. Mon.	*Georgii Monachi Chronicon,* ed. C. de Boor (Leipzig, 1904)
Grumel, *Regestes*	V. Grumel, *Les regestes des actes du Patriarcat de Constantinople,* vol. I, *Les Actes des patriarches, fasc. II, Les regestes de 715 à 1043* (Constantinople, 1936)
Janin, *CP*	R. Janin, *Constantinople byzantine,* 2nd ed. (Paris, 1964)

LIST OF ABBREVIATIONS

Janin, *Églises*	R. Janin, *La géographie ecclésiastique de l'Empire byzantin, I: Le siège de Constantinople et le Patriarcat oecuménique,* 3: *Les églises et les monastères,* 2nd ed. (Paris, 1969)
Janin, *Grands centres*	R. Janin, *Les églises et les monastères des grands centres byzantins* (Paris, 1975)
JÖB	*Jahrbuch der Österreichischen Byzantinistik*
Karathanasis	D. K. Karathanasis, *Sprichwörter* (Munich, 1936)
Karlsson, *Idéologie*^{2}	G. Karlsson, *Idéologie et cérémonial dans l'épistolographie byzantine,* 2nd ed. (Uppsala, 1962)
ΚΕΦΣ	Ὁ ἐν Κωνσταντινουπόλει ἑλληνικὸς φιλολογικὸς Σύλλογος
Laurent, *Corpus*	V. Laurent, *Le corpus des sceaux de l'Empire byzantin,* vols. II and V (Paris, 1963, 1981)
Lemerle, *Agr. Hist.*	*The Agrarian History of Byzantium from the Origins to the Twelfth Century: The Sources and Problems* (Galway, 1979)
Leo Gr.	Leonis Grammatici *Chronographia,* ed. I. Bekker, Corpus Scriptorum Historiae Byzantinae (Bonn, 1842)
Lequien, *OrChr*	M. Lequien, *Oriens Christianus in quatuor patriarchatus digestus,* 3 vols. (Paris, 1740)
Mango, "Two Lives"	"The Two Lives of St. Ioannikios and the Bulgarians," in *Okeanos: Essays Presented to Ihor Ševčenko on His Sixtieth Birthday by His Colleagues and Students = Harvard Ukrainian Studies* 18 (1983), 393–404
Mansi	*Sacrorum Conciliorun Nova et Amplissima Collectio,* ed. G. D. Mansi (Florence and Venice, 1759–98; reprinted Paris, 1901–)
MGH, *SS*	Monumenta Germaniae Historica, *Scriptores*
ΝέοςἙλλ.	Νέος Ἑλληνομνήμων
ODB	*The Oxford Dictionary of Byzantium,* 3 vols. (New York-Oxford, 1991)
Oikonomidès, *Listes*	N. Oikonomidès, *Les listes de préséance byzantines du IXe et Xe siècles* (Paris, 1972)
PG	Patrologiae cursus completus, series graeca, ed. J. P. Migne (Paris, 1857–66)
Ramsay, *Hist. Geogr.*	W. M. Ramsay, *The Historical Geography of Asia Minor* (London, 1890)
RE	Pauly-Wissowa, *Real-Encyclopädie der classischen Altertumswissenschaft*
REB	*Revue des études byzantines*

LIST OF ABBREVIATIONS

ROC	*Revue de l'Orient chrétien*
SC	Sources chrétiennes
Ševčenko, "Hagiography"	I. Ševčenko, "Hagiography of the Iconoclast Period," in *Iconoclasm,* ed. A. Bryer and J. Herrin (Birmingham, 1977)
Strömberg	R. Strömberg, *Greek Proverbs: A Collection of Proverbs and Proverbial Phrases which are not listed by the Ancient and Byzantine Paroemiographers* (Göteborg, 1954)
Suda	*Suidae Lexicon,* ed. A. Adler, 5 vols. (Leipzig, 1928–38)
Synaxarium CP	*Synaxarium Ecclesiae Constantinopolitanae,* ed. H. Delehaye, *Acta Sanctorum, Propylaeum ad Acta Sanctorum Novembris* (Brussels, 1902)
Theod. Stud.	*Theodori Studitae epistulae,* ed. G. Fatouros, Corpus Fontium Historiae Byzantinae, Series Berolinensis 31.1–2 (Berlin-New York, 1992)
Theoph.	*Theophanis Chronographia,* ed. C. de Boor, 2 vols. (Leipzig, 1883–85)
Theoph. Cont.	*Theophanes Continuatus,* ed. I. Bekker, Corpus Scriptorum Historiae Byzantinae (Bonn, 1842)
TM	*Travaux et mémoires.* Centre de Recherche d'Histoire et Civilisation byzantines (Paris, 1965–)
Treadgold, *Revival*	W. Treadgold, *The Byzantine Revival 780–842* (Stanford, Calif., 1988)
TU	*Texte und Untersuchungen zur Geschichte der altchristlichen Literatur* (Leipzig-Berlin, 1882–)
Vasil'evskij VGA	V. G. Vasil'evskij, *Žitija sv. Georgija Amastridskago,* in *Russko-Vizantijskija izsledovanija,* II (St. Petersburg, 1893) = *Trudy III* (St. Petersburg, 1915)
VGD	F. Dvornik, *La vie de saint Grégoire le Décapolite et les Slaves macédoniens au IXe siècle* (Paris, 1926)
VizVrem	*Vizantijskij Vremennik*
VN	C. de Boor, *Nicephori archiepiscopi Constantinopolitani opuscula historica* (Leipzig, 1880), 139–217
VT	I. A. Heikel, "Ignatii diaconi vita Tarasii archiepiscopi CP," *Acta Societatis Scientiarum Fennicae* 17 (1891), 389–430
Zacos-Veglery	G. Zacos and A. Veglery, *Byzantine Lead Seals,* vol. I (Basel, 1972); vol. II (Berne, 1984)
ZRVI	*Zbornik Radova Vizantološkog Instituta*

INTRODUCTION

DISCOVERY AND PUBLICATION OF THE CORRESPONDENCE

The correspondence of Ignatios, a collection of sixty-four letters, is preserved anonymously in a single MS, Vatopedi 588, which is described below. Its existence was first made public in January 1903 by Daniel Serruys, who presented a paper on this topic before the Académie des Inscriptions et Belles-Lettres.[1] A number of indications led Serruys to the conclusion that the author of the correspondence was named Ignatios, whom he incorrectly identified with the patriarch of that name (847–858; 867–877). He offered a brief analysis of the document he had discovered, drawing attention to the author's complete subordination to the imperial government, his conventional and mediocre mentality, and his frequent recourse to citations from classical literature.

In that same year 1903, all sixty-four letters were published by the prolific Greek scholar Manuel Gedeon in a collection entitled *Νέα βιβλιοθήκη ἐκκλησιαστικῶν συγγραφέων*.[2] They appeared under the title Ἀδήλου (*Θεοφάνους* Νι*καίας*) *ἐπιστολαί*, without any explanatory statement other than the shelfmark of the MS, incorrectly given as Vatopedi 1035. The edition, which contains many errors, was based not on the MS itself, but on a copy executed by the deacon Anthimos of Vatopedi.[3] Its first typographic sheet was somehow "leaked" to the Assumptionist J. Pargoire, who promptly equated Gedeon's sixty-four letters with those described by Serruys and was able to show that their author was neither Patriarch Ignatios nor Theophanes of Nicaea (i.e., St. Theophanes Graptos, d. 845), but Ignatios of Nicaea, better known as Ignatios the deacon.[4] The first fascicle of the Νέα *βιβλιοθήκη* (no more were published) was never put on the market. Under circumstances that are unknown to us, almost the entire edition was destroyed (as Gedeon himself later stated), which is why very few copies of it are now in existence.

Undaunted by this unfortunate experience, Gedeon reissued the correspondence in fascicle 4 of a new collection, called Ἀ*ρχεῖον ἐκκλησιαστικῆς ἱστορίας*,

[1] *Comptes rendus des séances de l'Académie des Inscriptions et Belles-Lettres* (1903), 38ff, 57.

[2] I, fasc. 1 (Constantinople, 1903), 1–64.

[3] On this person, a native of the island of Aphousia, and his reprehensible activity on Mount Athos, see Ch. Ktenas, Ἡ Σ*ύγχρονος* Ἀ*θωνιὰς σχολὴ καὶ οἱ ἐν αὐτῇ διδάξαντες ἀπὸ τοῦ 1845–1916* (Athens, 1930), 65–71.

[4] "Lettres inédites d'Ignace de Nicée," *EO* 6 (1903), 375–78. See also his review of Gedeon's edition in *VizVrem* 10 (1903), 633–34.

published on 10 July 1914.[5] This time he prefaced it with a short statement in which he gave the number of the MS (once again erroneously) as Vatopedi 388, acknowledged his debt to the deacon Anthimos, and defended his attribution of the letters to Theophanes against Pargoire's criticism. As far as we are aware, the fourth fascicle of the Ἀρχεῖον survives in a single copy, the property of the Gennadion Library, Athens. A manuscript note by one G. Arvanitidis on the last page of the book explains that the entire edition was stolen from the press before it could be distributed.

In the light of the above circumstances, it is hardly surprising that the correspondence of Ignatios should have remained virtually unknown to this day. The few scholars who have had an opportunity to refer to it[6] have done so for certain limited purposes without considering its significance as a whole. Only two of the letters have been republished in the original Greek,[7] and one has appeared in a German translation.[8]

THE MANUSCRIPT

Vatopedi 588 (= V) is a small parchment volume (17 × 12 cm) of 196 pages, written in single columns of 22–28 lines, in the early eleventh century.[9] As all other Vatopedi MSS, V was bound in 1870 by the monks Anthimos and Sabas of the skete of St. Demetrios. In its present state the MS is made up of twelve quires; the first quire lacks the first folio. To the last quire have been added three leaves corresponding to pp. 191–96.

The script is a *Perlschrift,* which, according to H. Hunger, should be located in eleventh-century Constantinople.[10] The text is negligently copied, having a number of spelling errors and mistaken compendia. In that respect, the comment of Photios' editors applies equally well to the rest of the MS: "Scriba parum doctus praesertim

---

[5] Pp. 420–87; cf. Ch. G. Patrinelis, *Δημοσιεύματα Μανουὴλ Γεδεών* (Athens, 1974), no. 454, who gives the publication date as 1913.

[6] In particular V. Grumel, V. Laurent, and W. Wolska-Conus as well as G. Karlsson, *Idéologie et cérémonial dans l'épistolographie byzantine* (Uppsala, 1959), 126 ff; 2nd ed. (1962), 125 ff. Some letters were recently discussed by A. Kazhdan, in *BSl* 53 (1992), 197–201. See also Postscript, below, p. 207.

[7] No. 25 by Karlsson, *Idéologie*², 128 ff; no. 41 by H. Wölke, *Untersuchungen zur Batrachyomachie* (Meisenheim am Glan, 1978), 249 (from Karlsson's collation).

[8] No. 37: G. Karlsson, "Eine Insel im Marmarameer," *Orientalia Suecana* 33–35 (1984–86), 211–14.

[9] See S. Eustratiades and Arcadios, *Catalogue of the Greek MSS in the Library of the Monastery of Vatopedi on Mt. Athos* (Cambridge, Mass., 1924), 115. The MS is mistakenly dated to the 12th century. We would like to thank the hieromonk Palamas and the monk Lazaros, librarians of the monastery of Vatopedi, for their warm hospitality and kind assistance while studying the MS *in situ.*

[10] *Studien zur griechischen Paläographie* (Vienna, 1954), 22–32.

in compendiis solvendis saepe erravit, interdum quae intellegere non poterat utcumque delineavit."[11]

V comprises works of three authors:

1. Pseudo-Nonnos' Commentaries on the mythical heroes and stories (*ἱστορίαι*) contained in three homilies of Gregory of Nazianzos (*Clavis Patrum Graecorum* 3011): (a) *Oratio I contra Iulianum* (pp. 1–32—first 50 chaps. missing); (b) *Oratio II contra Iulianum* (pp. 32–58);[12] (c) *Oratio in Sancta Lumina* (pp. 59–73).[13]

2. Correspondence of Ignatios (pp. 74–166).

3. Thirty-five letters of Photios: ed. Laourdas-Westerink, nos. 3–14, 16–18, 21, 22, 24, 25, 27–29, 32, 41–43, 45, 56, 58, 46–48, 52–54 (pp. 166–96).[14]

Chapter headings of Pseudo-Nonnos' scholia and titles of letters are written in accented capitals. V exhibits a considerable number of insignificant marginalia, most of them, it seems, of the twelfth–thirteenth centuries.

THE AUTHOR

In spite of several attempts to elucidate it,[15] the biography of Ignatios remains something of a puzzle: we have many of its constituent pieces but do not know how to put them together. A starting point is provided by the notice devoted to him in the tenth-century *Suda* lexicon (I, 84; ed. Adler, II, 607 ff):

> Ignatios, deacon and *skevophylax* of the Great Church of Constantinople, at one time (*γεγονώς*) metropolitan of Nicaea, a *grammatikos*. He wrote the Lives of Tarasios and Nikephoros, the holy and blessed patriarchs; funerary

[11] *Photii epistulae et Amphilochia*, ed. B. Laourdas and L. G. Westerink, vol. I (Leipzig, 1983), xiii.

[12] PG 36, 1036C–1058A; *Ps. Nonniani in IV orationes Gregorii Nazianzeni Commentarii*, ed. J. Nimmo Smith, Corpus Christianorum, Series graeca 27 (1992), where Vatop. 588 is listed (p. 17) as a 12th-century MS.

[13] Of which part is published in PG 36, 1065B–1072D.

[14] See vol. I, xiii.

[15] Among relatively recent studies we may mention E. E. Lipšic, "O pohode Rusi na Vizantiju ranee 842 goda," *Istoričeskie zapiski* 26 (1948), 312 ff; G. Marenghi, "Ignazio diacono e i Tetrastichi giambici," *Emerita* 25 (1957), 487–98; R. Browning, "Ignace le diacre et la tragédie classique à Byzance," *Revue des études grecques* 81 (1968), 401–10; W. Wolska-Conus, "De quibusdam Ignatiis," *TM* 4 (1970), 329–60; C. Mango, "Observations on the Correspondence of Ignatius, Metropolitan of Nicaea," *TU* 125 (1981), 403–10 = *Byzantium and Its Image* (London, 1984), XII; S. Efthymiadis, *The "Vita Tarasii" and the Hagiographical Work of Ignatios the Deacon*, D.Phil. thesis (Oxford, 1991), 74 ff (who argues for a slightly different reconstruction of Ignatios' career from the one adopted here, namely, that he became *skevophylax* during the patriarchate of Nikephoros (806–815) and metropolitan of Nicaea probably in 815–816); A. Kazhdan, as in note 6 and Postscript.

elegies; epistles; an iambic poem concerning Thomas the rebel, which is called τὰ κατὰ Θωμᾶν, and other works.

Short as the entry is, it raises several questions. First, why is it that Ignatios, who cannot be described as an intellectual figure of the first magnitude, was judged worthy of an entry in the *Suda,* which contains notices of only *two* other Byzantine authors later than the sixth century, namely, George of Pisidia and St. John Damascene? Second, what is the precise force of the perfect participle γεγονώς, which applies only to his tenure as metropolitan of Nicaea, and why, granted that he was a bishop, is he described by the inferior rank of deacon?

Ad primum, the following explanation has been offered. Hesychios of Miletos (first half of the 6th century) is known to have composed an *Onomatologos,* which was a biographical index of secular authors, excluding the Christian fathers (*Suda,* Adler, II, 594). A complementary series devoted to Christian authors had been provided earlier by the Greek translation (by Sophronios) of Jerome's *De viris illustribus.* In the second quarter of the ninth century (or so it has been surmised), these two works were combined and boiled down to an alphabetically arranged Epitome, which is thought to have been the common source of the biographical notices contained in both the *Bibliotheca* of Photios and the *Suda.*[16] Now, the *Suda,* as we have said, has notices of only three "Byzantine" authors. The inclusion of George of Pisidia (Adler, I, 517), regarded as a poet of the highest distinction throughout the Byzantine period, causes no surprise. In the case of St. John Damascene (Adler, II, 649), his struggle for the cause of icons as well as his numerous theological and philosophical works are, strangely enough, not mentioned in the *Suda,* which praises instead the beauty of his hymns. But why the relatively obscure Ignatios? The fact that both Jerome and Hesychios added to their compilations biographies of themselves has led to the supposition that Ignatios may have done the same in the Epitome, which was consequently his work.[17] If so, his biographical notice is a self-portrait. Since it mentions the Lives of Tarasios and Nikephoros, it could hardly have been written before 843. At the time, as we shall see, Ignatios was leaving no stone unturned in showing his devotion to "orthodoxy." It may be thought strange, therefore, that he would have omitted to comment on the Damascene's opposition to Iconoclasm, not to mention the apparent exclusion from the Epitome of a whole string of eminent orthodox authors from Sophronios of Jerusalem and Maximos the Confessor down to Patriarch Nikephoros.

The above argument is, admittedly, highly speculative. It may be that no

[16] G. Wentzel, *Die griechischen Übersetzungen der Viri illustres des Hieronymus, TU* 13.3 (1895). The issues raised by this unduly neglected study deserve to be reexamined.

[17] So W. T. Treadgold, *The Nature of the Bibliotheca of Photius* (Washington, D.C., 1980), 31 ff.

Epitome ever existed,[18] or, if it did, that Ignatios was not its author. The notice devoted to him in the *Suda* does, however, call for an explanation. If it was not written by Ignatios himself, it must be due to one of his associates, seeing that his reputation was not above reproach and is not likely to have outlived him by a long period of time. That brings us to our next question. The formula *γεγονώς* is not unknown. We find it, for example, in the title of the collected letters of another metropolitan of Nicaea, Alexander (tenth century): *Ἀλεξάνδρου τοῦ γεγονότος μητροπολίτου Νικαίας . . . ἐπιστολαί.* As the editor remarks, "L'expression *γεγονότος* signifie qu'Alexandre *a été* métropolite de Nicée mais qu'il ne l'était plus et qu'il ne l'est pas redevenu après son exil." [19] It may be thought, therefore, that Ignatios, at the time when his notice was written, was deacon and *skevophylax,* but was no longer bishop of Nicaea. Alternatively, if the notice was written after his death, it may mean that he was best known by the titles deacon and *skevophylax* or that those were the last titles he held, but that he had also, at one time, held the see of Nicaea. Before we come back to this matter, it may be useful to review the other items of information given in the notice.

i. *Deacon.* As deacon of the Great Church, Ignatios would have belonged to an élite group from which dignitaries of the Patriarchate and bishops were regularly chosen. In the sixth century the number of deacons attached to the cathedral of Constantinople was limited to one hundred,[20] but we do not know how many of them existed at any one time in the ninth century. The *Kletorologion* of Philotheos (899) states that twelve deacons of the Great Church were invited to the imperial table on Epiphany day.[21]

ii. *Skevophylax.* Keeper of religious plate, furniture, and liturgical books of the patriarchal cathedral, presumably appointed by the emperor.[22] Little as we know concerning the administrative structure of the Patriarchate in the first half of the ninth century, this was certainly an important office. Ignatios himself reports that when Leo V was applying pressure to remove Nikephoros from the patriarchal throne (in 815), he entrusted to a patrician (hence a layman) *τὰ τοῦ λόγου τῆς ἐκκλησίας καὶ τῶν ἱερῶν σκευῶν ἀναθήματα.*[23] This patrician, who was named Thomas,[24] seems,

---

[18] So J. Schamp, *Photios historien des lettres* (Paris, 1987), 53 ff.

[19] Darrouzès, *Epistoliers,* 68 note 1. We may also cite the example of James the hesychast, mentioned in the *Vita of St. Peter of Atroa,* who was former bishop of Anchialos and is designated by the same participle, *γεγονότα*: ed. Laurent (below, note 31), §65.5. On the same James see S. Efthymiadis, "Notes on the Correspondence of Theodore the Studite," *REB* 53 (1995), 146 note 24.

[20] *Nov. Just.,* 3.1 (a. 535).

[21] Oikonomidès, *Listes,* 185.25. For other references and bibliography, see *ODB,* 592.

[22] See Darrouzès, *Offikia,* 314 ff; see also *ODB,* 1909–10.

[23] See VN 190.16.

[24] *Scriptor incertus de Leone Armenio,* Bonn ed., 358.11 ff.

therefore, to have combined the functions of *oikonomos* (rather than logothete)[25] and *skevophylax.* He must have been in a position to make life uncomfortable for the recalcitrant patriarch—in part, as P. J. Alexander suggests,[26] because the *skevophylax* had charge of the icons.

iii. *Metropolitan of Nicaea.* This appointment must have occurred some time between 815, when the "orthodox" Peter was removed from his post,[27] and 843, hence certainly under iconoclastic rule. The two Lives of St. Ioannikios (those by Peter and Sabas respectively) relate a story about an iconoclastic bishop of Nicaea called Inger, whose imminent death was predicted by the great ascetic.[28] The incident, which is unfortunately undated, appears to have happened some time after 822, if we follow Peter's more reliable chronology.[29] Inger (who must have had, in addition, a Christian name) may have been, therefore, Peter's immediate successor. In that case, he was the person whom Theodore the Studite, in writing to the deposed Peter between 815 and 818, describes as "a piece of rubbish" (*κάθαρμα*) and *ὡς ἀληθῶς ἑτερόφθαλμος* (having different-colored eyes?).[30] If Ignatios came after Inger, he may have been ordained under Michael II, whose exploits against the rebel Thomas he celebrated in iambic verse. However, we cannot exclude the possibility that he came before Inger, in which case he was the subject of the Studite's uncomplimentary characterization.

Nicaea was surely a desirable bishopric, not so much in terms of patronage (the metropolitan had only six suffragans, all of them in minor localities) as because of its rank (8th in the order of precedence) and proximity to the capital. Besides, Nicaea was one of the few provincial towns that had not, at one time or another, fallen to the enemy, and so must have offered better amenities than a number of hierarchically more important but devastated cities.

We do not know how long Ignatios held the see of Nicaea. The next incumbent known to us is St. Theophanes Graptos (843–11 Oct. 845). Both the evidence of the Letters and the severity of Patriarch Methodios' policy toward the *lapsi* make it plain that Ignatios could not have been Theophanes' successor, as some scholars have supposed.[31]

---

[25] On the *oikonomos* see Darrouzès, *Offikia,* 16f, 36f, 303ff; on the ecclesiastical logothete, whose early functions are unclear, ibid., 359ff.

[26] *The Patriarch Nicephorus of Constantinople* (Oxford, 1958), 133–34.

[27] See S. Vailhé, "S. Michel de Syncelle et les deux frères Grapti," *ROC* 6 (1901), 634.

[28] *Vita* by Peter, c. 38, *AASS,* Nov. II.1, 408; *vita* by Sabas, c. 30, ibid., 360.

[29] The date of ca. 827, given by Van de Gheyn, ibid., 364 note 1, and reproduced by Vailhé, loc. cit., is simply a guess. See Mango, "Two Lives," 395ff, which attempts to show that the chronology of the Vita by Sabas has been deliberately doctored and should not be relied on.

[30] Theod. Stud., letter 313.19–20, ed. Fatouros, 456; for the date see ibid., 341*.

[31] E.g., V. Laurent, *La vita retractata et les miracles posthumes de saint Pierre d'Atroa* (Brussels, 1958), 152 note 3. Ignatios is listed after Theophanes Graptos in Lequien, *OrChr,* I, 644 and Fedalto, *Hierarchia,* I, 108.

iv. *Grammatikos.* In late antiquity, a *grammatikos* was a "secondary" teacher as distinct, on the one hand, from the *grammatistes* (primary teacher) and, on the other, from the rhetor or sophist, who conducted higher education, but it is a matter of doubt if this definition still held good in the ninth century. Two prominent contemporaries or near-contemporaries of Ignatios bore the title of *grammatikos:* George Choiroboskos, who is styled in manucripts *γραμματικὸς καὶ οἰκουμενικὸς διδάσκαλος*,[32] and the iconoclast John (patriarch of Constantinople, 838–843), but in neither case do we know the precise nature of their teaching activity. There is independent evidence that Ignatios was active as a teacher, and we shall return to this point later.

v. *The Life of Tarasios* (*BHG*[3] 1698).[33] There can be little doubt that this work (VT) was written in or after 843, as shown by the following considerations:

1. The author is styled "monk" in the title (Ἰγνατίου μοναχοῦ). We shall see that toward the end of his life Ignatios was relegated to a monastery by Patriarch Methodios. By itself, this datum is not conclusive because an earlier period of monastic reclusion is also recorded (below, p. 19f).

2. The author complains of his old age and ill health (p. 423.25: *ἀπορίᾳ λόγου καὶ γήρᾳ καὶ νόσῳ καμπτόμενος*).

3. Especially significant is the passage praising Tarasios for his moderation in 787 with regard to doctrinally compromised clergy (pp. 405.33–406.7). No injudicious charge, we are told, was made either before the council or after the council against any member of the clergy concerning the impiety that had previously prevailed; clerics and bishops who had been ordained by heretics were not suspended—instead, they were received with open arms on condition that they renounced their error in writing. In laying stress on the *oikonomia* evinced by Tarasios, Ignatios was tacitly contrasting it with the severity of Methodios, of which he himself had to suffer the consequences (see below, p. 11f).

In view of the apologetic nature of VT, we should be on our guard not to accept

---

[32] Cf. P. Lemerle, *Le premier humanisme byzantin* (Paris, 1971), 79ff; Darrouzès, *Offikia,* 22f and 68 note 1; N. G. Wilson, *Scholars of Byzantium* (London, 1983), 70ff. W. Bühler and Chr. Theocharidis, *BZ* 69 (1976), 397–401, argue that Choiroboskos should be placed between ca. 750 and the beginning of the ninth century, the earlier *terminus* being fixed by his use of John Damascene and the later by quotations of him in the *Etymologicum genuinum* (whose date and textual history are, however, subject to some doubt). His dependence on John Damascene had earlier been demonstrated by A. Papadopoulos-Kerameus, "K istorii grečeskih etimologikov," *Žurnal Ministerstra Narodnogo Prosveščenija* 319 (Sept. 1898), 115–33. Cf. C. Mango, "The Collapse of St. Sophia, Psellus and the *Etymologicum Genuinum,*" in *Gonimos: Neoplatonic and Byzantine Studies Presented to L. G. Westerink* (Buffalo, N.Y., 1988), ed. J. Duffy and J. Peradotto, 167–74. For the use and meaning of the word *grammatikos* in late antiquity, see R. A. Kaster, *Guardians of Language: The Grammarian and Society in Late Antiquity* (Berkeley-Los Angeles-London, 1988), 453–54.

[33] It may be noted that a late date of VT was first advanced by I. Andreev, *German i Tarasij, patriarhi Konstantinopol'skie* (Sergiev Posad, 1907), 61 note 1.

at face value all the information it provides.[34] We suspect in particular that Ignatios, in trying to establish his good reputation, may have exaggerated the extent of his familiarity with Tarasios, whom he probably knew less closely than he would have us believe. We need not doubt his presence at the patriarch's deathbed (p. 419.28), but some caution may be indicated in interpreting the oft-quoted passage in the peroration (p. 423.5–11):

> I shall not forget the useful instruction you gave me nor the devoted service, humble as it was, that I offered you. The former I enjoyed in the prime of my youth (*ἐν ἀκμῇ τῆς νεότητος*) when I was initiated by you in the best examples (*τὰ κράτιστα*) of the trimeter and the tetrameter, both trochaic and anapestic, and in dactylic verse; the latter I performed in noting with swift pen and ink the sacred discourses that you delivered with care, day after day, for the edification of souls and handed over to the best scribes to be artfully consigned to books.[35]

This passage is of importance for the biography of Ignatios since it shows that he acted as stenographer to Tarasios and so, presumably, must have had some notarial training; but we are not sure we can also conclude from it that Ignatios received from the patriarch (or the patriarch to be) a regular course of instruction in ancient prosody rather than some hints for further study.[36] If Ignatios had been closely acquainted with Tarasios, we might have expected VT to contain more personal information than it does.

vi. *The Life of Nikephoros* (*BHG*[3] 1335). If the dating and purpose of VT raise little difficulty of interpretation, the same cannot, unfortunately, be said of this work (VN), Ignatios' most elaborate work of hagiography. On this score two conflicting opinions have been expressed: (1) that VN was written in ca. 829;[37] (2) that its final version was produced between 843 and 846.[38] Our understanding of Ignatios' career is seriously affected if we adopt one or the other of these alternatives.

It should be said at the outset that VN cannot be earlier than October 829, as

---

[34] E. von Dobschütz, "Methodios und die Studiten," *BZ* 18 (1909), 59, already argued that VT was in the nature of a political tract and that it was composed at the instigation of Methodios. A more specifically anti-Studite stance is advanced by P. Speck, "Die Ursprünge der byzantinischen Renaissance," *17th International Byzantine Congress, Major Papers* (Washington, D.C., 1986), 568 ff.

[35] With the exception of the homily "On the Entrance of the Virgin Mary" (PG 98, 1481A–1500B), none of Tarasios' sermons has, however, survived; cf. Efthymiadis, *The "Vita Tarasii,"* 7–9. The practice of taking down sermons in shorthand is well attested in late antiquity.

[36] In Mango, "Correspondence of Ignatius," 407, this statement may have been taken too literally.

[37] So P. J. Alexander, "Secular Biography at Byzantium," *Speculum* 15 (1940), 204 note 3 (with references to the previous bibliography); Wolska-Conus, "De quibusdam Ignatiis," 339, 348.

[38] So von Dobschütz, "Methodios," 54 ff, and esp. Ševčenko, "Hagiography," 125.

Ševčenko has already pointed out, since it refers explicitly to the death of Michael II: in the words of our author, the emperor was enmeshed like a fish in the net of heresy and died together with his unsound doctrines (p. 209.10–11: *τοῖς τῶν δογμάτων σαθροῖς ἐναπέθανεν*). With this proviso, let us examine the case for an early date, which can be supported by the following arguments, the majority of which have been advanced by Vasil'evskij.[39]

1. In the exordium (pp. 139–40), Ignatios appears to be speaking of Nikephoros' death (5 April 828) as a recent event, which fills him with sorrow and dismay.[40]

2. In the concluding section (pp. 214.17–215.12), Nikephoros is compared to a lion whose death gave courage to the Iconoclasts, represented here as jackals, foxes, and hares. Now that the patriarch's lips have been stilled, our author adds, the heretics have mounted to the pinnacle of joy; they have laid aside all pretense and have been publishing their hair-splitting rigmaroles, "which, I am sure, will be scattered by the luminous shafts of our Father's discourses and will recede into nonexistence." In other words, the rigmaroles in question have not yet been refuted; the Iconoclasts, as Ignatios says, are still enjoying *παρρησία* (p. 214.26). It is difficult to square these statements with the situation after 843.

3. When the exiled Nikephoros was moved from the monastery *τῶν* 'Αγαθοῦ to the more remote monastery of St. Theodore (probably in 816), the emperor's nephew Bardas was delegated to oversee the transfer and did not have the courtesy to rise from his seat in the presence of the aged patriarch. Nikephoros warned him to learn a lesson from other people's misfortunes, a "prediction" that was fulfilled four years later: Bardas experienced a calamity, which reduced him to a sorry appearance, as anyone can see for himself (p. 201.25–26: *εἴ τῳ φίλον τὰ περὶ τούτου τελέως πιστώσασθαι, ἐντευξάσθω τοῦ ἀνδρός*). We are not told what the calamity was, but Alexander may well be right in suggesting that Bardas was mutilated on the accession of Michael II.[41] Although we do not know how long he survived his misfortune, the invitation to meet him in person would make more sense in ca. 829–830 than after 843.

4. Ignatios makes the heresy of Leo V responsible for various natural calamities and for civil war. He then adds: "From that time until this day, the disease of

---

[39] In *Russko-Vizantijskija izsledovanija,* II (St. Petersburg, 1893), xcvii note 3 (= *Trudy,* III [St. Petersburg, 1915]).

[40] It should be noted that neither the day nor the year of Nikephoros' death as transmitted by other texts accords with the day of Easter 828 recorded by Ignatios in VN 213.22–24. The *Synaxarium CP* and the *Menologia* agree that the patriarch died on 2 June 828, whereas the *Oration on His Exile and the Translation of His Relics* by the priest Theophanes (*BHG*[3] 1335–37f) places his demise after fourteen and not thirteen years of exile; see F. Halkin, *AnalBall* 76 (1958), 231–32.

[41] *The Patriarch Nicephorus,* 148.

internecine misfortune has prevailed" (p. 207.20–22: *ἐξ ἐκείνου γὰρ καὶ μέχρι νῦν τὸ δεινὸν τῆς ἐμφυλίου συμφορᾶς ἐπικρατῆσαι συμβέβηκε νόσημα*). He must be thinking, in the first instance, of the revolt of Thomas the Slav, which lasted until 823.[42] We are not informed of any other civil disturbance in the reign of Michael II, although it may be supposed that the effects of Thomas' rebellion persisted for a number of years. But what point would there have been in making such a statement after 843?

Now the case for a late date of VN.

1. It is virulently anti-iconoclastic in tone: a torrent of abuse is poured on Leo V, who, in addition to his other iniquities, is charged with treason (p. 163.6–8), and Michael II, too, is treated with scant courtesy. We have seen that Michael is described as being caught in the net of heresy; though appearing to be moderate, he concealed a disposition similar to Leo's. Furthermore, he is accused of ignorance, which he inherited in rich measure from the boorishness of his ancestors (p. 209.27–28). If Ignatios was publicly expressing such sentiments in ca. 830, he must have been exposing himself to considerable risk.

2. The lengthy peroration (pp. 215–17) is reminiscent of other abject admissions of guilt, which Ignatios made toward the end of his life. Here he prays to the dead Nikephoros to take pity on his "defeat and fall." He had been deceived (by his ordination?)[43] and polluted by communion (*κοινωνία*) with heretics, without, however, defiling his own conscience. he wishes to cleanse himself by means of repentance and "bitter penance," although he adds that he is not in need of instruction, having kept (presumably within his heart) the true doctrine. "I am certain," he continues, "that I shall suffer no small punishment on account of this, my fall; nay, I shall receive many blows for having acknowledged the Lord's will without carrying it out, and I shall weep without end for not having found the repentance I sought." He prays to be delivered from "the flood of unbelief" lest he be "drowned in the stormy waters of heresy." He had been entrapped not of his own free will, but under pressure "of threats both severe and shaky" (*δριμείαις εἰ καὶ ὑποσάθροις ἀπειλαῖς*). Now, however, he had ceased being a "Canaanite" and had renounced all "Canaanite" doctrines.

The difficulties we have noted may be partly resolved by the supposition that VN as we have it represents a revision of an earlier draft written, say, in ca. 830.[44] If

---

[42] On which see P. Lemerle, "Thomas le Slave," *TM* 1 (1965), 255–97.

[43] See VN 215.27: *χειρὶ κλαπέντας*, an obscure expression. Ševčenko, "Hagiography," 125 note 91, may well be right in explaining it as deceived by *cheirotonia*.

[44] The possibility of a revision is envisaged for other reasons by Lemerle, *Le premier humanisme*, 131.

that were so, it would follow that Ignatios had become a convinced anti-iconoclast by the early years of the reign of Theophilos, for it is hard to imagine that any biography of Nikephoros, no matter how worded, would have been other than anti-iconoclastic. The earlier draft, of course, would have been left unpublished, and when Ignatios exhumed it from his papers and proceeded to rewrite it, he may have neglected to alter a few passages that did not correspond any longer to the existing situation. The revision may have been carried out in 843 or later; indeed, the peroration appears to reflect the peculiar conditions that obtained during the patriarchate of Methodios, whose policy toward the iconoclastic clergy is highly relevant in this connection.[45]

Methodios himself admits to having been inclined to adopt a conciliatory line, but was dissuaded from doing so by his "brethren" (members of his synod) as well as by St. Ioannikios, who warned him quite bluntly: "If you receive the heretical ministers (*λειτουργούς*, i.e., deacons) and priests, you would be introducing into the Church not only Judaism, but also paganism."[46] In the event, the following course was adopted on the recommendation, it seems, of Sergios I, patriarch of Jerusalem: clerks who had been ordained by Tarasios or Nikephoros were to be readmitted and retain their original rank, but, as it were, in a lower category (*ἐν δευτέρᾳ τάξει*), provided they repented sincerely and anathematized the leaders of the heresy. The rest, that is, those who had been ordained by iconoclastic patriarchs, were to be permanently excluded from the clergy, anointed with oil like repenting Arians, and subjected to instruction (*κατηχήσεσι*).[47] In writing to the patriarch of Jerusalem in the spring of 846, Methodios regretfully admits that, even in the first group, none had shown any "fruit of repentance by way of self-abasing speech, harsh discipline of life, or voluntary reclusion (*ἠρεμίας ἐθελουσίου*); nay, they continued to behave in an arrogant and condescending manner."[48]

"None" is perhaps an exaggeration, and we may be sure that Ignatios was one of the exceptions. Having been ordained deacon in all probability by Tarasios or Nikephoros, he was entitled to keep that rank. He protested his repentance as loudly as possible, condemned the leaders of Iconoclasm in his writings, declared himself not to be in need of instruction (hence *μόνης ἐπιστροφῆς ἀλλ' οὐ διδαχῆς δεομένους τὸ σύνολον* in VN 215.30–216.1), and, after submitting to some kind of inquisition (letter 40), underwent, perhaps not altogether voluntarily, a period of

[45] See J. Darrouzès, "Le patriarche Méthode contre les iconoclastes et les Stoudites," *REB* 45 (1987), 15–57.

[46] Ibid., 54, fragm. 2.

[47] Ibid., 56, Testament = Grumel, *Regestes,* I.2–3, ed. Darrouzès (1989), 434 [435].

[48] Ed. J. B. Pitra, *Iuris ecclesiastici graecorum historia et monumenta,* II (Rome, 1868), 355–56.

reclusion in the monastery of Pikridion. In this manner he cleared his name and reestablished his position.

For the title of VN, see below, p. 20.

vii. *Funerary Elegies.* Three are preserved: *Anth. Pal.* xv.29 (an epitaph on himself containing a characteristic admission of sin, *Ἰγνάτιος πολλῇσιν ἐν ἀμπλακίῃσι βιώσας*); 30 (on a certain Paul, who died at the age of twenty-three); and 31 (on Samuel, deacon of the Great Church, hence a colleague of Ignatios). The authorship of the three short poems is indicated simply by the name *Ἰγνατίου*. Among ninth-century intellectuals, Ignatios may have been the first to cultivate the discontinued art of elegiac poetry.[49] We also possess in Barb. gr. 310 (10th century) a longer "anacreontic" poem with alphabetical acrostic (hence not an "elegy") on the same Paul, entitled *Ἰγνατίου διακόνου γραμματικοῦ εἰς Παῦλον τὸν ἴδιον μαθητήν*,[50] thus proving that Ignatios had indeed been a teacher. The anacreontic poem provides little additional information except that Paul was buried in a church of St. Stephen (vv. 75–76).[51]

viii. *Epistles.* See below, p. 18ff.

ix. *Poem concerning Thomas the Rebel.* This is lost, but it is reasonable to suppose that it has left some imprint on our historical sources concerning the revolt of Thomas the Slav, more particularly on Genesios who, as has already been observed,[52] appears to quote the actual title of the poem when he says (ed. Lesmueller-Thurn, 25.50) *οὕτως φασὶ τὰ κατὰ Θωμᾶν ἀκριβέστερον διεξιστορεῖσθαι*. It has also been remarked that the fanciful list of Thomas' heterogeneous supporters (24.17–21) has a poetic ring to it, and rather than suppose that it was derived from some "popular" poem,[53] it would be more plausible to argue that it was borrowed from Ignatios, the more so as several of the nationalities mentioned (Assyrians, Medes, Kabiroi, Huns, Vandals, Getai) have an antiquarian character. Without pursuing this line of argument any further, it is enough to note that Ignatios wrote a historical poem whose immediate purpose was to glorify Emperor Michael II and

---

[49] Cf. A. Cameron, *The Greek Anthology from Meleager to Planudes* (Oxford, 1993), 331ff.

[50] P. Matranga, *Anecdota graeca* (Rome, 1850), 664–67. Cf. S. G. Mercati, "Di un carme anacreontico spurio e mutilo di Gregorio Nazianzeno," *BZ* 17 (1908), 389–96, who attributes this piece to the later Ignatios of *Anth. Pal.*, I.109.

[51] In the MS there is a lacuna after Ignatios' poem. A. Mai, *Spicilegium romanum,* IV (Rome, 1840), xxxii, supposes on the evidence of the preserved *pinax* that there was another ode by Ignatios, an *ἀνακρεόντειον κατανυκτικὸν* contained in the MS, but it seems more likely that the *pinax* (ibid., xxxvi f) refers to the one poem on Paul.

[52] F. Barišić, "Les sources de Génésios et du Continuateur de Théophane pour l'histoire du règne de Michel II," *Byz* 31 (1961), 267; see also Lemerle, "Thomas le Slave," 268.

[53] As does H. Grégoire in A. A. Vasiliev, *Byzance et les Arabes,* I (Brussels, 1935), 31 note 2, who tries to reconstruct a poem in "politic" verse; rightly criticized by Barišić, "Dve verzije u izvorima o ustaniku Tomi," *ZRVI* 6 (1960), 165 note 47.

that, in so doing, he revived an old tradition that had probably been extinct since the days of George of Pisidia.

x. *Other Works.* A number of other compositions, in both verse and prose, have been attributed to our Ignatios either on the basis of titles in MSS or for reasons of style. Some of the works in question are of such slight interest that it does not particularly matter who their author was, but in other cases the question of authorship is of some moment. In trying to resolve it, we should bear in mind that there lived in the second half of the ninth century another Ignatios, styled *μαγίστωρ τῶν γραμματικῶν*, who composed a series of iambic epigrams on the church of the Virgin Mary "of the Source" (*τῆς Πηγῆς*). Since these epigrams (*Anth. Pal.* I.109–14) were occasioned by the restoration and redecoration of the church in question, which was damaged by the earthquake of 869,[54] and since *Anth. Pal.* I.109 names the reigning emperors as Basil, Constantine, and Leo, the last crowned in 870, it is highly unlikely that our Ignatios (born, as we shall see, not later than ca. 780) could have written these poems. To the later Ignatios (rather than to the patriarch of the same name) may also be attributed a seven-verse iambic poem on Lazarus and the Rich Man in Paris. suppl. gr. 690.[55]

We may now review briefly such miscellaneous works as may, with greater or lesser likelihood, be ascribed to our Ignatios.

Poems

1. *Acrostichon alphabeticum,* contained in a great number of MSS under different titles, for example, *Ἰγνατίου διακόνου Κωνσταντινουπόλεως ἀλφάβητον παραινετικόν* or *Ἰγνατίου τοῦ εὐσεβεστάτου σκευοφύλακος τῆς Μεγάλης Ἐκκλησίας παραίνεσις νέοις κατὰ στοιχεῖον.*[56] This is a poem of twenty-four lines addressed to schoolboys, hence consonant with Ignatios' teaching activity. We may note verse 8, *θήρευε τά κράτιστα τῶν νοημάτων*, which echoes a similar expression in VT 423.

2. *Versus in Adamum,* a longer iambic poem (143 verses) in the form of a dialogue between the Serpent, Eve, Adam, and God,[57] addressed to a friend "who

[54] *De sacris aedibus Deiparae ad Fontem, AASS,* Nov. III, 882; cf. R. Janin, *Églises,* 224.

[55] Ed. L. Sternbach, "Methodii patriarchae et Ignatii patriarchae carmina inedita," *Eos* 4 (1897), 151 ff. The reason for the attribution is that the poem in question, entitled *Στίχοι Ἰγνατίου*, is followed by three others on the Five Martyrs, of which the second mentions a church built(?) by Basil, perhaps Basil I.

[56] Ed. C. F. Müller, "Ignatii diaconi acrostichum alphabeticum," *Rheinisches Museum,* N.F. 46 (1891), 320–23.

[57] Ed. J. F. Boissonade, *Anecdota graeca,* I. (Paris, 1829), 436 ff; ed. C. F. Müller, *Ignatii diaconi tetrasticha iambica 53, versus in Adamum 143* (Kiel, 1886). Cf. idem, "Handschriftliches zu Ignatius Diaconus," *BZ* 1 (1892), 415 ff.

had fallen into misfortune" or perhaps rather into temptation, since he is invited to give thought to the original Fall after himself falling into a similar pit (Iconoclasm?).[58] The poem contains many quotations from Sophocles and Euripides.[59]

3. *Tetrasticha iambica,* a series of about fifty pieces that paraphrase and condense the Aesopic fables of Babrius. These have been transmitted in some twenty MSS under titles that vary a great deal. Only four mention the name of Ignatios, two without any qualification, one (Vind. phil. gr. 178 of 1429) with the addition *μαγίστορος*, and one (Paris gr. 2991A of 1420) with the addition of *διακόνου*. While the attribution remains, therefore, very doubtful, it may be noted that VT as well as the Letters of Ignatios show some knowledge of the Fables of Babrius.[60]

4. *Anth. Pal.* XV.39, a three-verse dedication of a MS of grammatical or possibly rhetorical content, which indicates that Ignatios either composed or edited such a textbook[61] and prided himself on having rescued the discipline of "grammar" from oblivion:

> *Ἰγνάτιος τάδε τεῦξε, σοφῆς πολύϊδρις ἀοιδῆς,*
> *Ἰγνάτιος τάδε τεῦξεν, ὃς ἐς φάος ἤγαγε τέχνην*
> *γραμματικήν, λήθης κευθομένην πελάγει.*

5. Two seven-line iconoclastic poems, presumably inscribed at the Chalke gate of the Imperial Palace, the first having the acrostic *Ἰγνατίῳ καύχημα ἐννοεῖν σταυρόν*, the second *Σταυρὸς Ἰγνατίῳ αἴνεσις*, quoted and refuted by Theodore the Studite.[62] It has been supposed that these and other iconoclastic poems refuted by Theodore dated from the first period of Iconoclasm,[63] but this has been shown to be

---

[58] Verses 8–9: *τῆς σῆς ἐν αὐτοῖς συμφορᾶς ἐπαισθάνου / ὡς καὶ λελαχὼς* [*λελουχὼς* cod.: *λελογχὼς* Boiss.] *τῶν ὁμοίων σκαμμάτων.*

[59] See Browning, "Ignace le diacre."

[60] The tetrasticha were edited as an appendix to *Babrii fabulae aesopeae,* ed. O. Crusius (Leipzig, 1897), 249 ff; recent edition by M. J. Luzzato and A. la Penna, *Babrii, Mythiambi Aesopei* (Leipzig, 1986). Further bibliography and discussion in Wolska-Conus, "De quibusdam Ignatiis," 335 ff, who raises considerable doubts concerning the authorship of this work. See, however, VT 403.5–6 (*οὐ νεβρῶν μυελοῖς*) and below, letter 37.

[61] It may be pointed out in this connection that an anonymous Byzantine treatise *Περὶ τῶν τοῦ λόγου σχημάτων*, ed. C. Walz, *Rhetores graeci,* VIII (Stuttgart-Tübingen, 1835), 617 ff (= L. Spengel, *Rhetores graeci,* III (Leipzig, 1856), 110 ff), is addressed to an Ignatios (*φιλοπονώτατον τέκνον καὶ εὐλαβέστατε Ἰγνάτιε*). It is attributed to Patriarch Tarasios by P. Nikitin, "O nekotoryh grečeskih tekstah žitij sviatyh," *Mémoires de Académie Impériale de Saint-Pétersbourg,* 8 ser., 1.1 (1895), 50 f.

[62] PG 99, 436 ff, 475–77.

[63] As still argued by Wolska-Conus, "De quibusdam Ignatiis," 351 ff; S. Gero, *Byzantine Iconoclasm during the Reign of Leo III* (Louvain, 1973), 113–26; and idem, in *Byz* 44 (1974), 27; A. Grabar, *L'iconoclasme byzantin*[2] (Paris, 1984), 152 ff.

untrue.[64] They must have been composed in or very shortly after 815. Their attribution to our Ignatios may be justified on the following grounds: (i) He is known to have collaborated with iconoclasts. (ii) The poems, which have an initial, a median, and a final acrostic, are very complex in structure and could only have been written by an experienced versifier. Ignatios the deacon was recognized as a specialist in this domain, and it is not likely that there was another equally qualified contemporary poet also named Ignatios. (iii) The iconoclastic poems were the work of four authors: John (most probably the future patriarch), Ignatios, Sergios, and Stephen, which brings us to the following.

6. A verse inscription (lost) in the ambulatory (*περίδρομος*) of the Sigma (a building erected in the Imperial Palace by Theophilos), the work *τοῦ οἰκουμενικοῦ διδασκάλου* (*Ἰγνάτιος τοῦτος ἐκαλεῖτο*). Another verse inscription in an adjoining hall called Pyxites was composed by the *asekretis* Stephen Kapitolites.[65] The conjunction of Ignatios, here designated as a teacher, with Stephen[66] leads us to suppose that these were two out of the four iconoclastic poets. The precise meaning of *οἰκουμενικὸς διδάσκαλος*, a title also bestowed on George Choiroboskos, remains unclear for the period in question.[67]

7. An indeterminate number of ecclesiastical kanons found in liturgical MSS with the designation *Ἰγνατίου*.[68] Among them five have a reasonable claim to be ascribed to our author.

i. A kanon on the Forty-Two Martyrs of Amorion (d. 6 March 845),[69] which begins with an admission of sin typical of our author:

> *Βυθῷ με πεσόντα ἁμαρτιῶν*
> *καὶ σοῦ τῷ πελάγει*
> *προσφυγόντα τῶν οἰκτιρμῶν*

---

[64] See E. E. Lipšic in *Istoričeskie Zapiski* 26 (1948), 326–27; C. Mango, *The Brazen House* (Copenhagen, 1959), 122ff; esp. P. Speck in *Ἑλληνικά* 27 (1974), 376–80; and M. F. Auzépy in *Byz* 60 (1990), 450–51.

[65] Theoph. Cont., 143. According to W. T. Treadgold, arguing from the order of entries in the Chronicle of Symeon the Logothete, the Sigma was built in 838–839; *DOP* 33 (1979), 173, 187. Cf. idem, *The Byzantine Revival* (Stanford, 1988), 445 note 421. If so, it may be thought that Ignatios was no longer bishop by 838.

[66] Cf. below, comment on letter 54.

[67] Discussed by Lemerle, *Humanisme*, 85ff. Cf. above, note 32.

[68] See A. Papadopoulos-Kerameus, Ὁ *ὑμνογράφος* Ἰγνάτιος, Ἐκκλησιαστικὴ Ἀλήθεια 22 (1902), 37ff; and for a more detailed presentation, Wolska-Conus, "De quibusdam Ignatiis," 334–35.

[69] Ed. V. Vasil'evskij and P. Nikitin, "Skazanija o 42 amorijskih mučenikah," *Mém. Acad. Impér.*, 8 ser., 7.2 (1905), 80. Cf. ibid., 262–68. For a new edition of the same kanon, see *Analecta hymnica graeca*, VII (Rome, 1971), 86–98.

πρεσβείαις, Χριστέ, τῶν ἀθλοφόρων
εἰς σωτηρίας λιμένα ὁδήγησον.

Since the same service also contains a *sticheron* attributed to Patriarch Methodios (Ἡ *ἐκκλησία σήμερον*), it was probably composed between 6 March 845 and 14 June 847.

ii. A kanon on the translation of the relics of Patriarch Tarasios (in 846), bearing the acrostichis: Ἀ*ρχιερέα θεοῖο* Τ*αράσιον ᾄσμασι μέλπω*.[70]

iii. A kanon on the translation of the relics of Patriarch Nikephoros (13 March 847).[71] Once again the kanon begins with an admission of the author's guilt:

Ἁ*μαρτιῶν τάφῳ δεινῷ συσχεθέντα με,*
τῇ ἀθανάτῳ νεύσει σου
καὶ τῇ εὐσπλάγχνῳ σου ἀναστήσας παλάμῃ,
ζώωσον ὡς οἰκτίρμων καὶ πολυέλεος.[72]

iv. A kanon on the iconophile bishop and confessor James (commemorated on 21 March).[73]

v. A kanon on St. Eustolia (commemorated on 9 November), including the following verses:

κἀμοῦ τὴν ἀχλὺν τοῦ πταίσματος
λῦσον λάμψασά μοι φῶς.[74]

If the attribution of the first three kanons to our Ignatios is justified, it may be inferred that he was still active in 847 and was in sufficiently good odor at the time to have been commissioned to take part in the composition of newly instituted and, indeed, officially sponsored liturgical services. Moreover, assuming that the kanon on the translation of the relics of Patriarch Nikephoros is to be credited to him, Ignatios' death must have occurred some time after 13 March 847. He might have survived Methodios (d. 14 June 847) if the kanon composed for the commemoration of the patriarch points to his hand too.[75] Apart from the acrostichis Ἀ*ρχιερέα θεοῖο* Μ*εθόδιον ᾄσμασι μέλπω*, this kanon contains a number of odes that were copied almost verbatim from the kanon on the translation of the relics of Tarasios (above, no. ii).

[70] Ed. Papadopoulos-Kerameus, Ὁ *ὑμνογράφος* Ἰ*γνάτιος*, 88, 90–91 (by "Ignatios the monk").
[71] Nineteen years after his death in 828: *Synaxarium CP*, 533.
[72] *Menaion* for March (Rome, 1898), 80ff.
[73] See ibid., 124–28.
[74] *Analecta hymnica gracea,* III (Rome, 1972), 260–68 (cited verses on p. 264.100–101).
[75] This kanon is transmitted anonymously in *Menaia,* V (Rome, 1900), 288–95.

Prose Works

1. *The Life of St. Gregory the Decapolite* (*BHG*³ 711). The attribution, though doubted by one scholar,[76] rests on good authority since it is given in three of the oldest MSS[77] (Βίος . . . *συγγραφεὶς ὑπὸ* Ἰ*γνατίου διακόνου καὶ σκευοφύλακος τῆς τοῦ* Θ*εοῦ μεγάλης ἐκκλησίας*) and is further supported by stylistic and thematic similarities with other works by Ignatios.[78] The date of St. Gregory's death is usually given as 20 November 842, but he may have died one or even two years earlier. Since several posthumous miracles are recorded, the Life can hardly have been written before 843; on the other hand, it does not appear much later.[79] Ignatios does not claim to have known the saint personally. He drew his information from two of Gregory's disciples, named Anastasios and John, and possibly from his uncle Symeon. It is worthy of note that the saint's most famous disciple, St. Joseph the Hymnographer, is not mentioned, perhaps because he had not yet returned from captivity (which he did soon after 843).[80] The tone of the Life is anti-iconoclastic throughout, and it may be conjectured that Ignatios undertook the commission of writing it in order to establish his orthodox credentials.

2. *The Life of St. George of Amastris* (*BHG*³ 668). The attribution of this work (VGA) to Ignatios has no manuscript authority and was advanced by V. G. Vasil'evskij on stylistic and historical grounds.[81] Further arguments have recently been marshaled by I. Ševčenko.[82] Without attempting to summarize here the vast (and largely unoriginal) literature that has grown round this text, especially in connection with the Russian attack on Amastris mentioned in its concluding part, we should like to make two brief points.

i. As shown conclusively by Ševčenko, VGA uses a series of typically iconoclastic formulations, which suggest that it was indeed written before 843. Yet George of Amastris was himself by no means an Iconoclast. On the contrary, he was on terms of friendship with Empress Irene and instigated the composition of an iconophile work on the translation of the relics of St. Euphemia by his suffragan, Constantine, bishop of Tios.[83] Hence the author's curious reticence on doctrinal matters. He is celebrating a man known to have been an iconophile in terms that would have been

---

[76] Wolska-Conus, "De quibusdam Ignatiis," 340 ff.

[77] Paris. gr. 501, 1525, and 1549.

[78] See Ševčenko, "Hagiography," 123 and note 71, and S. Efthymiadis, *JÖB* 41 (1991), 75–80.

[79] Note the reference to Iconoclasm as still vigorous (p. 75.4: *σὺν τῇ νῦν φρυαττομένῃ*) recalling VN 214.26.

[80] Cf. C. Mango, "On Re-reading the Life of St. Gregory the Decapolite," Β*υζαντινά* 13 (1985), 643 ff.

[81] *Trudy,* III (St. Petersburg, 1915), LXXXVIII–CVIII.

[82] "Hagiography," 121 ff. On its thematic similarities with VGD, see Efthymiadis, as in note 78.

[83] Ed. F. Halkin, *Euphémie de Chalcédoine* (Brussels, 1965), 81 ff.

acceptable in a period of iconoclastic ascendancy. Moreover, if we give credence to the author's statement in the preamble of VGA that this was his first venture in hagiography, we may obtain a *terminus ante quem* of 830, the year when the first draft of VN appears to have been composed.[84]

ii. George's fame appears to have been of a local character, and there are clear signs that the Vita was written for local consumption.[85] If Ignatios was indeed the author, we would have some reason for supposing that he was a native of Amastris or, at any rate, of Paphlagonia, a possibility to which we shall have occasion to return.[86]

Our rapid survey of Ignatios' literary oeuvre (as far as it can be defined) leads to the conclusion that he was, above all, a literary technician. He practiced a wide variety of genres—poetry in different meters, both secular and ecclesiastical, epistolography, hagiography—in addition to editing textbooks and, as we shall see (below, p. 198), compiling an anthology of proverbs. In classicizing hagiography he may have been narrowly anticipated by the Sicilian Methodios, but he went further in the use of classical reminiscences and even inserted into VN a kind of Platonic dialogue (pp. 169–86). As far as we can tell, he had, among the men of his generation, the widest knowledge of ancient authors.

Before we can add a few more touches to the portrait of Ignatios, we shall have to consider in some detail his correspondence.

THE LETTERS

Preserved as it is in a single MS, we have no guarantee that the collection of sixty-three items (plus one addressed to him) represents the entire corpus and is not merely a selection made by a later man of letters for purposes of study and imitation.

---

[84] VGA, 2.1–3: *ἡμᾶς δὲ καὶ πρὸ πείρας καὶ μηδὲν προεισενεγκόντας τοῦ παρόντος ἀγῶνος ἐπάξιον οἱ πνευματικοὶ πρὸς αὐτὰ συνωθοῦσιν ἀγωνοθέται τοῦ λόγου τὰ σκάμματα.* W. T. Treadgold, "Three Byzantine Provinces and the First Byzantine Contacts with the Rus," *Harvard Ukrainian Studies* 12–13 (1988–90), 132–44, argues that VGA was written between 820 and 839 on the assumption that the creation of three Byzantine themes in the Black Sea area resulted from the devastating raids of the Russes, one of them recounted in VGA.

[85] See esp. the peroration, p. 71.5: *τὴν πόλιν σου ταύτην φρούρησον* etc. We agree with Ševčenko, "Hagiography," 122–23 (cf. also the Addendum in the reprint of his article in *Ideology, Letters and Culture in the Byzantine World,* Variorum Reprints [London, 1982], V, 42) that the posthumous miracles (including the one relating to the Russes) are integral with the rest of the Vita. For a different opinion, see A. Markopoulos, *JÖB* 28 (1979), 75 ff.

[86] See below, commentary on letter 21; note also that Amastris is constantly called *πατρὶς*, perhaps with regard not only to the saint but also to the author; cf. Wolska-Conus, "De quibusdam Ignatiis," 348 note 110.

Chronology

The following letters contain some indication of relative or absolute date (discussed more fully in the Commentary):

1–4; possibly 6; 7–11, 13–15; probably 16; 17, 18: all of these pertain to Ignatios' episcopal period.

19, 20: written from Constantinople. The *chartophylax* (presumably Nikephoros) is referred to as the author's spiritual brother (no. 19).

21–24: before 826. Probably written at Constantinople.

27, 30: written under iconoclast rule, the latter probably ca. 823–829.

31: author describes himself as old and refers to having been a monk.

32: 842 or later.

33: before 846.

37: after ca. 830, perhaps by many years.

38–40: ca. 843.

41: possibly from monastery of Pikridion.

42: late in author's life.

43–46: from monastery of Pikridion, 843 or a little later.

49: 843–846.

52–55: to Patriarch Methodios (843–847).

58: refers to himself as having been a monk.

63: written in old age.

It is at once clear that the late letters are concentrated at the end of the collection and constitute about half of it (from no. 31 onwards, possibly with some exceptions). This being the case, one is naturally prompted to ask whether the entire collection may not be in chronological order. If it is chronological, we would have to conclude, in view of nos. 21–24 (which date from the reign of Michael II), that Ignatios was bishop of Nicaea before Inger, that he was, in other words, the *ἑτερόφθαλμος* referred to abusively by Theodore the Studite. He would then have been ordained bishop in ca. 815 and retired some time between 824 and 826. If, on the other hand, he was Inger's immediate or later successor, as can also be assumed, it would follow that the Letters are not in chronological order.

At a date surely before 843 Ignatios became a monk on the Bithynian Olympus, possibly at the monastery of Antidion, as conjectured by one of us.[87] He makes two references to this circumstance. In letter 31, writing to the monk Athanasios, he says:

[87] S. Efthymiadis, *The "Vita Tarasii,"* 84, who sees a pun on the name of Antidion in letter 43 (*ψυχῆς εἰδὼς κεραννύειν ἀντίδοτον*). Ignatios certainly had close links with Antidion (letter 34).

"Having broken the first promise made to Christ at my divine initiation [as deacon or priest] and having joined the Adversary [i.e., the Devil] through my unholy deeds, I then chose the solitary life. . . . But that life, too, I sullied and defiled by not abstaining from profane works and actions." The second reference is in letter 58 (to Leo *asekretis*): "Do you not, indeed, remember that you yourselves drew me away from my previous monastic quietude (*τῆς ἐν ἀρχῇ μοναδικῆς ἡσυχίας*) and dragged me down from Olympus? Not only that, but you also allowed me to be made a mockery through indigence. . . . How and why is it that I am poor and pressed hard by wasting hunger, whereas I ought to be enjoying pretty well all manner of benefit?" That can only mean that Ignatios was lured away from the monastery by the offer of a post, presumably at Constantinople, and that the offer came, if not from Leo *asekretis* himself, at any rate from his associates, that is, a group of dignitaries in the palace. Unfortunately, we know neither the date of letter 58 nor the nature of the post, although it may be conjectured that it was of an academic nature: we have seen that an Ignatios appears with the title of *oikoumenikos didaskalos* in the reign of Theophilos. Whatever the character of the post, it evidently did not bring the emoluments that Ignatios was led to expect.

We are still left with the period of his life when he was deacon and simultaneously *skevophylax* of St. Sophia. As we have seen, he is so styled in the *Suda* notice and in the titles of both VGD (ca. 842–843) and VN (first draft ca. 830; revised ca. 843), thus suggesting that his service as *skevophylax* (for which there is no other authority) should be placed toward the end of his life rather than earlier. Originally ordained deacon under orthodox auspices, he was, as already stated, entitled to keep that rank after 843. Indeed, if it is true that he became a monk on Olympus after he had been bishop, he would already have forfeited his episcopal status. Canon 2 of the Council of St. Sophia (879) forbids bishops to make themselves monks: if they do so, they are to lose their episcopal status.[88] The canonist Nikephoros the *chartophylax* (11th century) is even more specific: whereas priests who become monks are not suspended from officiating provided they have committed no other fault, bishops are suspended.[89] If the same discipline was applied in the first half of the ninth century, it would follow that Ignatios lost his *presbyterium* on becoming a monk. The question that remains is whether Ignatios was made *skevophylax* before or after the Feast of Orthodoxy. If before, would he not have been dismissed by Methodios? If after, would the patriarch, or rather the palace, have appointed a man compromised by iconoclastic association? While both alternatives present difficulties, the latter ap-

---

[88] P. P. Ioannou, *Discipline générale antique,* I.2 (Grottaferrata, 1962), 484–85.

[89] P. Gautier, "Le chartophylax Nicéphore," *REB* 27 (1969), 172. Cf. Grumel, *Regestes,* no. 983, ca. 1105.

pears to be more consonant with the evidence. If the kanons discussed above (p. 15f) are by him, he must have been of sufficiently good repute after 843 to have been entrusted with the composition of "officially sponsored" hymns. Perhaps the Paphlagonian empress Theodora, to whom he made himself useful (letter 32), interceded on his behalf. We would like to think that he died, a reasonably contented man, shortly after 847.

There is a modern tendency, especially evident in the works of F. Dvornik, to view the ecclesiastical politics of ninth-century Byzantium in terms of two "parties," the rigorist (represented by the Studites) and the moderate (represented by the patriarchs Tarasios and Nikephoros, among others). If there is any validity in this hypothesis (which certainly simplifies a much more complex web of individual and institutional interests), Ignatios should be classed among the moderates. There is no reason to believe that he was ever a committed Iconoclast: he simply went along with whatever party happened to be in power. His ties with St. Ioannikios, of which there are certain hints in the correspondence, would have placed him in the camp favorable to Methodios, but that is not to say that VN and VT were necessarily meant to be anti-Studite tracts or had any hidden purpose other than establishing his own orthodox credentials. In publishing his Letters he probably had similar objectives in mind: note, in particular, his exchange with Democharis, which places him on the right side already in the reign of Michael II. He also took care to present himself as an efficient bishop, mindful of the interests of the Church, and a protector of the needy. The important part he assigns to his correspondence with the *chartophylax* Nikephoros suggests that the latter had not only been fully rehabilitated, but continued to enjoy a position of esteem.

The Correspondents of Ignatios

By far the most frequent correspondent is Nikephoros, sometimes styled simply deacon (ten times: nos. 34–38, 51, 60–63), sometimes deacon and *chartophylax* (nineteen times: nos. 4, 14, 15, 25–30, 40–48, 59). It seems very likely that they were one and the same person. Otherwise one would have to assume that Ignatios had two close friends called Nikephoros whom he addressed in the same tone, with whom he had occasional tiffs and misunderstandings, of whose silence he complained, who sometimes wrote him letters of reproof, and who were both equally versed in classical literature. To our knowledge the *chartophylax* Nikephoros is not recorded elsewhere. He was already in office when Ignatios was bishop (no. 4), but it is not clear whether he was older or younger than Ignatios.[90] A man of iconophile sympathies (no. 27), he

[90] Ignatios addresses him as "brother and father" (letter 4) or as "father" (letter 40), but the same expression is used by Nikephoros in writing to Ignatios (letter 64).

either wrote or intended to write a refutation of iconoclastic doctrine (no. 30). He, too, however, compromised his position and had to recant (no. 40). At one time he withdrew to the barren island of Oxeia, but seems to have made a joke of it (no. 37). His literary interests were similar to those of Ignatios, his prose style even more convoluted (no. 64), and his handwriting minute and illegible (no. 38). The correspondence between the two pedants, who often sent gifts to each other (of olive oil, fish, and vegetables), forms the most intimate record of a friendship in ninth-century Byzantium.

The other correspondents of Ignatios are the following, those who are independently attested being marked with an asterisk:

A. *Secular*
Anonymous tax collector of Taion (17)
*? Constantine *asekretis* (32)
*? Constantine curator (56)
* Constantine *hypatos* (6)
* Constantine *spatharios* and *protonotarios tou dromou* (39)
Constantine, former student (57)
* Democharis, *logothetes tou genikou* (21–24)
*? Gregory *spatharokandidatos* (1–3)
*? Leo *protospatharios, asekretis* (58)
Nicholas, *spatharios* and *protonotarios* (7)
Theophanes *asekretis* (50)

B. *Ecclesiastical*
Anonymous bishop (12)
Anon. bishop of Helenopolis (13)
Anon. bishop of Noumerika (11)
Anon. bishop of Taion (10)
*? Athanasios (and Theophylaktos), monks (31)
Constantine metropolitan of Gangra (18)
* Ignatios metropolitan of Nicomedia (49)
John abbot of Komai (16)
John deacon and *kouboukleisios* (5)
* Joseph abbot of Antidion (33)
* Methodios, patriarch (52, 54, 55)
Nikephoros, metropolitan of Caria (9, 19, 20)
*? Theophilos deacon and *protonotarios* (53)

The high proportion of otherwise unattested persons is due to our poor knowledge of the Byzantine establishment of the 830s and 840s, that is, of the period that

falls between the correspondence of Theodore the Studite and that of Photios. For these intervening decades, Ignatios provides at the very least a kind of cultural sketch, while, unfortunately, telling us nothing or next to nothing about contemporary intellectuals like Leo the Philosopher, John the Grammarian, and (possibly) George Choiroboskos,[91] whom he ought to have known.

We may now attempt to summarize the results of the above discussion while frankly admitting its tentative nature. Ignatios may have been born in ca. 775–780 to a family that does not appear to have been rich. He was possibly of Paphlagonian origin, although that is far from certain. He had an elder brother who was in holy orders and who predeceased him (letter 54). We first meet him as a young man in the entourage of Patriarch Tarasios (784–806), who encouraged his studies and whom he may have served as notary. He was possibly ordained deacon by Tarasios. He was certainly acquainted with the next patriarch, Nikephoros (806–815),[92] but we do not know what position he occupied at the time. By 815, when Iconoclasm was reimposed, he was already a known literary figure and may have been called upon to compose two poems that were meant to be inscribed on the gate of the imperial palace. Soon after 823 he wrote a historical poem concerning the rebellion of Thomas the Slav, surely to please the reigning emperor, Michael II, although his own allegiance to Iconoclasm was less than enthusiastic, and he was himself, later, to vilify the same emperor (cf. VN—letters 24 and 30). At an unknown date he was ordained metropolitan of Nicaea, but does not seem to have remained very long in that post. After serving as a bishop, he became a monk on Mount Olympus, but was lured back to Constantinople, perhaps with the offer of a public teaching post, which brought him insufficient emoluments. Two of his students (Paul and Constantine) are recorded. In ca. 838 he composed an inscriptional epigram for Emperor Theophilos and, at about the same time, his first hagiographical work, VGA. In 843 he came under investigation for his dubious past. Reduced at first to the status of a monk and confined for a time in the monastery of Pikridion, he was, as an ordinand of Tarasios or Nikephoros, readmitted

[91] For the evidence that Choiroboskos was active in the 9th century see, *inter alia,* Mango, "The Collapse of St. Sophia," 172–74. The total lack of contemporary reference to this important and highly productive scholar is difficult to explain if he was active at Constantinople. Possibly he lived in the Arab empire, say in Egypt. An indication of that may be found in his Scholia on the Canons of Theodosius, ed. A. Hilgard, *Grammatici graeci,* IV.1 (Leipzig, 1889), 120: *Δεῖ γινώσκειν ὅτι νῦν μοναστήριον ἔστιν παρὰ τοῖς Ἀλεξανδρεῦσι καὶ λέγεται τοῦ Παία, ὡς ἀπὸ τοῦ Παίας· καὶ ἰδοὺ πάντα ἔχει τὰ τοῦ κανόνος, καὶ ὅμως οὐ κλίνεται διὰ τοῦ $\overline{\nu\tau}$· ἀλλ' οὐκ ἔστιν ἐν τῇ χρήσει τῶν Ἑλλήνων.*

[92] In the exordium of VN (pp. 139–40) Ignatios presents himself as a friend and "son" of the deceased patriarch. It may be added that VN shows an intimate knowledge, almost day by day of the patriarch's downfall in 815, whereas it has little to say about his exile.

to the diaconate. As a result of this crisis he roused himself to intense literary activity and set about glorifying recent iconophile saints in a series of polished biographies. His sins were forgiven, and his efforts may even have been rewarded by promotion to the post of patriarchal *skevophylax*. He died shortly after 847.

That is a possible reconstruction of the career of Ignatios, but, as we have seen, it is not the only possible reconstruction.

Some of his works enjoyed considerable popularity, as shown by the great number of manuscripts in which they are preserved. Furthermore, the incipit of VN is quoted verbatim in an epitaph of the year 882.[93] It is hardly surprising that his correspondence, obscure and cryptic as it is, should have attracted fewer readers.

---

[93] N. Bees, "Zu einer byzant. Inschrift aus Panion vom Jahre 882," *Rheinisches Museum* 71 (1916), 285–88. Cf. A. Heisenberg's remarks in *BZ* 23 (1914–19), 510.

SIGLA

V	Cod. Vatopedinus 588, saec. XI ineuntis
V[1]	Eiusdem codicis corrector
G	Editiones M. Gedeonis. In perpaucis locis discrepantiae inter primam (1903) et secundam (1914) editionem siglis G[1], G[2] notantur
Duffy, Efthymiadis, Polemis, Ševčenko	Correctiones vel coniecturae a viris doctis J. Duffy, S. Efthymiadis, I. D. Polemis, I. Ševčenko propositae
Karlsson	Coniecturae viri docti G. Karlsson in epistulis 25, 37
⟨ ⟩	addenda
[ ]	delenda
† †	locus corruptus
*	lacuna statuenda
. . .	spatium in codice vacuum relictum

TEXT AND TRANSLATION

1. Γρηγορίῳ σπαθαροκανδιδάτῳ

Ἡ ἐπιπελάσασα λύπη νῦν τῇ ἀνεξικάκῳ ὑμῶν ⟨καὶ⟩ μακροθύμῳ χρηστότητι ἐκ τῆς ἐμῆς ἐπνεύσθη ἀνεμιαίας φρενός· ἀλλ' εἴ τι τοῦ προσήκοντος διεσφάλημεν παραβλέψαι, θεομίμητε, δυσωπήθητι, καὶ μὴ πολὺν ἐπανατείνῃς τὸν κλύδωνα τοῖς ἐπὶ πελάγους ἀπορίας ἡμῖν σαλεύουσιν καὶ πυρσὸν ἐπιζητοῦσιν πρὸς ἀσφαλῆ λιμένα φαιδρῶς [καὶ] ἐγκαλούμενον. Ἐπὶ γὰρ τῷ πραχθέντι λόγος ἡμῖν ἀφίκετο ὡς ἐκ τῶν ἀπαναστάντων παροίκων τινὲς κατὰ τῆς ἐκκλησίας ἡμῶν ἐμμανῶς ἀνεβόησαν ἀδικίαν παρ' αὐτῆς ὑφεστάναι εἵνεκα τῶν γεωργημάτων, ὧν ἐν τοῖς τόποις αὐτῆς μισθοφόρων δίκην εἰργάσαντο· οὐ γὰρ ἀγνοεῖ ἡ θεοφιλὴς ὑμῶν σύνεσις ὡς οὐ τρέφει βοῦν ἀροτῆρα ἡ καθ' ἡμᾶς ἐκκλησία· οὐχ ἥρμοσέ ποτε πηκτὸν ἢ αὐτόγυον ἄροτρον· οὐχ ὕνιν παραδοῦσα πυρὶ στερρῶς ἀπελίπανεν, ἀλλ' ἐπιμετροῦσα τὴν ἑαυτῆς γῆν τοῖς τὰ περὶ γῆν ἠσχολημένοις, τὴν ἐκ τοῦ καρποδότου θεοῦ παροχὴν ἀπεκδέχεται, καὶ σὺν ἐκείνοις, κατὰ τὸν γεωργικὸν νόμον, ἐνδίκως καρπίζεται· ἣν μὴ στερηθῆναι τῆς δικαιοδοσίας καὶ τοῦ ἐπιβάλ || 75 || λοντος αὐτῇ μέρους ἐκτενῶς ἱκετεύομεν· ἀλλ' ἡνίκα γνωρίσοι καὶ ἐπιμετρηθείη τὰ ἴδια, ἡ ἐπίλοιπος συγκομιδὴ ἔστω τῶν ἐπὶ συμφώνῳ γεωργησάντων, καὶ μὴ τῷ ἐπαχθεῖ ζυγῷ τούτῳ ὑποπέσοι ἡ ἐκκλησία, ὅτι καὶ σιταρχία παρὰ τοῦ δημοσίου αὐτῇ ἀπεγράφη καὶ ἐξόδοις πολλαῖς ταῖς παντα . . . . . πλατύνεται, ὡς, εἰ καὶ ταύτην ὑποσταίη τὴν πεῖραν, οὐκ εἰς μακρὰν πᾶσαν γεωργήσει πενίαν, ἣν μὴ ὄψεσθαι ἡμᾶς εὐδοκήσοι θεός, τὴν ὑμετέραν ἔχοντας εἰς ἐπικουρίαν καὶ προστασίαν θερμοτάτην καὶ ὀξεῖαν ἀντίληψιν.

2. Τῷ αὐτῷ

Ἡμεῖς μὲν ⟨ἐν⟩ μέρει πληροφορίας ἐσμέν· μᾶλλον δὲ τὸ πᾶν ἔχομεν ὡς ἐκεῖνος τῶν προτελεσθέντων ἀτοπημάτων, ἐξ ἐπινοίας τοῦ εὑρετοῦ τῆς κακίας, ⟨ἐν⟩ λήθῃ καὶ ἀμνημοσύνῃ γέγονεν, καὶ οὐδὲν ὑπολέ-

---

1: 10 *βοῦν ἀροτῆρα*: Hes. *Op.* 405 || 11 *πηκτὸν ἢ αὐτόγυον ἄροτρον*: cf. Hes. *Op.* 432–33 || 11–12 *οὐχ ὕνιν – ἀπελίπανεν*: locum non invenimus

---

1: 3 *παράβλεψαι* V || 7 post *ἀπαναστάντων* lac. ca. quattuor litt. || 11 *αὐτόγυιον* V || 20 post *παντα* lac. ca. octo litt.

THE CORRESPONDENCE OF IGNATIOS THE DEACON

1. To Gregory the *spatharokandidatos*

The annoyance that has now befallen your forbearing and long-suffering Goodness was wafted from my vain mind. If I have been remiss in my duty, O imitator of God, deign to forgive me and do not inflict a violent storm upon me who am tossed on a sea of indigence and seeking a bright beacon that will guide me to a safe harbor. For regarding the event that has taken place, I have received a report that some of the *paroikoi* who had gone away protested frantically against our Church that they had suffered injustice at her hands on account of the produce that they, like hired laborers, had raised on her lands. Surely, your God-loving Prudence is aware that our Church does not nourish a single ox that pulls the plow; that she has never yoked a plow, be it of one piece or compacted of several, nor has she thoroughly greased a plowshare after singeing it in the fire. Nay, she parcels out her land to those who till the land and awaits the crop from God, the provider of harvest, which she justly enjoys with them according to the farmer's law. We therefore earnestly entreat you that she should not be deprived of justice and of the share that is due to her, but that, after she has taken stock of her own and received her measure, the remainder of the crop should go to those who have tilled the land under contract. Let not the Church submit to this burdensome yoke inasmuch as the provision of victuals has been imposed on her by the Treasury and she is overextended by numerous . . . expenses; for if she were to suffer this trial, too, she would soon reap abject poverty, which may God grant us not to see happen, having as we do your most ardent and swift succor for our assistance and protection.

2. To the same

I am assured—indeed, I have all the evidence that this man, inspired by the Inventor of evil, has become unaware and forgetful of his previous offenses and all

λειπται, ὃ πεποιήκαμεν ἢ πεπόνθαμεν. Τοῦτο γὰρ τεκμηριοῖ τὸ τοῦ χριστιανοῦ τέλειον ἐν τῷ πάσχειν μὴ λογίζεσθαι μηδὲ ἀντιδιδόναι τῷ ὑπὲρ οὗ τὸ πάσχειν γεγένηται. Εἰ οὖν ταῦτα οὕτως, σὲ δὲ ἴσμεν ἀξίως τὸ τοῦ χριστιανοῦ καὶ τελείως ἐνδεδυμένον ἐπάγγελμα, δεῖξον τῇ ἐνούσῃ σοι ἀμνησικάκῳ συνέσει, καὶ δὸς τόπον τῇ ὀργῇ, κατὰ τὸν μακάριον καὶ ‖ 76 ‖ πρῶτον διδάσκαλον Παῦλον, ἕνεκεν τῆς ἐκ τοῦ οἰκονόμου ἡμῶν ἀπροσεξίας, καὶ μὴ τὸ ἐκείνου πλημμέλημα τῇ ἐκκλησίᾳ λογισθήτω· αὐτὸς γὰρ τὸ τῆς ἀφροσύνης φορτίον ἐπὶ τῶν ὤμων ἄρας οἴχεται· ἀλλ' ἡ ἐκκλησία μηδὲν πειρασθείη ὧν ἀπεύχεται, μηδὲ τὰ ὑπὲρ δύναμιν εἰσπραττέσθω· μᾶλλον δὲ καὶ ἐκ τῶν ἤδη προγεγονότων ἐπικουφισθήτω διὰ τῆς ὑμετέρας εὐμενοῦς παρακλήσεως, καὶ ἑτέρου βλάβην προξενοῦντος μὴ πειρασθήτω· ἔσται δὲ τοῦτο εἰ διὰ τῆς ὑμετέρας φιλοσυμπαθοῦς ἡμερότητος ἀνθυπονοστήσει ὁ οἰκονόμος τῆς ἐκκλησίας ἐν τῇ διακονίᾳ αὐτοῦ, ἵνα μὴ ὁλοσχερὴς τοῖς τῆς ἐκκλησίας πράγμασιν ἐπακολουθήσῃ φθορά· ἱκανὴ γὰρ αὐτῷ ἡ ἐπιτιμία· μὴ οὖν ἀνιάτρευτος ⟨εἴη⟩· ἀλλὰ τῇ διακριτικῇ ὑμῶν μοτώσει θεραπείαν δέξαιτο τὸ ἀναφυὲν ἄλγος ἐπ' αὐτῷ, ὃ καὶ πρὸ τῶν γραμμάτων ὄψεσθαι ἐν ἐλπίδι ἦμεν. Τὴν δὲ τοῦ οἰκονομείου κλεῖδα, ἐν ᾧ τὰ ἑτοιμασθέντα εἰς τροφὴν τοῦ παρ' ὑμῶν κυβερνωμένου λαοῦ ἀποτέθειται, πεπόμφαμεν· ἣν ὑπανοιγνὺς καὶ τὰ ἔνδον ἐπιμετρῶν, ὡς παρίσταται τῇ ὑμετέρᾳ ἀκριβεῖ ὑπεροχῇ, διανεῖμαι· καὶ Κύριος ὁ θεὸς ἡμῶν, ὁ πάντων ἀγαθῶν χορηγὸς καὶ παροχεὺς ἀφθονώτατος, ‖ 77 ‖ ἀνοίξει ὑμῖν τῆς αὐτοῦ βασιλείας τὴν εἴσοδον, ταῖς τοῦ κορυφαίου τῶν ἀποστόλων καὶ κλειδούχου τῶν οὐρανῶν Πέτρου πρὸς αὐτὸν ἐντεύξεσιν, καὶ λύσιν ὑμῖν τῶν πλημμελημάτων παρέξει, δι' ἧς ἔστι τοῦ πρώτου τυχεῖν ἐφετοῦ καὶ τῆς ἐν ἐλπίσι κειμένης μακροῦ αἰῶνος λήξεως.

3. Τῷ αὐτῷ

Ἰδού σοι καὶ ὁ πολυζήτητος κουράτωρ ἥκει· ὃν εἴτε ποθῶν εἴτε ἀπειλῶν ἐπιζητεῖς ἀγνοούντων σοὶ μόνῳ τοῦτο παραχωροῦμεν εἰδέναι.

2: 5–6 *ἐν τῷ πάσχειν – γεγένηται*: cf. Mt. 5.39 ‖ 8 *δὸς – ὀργῇ*: Rom. 12.19 ‖ 11 *τὸ τῆς ἀφροσύνης φορτίον*: cf. Ps. 37 (38).13–14

2: 4 ὃ: fort. *ὧν* legendum ‖ 19 post *ἀνιάτρευτος* vox *ὑγυῆ* (?) erasa ‖ 21 *οἰκονόμου* V: corr. G ‖ 23 *ἣν* V: *ἵν'* G fort. recte ‖ 24 *ἀκριβῆ* V: corr. G ‖ 27 *ἐντεύξευσιν* V: corr. G ‖ 29 an *μακραίωνος* legendum?

3: 2 Fort. *ἀγνοοῦντες* cum G vel *ἀγνοούντων ἡμῶν* legendum

my actions and suffering have been to no avail. For this is proof of Christian perfection, namely, to take no account of one's own suffering nor to repay him on whose account the suffering was caused. If then that is so, and since I know that you are deservedly and fully invested with the profession of a Christian, show it by the forgiving prudence that is within you and give place unto ⟨God's⟩ wrath (as our blessed and foremost teacher Paul saith) regarding the heedlessness of our *oikonomos,* and let not his transgression be charged against the Church. For he, having taken upon his shoulders the burden of his folly, has departed. As for the Church, she should not be tried for what she deplores, nor should she be made to pay what is beyond her capabilities; rather, she should be relieved by your kindly exhortation of her past tribulations and should not experience the damage caused by another man. This shall be so if, thanks to your gentle sympathy, the *oikonomos* of the Church returns to his duties so as not to cause complete disaster to the affairs of the Church. The penance is sufficient unto him. Let him not, therefore, ⟨remain⟩ uncured; rather let his disease be healed by your discerning ministration—an outcome I hoped to see even before ⟨writing⟩ this letter. As for the key of the *oikonomeion,* wherein is stored the food set aside for the sustenance of the host that is governed by you, I have sent it to you, so that you may open ⟨the door⟩ and, after counting the contents as your meticulous Excellence sees fit, distribute them.

May our Lord God, the granter and bountiful dispenser of all good things, open to you the entrance to His Kingdom by the prayers of Peter, the chief of the apostles and key-bearer of heaven, and grant you release from your sins, whereby you may attain that which you most desire and the eternal end that lies within your hopes.

3. To the same

Behold, the much-sought *kourator* is coming to you. Whether you have been searching for him because you desired ⟨his company⟩, or ⟨wanted⟩ to threaten him, you alone can tell since I am ignorant of the matter. Had he not been crooked in both

Εἰ μὴ γὰρ ἦν ἀμφοτέραις ταῖς ἰγνύαις ὀκλάζων καὶ βακτηρίᾳ τὸ χωλὸν ὑπερείδων, τάχα ἂν σὺν τῷ οἰκονόμῳ ἐπὶ τὴν τῶν παροίκων ἀποικίαν ἐστέλλετο. Ἐπειδὴ δὲ φέρειν αὐτὸν ἐξ ἀσθενείας οὐχ οἷός τέ ἐστι, πῶς ἑτέρων ἐνεγκεῖν βίαν δυνήσεται ἄνθρωπος ἡμιθανὴς καὶ τομίας, ὑπὲρ οὗ λέγειν οὐκ ἔχομεν ἕτερον, ἢ εὐχαριστεῖν Κυρίῳ ὡς ἑνὸς εὐνούχου καὶ χωλοῦ περικρατῆσαι ἰσχὺς ἡμῖν οὐκ ἐγένετο; Τοιαύτη τῆς περὶ ἡμᾶς σου κηδεμονίας φροντίς· τοῦτο τὸ μέγεθος τῆς πρὸς ἡμᾶς ἀντιλήψεως. Εἰ μὴ γάρ ⟨οὐκ⟩ ᾔδει τὴν ἐκκλησίαν καὶ τὰ περὶ αὐτὴν κατὰ μικρὸν ὑπορρέοντα καὶ μηδεμιᾶς παρ' ὀλίγον ἐχόμενα στάσεως, διὰ τὴν ἐρημίαν τῶν αὐτὴν διεξαγόντων, || 78 || ἔδοξέ τισιν ἴσως λέγειν ὑπ' ἀνοίας ταῦτα προστάσσειν τὴν περίβλεπτον ὑμῶν ὑπεροχήν· νυνὶ δὲ πάντων τῶν ἐπιτροπευόντων τὰ τῆς ἐκκλησίας παρ' αὐτοῦ ἀπαχθέντων καὶ κατ' ὀφθαλμοὺς αὐτοῦ ὁσημέραι παρεστώτων καὶ τὴν τῶν βασιλέων ἐπιεικῶς τελούντων δουλείαν, τί λοιπὸν ὑπολείπεται; Τί ἄλλο γε ἢ πάντως ἡμᾶς αὐτοὺς παρεῖναι καὶ τὸν λόγον τῶν δραπετευσάντων ὑπέχειν. Τήρησον οὖν μετ' εὐνοίας, καὶ πρὸς τὴν ἐκκλησίαν ταῦτα, τὸ πρόσωπον, καὶ στῆσον αὐτὴν ἐπὶ στερεὰν τῆς ἀντιλήψεως πέτραν, χωλεύουσαν, καὶ δὸς αὐτῇ πραγμάτων βάσιν ἀσάλευτον, ὡς ἂν θεός, κατευθύνων τὰ πρὸς αὐτὸν ὑμῶν διαβήματα, καὶ πᾶν σκῶλον καὶ σκάνδαλον κατενώπιον ὑμῶν ἐκβάλλων, λείαν καὶ προσιτὴν τὴν εἰς ⟨τὴν⟩ αὐτοῦ βασιλείαν ὑπανοίξειεν εἴσοδον, πρεσβείαις τῆς αὐτὸν τεκούσης Θεοτόκου καὶ τῶν ἀπ' αἰῶνος αὐτῷ εὐαρεστησάντων ἁγίων.

4. Νικηφόρῳ διακόνῳ καὶ χαρτοφύλακι

Ἰλιάδα συμφορῶν ὁ τῆς ἱερωσύνης ζυγὸς ἡμῖν ἀποτέτοκεν· μὴ γὰρ φέρων τὸ τῆς ἀναξιότητος ἡμῶν ἐπαχθὲς ταύτῃ ἡμᾶς ἐπεβάρησεν καὶ

3: 3 *ἀμφοτέραις ταῖς ἰγνύαις*: 3 Reg. 18.21 || 20–21 *θεὸς – διαβήματα*: cf. Lc. 1.79; 1 Th. 3.11

---

3 *ἰγνύες* V: corr. G || 10 *εἴδη* V: corr. G || 14 *ἀπαχθέντα* V: corr. G || 15 *ὡσημέραι* V || *παρεστῶτα* V: corr. G || 21 *σκολον* V || 22 *λίαν* V: corr. G || *τὴν* suppl. G

4: 1 *ἰλιάδα συμφορῶν*: cf. Zen. IV.43; Diogen. V.26; Karathanasis 38

4: 1 *ἱεροσύνης* V: corr. G || 2 *ταύτης* V

legs and been supporting his lameness with the help of a staff, he would probably have been dispatched, together with the *oikonomos,* to the settlement of the *paroikoi.* Since, however, he is unable, because of his infirmity, to carry himself, how will a half-dead castrate manage to resist violence from others (to whose credit I can say this only, that I am grateful to God for having been unable to prevail over one eunuch who is, in addition, lame)? Such is your solicitude on our behalf, so great is your assistance to us! For unless you did not know that the Church and her affairs were slowly ebbing away without the slightest pause because of the absence of anyone who could lead her out of difficulty, it might perchance have occurred to some persons to say that these orders were given senselessly by your distinguished Supremacy. Now, however, that all the men who administer the affairs of the Church have been removed by you, stand in your presence every day and are meekly performing the emperors' service, what else remains to be done? Nothing, surely, except that I should present myself and take responsibility for the fugitives. Keep, therefore, a gentle countenance, especially with regard to the Church, and set her up, lame as she is, upon the firm rock of your succor; grant her an unshakable foundation so that God, in guiding your steps toward Him, may remove from your path every hindrance and stumbling block and open a smooth and accessible entrance to His Kingdom; by the prayers of His Mother, the Theotokos, and of all the saints who have found favor in His sight from the beginning of time.

4. To Nikephoros, deacon and *chartophylax*

The yoke of priesthood has caused me an Iliad of misfortunes; for, being unable to bear the burden of my unworthiness of it, it has weighed me down with them,

χειμῶνι πραγμάτων ἐπέκλυσεν καὶ καταιγίσιν ἃ || 79 || *βουλήτων πειρασμῶν ἐπετάραξεν, ὥστε, εἰ μὴ τὸ τῆς ὑμετέρας ἡδυεποῦς καὶ μειλιχίου γλώσσης ἡμᾶς ἀνεκτήσατο λόγιον, ἦν εἰπεῖν ποιητικῶς Ἰλιόθεν με φέρων ἄνεμος Κικόνεσσι πέλασσεν. Τοσαύταις φροντίδων ἐπιρροαῖς καταντλούμεθα, καὶ τοιούτοις εἴδεσιν ἀνιαρῶν † ποικιλλόμεθα, † καὶ οἵᾳ τῷ μύθῳ δοκεῖ ὕδρᾳ πολυκεφάλῳ, ὁσημέραι περιστοιχιζόμεθα ἧς, εἰ καὶ μιᾶς τῶν δεινῶν ἐκείνων κεφαλῶν περιεσόμεθα, ἑτέρα ὅσον οὔπω δεινοτέρα ἐπικυΐσκεται καὶ ⟨εἰ⟩ ταύτην αὖθις ἐκτιλλόμεθα, ἄλλη λοιπὸν ἐπανατέλλει καὶ φρικτὸν ἡμῖν μορμολύττεται· ὥστε πρὸς ταύτας ἡμῖν ὁ πᾶς ἀγὼν κἂν εἰ μὴ καταγωνιεῖσθαι τοῦτον δυνάμεθα.*

Τοῦτο ἡμῖν τῆς πρὸς σὲ σιγῆς ὑπῆρξε κεφάλαιον· ὅθεν αἰτοῦμεν τῆς μέμψεως ἡμᾶς ἀφεῖναι καὶ τῆς βραδυτῆτος τὴν αἰτίαν λῦσαι εἰδὼς οἵαις καὶ ὅσαις ἐπηρείαις βαλλόμεθα· ὑμῶν δὲ καὶ ἄλλως ἐθαυμάσαμεν τὸ ἐπιεικὲς καὶ σεβάσμιον ὅτι καὶ γράμμασιν πρῶτος ἡμῖν προσωμίλησας καὶ τὸ τῆς ἀηδίας καὶ λύπης ἡμῶν διὰ τῆς σῆς θεραπευτικῆς ἀντιδότου πικρὸν κατεγλύκανας· ἧς ἐγγευσάμενοι καὶ πᾶσαν καχεξίαν ἀποσεισάμενοι, ῥωστικῆς ἐνεφορήθημεν χάριτος, καὶ εὖγε ἀδελφῶν ἐμοὶ καὶ πατέρων ἐρασμιώτατε· σὲ δὲ ἴσμεν ὡσεὶ ἐλαίαν ἐν τῷ οἴκῳ Κυρίου || 80 || *κατάκαρπον, ταῖς ἄνωθεν πνευματικαῖς ἐπομβρίαις ἀρδευομένην πιαίνεσθαι, καὶ ἑτέροις τὸ ἐλεεῖν ἐπιμετροῦσαν καὶ ἐπαλείφειν· αἰδούμεθα· τόλμῃ δὲ χρησάμενοι ἐξ αὐτῆς τῆς παρ' ἡμῖν ὀντότητος μικρὰν ἐλαίου ὁλκὴν πεπομφέναι προτεθυμήμεθα, ἣν δεχθῆναι μὴ ἀπαξιώσῃ ἡ ὑμετέρα πολυέλεος προαίρεσις, τὴν ἄτεγκτον ταῖς ἁμαρτίαις καὶ ἄνικμον ἡμῶν ψυχὴν ταῖς θείαις πρὸς τὸ κρεῖττον ἐντεύξεσιν ὑμῶν πρὸς εὐκαρπίαν ἀρετῶν ἐπιρραίνουσα· καὶ ἐρρῶσθαι ὑμᾶς εὐχόμεθα, καὶ εὔχεσθαι ὑπὲρ ἡμῶν δυσωπήθητι.*

5. *Ἰωάννῃ διακόνῳ καὶ κουβουκλεισίῳ*

Ἐγὼ μὲν ἡνίκα τῆς ὑμετέρας διεζεύχθημεν παρουσίας ὡς λύπῃ πολλῇ συνήφθημεν. Τί γὰρ οὐ συνήντησεν ἡμῖν τῶν ἀβουλήτων; Τί δαὶ

5–6 *Ἰλιόθεν – πέλασσεν*: *Od.* 9.39 || 20–21 *ὡσεὶ – κατάκαρπον*: Ps. 51(52).10

---

7 *ποικιλλόμεθα* V: an *πημαινόμεθα* legendum? || 8 *οἷα . . . ὕδρα πολυκέφαλος ὡσημέραι* V || *περιστυχιζόμεθα* V: corr. G || 9 *τῶν* nos: *τοιούτων* V || *ποιησόμεθα* V: *περιεσόμεθα* G || 10 *δεινότερα* V || *ταύταις* V || 11 *ταύταις* V || 14 *ἀφῆναι* V: corr. G || 15 *ἐπιρείαις* V: corr. G || 18 *ησεγγευσάμενοι* V: *ἧ συγγευσάμενοι* G || 25 *πολυέλαιος* V: corr. G || 27 *ἐπιραίνουσα* V: *ἐπιρρωνύουσα* G

flooded me with a gale of concerns, and confounded me with squalls of unsought temptations, so that, had I not been revived by the words of your sweet and soothing tongue, I could say with the Poet, "From Troy the wind bore me and brought me to the Cicones." I am inundated by such floods of cares, injured by so many kinds of distress that beset me every day—it is like the many-headed hydra of the myth: if I overcome one of those dreaded heads, another, more terrible, straightaway sprouts up; and if, in turn, I pluck this one out, yet another rises up and frightens me horribly. My whole struggle is against these, even if I am not equal to it.

This has been the main reason of my silence toward you. Hence I beg you to absolve me of blame and not hold me responsible for my tardiness, knowing as you do all the injuries that assail me. Besides, I have admired in other respects your gentle and venerable character in that you took the first step in addressing me by letter and by your healing remedy sweetened my bitter sorrow and depression. Having tasted it and shaken off my whole disaffection, I have been filled with fortifying grace. Well done, most beloved brother and father! I know you are "like a fruitful olive tree in the house of our Lord"; watered by spiritual showers from above, you are increased and are dispensing mercy and assuagement to others. I am embarassed; yet, summoning up my courage, I have eagerly resolved to send you a small quantity of oil from our property which, I trust, your merciful Goodness will not refuse and, by means of your holy prayers to God, moisten my soul, which is hardened and desiccated by sin, that it may produce a harvest of virtue. I pray for your good health and beseech you to pray for me.

5. To John, deacon and *kouboukleisios*

When I was parted from your presence I experienced great sorrow. Indeed, every undesirable thing befell me, and I was overcome by every circumstance that

οὐ κατέσχεν ἡμᾶς ὅσα τις διαφεύγειν ἐπεύχεται, ὥστε ἀπολέγεσθαι ἡμᾶς, κατὰ τὸν μακάριον Ἰωνᾶν, καὶ αὐτοῦ τοῦ ζῆν; Οὐ γὰρ γράφειν ἱκανῶς ἔχομεν τῶν συμβάντων ἡμῖν ἀνιαρῶν τὰ δεινά· ἀλλ' ὁ παρακαλῶν τοὺς ταπεινοὺς παρεκάλεσεν ἡμᾶς, καὶ τῇ ἀνεξιχνιάστῳ αὐτοῦ καὶ ἀνεικάστῳ χρηστότητι τὸ βάρος τῶν ἐπελθόντων, ὀψὲ καὶ μόλις, κατελαφρῦναι κατένευσεν· τοσαύτη τῶν κύκλῳ συνεπιτιθεμένων ἡμῖν ἀλγεινῶν ἡ ἐπισύστασις. Εἰ γὰρ ‖ 81 ‖ ἑκάστου σκόλοπος ἀπογυμνῶσαι τὴν βίαν θελήσαιμεν, ἐπιλείψει ὁ παρὼν χρόνος διηγουμένους ἡμᾶς· ἀλλὰ δόξα θεῷ τῷ μὴ κατ' ἀξίαν τὰ τῆς παραχωρήσεως αὐτοῦ ἐφ' ἡμῖν τελοῦντι, ἀλλὰ ποιοῦντι σὺν τῷ πειρασμῷ καὶ τὴν ἔκβασιν. Τῆς δὲ ὑμετέρας θεοπαρόχου ῥώσεως ἐνωτισάμενοι τὸ ἥδιστον ἄκουσμα, πᾶν εἴ τι λύπης ἡμῖν ἐμφωλεῦον ἐνῆν λείψανον ἀπεκρουσάμεθα καὶ ὅλοι τῆς χαρᾶς γενόμενοι, τῷ δοτῆρι ταύτης θεῷ θυσίαν εὐχαριστίας προσήξαμεν· ἀλλὰ καὶ ἀπολαβέσθαι ὑμᾶς ἐρρωμένους, καὶ ὑπὸ θείας ῥοπῆς σκεπομένους, ἡ παντοδύναμος εὐδοκήσοι τοῦ θεοῦ ἡμῶν χρηστότης, ὡς ἂν τὰ τῷ γράμματι ἡμῶν λείποντα εὐκαίρως ἀποπληρώσωμεν.

6. Κωνσταντίνῳ ὑπάτῳ

Ἐν πᾶσιν ὑπὸ τῆς ἄνω ῥοπῆς κοσμουμένην τὴν ὑμετέραν μεγαλόνοιαν τοῖς θείοις πλεονεκτήμασι πάλαι διέγνωμεν. Οὐ γὰρ μόνον ἐν ταῖς τῶν δημοσίων πραγμάτων προκοπαῖς εὐοδουμένην βλέπομεν, ἀλλὰ καὶ ἐν τοῖς τῷ θεῷ ἀνήκουσι ζῆλον εὐσεβείας ἐνδείκνυσθαι πεπειράμεθα· ὅθεν καὶ νῦν, ἐκκλησιαστικοῦ τινος παραπεσόντος κεφαλαίου, ἐν ἄλλῳ οὐδενὶ τοῦτο θαρροῦμεν ἀναθεῖναι ἢ ἐν τῇ ὑμετέρᾳ ὀρθοτάτῃ κρίσει.

Ὁ γὰρ ἀποδιδοὺς τὸ γραμμάτιον ⟨τοῦ⟩ θεοφι ‖ 82 ‖ λοῦς ἐπισκόπου Νικομηδείας *ἡμᾶς ἐδίδαξεν ὡς τὰ ὑπὸ τὴν ποίμνην αὐτοῦ τελοῦντα εὐαγῆ μοναστήρια, δι' ἣν πρόφασιν εἰπεῖν ἀποροῦμεν, ὁ τοῦ ξενοδόχου* Πυλῶν *κουράτωρ ὑπεισελθὼν χρυσίου τινα ποσότητα παρ' αὐτῶν*

5: 3–4 *ἀπολέγεσθαι – τοῦ ζῆν*: Ion. 4.8 ‖ 5–6 *ἀλλ' ὁ – ἡμᾶς*: 2 Cor. 7.6 ‖ 8 *τῶν – ἡμῖν*: Ps. 3.7 ‖ 10 *ἐπιλείψει – ἡμᾶς*: cf. He. 11.32 ‖ 12 *ἀλλὰ ποιοῦντι – ἔκβασιν*: 1 Cor. 10.13

5: 3 *ἀπεύχεται* V ‖ 17 *εὐδοκήσει* V

6: 9 Νικομηδείας nos: *ἡκοῦ* V: *Ἰκονίου* G ‖ 10 *ξενοδοχείου* G

one would wish to avoid so that, like the blessed Jonah, I despaired of my very life. I am unable to describe adequately the terrible misfortunes that happened to me; but He that comforteth those that are cast down comforted me and, through His unfathomable and incomprehensible goodness, deigned to lighten, though barely and at the last moment, the burden that had been placed upon me. So great was the mass of sufferings that had set itself against me round about; for, if I were to reveal the severity of each torment, the present time would fail me to tell all. But glory be to God, who does not perform His dispensation over me according to my deserts, but "with the temptation also makes a way to escape." Having heard the sweet tidings of your God-provided recovery, I have ejected every remnant of sorrow that lay lurking within me and, having entirely given myself over to joy, I offered a sacrifice of thanksgiving to God who grants this joy. May our God's all-powerful goodness grant me to find you in good health and under the protection of the divine will, so that I may have an opportunity of telling you all the things that have not been said in this letter.

6. To Constantine, *hypatos*

I have long recognized that your Magnanimity was in all respects adorned with divine qualities by the will of the Highest. For not only do I see your success in the transaction of public affairs, but I also know by experience the pious zeal you manifest in those things that pertain to God. This is why, now that a certain ecclesiastical matter has arisen, I dare entrust it to no one else except to your most righteous judgment.

The messenger who delivered the letter of the godly bishop of Nicomedia has informed me that the curator of the *xenodochos* of Pylai had insinuated himself (on what pretext I am unable to say) into the holy monasteries that are placed under the bishop's pastoral jurisdiction and had removed from them a certain sum of gold. The

σφετερίζεται, τοῦτο λέγειν μόνον ἔχων εἰς ἀπολογίαν ὑπόψυχρον, ὡς διὰ τὸ πλησίον ἱδρῦσθαι τοῖς κτήμασι τοῦ ξενοδοχείου τὰ προρρηθέντα εὐαγῆ μοναστήρια τὴν ταύτην ἀποτιννύναι δόσιν· ὅπερ ἔξω καθέστηκεν καὶ πολιτικῆς καὶ πνευματικῆς καταστάσεως· πάντως γὰρ τοὺς τῷ θεῷ ἑαυτοὺς ἀναθέντας καὶ αὐτῷ ζῆν ᾑρημένους καὶ τῶν τοῦ κόσμου φροντίδων ἑαυτοὺς ἐξωθήσαντας, ἐλευθερίαν ἔχειν οἱ θεῖοι νόμοι θεσπίζουσι, καὶ μηδὲν παρὰ τῶν εὐσεβῶς διατεταγμένων εἰς αὐτοὺς πράττειν κελεύουσιν· οὕτω γὰρ ἔσται προσέχειν ἑαυτοῖς καὶ ὑπὲρ ῥώσεως καὶ πολυχρόνου εὐετηρίας τῶν ἐκ θεοῦ προλαμπόντων βασιλέων ὑπερεύχεσθαι.

Ταῦτ᾽ *οὖν διακούσασα ἡ ἀκριβὴς ὑμῶν σύνεσις καὶ τῷ θείῳ ζήλῳ πυρουμένη, τὸ ἀνόσιον τοῦτο τῆς εἰσπράξεως μὴ ἐπαφήσοι τελεῖσθαι ἐν οἷς τὸ θεῖον εὐαγῶς καὶ ἀκαταπαύστως λατρεύεται σεμνείοις· ἀλλ᾽ εἰ καί τι παρὰ τοῦ προφάσει ἀδικίας τοῦτο ἐπινοήσαντος ἀπῄτηται, ἀνταπαιτηθήτω καὶ τοῖς ἀδικηθεῖσιν ἀποδοθήτω, καὶ ἔστω ὑπὸ τὴν γνώμην* || 83 || *καὶ χεῖρα τοῦ ἐπισκόπου τελοῦντα τὰ ὑπ᾽ αὐτὸν μοναστήρια μὴ ὑφορώμενά τινα τῶν πα . . . ν τῆς τοῦ ἐπισκόπου χωρὶς ἐπισκήψεως ἐπὶ βλάβη τῆς αὐτῶν γενέσθαι βιώσεως.* Τοῦτο *γὰρ ποιῶν εὐάρεστος ἀναδειχθήσῃ θεῷ καὶ παρ᾽ αὐτοῦ συνεργούμενος καὶ ἐν τοῖς βεβουλευμένοις σοι πᾶσαν προκοπὴν εἰσδεχόμενος, μηδὲ τῆς ἐκεῖ διαμάρτοις τῶν ἀγαθῶν μετουσίας ἐν τῇ τῶν ἁγίων λαμπρότητι.*

7. Νι*κολάῳ σπαθαρίῳ καὶ πρωτονοταρίῳ*

Ἔ*δει μὲν ἡμᾶς πρὸς τὴν περίβλεπτον ὑμῶν μεγαλόνοιαν ποιουμένους τὸν λόγον, γηθομένῃ καρδίᾳ καὶ χαρίεντι προσώπῳ ποιεῖσθαι τὴν πρόσρησιν· τοῦτο γὰρ ἂν ἡμῖν ὑπῆρξε πάσης θυμηδίας ἀνώτερον καὶ ἑορτῆς μεγίστης ἐρασμιώτερον.* Ἐ*πειδὴ δὲ ἡ τῆς χαρᾶς φαιδρότης ἐκλέλοιπεν, λύπη δὲ πάντοθεν πιέζει καὶ θλίψεως τάραχος σφοδρὸν ἡμῖν ἐπανατείνει τὸν κλύδωνα, μέλανι τοὺς ἡμῶν ἐπιχρώσαντες λόγους, ὀδυνηρόν τι καὶ στυγνὸν προσφθεγγόμεθα.* Μ*ὴ γὰρ ἱκανῶς ἔχοντες φέ-*

6: 19–21 *καὶ ὑπὲρ – ὑπερεύχεσθαι*: cf. Just. *Nov.* 133.5

---

13 *προρηθέντα* V || 14 *ἐξ οὗ* V: corr. G || 17 *ἐξωθίσαντας* V: corr. G || 18 *πέρα* G: *παρὰ* V || 24 *σεμνοῖς* V: corr. G || 25 *ἀδικίας* V: an *ἀδίκῳ* legendum? || *ἠπέτηται* (αι supra ε) V: corr. G || 26 *ἀνταπέτηθήτω* (αι supra ε) V || 28 post *πα* rasura c. trium litt.: *τῶν παρὰ τῆς* G: *τῶν πάντων* proposuit Duffy: an *τὸ παράπαν* ? || 27 *ἐπισκήψεως* ex *ἐπισκέψεως* V litt. *η* in marg. scripta

only excuse he could offer was the rather weak one, namely, that the said holy monasteries ought to pay this contribution because they adjoined the properties of the hostel. This act contravenes both civil and religious order; for surely the sacred laws ordain that those men who have dedicated themselves to God, have chosen to live for Him, and have severed themselves from the cares of this world should enjoy immunity, and that nothing should be done to them contrary to these pious decrees. In this way they will be able to keep watch over themselves and to pray for the health and lasting prosperity of the emperors whose illustriousness comes from God.

Having heard this case, may your righteous Prudence, fired as it is by divine zeal, forbid this unholy exaction from the monasteries wherein the Deity is piously and unceasingly worshiped. Let the sums that the instigator of this matter has collected on an unjust pretext be demanded back of him and returned to the injured parties; and may the monasteries that are subject to the bishop remain under his judgment and control and not suspect anyone at all (?) of being detrimental to their way of life without the bishop's injunction. By doing so you will find favor with God by whose help you will receive all manner of success in your counsels; and may you without fail enjoy hereafter your share of the reward in the glorious estate of the saints.

7. To Nicholas, *spatharios* and *protonotarios*

In addressing your admirable Magnanimity it would have been only proper for me to salute you with a rejoicing heart and a smiling countenance. That, indeed, would have been the highest joy for me and an occasion more agreeable than the greatest feast. Since, however, the brightness of joy has faded, while sorrow oppresses me on every side and a turmoil of troubles is roused up against me like a violent storm, I have dyed my words in black and am addressing you in a distressed and gloomy manner.

7

ρειν τῶν ἐκ τοῦ δημοσίου δίκην νεφῶν ἐπιφυομένων εἰσπράξεων τὰ ἐπώδυνα, τὴν ὑμετέραν ἐγκαλοῦμεν μετὰ θεὸν θερμὴν καὶ ὀξυτάτην ἀντίληψιν· ἡ γὰρ ἐκκλησία ἥν, πολλῷ βάρει ἁμαρτιῶν συνωθούμενοι ἀλλ' οὐ διά τινα προκοπὴν ἀρετῆς, γνωρίσαι παρὰ θεῷ κατεκρίθημεν, πάσης πρὸ τούτου δαψι || 84 || λῶς ἀπέλαυεν ἡμερότητος, καὶ παντελοῦς ἀπήλλακτο τῆς τοῦ δημοσίου περιφορᾶς τε καὶ γεύσεως· οἷον εἰπεῖν συνωνῆς, ἀγγαρείας, καὶ παντοδαποῦς ἐπηρείας· καὶ ἦν αὐτῇ κεφάλαιον τοῦτο καυχήσεως καὶ πάσης ἀξίας καὶ φαιδρότητος τιμιώτερον. Νυνὶ δὲ ἡμέρᾳ πολὺν ὑφίσταται ῥαγδαίων νιφάδων ἐπιζήμιον κλύδωνα, καὶ ὁ συναλγῶν ἢ ἐπικουρῶν οὐδαμοῦ. Διὰ τοῦτο τὴν ὑμετέραν δυσωπεῖν προήχθημεν μεγαλόνοιαν, καὶ ὡς ἤδη πρὸ τῶν ἰχνῶν αὐτῆς τὴν ἱκετείαν ποιούμενοι, λιπαροῦμεν κλιθῆναι ὑπὸ τῆς ἄνω ῥοπῆς καὶ τὴν ἐπελθοῦσαν τῇ ἐκκλησίᾳ ἐκδήμου νέφους δριμυτάτην σκοτόμαιναν σκεδάσαι καὶ ἐπιγλυκάναι τῇ μειλιχίῳ καὶ μελισταγεῖ αὐτῆς πρὸς αὐτὴν ἡμερότητι. Πρὸ γὰρ τοῦ ἤδη παρωχηκότος ἰουλίου μηνὸς ὁ λόγος τῆς ὁρισθείσης συνωνῆς ἀπητήθη καὶ ἀσφαλὴς ἀπόδειξις ἐγράφη πρὸς τὸ μὴ ἑτέραν ὑποστῆναι εἴσπραξιν. Ὡς ὁρῶμεν δὲ καὶ παγίᾳ πληροφορίᾳ βεβαιούμεθα, καταιγὶς ἀπαιτήσεως συνωνῆς τῇ ἐκκλησίᾳ καὶ αὖθις ἐπέπνευσε, πρὸς βυθὸν ἕλκουσα τὸν κλῆρον πενίας· ἀνὰ γὰρ μοδίους ἓξ εἰσπράττεται πᾶς ἀπὸ νηπίου θηλάζοντος ἕως καθεστηκότος πρεσβύτου ἢ καὶ ὠμογέροντος, καὶ ὁ καιρὸς ἀφορίας ἐπ' ὄρους ὑψηλοῦ ἀναδραμὼν μέγα βοᾷ καὶ τὴν στένωσιν τοῦ παντὸς ἀνακηρύττει τρανότατα. || 85 || Ἀκουτισθείη οὖν παρ' αὐτοῦ καὶ ἡ ὑμετέρα ἑτοιμοτάτη ἀντίληψις τὴν τῆς ἐκκλησίας βίαν, καὶ μὴ χρονίσῃ εἰς τὴν αὐτῆς ἀπερίστατον ἀπορίαν, ὡς ἂν μὴ τὸ δυσαχθὲς τοῦτο φορτίον ὄκλασιν αὐτῇ τὴν ἐπὶ γόνυ προξενήσοι καὶ καταρράξῃ, κατὰ τὸ λόγιον, εἰς πέταυρον ᾅδου· μᾶλλον δὲ τῇ ἀντιληπτικῇ προνοίᾳ τῆς ὑμετέρας χειρὸς ἀνασωθήτω καὶ κηδεμονίας ἀξιωθήτω, καὶ μηδὲ μιᾶς βλάβης πεῖραν δέξοιτο, ἵνα καὶ ἐν τούτῳ καὶ διὰ παντὸς ὁ δι' αὐτῆς ἐπευφραινόμενος Κύριος [καὶ] παρ' αὐτῷ φυλαττομένην διατηρήσοι, παρέχων αὐτῇ πᾶσαν εὐκολίαν ἐν οἷς ἂν βουλεύηται καὶ ἐπιτηδεύῃ, καὶ τὴν ἐκεῖθεν προξενήσοι τῶν αἰωνίων ἀγαθῶν ἀμοιβὴν καὶ ἀπόλαυσιν.

7: 33–34 *εἰς πέταυρον ᾅδου*: Prov. 9.18

7: 8 *τὸν* V: corr. G || 14 *συνονῆς* V: corr. G || *ἐπιρείας* V: corr. G || 16 *πολὺν . . . ῥαγδαιον νιφάδα* V || 20 *ἔκδημον* V: corr. G || 26 *ἐνέπνευσε* V || 30 *ἡμέρα* V: *ὑμετέρα* G || 33 *καταράξῃ* V: corr. G || 35 *κηδαιμονίας* V: corr. G

7

Indeed, being unable to endure the pains of the tax exactions that spring up from the Treasury like clouds, I invoke, after God's, your fervent and speedy support. For the Church, which I have been condemned by God to become familiar with, impelled as I was by the burden of my sins and not on account of any progress in virtue—that Church heretofore used to enjoy in abundance every manner of tranquillity and was altogether exempt from tasting the dishes served up by the Treasury, namely, the *synone,* compulsory service, and all kinds of vexation. That was to her a source of pride more precious than any dignity and splendor. But today she suffers a violent snowstorm, an injurious flood, and there is none to comfort her or to help her. For this reason I have been induced to implore your Magnanimity, and, as if I were already making my supplication before your feet, I beseech you to be swayed by the influence of the Highest, to scatter the alien cloud of bitter darkness that has swept over the Church, and to soothe her with the honeyed sweetness of your gentleness on her behalf. For, before the month of July that has just gone by, the account of the appointed *synone* was demanded and a certification was given in writing that the Church would not be liable to another exaction. But, as we now see and are assured by trustworthy evidence, a claim for *synone* has, once again, come blowing upon the Church like a hurricane, dragging the clergy into the abyss of poverty: for every person, from the suckling babe to those in advanced or vigorous old age, is to be charged six *modii* each, while the sterile season cries out loud and clearly proclaims, as from a high mountain, the dearth of everything. May you, ready and helpful as you are, become aware thereby of the violence that is done to the Church and do not delay in the face of her helpless poverty, lest this heavy burden bring her to her knees and cast her, as the saying goes, into the trap of Hell. On the contrary, may she be delivered by your provident and helpful hand and be deemed worthy of protection without experiencing any harm whatever, so that, both in this case and for evermore, our Lord, delighted as He is by you, may continue guarding you and grant you every facility in all your counsels and pursuits as well as rewarding you with the enjoyment of the eternal blessings in heaven.

8. Τῷ *αὐτῷ*

Ἐντροπή μου καὶ λύπη τὸ πρόσωπον καὶ δειλία βάλλει με πάντοθεν ὑφορώμενον μὴ οὖσαν τὴν ὑμετέραν ὑπεροχὴν ὡς χθὲς καὶ τρίτην ἡμέραν πρὸ ἐμοῦ. Τοῦ γὰρ προβάντος σκανδάλου τὸ δριμὺ καὶ πικρότατον βέλος νύσσει τὴν ἐμὴν ψυχήν, καὶ οὐκ ἐᾷ καθαρᾷ συνειδήσει καὶ λόγῳ πεπαρρησιασμένῳ γράφειν· ἀλλ' ἀνθέλκει με ὁ θεομίμητος τρόπος καὶ ἡ περὶ τὸ κρεῖττον ὑμῶν γνησία στοργὴ καὶ ἡ περὶ τὰς τοῦ θεοῦ ἐκκλησίας ἀγαθὴ καὶ ἑδραία διάθεσις καὶ οὐκ ἐννοεῖν ταῦτα συμπείθουσι. Βλέποντες δὲ τὴν φθάσασαν καὶ νυνὶ προσπελάσασαν τῇ ἐκ || 86 || *κλησίᾳ* Νικαίας *ἐξαπίνης ἀγρίαν λαίλαπα, ἀπειρήκαμεν καὶ ἀφασίᾳ παντελεῖ συνεχόμεθα ὅτι, μήπω τῆς τελεσθείσης παρ' ἡμῶν σιταρχίας ἐν τοῖς τοῦ δημοσίου ταμιείοις ἀποκληρωθείσης, ἄλλος ἡμᾶς ἐπεβρόντησεν ἀρχισιτάρχης· μᾶλλον δὲ τὴν ἐκκλησίαν ἀστραπαῖς ἀπειλῶν ἐδειμάτωσεν, ἀνὰ ἓξ μοδίους σίτου ἕκαστον κληρικὸν ἀπὸ βρέφους καὶ παιδίου καὶ βούπαιδος καὶ ἕως ἐσχατογήρου καὶ πρωτογέροντος εἰσπραττόμενος.* Καὶ *πῶς ἀπεκρύβη τοῦτο τῇ ἀκριβεῖ ὑμῶν συνέσει εἰπεῖν ἀποροῦμεν, ὡς πρόσταξις βασιλέων καὶ ἀρχαῖον ἐπεκράτησεν ἔθος ἐν ἀδείας μέρει πάντα τὸν ἱερωμένον τῇ ἐκκλησίᾳ ταύτῃ τελεῖν καὶ πάσης ἀπηλλάχθαι κακώσεως.* Ἀλλ' *ὡς ἐγῷμαι καὶ συνορῶ καὶ μετρεῖν ἔχω, τοῦτο τῆς ἐμῆς ὑπάρχει ταλαίνης ψυχῆς τὸ ἀπότευγμα· ὃ στήσαις διὰ τῆς σῆς εὐμενείας, διδοὺς τῆς σκληρᾶς ταύτης εἰσπράξεως ἀνακωχήν, ἵνα μὴ γαγγραίνης δίκην νομὴ τῇ ἐκκλησίᾳ προσγένηται καὶ τὴν θεραπείαν ὁλοσχερῶς ἀπαρνήσηται.* Οὕτω *γὰρ παρὰ θεῷ κομιεῖται τὴν ὑπὲρ τούτων ἑκατοντάκις ἀμοιβήν· οὐ γὰρ ἡ ἐπ' ἄκρον ἀφορία καὶ ἀπορία τοῦ καιροῦ λανθάνει, ὡς καὶ εἰς αὐτῆς τῆς ἐφημέρου ζωῆς εὐφορίαν στένωσις οὐ μετρουμένη συμβέβηκε, καὶ εἰς ἀνάγκην μεγίστην πᾶσα περιέστη ψυχή.* Τ*ὴν οὖν ἱκετείαν τῆς ἐκκλησίας μὴ ἀπώσῃ, θεάρεστε· ἀλλ' ἵλεῳ ὄμματι καὶ προσηνεῖ καρδίᾳ τὸν εἰς αὐτὴν ἔλεον μετὰ θεοῦ συνεργάσασθαι προθυμήθητι,* || 87 || *ὡς ἂν καὶ* [*εἰ*] *ὑμᾶς ἡ παρ' αὐτοῦ ἐλέους ἐπισκιάσῃ εὐμένεια, πᾶν, εἴ τι δυσχερὲς καὶ ἄναντες, κατευμαρίζουσα σκάνδαλον, καὶ ταῖς κατὰ*

8: 1 *ἐντροπὴ – πρόσωπον*: cf. Ps. 68 (69).8

8: 10 *παντελῆ* V: corr. G || 11 *ημ(ει)ς* vel *ημ(ης)* V: corr. G || 12 *ἀρχισιτοχ* V: corr. G || 13 *σῖτον* V || 21 *ἀνακοχὴν* V: corr. G || *γαγραίνης* V: corr. G || 25 *ευφορ(ην) στενουσ(ης)* V || 27 *προσηνῆ* V: corr. G

8. To the same

Shame, sorrow, and timidity assail my face from every direction as I suspect that your Eminence is no longer on my side as it was yesterday and the day before. For the grievous and bitter shaft of the offense that has occurred pierces my soul and does not allow me to write with clear conscience and frank speech; yet your manner that is modeled after God, your genuine love of the higher state, and your steadfast goodwill toward God's churches draw me in the opposite direction and persuade me not to take thought of these matters.

When I see the violent storm that has now suddenly approached and fallen upon the Church of Nicaea, I despair; I am gripped by utter speechlessness in that, even before the produce (*sitarchia*) provided by us had been deposited in the stores of the Treasury, another chief commissar of the grain tax has struck us with his thunder or, to put it better, has terrified the Church by the lightning flashes of his threats in exacting six *modii* of corn from every cleric, starting with infants, children, and big boys, and ending with the decrepit old men and the middle-aged. I am at a loss to explain how it has escaped your meticulous Prudence that by imperial command and ancient custom every clergyman of this Church has enjoyed exemption and been freed from all manner of vexation. But, as I think, as I perceive and can reckon, this ⟨disaster⟩ is due to my miserable self. May you arrest it by your goodwill and give us relief from this cruel exaction lest the Church be affected with a spreading gangrene that defies all treatment. In so doing you will receive a hundredfold reward from God; for you are not unaware of the extreme dearth and poverty of the season—indeed, the very well-being of everyday life has experienced an infinite deterioration, and everyone has been reduced to the utmost need. Do not, therefore, dismiss the supplication of the Church, you who are so agreeable to God; be willing, with kindly eye and gentle heart, to help, along with God, in showing her mercy so that His merciful goodwill may overshadow you also, smoothing every vexatious stumbling block that

θεὸν ὑμῶν διεξαγωγαῖς συμπνέουσα, τῶν ἐκεῖθεν ἀκηράτων μισθῶν δι᾽ ἀγαθοεργίας προξενήσοι τὴν αἰωνίαν ἀντίδοσιν.

9. Νικηφόρῳ ἐπισκόπῳ Καρίας

Πάσης ἱερᾶς ἐμπνεύσεως πλῆρες γράμμα ἡμῖν παρὰ τῆς ὑμετέρας ὁσιότητος κομισθέν, ὃ καὶ ὑπτίαις χερσὶν δεξάμενοι καὶ δι᾽ αὐτοῦ τὰ θεῖα νουθετηθέντες καὶ τὰ τῆς ἱερωσύνης τέλεια μυηθέντες, τὸ πολὺ τοῦ κατασχόντος ἡμᾶς ἐξ ἀθυμίας νέφους ἀπεσκευασάμεθα κάλυμμα. Καὶ μικρὸν ἀνασφήλαντες, τὸ τῆς ἱερᾶς ζεύγλης ἄχθος ὁποῖόν ἐστιν ἐδιδάχθημεν, καὶ ἰατρεία τις ἡμῖν τοῦ δυσαλγοῦς ἀνέκυψε μώλωπος καὶ τῆς συνεχούσης σκοτοδινίας ἀνανεῦσαι συμβέβηκεν. Ἀλλὰ μὴ μέχρι τούτου σταίη τὰ τῆς νουθεσίας ὑμῶν ἐπαλείμματα, ἀλλὰ καὶ αὖθις τούτοις ἡμᾶς ἰατρεύοιτε καὶ τὰ τῆς ἀνίας ἐπώδυνα περικόπτοιτε, ὡς ἂν μὴ μετρηθείη παρὰ θεῷ τὰ τῆς ἁμαρτίας ἡμῶν ἐλαττώματα, καὶ ἡ προπετὴς πρὸς τὴν ἱερωσύνην ταχυτὴς ἐλεγχθείη, καὶ χεῖρας καὶ πόδας δεθείημεν, καὶ εἰς πῦρ βληθείημεν ὡς ἀνάξιον τοῦ ἐπαγγέλματος περικείμενοι ἔνδυμα· ἀλλὰ βλέπων παραβλέψοι τῶν παραπτωμάτων τὸ μέγεθος, καὶ ἐλέῳ χρηστότητος ἐξιάσεται.

Ἡ δὲ παρουσία ὑμῶν ἐν ἐλ ‖ 88 ‖ πίδι ἦν ἡμῖν διὰ Νικαίας γενέσθαι· τούτου μὲν διημάρτομεν· τῷ δὲ ὑμετέρῳ γράμματι ἐνοπτρίζεσθαι ταύτην οἰόμενοι παρεκλήθημεν. Τῇ γὰρ ἡμέρᾳ τῆς καθιδρύσεως ἡμῶν τοῦτο δεξάμενοι, μεγίστης χαρᾶς ἀφορμὴν συνελεξάμεθα· διὰ δὲ τὸ πολλὴν ἐνταῦθα συρρεῦσαι τοῦ δημοσίου ἐπίκλυσιν, τὴν ἡμέραν τῆς ἁγίας Χριστοῦ ἀναστάσεως ἐν τῇ βασιλευούσῃ ἑορτάσαι συνείδομεν· ἐν ᾗ καὶ ἀποληψόμεθα σὲ καὶ ἐν ἁγίῳ ἀσπασμῷ προσδεξόμεθα καὶ τὰ τῷ γράμματι λείποντα οἰκείῳ προσαναπληρώσομεν στόματι. Καὶ ἔρρωσο ἐν Κυρίῳ καὶ εὔχου ἡμῖν εὐαρεστεῖν αὐτῷ.

---

31 $\overset{\sigma\theta\theta}{\mu\iota\sigma}$ . . . V: corr. G ‖ 32 προξενίσοι V

9: Tit. Καρείας V: corr. G ‖ 5 ἀνασφείλαντ(ες) V: corr. G ‖ 7 ἀνανεῦσαν V: corr. G ‖ 17 ἡμέρᾳ G: ἡμετέρα V ‖ 18 τὸ G: τὴν V ‖ 19 ἡμέραν G: ἡμετέραν V ‖ 21 προσδεξάμεθα V: corr. G ‖ 22 προσαναπληρώσωμεν V: corr. G

rises in your way, wafting you on your godly course, and so, through your good works, grant you eternal reward in the other world.

9. To Nikephoros, bishop of Caria

A letter full of sacred inspiration has been brought by your Holiness, and I received it with open hands. It has instructed me in things divine and initiated me into sacerdotal perfection, thus scattering the thick cloud cover of despondency that had enveloped me. Having recovered a little, I learned what kind of burden is ⟨imposed by⟩ the priestly yoke; a remedy of my painful wounds appeared, and I was able to revive from the dizziness that gripped me. Let not the remedy of your instruction cease at this point: nay, would you but cure me thereby once again and remove the pain of my grief, so that my sinful shortcomings should not be reckoned by God, my rash eagerness for the priesthood should not be condemned, that I should not be bound hand and foot and cast into the fire for wearing a garment that is not worthy of my profession. But may He indeed overlook the greatness of my sins and cure me with the mercy of His goodness.

I had hoped that you would visit me at Nicaea. Of this I was disappointed, but was consoled by imagining your presence reflected in your letter. For, having received it on the day of my ordination, I derived great joy from it. Since a great throng of Treasury officials has gathered here, I have resolved to celebrate Christ's Resurrection in the capital. There I shall meet you again, receive you with a holy embrace, and supply with my own mouth what is lacking in this letter. Fare thee well in the Lord and pray that I should please Him.

10. Τῷ ἐπισκόπῳ τοῦ Ταΐου

Πῶς οὕτω ταχέως ἐπιλελῆσθαι συμβέβηκεν τῇ ὁσιότητί σου ὧν παρ' ἡμῶν ἤκουσε καὶ ἐνετάλθη ἐν τῇ πανευδαίμονι καὶ βασιλίδι πόλει; Οὐ γὰρ παίζοντες ἀλλὰ καὶ λίαν σπουδάζοντες διελέχθημεν καὶ παρηνέσαμεν αὐτῇ περὶ τῶν ἀφαιρεθέντων ἐκ τῆς ἱερᾶς ἐκκλησίας ἡμῶν σεπτῶν κειμηλίων παρὰ τοῦ τὴν ἐπισκοπὴν ὑμῶν καινίσαντος μητροπολίτου, καὶ παρασχεθέντων ὑμῖν χρείας μικρᾶς ἕνεκα· καὶ τί λογίσασθαι ἀγνοοῦμεν· λέγομεν δὲ ὅτι λήθη καὶ αὔραις ταῦτα παρέπεμψεν περικρατὴς ἐκείνων οἰομένη φανήσεσθαι. Ἀλλὰ τοῦτο μὴ ἐν ἐλπίδι κείσθω παρ' ὑμῖν. Ἰδοὺ γὰρ καὶ τῇ διὰ γράμματος ὁμιλίᾳ χρησάμενοι ἐπιβεβαιοῦμεν ὡς ἄν, πᾶσαν ἀναβολὴν ἀπορρί || 89 || ψασα, καὶ τὴν εἰς αὔριον προσδοκίαν ἀπωσαμένη, διὰ θερμῆς ταχυτῆτος τὴν ἀπόδοσιν τῶν ἱερῶν κειμηλίων ποιήσηται, καὶ μὴ δι' ἀμελείας καὶ καταφρονήσεως ἔνοχον ἑαυτὴν τῇ μεγάλῃ ἐκκλησίᾳ ταύτῃ ἐγκαταστήσοι. Εἰ γὰρ καὶ προφάσεις ἀνακινεῖν ἐθέλοι ὡς προῖξ καὶ δῶρον δέδοται αὐτῇ παρὰ τοῦ εἰρημένου μητροπολίτου, ἀλλ' οὐκ ἔστιν ὁ συνιστῶν τοῦτο καὶ ἐπιμαρτυρῶν, ἀλλ' οὐδὲ παρεγράφη ἐν τοῖς βρεβείοις τῆς ἐκκλησίας ὡς μὴ μέλλοντα ἀνθυπονοστεῖν, ἀλλὰ καὶ λίαν ἀκριβὴς ἐν αὐτοῖς ἀπογραφὴ ἐνεσημάνθη, πρὸς τὸ τῶν ἰδίων κυρίαν τὴν ἐκκλησίαν γενήσεσθαι. Ἵνα δὲ καὶ κατὰ τὸν τῆς ἱερωσύνης θεῖον θεσμὸν λέγειν ἔχωμεν, οὐδεμία τις ἐξουσία ὑπῆν τῷ ῥηθέντι μητροπολίτῃ τὰ τῆς εὐαγεστάτης καὶ καθολικῆς ἐκκλησίας ἀπαλλοτριοῦν κειμήλια. Ταῦτα τοίνυν τὰ νῦν καὶ τὰ πρότερον ἐνωτισθήτω, καὶ τὴν τῶν ἱερῶν μεθ' ἑαυτῆς ποιήσεται παρουσίαν, ἀποθησαυρίζουσα ταῦτα ἐν τοῖς ἱεροῖς ταμιείοις τῆς ἐκκλησίας· καὶ ἡ ὑμετέρα ὁσιότης ἐξ ὧν ὑπεμνημάτισεν καὶ ὑπέσχετο ἐν αὐτῇ τῇ χειροθεσίᾳ αὐτῆς παρασχεῖν τῷ μέρει τῆς ἐπισκοπῆς, χρυσίου ποσότητα ἀποτιννύτω, καὶ τὴν ἐκκλησίαν ἑαυτῆς ἀνασωσάσθω, ἵνα καὶ ἡ μνήμη αὐτῆς διαρκέσῃ ἐν τῷ ποιμνίῳ αὐτῆς. Ἀλλὰ μὴ ἐκ τῆς τῶν ἀλλοτρίων συνεισφορᾶς κολοιοῦ δίκην ἐπιμορφάζειν τὴν ἑαυ || 90 || τῆς ἐκκλησίαν σπουδάσειεν· ἐπεί, τῶν ἀλλοτρίων ἀφαιρεθέντων, τὸ λοιπὸν κἂν ἡμεῖς μὴ λέγωμεν, αὐτὴ συναγέτω. Καὶ ἔρρωσο καὶ εὔχου ὑπὲρ ἡμῶν.

10: 3 *οὐ γάρ – σπουδάζοντες*: cf. Pl. *Leg.* I.636c etc. || 28 *κολοιοῦ δίκην*: cf. Aesop. *Fab.* 200[b]; Lucian. *Apol.* 4; Greg. Naz. *Carm.* I.29, 55–57, etc.

10: 12 *κειμιλίων* V: corr. G || 14 *ὡς προῖξ* in marg., *ὡς προῖκα* in textu V || 20 *ἔχομεν* V: corr. G || 21 *κειμίλια* V || 23 fortasse *ποιησάτω* legendum || 30 *αὔτη* V

10. To the bishop of Taion

How has your Reverence managed to forget so quickly what I have told you and instructed you to do in the felicitous imperial city? It was not in jest, but most seriously that I spoke to you and admonished you concerning the sacred vessels that had been removed from our holy Church by the metropolitan who restored your bishopric and lent to you for a temporary need. I do not know how to regard ⟨your behavior⟩; I am saying, however, that you have consigned this matter to oblivion and to the breezes in the expectation of taking possession of the vessels. But of this you should have no hope. For behold, here is my confirmation in writing: abandon all delay and, without postponement until the next day, return the sacred vessels with all speed lest, through indifference and contempt, you make yourself guilty before this great Church. If you wish to invent excuses that these things had been given to you as a free gift by the said metropolitan, there is no one to confirm it or witness it, nor have they been deleted in the inventory of the Church as objects that would not be returned; on the contrary, a clear annotation has been entered therein to the effect that the Church would remain mistress of her own property. If I may, furthermore, quote the holy law of priesthood, the said metropolitan had no authority whatsoever to alienate the vessels of our most-holy catholic Church. Taking heed of my present and my previous words, you should present yourself together with the sacred objects and deposit them in the holy treasury of the Church. Furthermore, your Reverence should pay in respect of your bishopric a sum of money out of what you covenanted in writing to contribute at the time of your ordination, and so redeem your Church that your memory may remain among your flock. You should not, like a jackdaw, strive to deck out your Church with the contribution of others; for once these contributions have been taken away, you can understand the rest even if I do not say it. Farewell and pray for me.

11. Τῷ ἐπισκόπῳ τῶν Νουμερικῶν

Πολλὰ μὲν ἦν τὰ πρὸς πληροφορίαν ἡμᾶς ἐκκαλούμενα περὶ τῆς ὑμετέρας ὁσιότητος καὶ δεικνύντα ὡς οὐ κατὰ τοὺς ἱεροὺς κανόνας ἑαυτὴν ἄγει καὶ διευθύνει καὶ τῆς ἀποστολικῆς κατ' οὐδὲν παράπτεται τρίβου· οἷον τὸ τῷ θεῷ πάλαι καθιερῶσθαι· τὸ ἐν τοῖς θείοις ἐσχολακέναι λογίοις· τὸ ἐν τῷ μεγίστῳ τετάχθαι βαθμῷ τῆς μητρὸς καὶ βασιλίδος πασῶν τῶν ἐκκλησιῶν. Καὶ ἰδοὺ ὁρῶμεν ὀλίγα τούτων ὑμᾶς φροντίσαι. Εἰ γὰρ ἐν ἐρεύνῃ καὶ μελέτῃ τῶν εἰρημένων καθίστατο, οὐκ ἂν ἐν λήθῃ γέγονεν, τί τὸ προκαθεζόμενον καὶ τί τὸ ὑποβεβηκός· τίς ἡ κεφαλὴ καὶ τί τὸ τῶν ποδῶν ἔχον ἀξίωμα. Ἔδει γὰρ μηνυθεῖσαν τὴν ἡμῶν παρουσίαν σκυλῆναι καὶ ἐπισκέψασθαι ἡμᾶς, ἢ καὶ παρ' ἡμῶν ἐπεσκέφθαι· ἔπραξε γὰρ ἂν οὐδὲν ἐκτόπως, ἀλλὰ καὶ λίαν ἐπῃνέθη παρὰ θεῷ τε καὶ ἡμῖν· οὐδὲ γὰρ εἵνεκέν τινος δόσεως ἢ λήψεως τὰ τῆς παρουσίας ὑμῶν πρὸς ἡμᾶς γενέσθαι πόθον εἴχομεν, ἀλλ', ἀποστολικῶς φάναι, μὴ ζητεῖν ἡμᾶς τὰ ὑμῶν ἀλλ' ὑμᾶς· ἀπολαῦσαι δὲ μᾶλλον ὑμῶν καὶ ὅσα πρὸς ἐκκλησιαστικὴν συντείνει ὠφέλειαν ὁμιλῆσαι, καὶ τὸ ὑστεροῦν δι' ἐμμελείας ἐπιμελοῦς ἀνασώσασθαι. Ἐπεὶ δὲ ταῦτα || 91 || μὴ γέγονεν, ποίᾳ χρήσασθαι βούλεται ἀπολογίᾳ περὶ τούτων ἐρωτωμένη, αὐτῇ καὶ μόνον τυγχάνει γνωστόν. Οὐκοῦν εἰ τὴν ἐπιτεθεῖσαν αὐτῇ τῆς ἱερατείας ζεύγλην ἕλκειν βούλεται, καὶ προῄρηται τὴν τῆς ἐκκλησίας αὔλακα τέμνειν καὶ πολύχουν ἐξ αὐτῆς δρέπεσθαι κέρδος, ἐπιγνώτω τὸν ἑαυτῆς ποιμένα καὶ καλοῦντα· κλινάτω οὖς εὐήκοον, καὶ μὴ ἀπωσάσθω λόγον ὠφελείας πρόξενον, καὶ μὴ μακρυνάτω τὴν ἑαυτῆς ἀπουσίαν, ἀλλ' ἐγγίσαι ἡμῖν διὰ τῆς παρουσίας αὐτῆς ἐπικρινάτω· ἵνα μὴ ἐπὶ πλεῖον ἀφηνιάζουσα καὶ τῶν κεκανονισμένων ὅρων ἐκτὸς ἀπονεύουσα τὴν ἐκκλησιαστικὴν ἐπιτιμίαν ἐφ' ἑαυτὴν ἐπισπάσοιτο· καὶ ἔρρωσο· καὶ τὴν τῶν γεγραμμένων τάχιον ἐκτέλεσον ἔκβασιν, ἵν' ἐπὶ τούτοις πνευματικῶς ἑορτάσωμεν καὶ τὰ μεσιτεύσαντα σκῶλα ἐκ τῆς ἑαυτῶν ἐκκαθάρωμεν διανοίας.

11: 12 *δόσεως καὶ λήψεως*: cf. Phil. 4.15 || 14 *μὴ ζητεῖν – ὑμᾶς*: 2 Cor. 12.14 || 18–19 *τῆς ἱερατείας ζεύγλην*: cf. Theodoreti *Hist. rel.* XV.4, ed. P. Canivet and A. Leroy-Molinghen, SC 257 (Paris, 1979), p. 22 || 21 *οὖς εὐήκοον*: cf. Pr. 25.12

11: 2 *ου* supra versum scriptum V || 5 *λόγοις* V iota supra versum add. V[1] || 15 *συντείνει* in marg. V || 18 *αὐτη* V || 20 *τέμνειν* supra versum scriptum V

11. To the bishop of Noumerika

Many circumstances have been urging me to gain full knowledge concerning your Reverence and showing me that you are not behaving and directing yourself in accordance with the sacred canons and not following in any way the apostolic path: I mean the fact that I have been consecrated to God for a long time, that I have studied the holy Scriptures, and have been appointed to the highest rank of the Mother and Queen of all the Churches. Yet I see that you have set little store by these things. For, had you investigated and studied the aforesaid, you would not have forgotten who it is that presides and who has lower place; who is the head and who ranks with the feet. When you were informed of my presence, you ought to have bestirred yourself and visited me or else received me: in this you would have done nothing extraordinary—on the contrary, you would have won both God's and my approval. Indeed, I was desirous of your presence not for the sake of giving or receiving anything, but, to quote the Apostle, I sought you and not yours—to enjoy your company, to converse of those matters that are beneficial to the Church, and to retrieve with due care what has fallen behind. Since, however, this has not happened, you alone can know what excuse you wish to use when you are questioned on this score. Surely, if you wish to draw the yoke of the priesthood that had been laid upon you; if you have chosen to cut the furrow of the Church and reap therefrom a rich reward, you should recognize your shepherd when he calls you; you should bend an obedient ear and not ignore words productive of benefit; you should not prolong your absence, but consent to approach me with your presence, lest by rebellion against the reins and straying from the appointed bounds, you draw upon yourself the penalty of the Church.

Farewell and give a speedy issue to what I have written so that we may celebrate this event spiritually and sweep from our minds the obstacles that have intervened.

12. Τῷ ἐπισκόπῳ . . .

Πολὺς πόθος ἡμᾶς ἐπικάμπτει καὶ ἀγάπης ἐπίτασις τοῦ σὲ καὶ θεᾶσθαι καὶ πνευματικῶς περιπτύσσεσθαι τὴν σὴν θεοφιλίαν· ἀλλ' ἐπεὶ νοσεῖν αὐτὴν καὶ πονηρῶς περὶ τὸ σῶμα διακεῖσθαι, συμβὰν οὕτω, διέγνωμεν, τὸ ὅπως ἀλγεινῶς διετέθημεν πληροφορεῖν οὐδένα βουλόμεθα, ἐνδομυχοῦσαν καὶ σμύχουσαν τὴν λύπην ὁσημέραι περιφέροντες. Ἀλλ' αἰτοῦμεν τὸν πάντων ἰατρόν τε καὶ Κύριον τῇ ἄνωθεν αὐτοῦ ἑτοίμῃ χρηστότητι τὸν ἔλεον ὑμῖν ἐπιχέαι δαψιλῶς τῆς ἰάσεως, ὡς ἂν διὰ τάχους εὐαγγέλια τῆς ὑμῶν ὑγιείας δεξαίμεθα, καὶ τὸ τῆς ἡμῶν ἐφ' ὑμῖν ἀνίας ‖ 92 ‖ παῦλαν δέχηται ἄλγημα. Καὶ γένοιτο, θεοῦ διδόντος φιλανθρώπως τὴν αἴτησιν. Τὰ δὲ ἀπεσταλμένα δεξάμενοι ἥσθημεν καὶ λίαν ἠγάσθημεν τῇ ἐν ὑμῖν προαιρέσει, ἃ καὶ ἀντὶ πολλῆς ὁλκῆς ἀργυρίου τερπνότητα λελογίσμεθα.

13. Τῷ ἐπισκόπῳ Ἑλενουπόλεως

Οὐ μῆκος παρῳχήκει χρόνου ἀφ' οὗ τὴν πορείαν ἐν Πραινέτῳ καὶ πρὸς ὑμᾶς ἐστειλάμεθα, ἐν ᾗ τὴν ὑμετέραν ἱστορῆσαι πόθον εἴχομεν ὁσιότητα. Ἀλλ' ἐν στερήσει ταύτης γενόμενοι βαρέως ἠνέγκαμεν· ὅθεν ἐπὶ τὴν διὰ γράμματος ὁμιλίαν, προφάσεως εὐκαίρου δραξάμενοι, τραπῆναι συνείδομεν· ἥτις ἐν τούτοις ἐστίν· ἁλὸς χρείαν εἰς τὰ περὶ τὸ ζῆν ἐπιτήδεια δεδεήμεθα. Οὐ γὰρ βρωθήσεται, κατὰ τὸ λόγιον, ἄρτος ἄνευ ἁλός, καὶ πᾶν ὃ συντελεῖ πρὸς ἡδεῖαν γεῦσιν τῷ λάρυγγι, εἰ μὴ τούτῳ στυφθείη τῷ ἁλικράματι, οὐδὲ τροφὴ λογισθήσεται· διὰ δὴ τοῦτο ἐπὶ τὴν ὑμετέραν νόστιμον κεχωρήκαμεν δεξιάν, ἵν' ἐκ τῶν παρ' ὑμῖν πονηθέντων ἁλῶν καὶ τοῖς χρήζουσι τιμήματος νεμομένων καὶ ἡμᾶς ἁλισθῆναι δαψιλῶς, εἰ προαιρέσεως ἔχοιτο, οὐ προῖκα, ἀλλὰ μισθοῦ τοῦ προσήκοντος· ὅρῳ γὰρ ἀρραβῶνος χρυσίνους τρεῖς ἐκπεπόμφαμεν, ἕως

12: 1 *ἐπίστασις* V: corr. G ‖ 2 *τὴν σὴν θεο* . . . supra versum scriptum V ‖ 5 *ὡσημέραι* V ‖ 7 *ἡμῖν* V: corr. G ‖ 8 *ὑγείας* V: corr. G ‖ 8–9 *ὑμῶν ἐφ' ἡμῖν* V ‖ 9 *γένηται* V

13: 2 *ἱστορῆσαι*: cf. Gal. 1.18 ‖ 6–7 *βρωθήσεται – ἁλὸς*: Jb. 6.6

13: 6 *ἐπιτήδια* V ‖ 9 *ἣν* V ‖ 12 *ἕως*: *ὡς* V

12. To the bishop of . . .

I am pressed by great desire and intense longing to see your Reverence and give you a spiritual embrace, but since I learned that you happened to be ill and in sore bodily condition, I am unwilling to inform anyone of my pain as I carry with me, all day, grief deep in my heart and smoldering. I beseech the Lord, who is the physician of all men, to grant you in His ready goodness an abundant stream of healing from above, so that I may quickly receive the glad tidings of your recovery and that my sorrow on your behalf may cease. May this happen, God mercifully granting my prayer.

I received with pleasure the things you sent me and was overjoyed by your intention—they were a delight which I value more than a great mass of silver.

13. To the bishop of Helenopolis

It is not long since I went on a journey to Prainetos and to you, in the course of which I was desirous of visiting your Reverence. But, being deprived of your presence, I was grieved. Hence, seizing a favorable occasion, I have decided to have recourse to epistolary conversation. The occasion is this: we beg the use of salt for our provisions. For, as Scripture has it, bread cannot be eaten without salt, and everything that is tasty to the throat, unless it be seasoned with this condiment, shall not be accounted as food. For this reason I am having recourse to your nutritious hand: may we, too, be supplied in abundance, if you so approve, with the salt that is produced by you and is dispensed against payment to those that need it—not free of charge, but for a suitable price. By way of surety I have sent you three gold pieces

ἂν ἡμῖν ἐπιμετρηθῇ τὸ ἐκ συμφωνήσεως ποσὸν καὶ τηνικάδε χορηγηθείη πρὸς ἡμᾶς, θεοῦ τοῦτο ἐπὶ καιροῦ ἐπιτρέποντος, τῆς πάσης τιμῆς ἀνασωθείσης ὑμῖν· εἰς γὰρ δωδεκάτην αὐξήσει χρυσίου ποσότητα· ‖ 93 ‖ *καὶ εὔχεσθαι δυσωποῦμεν ὑπὲρ ἡμῶν, ἱερώτατε.*

14. Νικηφόρῳ *διακόνῳ καὶ χαρτοφύλακι*

Τὴν *σὴν ἑκάστης . . . περιστέφουσι τράπεζαν, μετ᾽ ἐκεῖνον τὸν ἡδύνοντα ἄρτον καρδίας στηρίζοντα, ὄψα μὲν ἀτταγᾶς τε καὶ φάτται καὶ πέρδικες καὶ ὅσα, κατὰ τὴν ποίησιν, τοῖς καϋστρίοις θαμίζουσι ῥεύμασι, γένη χηνῶν καὶ κύκνοι καὶ γέρανοι· ἀλλ᾽ οὐδ᾽ ὅσα κύνες πρὸς τροφὴν ἀνθρώπων θηρεύειν εἰώθασιν τῆς ὀψοποιΐας τῆς ὑμετέρας ἔξω που περιθέουσιν· σὺν ἐκείνοις δὲ διὰ τῆς τῶν μαγείρων τέχνης ὁδεύοντα καὶ δι᾽ ἐμμελοῦς ἐρεύνης πάσης ἀφαιρεθέντα κηλῖδος, οὕτω μεθ᾽ ἁλῶν ὀριτρόφων παττόμενα, καρυκευτικαῖς εὐωδίαις κεράννυνται, καὶ διὰ πεμπωβόλων ὀργάνων τὴν φλόγα καλῶς ὑπερχόμενα, ἢ καὶ ζωμοῖς ἀρωματίζουσιν ἐννηχόμενα, ἡδεῖαν πνοὴν καὶ τροφὴν ἀπερεύγονται καὶ τοῖς αἰσθητηρίοις εὐετηρίαν χαρίζονται.* Τούτοις *οἱ παρὰ σοὶ δαιτυμόνες ἐπ᾽ ὀνείασι χεῖρας ἰάλλουσι.*

Καὶ *ταῦτα μὲν οὐχ ὡς ἐρῶντά σε τρυφῆς γράφειν ἠπείχθημεν· ἴσμεν γὰρ τὴν ὀλιγάρκειαν παρὰ σοὶ σιτευομένην ὁσημέραι, καὶ τὴν τρυφὴν ἐν τῇ σῇ διαίτῃ λιμώττουσαν· ἀλλ᾽ ἵνα τὸ παρ᾽ ἡμῖν λιμναῖον ὄψον ὡς πρῶτον αἶσχος ἐπικαλύψωμεν, πᾶσαν ἐλαχιστείαν ἐξ αὐτῆς ἐντεύξεως περικείμενον* ‖ 94 ‖ *καὶ ὅλην ἀηδίαν ἐκ τῆς ἐμφύτου καὶ βρομώδους ὀσμῆς προϊέμενον, καὶ διὰ τοῦτο μηδὲ δῶρον καλεῖσθαι δυνάμενον, τὴν ὑμετέραν ἐξηλλαγμένως ἐξήραμεν τράπεζαν.* Ἀλλ᾽ *ὡς εἰδυῖα τοῖς τελείοις καὶ πνευματικῶς τρέφουσι καὶ τοῖς ταπεινοῖς συναπάγεσθαι ἡ ὑμετέρα προαίρεσις, καὶ τοῦτο δυσωπηθείη προσδέξασθαι· ἀπορίᾳ γὰρ ἡμεῖς τοῦ μὴ κατ᾽ ἀξίαν τι προσαγηοχέναι, ταῦτα καὶ λέγειν καὶ γράφειν παρωρμήθημεν.*

14: 2 *ἄρτον – στηρίζοντα*: Ps. 103 (104).15 ‖ 4 *γένη – γέρανοι*: *Il.* 2.460 ‖ 9 *πεμπωβόλων*: *Il.* 1.463; *Od.* 3.460 ‖ 12 *ἐπ᾽ ὀνείασι – ἰάλλουσι*: *Od.* 1.149 et al. ‖ 20–21 *τοῖς ταπεινοῖς συναπάγεσθαι*: Rom. 12.16

14: 1 post *ἑκάστης* (sine accentu) lacuna ca. 10 litt. ‖ *εκείνιον* V ‖ 2 *ἡδύνὀντα* V ‖ *ἀτταγάς* V: *ὄρτυγες* G ‖ 3 *καϋστηρίοις* V: corr. G ‖ 9 *πεμποβόλων* V ‖ 11 *εὐητηρίαν* V ‖ 13 *ὅς*: V corr. G ‖ 14 an *ὀλιγαρκίαν* scribendum? ‖ *ὡσημέραι* V ‖ 15 *λιμόττουσαν* V corr. G ‖ 18 *ὁρμῆς* V ‖ 22 *ἡμᾶς το* V corr. G ‖ *προσαγειοχέναι* V corr. G

until the agreed quantity is delivered and handed over to us at a future time (God allowing it then), when you will recover the entire sum; for the amount of gold shall increase to twelve pieces. I beg your Holiness to pray for me.

14. To Nikephoros, deacon and *chartophylax*

⟨Delicacies⟩ surround your table every day, namely—in addition to bread that soothes and sustains the stomach—dishes such as francolin, pigeons, and partridges, and those fowl that, according to the Poet, frequent the Caystrian stream—geese of different kinds, swans, and cranes. Not even the game that dogs are wont to hunt to provide food for men is excluded from your cuisine; but, passing through the hands of skillful cooks—the game as well as the fowl—freed, after careful scrutiny, from every blemish, they are then besprinkled with mountain-nurtured salt, mixed with savory sauces, and thoroughly roasted on five-pronged spits or submerged in aromatic gravy so as to exude a sweet smell and taste and bestow pleasure on the senses. To such victuals do your guests put forth their hands.

I have been driven to write these things not because you are a lover of luxury—indeed, I know that frugality prevails in your house every day, whereas luxury is left starving in your regimen—but that I may conceal as a signal disgrace the fish of our lake whose exiguity is apparent at first sight and which, by its inherent bad odor, produces nothing but disgust. For this reason—since it cannot even be called a gift—I have extolled your table so extravagantly. But since your Judgment knows how to accommodate itself to perfect spiritual nourishment as well as to the lowly, may it please accept this present; for, being at a loss to make a worthy offering, I have been urged to say and write these things.

15. Τῷ *αὐτῷ*

Λακωνίζειν οὐκ ἀττικίζειν καιρός· μακρὰ γὰρ περὶ μικρῶν λέγειν ἀσύμφορον. Πῶς εἰρωνείαν καλέσαι τὴν ἡμῶν πρὸς σὲ φιλίαν ὑπέμεινας, ἀδελφῶν ἐμοὶ καὶ φίλων ἀκρότατε; Οὐκ εἴρωνες ἡμεῖς, οὐκ ἀστεϊσμόν, οὐ σαρκασμόν ποτε κατὰ φιλίας τροπολογεῖν ἐσπουδάκαμεν. Εἰ γὰρ τὰ νῦν ἐπεσταλμένα τοῖς πάλαι παιχθεῖσι συνέβαλες, πόρρω που τὴν εἰρωνείαν ἀπώσειας· ἐκείνων δέ, ὡς ὁρῶμεν, ἀμνημονήσας καὶ ταύτῃ τὰ πρωτεῖα δοὺς παρ' ἡμῖν ἀποφέρεσθαι, τί ἄλλο γε ἢ κεκλῆσθαι τῷ ταύτης ἡμᾶς ἐπιφημίζεις ὀνόματι; Ἀλλ' ἐπεὶ τῇ ὑμετέρᾳ τελείᾳ νήψει ἡ τοῦ γράμματος ἁπλότης ἐνομίσθη διπλόη, τοῦτο μέν, κατὰ τὸν εἰπόντα, φέροιεν ἀναρπάξασαι ἄελλαι· μενέτω δὲ τῶν ἑαυτῆς ὅρων ἡ ἀδιάβλητος ἐντὸς ἀγάπη, εἰρήνην ταῖς ἡμετέραις καρδίαις βραβεύουσα. ‖ 95 ‖

16. Ἰ*ωάννῃ ἡγουμένῳ* Κ*ωμῶν*

Οὐδὲν τῆς τοῦ θεοῦ περὶ ἡμᾶς κηδεμονίας ἀνώτερον, καὶ οὐδὲν τῆς τῶν ἀνθρώπων ταλαιπωρίας πρὸς κακίαν ἐπιρρεπέστερον· ὅτι αὐτῷ μὲν τὸ ἀγαθὸν συνουσίωται, ἡμῖν δὲ τὸ ἐναντίον ἐκ προαιρέσεως συνῳκείωται. Ἐπιγνώτω οὖν ἡ ἀμίμητος ὑμῶν ἐπ' ἀρετῇ τελειότης τὸν τὸ γράμμα τῆς ἡμετέρας κομίζοντα μετριότητος· ὅτι, πτώματι περιπαρεὶς ὑπὸ τοῦ εὑρετοῦ τῆς κακίας δαίμονος, ἑκουσίου φόνου αὐτουργὸς κατέστη· ὅς, τὸ τοῦ μύσους δεινὸν ὑφορώμενος, τῇ ἐκκλησίᾳ προσπέφευγεν· εἶτα τῇ φιλανθρώπῳ κρίσει καὶ διακρίσει τοῦ ἁγιωτάτου καὶ οἰκουμενικοῦ πατριάρχου ἐντυχών, καὶ τὰ κατ' αὐτὸν οἰκείῳ στόματι ἐξαγορεύσας, τῇ κανονικῇ ἀποφάσει καὶ δικαίᾳ ἐπιτιμήσει ἑαυτὸν ἐν ὑποπτώσει παρέδωκεν. Ὅθεν, ὡς ἀκλινεῖ τῶν ἱερῶν κανόνων φύλακι καὶ εἰδήμονι, τῇ ὑμετέρᾳ εὐλαβεῖ διακρίσει τοῦτον πεπομφέναι

15: 1 *λακωνίζειν οὐκ ἀττικίζειν*: cf. Xen. *Hell.* VI.3.14 ‖ *μακρὰ – λέγειν*: cf. Eur. *Or.* 758 ‖ 10 *φέροιεν – ἄελλαι*: *Od.* 8.409

15: 1 *μικρον* V: corr. G

16: 3 *τῶ ἀγα*^{θ} V: corr. G ‖ 4 *συνοικείωται* V

15. To the same

It is time to use the Laconian, not the Attic style, for it is unprofitable to speak at length about trifling matters. How could you have suffered to give the name of irony to my friendship toward you, O best of my brethren and friends? I am not ironic; I have never sought to use the tropes of humor or sarcasm against friendship. Had you compared my last letter to our previous jokes, you would have dismissed any notion of irony. But, as I see, having forgotten those jokes and decided that irony stands foremost in my mind, what else can you declare but to label me with that name? Since the simplicity of my letter appeared duplicitous to your prefect Moderation, let that, as the saying goes, be carried off by the wind; but let love that does not listen to calumny remain within her bounds and bestow peace on our hearts.

16. To John, abbot of Komai

Nothing surpasses God's solicitude on our behalf just as there is nothing more inclined to evil than man's miserable estate; for goodness is joined essentially with Him, while the opposite dwells with us by our choice.

May, therefore, your Perfection, inimitable as it is in virtue, take due cognizance of the bearer of this letter from my mediocrity; namely, that, having been entangled in sin by the Devil (the inventor of the evil), he has voluntarily committed murder. This man, in fear of the dreadful defilement, sought refuge with the Church. Later, having met with the merciful judgment and discernment of the most-holy ecumenical patriarch, and having confessed his affairs with his own mouth, he delivered himself in submission to the canonical sentence and just penance. For this reason ⟨the patriarch⟩ deemed it proper that he be sent to your pious Discernment inasmuch as you are a steadfast guardian and expert of the holy canons; so that, administered by you or, rather, by the customary regulations, he may rub off the stain of this calamity

καλῶς ἐδικαίωσεν, ὡς ἂν ταῖς αὐτῆς, μᾶλλον δὲ ταῖς πρακτικαῖς οἰκονομούμενος διατάξεσι, τὸ τοῦ πάθους ἀποτρίψηται σπίλος καὶ τοῦ πολυμόχθου τούτου καθαρθείη μιάσματος. Τοῦτον οὖν οἰκονομήσει ἡ ὑμετέρα ἐξαίρετος εὐλάβεια, τῷ κανόνι τοῦ ἱεροφάντου πατρὸς ἡμῶν Βασιλείου τῷ φάσκοντι "ὁ ἑκουσίως φονεύσας μετὰ δὲ τοῦτο μεταμεληθεὶς εἴκοσιν ἔτεσιν ἀκοινώνητος ἔσται || 96 || τοῖς ἁγιάσμασιν." Ἡ δὲ τοῦ χρόνου οἰκονομία ἡμῖν δήλη καθέστηκεν· ἥν, κατὰ τὸν κόπον τοῦ ἐπιτιμωμένου καὶ τὴν ἐπὶ τῷ ἀγαθῷ προκοπήν, ἡ ὑμετέρα ἐπιμετρήσει εὐμενὴς διάκρισις. Καὶ εὔχεσθαι ὑπὲρ ἡμῶν δυσωποῦμεν, ὡς παρρησίαν πρὸς τὸ κρεῖττον καὶ οἰκειότητα φέροντας.

17. Τῷ διοικητῇ τοῦ Ταΐου

Ἔδει μὲν ἡμᾶς, ἀνθρώπους ὄντας καὶ συνειδήσεως κριτηρίῳ τὸν λογισμὸν προκαθήμενον φέροντας, σφᾶς αὐτοὺς ἑαυτῶν καθιστᾶν ἐπιγνώμονας καὶ διορθώσει τῶν πεπραγμένων πρὸς βελτίωσιν ἐπανάγεσθαι, ἀλλὰ μὴ δι' ἑτέρων νουθεσίας πρὸς τὸ ἀγαθὸν ἀπευθύνεσθαι καὶ τὴν ἀρετὴν κατεργάζεσθαι. Ἐπειδὴ δέ, κατὰ τὸ γεγραμμένον, οὐ πάντων ἡ γνῶσις, χρεὼν διὰ τῆς τῶν ἀγαθῶν συνουσίας καὶ συμβουλῆς τὸ κρεῖττον ἐκλέγεσθαι καὶ ζημίας ψυχικῆς ἀπαλλάττεσθαι.

Τὴν οὖν ὑμετέραν κατὰ Χριστὸν τελειότητα δι' ἀκοῆς ἴσμεν μεγίσταις ἀρεταῖς ἐγκαλλωπίζεσθαι, ὥστε οὐδὲ γράφειν βουλῆς ἦμεν, ἤδη τὸ ἀγαθοεργεῖν καὶ πρὸ τῶν γραμμάτων ἐπιεικῶς μεμεριμνημένον ἔχουσαν· ἵνα δὲ τελείαν αὐτῷ τὴν ὠφέλειαν προξενεῖν νομισθείημεν * Οὐ γὰρ ἀγνοεῖν οἰόμεθα τὴν μεγίστην ὑμῶν ἐπὶ συνέσει ἀγχίνοιαν, ὡς ἡ ἐπισκοπὴ τοῦ Ταΐου πολλοῖς χρόνοις τὸ τῆς ἐπισκοπῆς ἀπώλεσεν ὄνομα, καὶ || 97 || σὺν αὐτῷ τὰ κατ' αὐτὴν δικαιώματα. Χήρα γὰρ καὶ ἄνανδρος μέχρι που τῶν ἄρτι χρόνων ἐκάθευδεν καὶ τὴν ἑαυτῆς ἀτεκνίαν, μᾶλλον δὲ τὴν τῶν τέκνων ἐρημίαν, πενθήρη σάκκον καὶ κατη-

---

16: 17–18 *ὁ ἑκουσίως – ἁγιάσμασιν*: Basil. *Can.* 40 (56). Cf. M. Arranz, *I penitenziali bizantini* (Rome, 1993), 60

13–14 *οἰκονομούμενον* V || 14 *σπῆλος* V: corr. G || 16 *τὸ κανόνι* V

17: 5–6 *οὐ πάντων ἡ γνῶσις*: 1 Cor. 8.7 || 10 *ἀγαθοεργεῖν*: 1 Tim. 6.18; Acta 14.17

17: 11 post *νομισθείημεν* lacunam statuimus || 13 *ταιοῦ* V

and be cleansed of this painful pollution. Your exceptional Piety will treat him according to the canon of that sacred teacher, our Father Basil, which proclaims: "He who has killed voluntarily and then repented shall be excommunicated from the sacraments for twenty years." The disposition with regard to the period of time is known to us, and your kindly Discernment will apply it according to the toil of the penitent and his progress toward betterment. We beseech you to pray for us inasmuch as you have liberty of approach and familiarity with the Godhead.

17. To the tax collector of Taion

Since we are men and reason presides at the tribunal of our conscience, we should become our own appraisers and, by correcting our actions, be led to improvement, instead of being directed toward the good and achieve virtue through the admonition of others. Seeing, however, that, as Scripture has it, knowledge is not in every man, it is needful that through the company and counsel of good men we choose what is best and liberate ourselves from spiritual damage.

We know by report that your Christian Perfection is adorned with the greatest virtues, and so I was not intending to write to you at all, inasmuch as you had probably bethought yourself already of doing good even before ⟨receiving⟩ my letter. But that I may appear to be causing you a perfect benefit . . . For I suppose that your Sagacity (great as it is in intelligence) is not unaware of the fact that the bishopric of Taion had for many years lost the title of a bishopric and therewith the property deeds appertaining to her. Until fairly recent times she remained dormant, a widow deprived of her husband, and, clad in the sackcloth of mourning and robes of despondency, she lamented her childlessness or rather the desolation of her children. Since,

φείας ἐνδεδυμένη στολήν, ἀπωδύρετο. Ἐπειδὴ δὲ θεός, ὁ τὰ παλαιὰ καὶ γηράσκοντα καὶ εἰς ἀφάνειαν ἐληλακότα δι' ἀνακαινώσεως νεάζειν διδούς, καὶ τὰ πόρρω ἐγγὺς ἄγειν εὐδοκῶν, καὶ ταύτην παλαιᾷ πτώσει περιπαρεῖσαν ἀνακύψαι καὶ φῶς ἰδεῖν ἐλεύθερον ἐδικαίωσεν, καὶ τὸ ἀρχαῖον ἀξίωμα δέξασθαι, καὶ τὴν ἑαυτῆς τιμὴν ἐπενδύσασθαι κέκρικεν· καὶ τοῦτο οὐκ αὐτονόμῳ προπετείᾳ, ἐπινεύσει δὲ μᾶλλον τῶν ἐκ θεοῦ προλαμπόντων μεγάλων βασιλέων, καὶ τῆς καθολικῆς ἐκκλησίας συνεπιβαλλομένης, τὴν περαίωσιν ἔλαβεν· καὶ ἰδοὺ χρηματίζει πόλις καὶ ἐπὶ θρόνου προκάθηται καὶ ποιμένα βακτηρίᾳ διδασκαλίας ἐπερειδόμενον καὶ ἐπὶ νομὰς ζωηφόρους τὸ ποίμνιον προκαλούμενον, ἐνιδρυμένον καὶ τῇ τοῦ Πνεύματος προβεβλημένον ἔχει νεύσει καὶ χάριτι· πενία δὲ τὴν αὐτῆς περιστοιχίζει προεδρίαν διὰ τὴν τῶν δικαιωμάτων ἀφαίρεσιν· ἔνθεν καὶ τὸ ἀπαρρησίαστον ἔχουσα πένεται, καὶ τῶν ταύτην πιεζόντων καὶ συνεχόντων ἡ προαίρεσις ὑπνοῖ, λήθην λαβόντων τῆς ἠπειλημένης τοῖς ἀδικοῦσι δεινῆς ‖ 98 ‖ *ἀποφάσεως. Ἵνα δὲ τὸ πᾶν ὑμῖν ἐκκαλύψωμεν, λόγος παρὰ πολλῶν ἦλθεν εἰς ἡμᾶς ὡς καὶ ἡ ὑμετέρα ἐν Χριστῷ σύνεσις ἀποκεκληρωμένον τόπον τῇ ἐκκλησίᾳ ἐκείνῃ ἐκ πατρικῆς κληροδοσίας νενέμηται· ὅθεν ὑποτιθέμεθα καὶ τὸ καλὸν ἐνώπιον αὐτῆς προτίθεμεν, ὡς ἂν μὴ τὸ ἀλλότριον, μᾶλλον δὲ τὸ τοῦ θεοῦ, παρ' ἑαυτῇ μένοι· ἀλλὰ τῇ πολλοῖς χρόνοις στερηθείσῃ τῶν ἑαυτῆς δικαιωμάτων ἐκκλησίᾳ τούτων ἐγγραφῆναι κυρίαν, καὶ μὴ τὸ ἐλάττωμα τῆς ἁρπαγῆς τοῦ ὑμετέρου πατρὸς εἰς κληρονομίαν ὑμῖν λογισθείη· μᾶλλον δὲ καὶ αὐτὸν ἐκ τούτου ἀνακαλέσασθαι μιάσματος προθυμηθείη ⟨πρὶν ἢ⟩ ἐπ' ἐξουσίαν καὶ κριτήρια μείζονα καταστῆναι, μήπως, οὐδεμιᾶς μοίρας τοῦ δικαίου συνηγορούσης, τὴν ἧτταν ἐξ αὐτῆς βαλβῖδος καὶ προσβολῆς ἀπενέγκοιτο. Σπευσάτω οὖν καὶ ἑαυτῆς γενέσθαι καὶ τῆς ἐκκλησίας καὶ τὸ ἐπιβάλλον τῆς ἀρχαίας αὐτῇ περιουσίας κατέχειν μὴ προαιρείσθω· ὡς μὴ ἐπὶ πολὺ τοῦτο παρ' ἑαυτῇ κατέχουσα ἀπαραίτητον εὕροι τὴν ἐκεῖ τοῦ ἀπαραλογίστου κριτηρίου ἀπόφασιν. Καὶ ἔστω Κύριος ὁ θεὸς ἐπιχορηγῶν ὑμῖν τὰ παρ' ἑαυτοῦ ἀγαθὰ καὶ τῶν ἀλλοτρίων ἀφέξεσθαι εὐδοκήσοι καὶ ἀναδείξοι ἀγαθοεργοῦντα τῆς ἄνω τυχεῖν ἀκηράτου τῶν ἀγαθῶν μετουσίας καὶ ἀνταποδόσεως.*

17–18 *τὰ παλαιὰ – ἐληλακότα*: cf. He. 8.13 ‖ 19 *τὰ πόρρω ἐγγὺς ἄγειν*: cf. Eph. 2.13 ‖ 29 *τὸ ἀπαρρησίαστον – πένεται*: cf. Chrys. *Hom. XVIII in Hebraeos,* PG 63, 137 ‖ 31 *τῆς ἠπειλημένης – ἀποφάσεως*: cf. Lc. 13.27 sqq. ‖ 41–42 *ἐξ αὐτῆς βαλβῖδος*: Zen. II.7; Greg. Cypr. Leid. I.56; Karathanasis 153

---

17 *ἐνδεδυμένην* V ‖ *ἀπωδύρατο* V ‖ 18 *ἀνακενώσεως* V: *ἀνανεώσεως* G ‖ 40 *ἐξουσία* V ‖ *κριτηρίῳ μείζονι* G ‖ 41 *μύρας* V: corr. G ‖ 43 *τῇ ἐκκλησία* V ‖ 44 *ὡσεὶ* V ‖ 45 *κρητηρίου* V: corr. G

however, God, who grants that things that are old and aging and have sunk into obscurity should be restored to youth by renewal, who deigns to bring close things that are distant, has also deemed fit that she, who had fallen upon an old calamity, should rise again and see the light of freedom; and He has decreed that she should receive her ancient title and be invested with her own dignity. And this was accomplished not through self-willed eagerness, but by the approval of the great emperors who shine forth by God's decree and the consent of the universal Church. And behold, she is become a city and presides on a throne, and has an established shepherd, appointed by the command and grace of the Spirit, who leans upon the staff of teaching and leads his flock to life-giving pastures. Yet poverty encompasses her episcopal see because of the removal of her property deeds. Wherefore, being deprived of her liberty, she is in need, and the goodwill of those who oppress and constrain her is slumbering, for they have forgotten the terrible sentence that has been uttered in threat against the unjust.

But, so that I may make the whole matter clear to you, word has come to me from many quarters that your Christian Sagacity, too, is holding by virtue of inheritance from your father a piece of land that had been allotted to that Church. Wherefore, I enjoin on you and propose that which is good, namely, that you should not keep what belongs to another, or rather to God; nay, that the Church, which for many years has been deprived of her deeds, should be registered as owner, lest the fault of your father's rapacity be reckoned as your inheritance. Rather should you seek to redeem him also from this pollution ⟨in anticipation of⟩ appearing before a higher authority and ⟨a higher⟩ tribunal, so that, no article of justice pleading on your behalf, you should not stand condemned from the very start. Hasten, therefore, to be master of yourself and do not choose to withhold from the Church what is due to her from her former property, lest, by withholding it for a long time, you meet with an inexorable sentence at the infallible Tribunal yonder. May the Lord our God provide you with the good things at His disposal and grant you to abstain in the future from the property of others and cause you by your good works to obtain the eternal participation in blessedness and recompense above.

18. Κωνσταντίνῳ ἐπισκόπῳ Γαγγρῶν || 99 ||

Ἐξ αὐτῆς καὶ μόνης ἐντεύξεως τὴν ὠφέλειαν διαπορθμεύειν οἶδε τοῖς πλησιάζειν ἐθέλουσιν ἡ ἀρχικὴ ὑμῶν καὶ πατρικὴ τελειότης· τὸ δὲ συνεῖναι αὐτῇ καὶ συναυλίζεσθαι τίνος οὐκ ἂν εἴη μεταδοτικὸν ὁλοσχεροῦς εὐλογίας; Τοιοῦτον *γὰρ ἡ ἀρετή· ἐν πᾶσι μὲν βιωφελῶς ἐξαπλουμένη, ἐν αὐτῇ δὲ μείωσιν ἥκιστα δεχομένη.* Οὕτω *σὲ καὶ ἴσμεν καὶ ἔχομεν, ὦ ἱερὰ καὶ φίλη θεῷ κεφαλή· ἡνίκα γὰρ τῆς παρουσίας αὐτῆς κατετρυφῶμεν, πολλῆς ἀπελαύομεν τῆς κατὰ ψυχὴν δαψιλείας· ἐπεὶ δὲ τῆς ἀπουσίας αὐτῆς ἐπησθόμεθα, ἔγνωμεν ὧν ἐστερήθημεν ὡς καλῶν τε καὶ ἀγαθῶν καὶ τοῦ παντὸς ἐπαξίων· ἀλλ' εἰ καὶ πορρωτέρω διέστηκεν, ἐγγισάτω ἡμῖν διὰ τῶν ἱερῶν αὐτῆς πρὸς θεὸν ἐντεύξεων, αἷς ἐπευφραίνειν τὸ θεῖον αὐτὴν ἀεὶ τεθαρρήκαμεν.* Ταύταις *τὸ ποίμνιον καταρτίσει στηρίξατε· ταύταις ὡς ῥάβδῳ καὶ βακτηρίᾳ λογικῶς ἐπερειδομένους κατανύξατε, ὡς ἂν ἡμᾶς ἑαυτοὺς κατευθύνωμεν καὶ τῶν ἐπερχομένων ἁρπάγων λύκων τὰς προσβολὰς κατευνάζωμεν· καὶ γὰρ εἰς τοῦτο πολλῆς τῆς ἐξ ὑμῶν ἐπικουρίας καὶ συνδρομῆς δεδεήμεθα, δι' ἧς τὰ συνοίσοντα καὶ σωτηρίας ἐχόμενα ἑαυτοῖς προξενήσαιμεν.* Ἔκ*τεινον τοιγαροῦν ὡς ὁ θεόπτης ἐκεῖνος τὰς χεῖρας* Μωϋσῆς *πρὸς τὸν ἐν οὐρανοῖς πατέρα, καὶ πᾶσαι κακεργέτιδες τῆς ἁμαρτίας ἡμῶν ἐπισυστάσεις* || 100 || *καλῶς τροπωθήσονται, καὶ ὁ κατὰ ψυχὴν ἡμῖν ἀμαληκίτης λωφήσει πόλεμος.* Στῆθι *κατενώπιον* Κυρίου, *ταῖς μυστικαῖς κοσμούμενος χάρισι, καὶ τὸν ποδήρη τῆς ἀρχιερωσύνης εὐσταλῶς στολισάμενος καὶ τὴν ἐπωμίδα καὶ κίδαριν ἱερῶς περιθέμενος, καὶ τὸ λόγιον τῆς θεολογίας διδασκαλικοῖς πίναξιν ἐνστερνισάμενος, καὶ τὰς ἀναίμους θυσίας ἀνεπιλήπτῳ νοῒ προσάγων καὶ προθυόμενος, δι' ὧν οἶκος θεοῦ καὶ ναὸς ἐχρημάτισας, καὶ ἡμεῖς, οἱ τὸν ἑαυτῶν ναὸν κηλιδώσαντες καὶ πολλὴν ἁμαρτίαν σύνοικον ἔχοντες, οἰκοδομῆς τῆς εἰς ἀρετὴν οὐκ εἰς μακρὰν ἐπιτύχοιμεν.* Γενοῦ *τοῦ μικροῦ ποιμένος ἐμοῦ μέγας ἀρχιποίμην, καὶ τῆς ἐμῆς ἀτελοῦς εἰς ποιμαντικὴν ἕξεως τελειωτὴς περιδέξιος· ἐπὶ γὰρ τῷ ὑμετέρῳ κανόνι ἀπευθύνεσθαι προθυμούμεθα καὶ τούτῳ τὴν σωτηρίαν ἡμῖν πρυτανεύεσθαι πίστιν ἔχομεν.*

18: 12 *καταρτίσει στηρίξατε*: cf. 1 Pet. 5.10 || 14 *ἁρπάγων λύκων*: cf. Mt. 7.15 || 16–17 *ἔκτεινον – Μωϋσῆς*: cf. Ex. 4.4 || 19–20 *ἀμαληκίτης – πόλεμος*: cf. Ex. 17.8 sqq. || 22 *ἐπωμίδα καὶ κίδαριν*: cf. Ex. 25.7; 28.4; 29.5

18: 8 *ἐπησθώμεθα* V || 11 *ἀεὶ* supra versum scripsit V || 12 *καταρτίσει* nos: *καταρτίζειν* V: *καταρτίζοντες* sugg. Duffy || 16 *ἑαυτοὺς προξενίσαιμεν* V || 25 *ἑαυτὸν* V: corr. G || 28–29 *τελειότης*

18. To Constantine, bishop of Gangra

Your eminent and paternal Perfection is able, by means of a mere meeting, to confer benefit on those who wish to approach you. But to be and to dwell with you—would that not cause complete blessing? For such is ⟨the nature of⟩ virtue: while it reaches out in every way so as to benefit life, yet in itself it suffers no diminution. This is how I know and regard you, O holy man who are dear to God. For when I delighted in your presence I enjoyed an abundant spiritual benefit; but when I became aware of your absence I realized what good, excellent, and worthwhile things I had been deprived of. Yet, even if you are farther away, may you draw near to me through your holy prayers to God in which, as I have always confidently believed, God is pleased. Restore and strengthen your flock by means of these ⟨prayers⟩; use them as a staff or rod to goad to compunction those who lean on you spiritually, so that I, too, may be corrected and assuage the attacks of the rapacious wolves that are coming upon me. For this purpose, too, I need from you much help and assistance, so as to bring about to myself those things that will profit me and pertain to salvation. Stretch out, therefore, your arms toward our Father that is in heaven, like Moses who saw God, and all the evil-doing uprisings of my sin will be roundly defeated, and the war with Amalek that is in my soul shall abate. Stand before the Lord, adorned as you are with the mystical graces, fittingly clad in the robe of the high priesthood, wearing in holy fashion the ephod and headdress, bearing on your breast the breastplate of divine knowledge ⟨like⟩ a teacher's tablets, as you bring forth and offer with blameless spirit the bloodless sacrifice—thanks to which ⟨actions⟩ you have become the house and temple of God. And may I, who have defiled my own temple and live in the company of much sin, be granted shortly the edification that leads to virtue. Be a great chief-shepherd to me, who am a paltry shepherd, and an expert perfector of my own insufficient shepherdly skill. For I wish to be directed by your rule and am confident that

Λέξον οὖν πρὸς ἡμᾶς ὡς ἡ ζῶσα χάρις Χριστός “*κατὰ τὴν πίστιν σου γενηθήτω σοι*”· *καὶ εὕροιμέν γε παρ’ αὐτοῦ τὴν ἔκβασιν ὧν ᾐτήκαμεν.*

Καὶ περὶ μὲν τούτων ἅλις. Ὁ *δὲ ὑμέτερος* Θεόφιλος *νυνὶ δὲ καὶ ἡμέτερος, ὃν ἐν χερσὶ ταῖς ἡμετέραις παρέθετο, ταῖς θείαις ὑμῶν ὁσημέραι καταντλούμενος εὐκτικαῖς ἐπιλιμνάζεται προκοπαῖς, καὶ τέως ταῖς γραμμα* ‖ 101 ‖ *τικαῖς ἐμπειρίαις στοιχειωθείς, ἐπὶ τὰ τελεώτερα ἑαυτόν, θεοῦ συνεπαμύνοντος, ἐπιδίδωσιν, οὗ μνείαν ποιούμενος καὶ γεγωνότερον πρὸς θεὸν ἀναβοῶν, ἔσο πρὸς τὰ ἑξῆς καὶ κρείττονα καθηγούμενος.* Ἡμῖν *δὲ μὴ διαλίποις τὸ θεῖον ἐξιλεούμενος, ὡς ἂν τὸ ζοφῶδες τῆς ἐπικειμένης ἁμαρτικῆς ἀχλύος ἀποσεισάμενοι, τῆς ἐκεῖθεν μεγάλης ἡμέρας τῷ φωτὶ πλησιάσαιμεν, πρεσβείαις τῆς πανυμνήτου* Θεοτόκου *καὶ πάντων τῶν ἁγίων καὶ ταῖς ὑμετέραις θεοπειθέσιν ἐντεύξεσιν.*

19. Νικηφόρῳ ἐπισκόπῳ Καρίας

Εἰ *τὸ ἀποστολικὸν ἡμᾶς οὐχ ἱκανόν ἐστι δυσωπεῖν ἐκεῖνο νουθέτημα, τίνι λοιπὸν προσέξωμεν μεγαλοφωνότερον ἡμῖν συμβουλεύοντι;* Τί *δὲ τὸ τῆς νουθεσίας ὑπαινίττεται λόγιον;* “Εἰ *γὰρ ἃ κατέλυσα ταῦτα πάλιν οἰκοδομῶ, παραβάτην ἐμαυτὸν συνίστημι.*” Τοῦτο *μικρὸν ὑπαλλάξαντας ἐπὶ καιροῦ καὶ νῦν ἐστιν ἐφ’ ὑμῖν ἀναφθέγξασθαι· εἰ γὰρ ἅπερ καλῶς ἐπῳκοδομήσατε, ταῦτα πάλιν καταλύειν πειρᾶσθε, τὸ ἑξῆς ὑμεῖς συναγάγετε.* Πάντως *οὖν ἔγνω ἡ ἱερὰ ὑμῶν νῆψις τὸ προοιμιασθέν, ὡς ἐξ ὀνύχων τὸν λέοντα· μᾶλλον δὲ καὶ ὁλοσώματον τὸ τοῦ πράγματος κεφάλαιον καὶ τὴν τούτου περιέβλεψε περιπέτειαν.* Τῇ *γὰρ αὐτῆς* ‖ 102 ‖ *μεσιτείᾳ, μᾶλλον δὲ παρουσίᾳ, τὸ τῆς γαμικῆς ἐκείνης* * *ἐνθέσμως ἐπερατώθη συνάλλαγμα, φαμὲν δὴ τοῦ πανευφήμου ἀνδρός, τοῦ βασιλικοῦ στράτορος ἐν ταύτῃ τῇ πανευδαίμονι καὶ βασιλευούσῃ*

31–32 *κατὰ – σοι*: Mt. 9.29 ‖ 40–41 *τῆς – ἡμέρας*: cf. Joel 3.4; Acta 2.20

34–35 *ὡσημέραι* V ‖ 39 *διαλείποις* V

19: 3–4 *εἰ γὰρ – συνίστημι*: Gal. 2.18 ‖ 8 *ἐξ ὀνύχων τὸν λέοντα*: Diogen. V.15; Macar. III.95; Apostol. VII.57

19: Tit. *Καρείας* V deinde corr. ‖ 10 lacunam statuimus. Supple *ὑποθέσεως* vel simile

salvation will be granted to me thereby. Say, then, to me, like Christ, the living Grace, "According to your faith be it unto you," and may I obtain from Him the issue that I have asked for.

But enough of these things. As for your Theophilos, who is now also mine, since you have placed him in my hands, he is every day irrigated to overflowing by your holy admonitions toward improvement, and having in the meantime acquired a grounding in grammatical practice, is devoting himself, with God's help, to higher pursuits. May you, by mentioning him in your prayers and crying out loudly to God, be his guide toward the better things that lie in store for him. Do not cease also from beseeching the Divinity on my behalf, so that I may dispel the mist of sin that lies upon me and draw nigh to the light of the great day hereafter. Be it by the intercession of the all-praised Mother of God and of all the saints and by your prayers to which God hearkens.

19. To Nikephoros, bishop of Caria

If that apostolic injunction is not sufficient to persuade us, to whom then should we pay heed who can give us clearer advice? But what is it that the scriptural admonition hints at? "For if I build again the things which I destroyed, I make myself a transgressor." By changing this a little, it is appropriate at the present time to apply this comment to you. For if you try to destroy again the things which you built up well—you will understand the rest. Surely, your holy Sobriety has comprehended my preamble, like the lion by his claws; indeed, you have seen from every side the whole body of the matter and its vicissitudes. For it was by your mediation, or rather in your presence that that painful marriage contract was lawfully completed, I mean that of the illustrious *strator* in this most felicitous capital city, and the entire admin-

πόλει, καὶ ἐφ' ὑμῖν ἡ πᾶσα τῶν συμφώνων ἀνηρτήθη διοίκησις, ὡς σὺν ἡμῖν ἐπιμαρτυροῦσι πολλοί· νυνὶ δὲ τὸ πρόσωπον ἐπὶ τῷ προτέρῳ γαμβρῷ πῶς εἰπεῖν οὐκ ἔχομεν ἐστηρίσατε, καὶ ταῦτα οὐδὲ εἰς γαμβροῦ γνησιότητα φθάσαντι, καὶ τὸ τῆς ἐπιβαλλούσης οὐσίας τῷ οἴκῳ τοῦ ἐν μακαρίᾳ τῇ λήξει συντέκνου ὑμῶν πρὸς ἐκεῖνον μεταστῆσαι διὰ τῆς ὑμετέρας μαρτυρίας βεβούλησθε· μὴ δὴ τοῦτο ἐννοηθείητε, μηδὲ τῷ γνησίῳ νόθον σύγκληρον ποιῆσαι θελήσοιτε· ἀσύμβατον γὰρ καὶ τοῦ εἰκότος ἀλλότριον. Ἀλλὰ δότε τόπον τῇ οἰκουρῷ καὶ δεσποίνῃ τῶν τοιούτων, ὡς ἂν βούλοιτο τὰ ἑαυτῆς διεξάγειν· αὕτη ἐπιτροπευέτω καὶ ἐπικρινέτω καὶ διαμενέτω τοῖς τέκνοις παρὰ γνησίου συνεύνου κυρία καταλειφθεῖσα ἐγκάτοχος. Ἡμεῖς δὲ μὴ κριτῇ τούτου γε εἵνεκεν ἑαυτοὺς παρεστάναι προδοίημεν· μηδὲ ὑπὸ τῶν ἔξω κριτηρίων εὐθύνεσθαι δεηθείημεν, ἐνὸν σιγῶντας μηδὲ μιᾷ μώμου κηλῖδι προστρίβεσθαι. "Ἵνα τί γὰρ ἡ ἐλευθερία μου," φησὶν ὁ μέγας ἀπόστολος, "ὑπὸ ἄλλης συνειδήσεως κρίνεται;" || 103 || *Εἰ μὲν δυνατῶς ἔχοιτε τῷ μέρει τούτῳ συμβαλεῖσθαι καὶ προστεθήσεσθαι, ὡς ὑμετέρῳ φανέντι γεωργίῳ, ἐπαινετόν· εἰ δὲ τοῦτο προκεῖσθαι ἢ ἐπικουρῆσαι δυσανασχετεῖτε, δότε τῇ ἐπαινουμένῃ σιγῇ τὸ πᾶν, καὶ ὠφελήσοιτε μᾶλλον τὰ μέγιστα. Ἵνα οὖν ἀπαλλάξητε πολλῶν καὶ ἡμᾶς ἐνοχλήσεων καὶ συνεχῶν αὐτοὺς θορύβων, μηδὲν ἔξω τῶν συμβουλευομένων ὑμῖν παρ' ἡμῶν ποιῆσαι προθυμηθείητε· ἐπὶ γὰρ τῷ ἁγιωτάτῳ πατριάρχῃ τὰ τῆς ὑποθέσεως ἀνενεγκεῖν ὁ εἰρημένος πανεύφημος ἀνὴρ βουληθείς, ὡς ἂν ἐξ αὐτοῦ λόγος πρὸς ὑμᾶς ἀφίκοιτο ἢ καὶ γράμμα τὴν αὐτὴν ὑμῖν κομίζον ἀπαγγελίαν, ὑφ' ἡμῶν ἀνεστάλη καὶ τοῦ σὺν ἡμῖν λογιωτάτου καὶ τῆς ἐκκλησίας ὀφθαλμοῦ καὶ πνευματικοῦ ἡμῶν ἀδελφοῦ τοῦ χαρτοφύλακος, ὡς ἡμῶν ἱκανῶν ὄντων διὰ τῶν ἡμετέρων προρρήσεων πεῖσαι τοῦτο ποιῆσαι τὴν ὑμετέραν πατρικὴν ἁγιότητα. Δειξάτω οὖν τὴν ἡμετέραν πρὸς αὐτὴν ἰσχὺν καὶ τὴν εἰρήνην ἐν τῷ οἴκῳ ἐκείνῳ βραβευσάτω, ὡς ἂν τῶν εἰρηνοποιῶν τὸν μακαρισμὸν ἀπενέγκοιτο. Πρὸ δὲ τοῦ παριππεύσαντος χρόνου, διά τινος κληρικοῦ τῆς καθ' ὑμᾶς ἐκκλησίας, γράμμα πεπόμφαμεν τῇ ὑμετέρᾳ ὁσιότητι, δι' οὗ σεσημαγκέναι αὐτῇ τὰ καθ' ἡμᾶς εὖ ἔχειν ἐκρίναμεν·* || 104 || *ἔνθεν ἀρκεσθέντες ἐκείνῳ σιωπῇ τὰ*

14–15 *τὸ πρόσωπον – ἐστηρίσατε*: cf. Lc. 9.51 || 26–27 *ἵνα – κρίνεται*: 1 Cor. 10.29 || 41 *τῶν εἰρηνοποιῶν – ἀπενέγκοιτο*: Mt. 5.9

---

15 *ἐστερήσατε* V || 18 *βεβουλῆσθαι* V || 22 an *διανεμέτω* scribendum? || 25 *σιγῶντες* V || 28 *προτεθήσεσθαι* V || 30 *ὀφελήσοιτε* V || 31 *συνεχων* V || 35 *εἰ καὶ* V || *κομίζων* V || 38 *προρήσεων* V || 39 an *δεξάτω* scribendum?

istration of the agreement was entrusted to you, as many persons join me in testifying. Now, however, for some unknown reason, you have set your face upon the former in-law, and this in spite of the fact that he is not even a genuine in-law, and you intend to confer on him by means of your testimony the property that pertains to the household of your deceased co-parent. Do not conceive such a plan! Do not propose to make the legitimate and the illegitimate share the same lot! For that would be incongruous and unreasonable. Grant, on the contrary, leave to the mistress of the house to arrange her affairs as she may wish. Let her administer, decide, and remain with her children in possession of the goods bequeathed to her by her legitimate husband. Let us not on this account deliver ourselves to appear before a judge; nor should we need to be set right by external tribunals, when it is possible, by keeping silent, to be untouched by any blot of reproach. For, as the great apostle says, "Why is my liberty judged by another man's conscience?" If you find it possible to agree and consent to this course as if it appeared to be your own doing, well and good; if, however, you are reluctant for this to be proposed or to give help, then have recourse to silence that is golden, and you will cause the greatest good. Do not be eager to do anything beyond the advice I have given you so that you may rid me of much annoyance and yourself of continual disturbance. For the aforesaid illustrious man was intending to refer this matter to the most holy patriarch with a view to your receiving a message from the latter or an epistle containing the same injunction, but was prevented by me and my colleague, the most learned eye of the Church, my spiritual brother, the *chartophylax,* on the grounds that we were able, by means of our warnings, to convince your paternal Holiness to act in this manner. May you acknowledge our influence over you, and confer peace on that household so that you may be rewarded with the blessing of peacemakers.

Before the year that has gone by, I dispatched, through the offices of a cleric of your Church, a letter to your Holiness in which I thought fit to notify you that I was

νῦν τιμῶ, μέχρι τῆς ἐξ ὑμῶν ἐπιτύχοιμεν ἀποκρίσεως. Καὶ ἔρρωσο, καὶ εὔχου ὑπὲρ ἡμῶν, ἱερώτατε.

20. Νικηφόρῳ ἐπισκόπῳ Καρίας

Ὁ τῆς ὀρθῆς ἀγάπης θεσμὸς εἰ καὶ βραχύ τι τοῦ ποθουμένου πεῖραν ἀποστάσεως δέξαιτο, ὡς ἤδη μακροῦ χρόνου παρῳχηκότος, ὁρᾶν ἐπιζητεῖ τὸ ποθούμενον. Ἡμεῖς δὲ οὐχὶ βραχείας ὥρας παριππευσάσης, οὐδὲ τελείας ἡμέρας μεταβάσης, ἀλλὰ χρόνου δεξαμένης ἐπίτασιν τῆς ἱερᾶς ὑμῶν ἀπολείψεως, ἀθυμίας οὐ μετρουμένης ἐπλήσθημεν καὶ τὸν ὀφθαλμὸν ὧδε κἀκεῖσε περιάγειν διὰ σπουδῆς ἐγενόμεθα, ὡς ἂν τοῦ ποθουμένου περιδραξαίμεθα· ἀλλ' οὕτω διακειμένοις ἀνίᾳ, ὥσπερ τις ἀστὴρ ἐπιφανὲν ἀπλανέστατος τὸ ἱερὸν ὑμῶν γράμμα τὴν ἐν ἀθυμίᾳ καὶ λήθης ἀχλΰϊ τελοῦσαν ἡμῶν καρδίαν κατηύγασεν. Ὅθεν σὺν τῇ τοῦ γράμματος ἀποδοχῇ καὶ τῆς ἀγάπης συνανέτειλεν ἔρως καὶ εὐχαῖς ἐν τούτῳ τὸ θεῖον ὑμνεῖν ἡμᾶς παρεσκεύασεν, καὶ γράμμασι χρήσασθαι συνηνάγκασεν, ὥστε τὸν τῆς φιλίας πυρσὸν ἀνάψαι καὶ τηλαυγῶς πρὸς τὸ ποθούμενον διαπορθμευθῆναι.

Καλῆς δὲ βουλῆς γέγονεν ἡ ὑμετέρα ἱερὰ ὁσιότης μὴ τῆς ὁδοῦ νῦν τῆς πρὸς ἡμᾶς ἐφαψαμένη· ἡ γὰρ τῆς ὥρας δυσχέρεια καὶ τῆς ὁδοῦ τεναγώδης ἐπάχθεια, καὶ τοῖς διὰ παντὸς οἴκαδε ἠρεμοῦσιν συ ‖ 105 ‖ *στολὴν τὴν ἐκ τοῦ κρύους οὐ μικρὰν προεξένησεν, ὥστε, εἰ σκυλμὸς συνέβη τῇ ὑμετέρᾳ γενέσθαι τελείᾳ νήψει, καὶ πόνος ὑμῖν συνωδοιπόρησε μέγιστος καὶ μεταμέλεια πολλὴ προσεγένετο. Περὶ δὲ τῶν πραγμάτων, ὧν ἡ ἱερὰ ὑμῶν ὁσιότης ἐπιστατικῶς μανθάνειν ἐπείγεται, πᾶσα σιγὴ ταῦτα καλύψασα καὶ τέλος οὐδὲν ἐξενεγκεῖν συγχωρήσασα, μέχρι τήμερον ἀνέκφορα διαμένει. Ὅθεν, τοῦ γράψαι τι ἢ ἀποκρίσεως πόρον δοῦναι ἐν ἀπορίᾳ τυγχάνοντες, σιγᾶν προειλόμεθα· λέγομεν δὲ καὶ ἐλπίζομεν ὅτι οὐκ εἰς μακρὰν ἡ ἐπὶ τούτοις ὁδὸς ἀνοιχθήσεται, καὶ πέρας ἡ τοῦ κεφαλαίου περιπέτεια δέξεται, καὶ τότε γράψαι καὶ καταμηνύσαι τῇ ὑμετέρᾳ ἱερᾷ τελειότητι οὐκ ἀποκνήσαιμεν. Εὔχου δὲ ὑπὲρ τῆς ἡμετέρας μετριότητος τῆς θελούσης καὶ σπουδαζούσης ἀποπληροῦν πᾶσαν ἱερὰν ὑμῶν ἐπιθυμίαν καὶ θέλησιν.*

20: Tit. Καρείας V ‖ 12 *συνηνέγκασεν* V: corr. G ‖ 16 *ηρεμασιν* V ‖ 17 *προεξένισεν* V: corr. G

well. Deeming that sufficient, I now keep silent until I am favored with your reply. Be in good health and pray for me, your Holiness.

20. To Nikephoros, bishop of Caria

If the nature of true love experiences even the shortest separation from the object of its affection, it desires, as if a long time had gone by, to see the beloved. As for me, since it is not a short hour that has elapsed, nor a whole day that has gone by, but the absence of your Holiness has been extended for a length of time, I have been filled with immeasurable sadness and have been eagerly casting my eye hither and thither that I might attain the object of my desire. As I was in this despondent state, your holy letter appeared like some fixed star and illuminated my heart that was covered with the mist of sadness and oblivion. And so, a glow of love dawned with the reception of your letter and caused me to glorify God for this in my prayers. And it compelled me to write you a letter so as to kindle the pyre of friendship and convey afar its bright light to the beloved.

Your sacred Holiness has been well advised in not having undertaken at this time a journey hither. For the harshness of the season and the troublesome quagmires of the road have caused no small hardship from the cold even to those who always remain quietly at home. And so, if your perfect Sobriety had happened to undertake a journey, great toil would have followed you and much regret would have ensued.

Concerning the matters of which your Holiness is insistently anxious to be informed, complete silence has veiled them and has not allowed any result to be produced, so that they remain to this day in the dark. Being, therefore, at a loss to write anything or provide an answer, I preferred to be silent. I say and hope, however, that at no distant time a way will be opened in this connection and the vicissitudes of this affair will be concluded; and then I would not hesitate to announce it in writing to your holy Perfection. Pray for my mediocrity who am willing and anxious to fulfill your every holy wish and desire.

21. *Δημοχάρει γενικῷ λογοθέτῃ*

Εἰ μὲν ὡς σὺ πρὸς ἑαυτὸν οἴει με πρὸς σὲ διακεῖσθαι, ὄντως τὸν τῆς φιλίας πυθαγόρειον ὅρον ὀρθῶς μεμελέτηκας· ἑαυτὸν γὰρ ἄλλον ἐκεῖνος τὸν φίλον ὡρίζετο. Εἰ δὲ ἄλλως πως ἔχειν πρὸς σὲ παρὰ σοὶ λελόγισμαι ἢ Πυθαγόρας *καλῶς διωρίζετο φίλον ὄντα, μηδαμῶς τὸν τοιοῦτον ὅρον ὑπ' ἐμοῦ παραβλάπτεσθαι· ἀλλὰ μὴν κἀκεῖνος ὀρθῶς διωρίσατο καὶ ἄλλως ἐγώ σοι καθέστηκα· καὶ εἰ ἄλλως* ‖ 106 ‖ *ἐγώ σοι καθέστηκα, ὀθνεῖον οὐδέν σοι καὶ ξένον βουλεύσαιμι.* Πᾶς *γὰρ αὐτὸς ἑαυτῷ τὰ συνοίσοντα καὶ θέλει καὶ βούλεται· συνοίσει δ' εἰ ἄλλο τι καὶ ὁ πρὸς τοὺς ὁμοιοπαθεῖς θεομίμητος ἔλεος. Τί δέ ἐστι τὸ ὑπ' ἐμοῦ προτεινόμενον, λέξων ἔρχομαι.*

"Ανδρες τινὲς χθές, ἤδη τῆς ὥρας καλούσης πρὸς τράπεζαν, οἷά τινες ἔκφρονες καὶ λύπῃ μαινόμενοι, τὰς θύρας ἐπιστάντες τοῦ ἐμοῦ συνέθλιβον δώματος· ὡς δ' ἐγὼ τούτοις ὑπανοιγνὺς τὰς πύλας ἑώρακα, θάμβους ἐπληρούμην καὶ δείματος μήπως ἄρα τινὶ κακῷ συνεκύρησα· ἦσαν γὰρ αὐχμηροὶ καὶ ὠχριῶντες ὑπ' ἀλουσίας, ὡς ἐγῷμαι, τὴν πρόσοψιν· κρηδέμνοις τε τὰς κεφαλὰς ὑπεκάλυπτον, τὴν τῆς κόμης συμβᾶσαν ἐξ ἐπηρείας ἀπόκαρσιν, ὡς ἐτόπαζον, περιστέλλοντες· καὶ ἁπαξαπλῶς οἷά τινες προάγγελοι τῆς συνεχούσης λύπης ἐβλέποντο. Ἐ*ρομένῳ δέ μοι τί ἄρα καὶ βούλοιντο, "ἐκ τοῦ δυσκλεοῦς σχήματος δέχου τὴν ἀπόκρισιν," ἔφασκον· "νῶτα γὰρ κατεξαμμένα πληγαῖς καὶ κόμας πιναρὰς καὶ ψιλὰς ἐκ σιδήρου θεώμενος, αὐτόθεν ἀκριβῆ τὴν ἀπόφασιν εἴληφας.* Εἰ *δὲ καὶ λόγῳ τὴν συμφορὰν γνωρίσαι βεβούλησαι, τὴν ἀκοὴν ὑποσχὼν δέχου τὴν εἴδησιν· καὶ γὰρ νησιδίου τινὸς οἰκήτορες ἐσμέν, ὡς μὴ ὤφειλεν, ὅπερ* Ἀ*νδρωτὴν οὐκ εὐαγῶς οἱ πάλαι κεκλήκασιν· δημοσίῳ δὲ νῦν ἐξ ἀβουλίας ἡλώκειμεν πτώματι, οὗ* ‖ 107 ‖ *σὺ εἴπερ ἄλλος τις ἐς τάχος ἡμᾶς ὑπεκλύσειας· πλοίων γὰρ σιτηγούντων ὑπάρχομεν ναύκληροι, ἃ τὸν φόρτον τῷ δημοσίῳ λόγῳ εἴωθε κομίζειν ἐπέτειον· ἐξ οὗ μικρόν τι σίτου διὰ λιμὸν ὑφελόμενοι καὶ κριθῆ*

21: 2 *ἑαυτὸν – ἄλλον*: cf. Arist. *EN* 1166a 31; Porphyrius *Vita Pythagorae,* 33, ed. Nauck (1886) 34.21; Hermias *in Phaedr.* 253b ed. Couvreur, 192.11; Ps. Plutarchus *Vit. Hom.* 151 et Scholion in Iliad. Σ. 82; Strömberg 76; Delatte, *Études sur la litt. pythagoricienne* (Paris, 1915), 119

21: 5 post *παραβλάπτεσθαι, νόμιζε* vel sim. verbum excidisee arbitrari potest ‖ 6 *ἄλλως* V: an *ἄλλος* scribendum? ‖ 13 *τούτοις*: fort. *τούτους* legendum ‖ 15 *πρόσωψιν* V ‖ 16 *⟨κ⟩άλυμα κεφαλῆς παρειμένον τοῖς ὤμοις . . .* in marg. glossa a manu recentiori ‖ 24 *ἀνδροτὴν* V ‖ 25 *οὓς* V: corr. Ševčenko ‖ 28 *ἐπαίτιον* V: corr. G

21. To Democharis, logothete of the Genikon

If you think that my attitude to you is like yours to yourself, then indeed you have noted correctly the Pythagorean doctrine of friendship; for he defined a friend as another self. But if you consider that I am inclined to you in a way that differs from Pythagoras' good pronouncement of what a friend is, ⟨do not think⟩ that this definition has in any way been contravened by me. But he indeed made a sound definition, yet I am regarded by you in a different light; and even if I am regarded differently, I would advise you nothing that is alien or strange. For, every man wants and desires what will benefit himself; and, more than anything else, a godlike pity toward our fellow sufferers will confer benefit. What it is that I am putting forward I shall now explain.

Yesterday, at dinnertime, certain men who seemed out of their senses and mad with grief came crowding before the doors of my house. When I opened the gates and saw them, I was filled with terror and fear lest I should meet with some mishap. For they were squalid and their faces gray through lack of washing, or so I think. They covered their heads with veils concealing, as I believed, the fact that their hair had been cropped in dishonor. Altogether they looked like the harbingers of the grief that possessed them. When I asked what it was they wanted, they said: "Take our wretched appearance for an answer. For when you see our backs torn with scourging, our hair ragged and cut short by the shears, you will have found the correct verdict. But if you also wish to know of our distress in words, lend your ear and receive the information. We dwell on a little island (where it not so!) which men of old have called by the indecent name of Androtê. And now, out of senselessness, we have been caught in a civil offense from which you, more than anyone else, might free us quickly. For we are the captains of the grain ships that normally transport the annual cargo for the Treasury. Because of hunger we removed from it a small quantity of

τὸ λεῖπον ἀνασωσάμενοι, φωραθέντες τὴν δίκην πολυπλασίως ἐκτίννυμεν." "Καὶ τίς ἄρα," ἔφην, "οὗτός ἐστιν, ὃς τὸ τοῦ δημοσίου λόγου αὐστηρὸν παρωσάμενος, τοῖς ἐμοῖς λόγοις πειθήνιος γένοιτο, καὶ ὑμᾶς ἀπαλλάξει τοῦ πτώματος;" Ὡς δ' ἐπὶ σοὶ τῷ τῆς χαρᾶς φερωνύμῳ ἡ ψῆφος ἐδίδοτο, θαρσεῖν τούτους συντόμως ἐκέλευον, ὡς οὐ τῆς ἐνεγκούσης αὐτοὺς ἐλπίδος πρὸς μὲ ψευσθείησαν· ἑώρων γὰρ ἀγχίθυρον ἔχον τὸ πταῖσμα τὴν ἄφεσιν, ὡς οὐ πολλὴν τῷ δημοσίῳ λόγῳ τὴν βλάβην προέμενον. Εἰ οὖν ἀνύποιστον οὐδὲν οἱ τῆς Ἀνδρωτῆς οἰκήτορες ἥμαρτον, μὴ διαμάρτοιεν τῆς ἐφέσεως· Ἀνδρωτῆς ἐκείνης, ἣν πάντοθεν περιστοιχίζουσα θάλασσα μικρὰν ποιεῖ καὶ ταπεινὴν καὶ περίγραπτον, ἄνυδρόν τε καὶ ἄξυλον, καὶ παντὸς ἄλλου τοῦ τὴν ἐφήμερον ζωὴν τῶν ἀνθρώπων ὑπερείδοντος εἴδους ἀμέτοχον· ἣν ποτ' ἐγώ, κἀκεῖσε γενόμενος, || 108 || κατεθρήνησα, ὡς ἑώρων ὑπ' ἀνάγκης ἠπειρόθεν περαιούμενα καὶ ξυλευόμενα καὶ ὑδρευόμενα γύναια. Αὕτη οὖν, εἰ μή τι ἄλλο, δυσωπείτω τὴν ὑμετέραν ἀμνησίκακον τελειότητα· ἱκανὸν γὰρ τὸ τῆς πληγῆς καὶ τῆς ἐπιθρίξεως ἐπιτίμιον· μὴ δὴ ταύταις ἐπακολουθήσοι καὶ ζημία ἐπιξαίνουσα τοῦ τραύματος τὸ ἐπώδυνον, ἀλλ' ὡς τῶν τοιούτων μωλώπων ἰατρὸς γαληνότατος καὶ παντὸς κινδυνώδους κλύδωνος στορεστὴς ἀμφιδέξιος, λωφῆσαι τὴν ἐπηρτημένην αὐτοῖς τῆς ζημίας καταιγίδα ταῖς μειλιχίοις αὔραις τῆς σῆς κελεύσεως θέλησον, ὡς ἂν παρὰ τῆς ἄνω θείας νεύσεως ἀεὶ κυβερνώμενος, τὴν τῆς ψυχῆς ὁλκάδα, τοῖς ἀγωγίμοις τῶν ἀρετῶν ἐπιβρίθουσαν, ἀκυμάντως εἰς τὸν ἀχείμονα καὶ μακραίωνα ὅρμον τῆς ἐλπιζομένης ζωῆς διασώσειας.

22. Τῷ Δημοχάρει γενικῷ λογοθέτῃ

Καὶ δεύτερος γράφεις καὶ πρῶτος ἐγκαλεῖς, ἡμεῖς δὲ καὶ πρῶτοι γράψαντες πρὸς τὴν ἔγκλησιν δευτερεύσωμεν. Πῶς ἀεὶ πρὸς τὰ καλὰ ταχὺς τυγχάνων ἐπὶ μόνης φιλίας τὴν βραδυτῆτα τετήρηκας; Εἰ γὰρ ἄλλος ἐγώ, κατὰ τὸν Πυθαγόραν, ὁ φίλος ὁρίζεται, ἄλλους ἑαυτοὺς οἱ πέλας || 109 || τοὺς φίλους ἡγείσθωσαν. Τοιοῦτον δή τινα σύνδεσμον καὶ

30 *ὡς* V: corr. G || 36 *ἀνδροτῆς* V || 37 *ἀνδροτῆς* V || 41 an *ἠπειρόσε* legendum? || 51 *ἀχημονα* V || *ὅρμον* Duffy: *οἶμον* V

22: 4 *ἄλλος ἐγὼ – ὁρίζεται*: v. ad ep. 21.2 || 5–7 *τοιοῦτον – ἀπεγέννησας*: cf. Iamblichus, *In Nicomachi arithmeticam introductionem liber*, ed. H. Pistelli and U. Klein (Stuttgart, 1975), 35

wheat and made up the difference with barley, but we were detected and are now paying the penalty many times over."

"And who is it," I said, "who, setting aside the strict rules of the Treasury, might be persuaded by my words and free you from your misfortune?" When the choice fell on you who bear the name of joy, I immediately bade them be of good cheer, for they would not be deceived in the hope that had brought them to me. For I saw that their misdeed had its forgiveness near at hand, since it had not caused great harm to the Treasury. If then the inhabitants of Androtê have not committed an insufferable offense, let them not be disappointed in their appeal. As for Androtê, the sea surrounds it on all sides, making it small, wretched, and confined, without water and wood, and lacking every other commodity that sustains man's daily life. I visited it once and wept over it when I saw that its women were compelled to cross to the mainland to fetch wood and water. Let the island then, if nothing else, implore your merciful Perfection. For the penalty of scourging and cropping is sufficient; do not let a fine that further irritates the pain of the wound be added, but, like a physician who gently heals such bruises and a man who dexterously calms all dangerous storms, be willing to quell by the honeyed breezes of your bidding the tempest of the fine that hangs over them. Thus, ever directed by the divine will from above, you may bring the vessel of your soul, weighed down by its cargo of virtue and tossed by no waves, into the calm and eternal harbor of the life for which we hope.

22. To Democharis, logothete of the Genikon

You are the second to write and the first to accuse me, whereas I wrote first, yet would take second place in accusation. How is it that you who are always prompt in good works have been so slow in friendship alone? For if, according to Pythagoras, a friend is defined as another "I," one's fellows should consider their friends as sec-

ἐν ἀριθμοῖς, ὡς ἔμαθες, εὕρηκας, ὧν εἰ πρὸς [ἡ] μέρη λεπτύνεις τὸν ἕτερον, ὁλικῶς τὸν ἕτερον ἀπεγέννησας· καὶ ταῦτα, μηδεμιᾶς τούτοις ὑπούσης ἐρωτικῆς, ὡς οἶσθα, θελήσεως· ψυχῆς γὰρ καὶ ἡδονῆς ἅπας ἀριθμὸς ἀπεστέρηται· ὡς εἰ τοιαύτη τις τοῖς λογικοῖς καὶ ἐμψύχοις ὑπῆν φιλίας συνούλωσις, τάχα ἂν ὑπὲρ ἀλλήλων κατετολμᾶτο καὶ θάνατος, καὶ πᾶν τὸ ἀλγεινὸν ὡς ἥδιστον ἐλελόγιστο, καὶ πᾶν τὸ μικρῶς διιστῶν ὡς χρόνος μακρὸς ἐνενόμιστο. Νυνὶ δὲ τούτων μὲν οὐδέν· ἕκαστος δὲ μένων ἐπὶ χώρας ἑαυτοῦ, καὶ φίλος οἰκεῖος καθίσταται, χλούνης τις ἢ μονιός, ἅπαν τὸ φιλικὸν ἀπαγορεύων καὶ σύννομον, καὶ ὑπὸ τὸ ἀγριαῖνον ἦθος φερόμενος. Καὶ ταῦτα οὐ σοῦ κατηγορῶν προήχθην λαλῶν—μὴ γὰρ ἐπὶ τοσοῦτο φρενὸς ἔξω πέσοιμι—σοὶ δὲ συνηγορῶν, ἐμαυτοῦ κατηγόρησα· ἀλλὰ ταῦτα μὲν Ὅμηρος· μεταφρασόμεσθα καὶ αὖτις· σὺ δὲ εἰ μέλλοις καὶ παρὼν κατηγορεῖν ἡμῶν, οὐχ ὑπερθήσῃ περαιτέρω τὴν ἔλευσιν· μάλα γὰρ τοῖς σοῖς ἡδόμεθα σκώμμασιν· εἰ δὲ ταύτην ἀναβάλλῃ, ἡμεῖς ἑαυτοὺς πρὸς τὰς ἑαυτῶν κατηγορίας ὁπλίσαιμεν. || 110 ||

23. Τῷ αὐτῷ

Ὡς μὲν σὺ λέγεις καὶ ἐγὼ πείθομαι, τῆς σοὶ περικειμένης ἀξίας κατωλιγώρησας· ὅθεν καὶ ὡς ἤδη ταύτης ἐκτὸς ὤν, μικρὰ ἢ οὐδ' ὅλως περὶ ταύτην ἠσχόλησαι· καὶ ὅτι ταῦθ' οὕτως ἔχει, ὁ ἱκετήριος τῆς χήρας χάρτης τὴν πίστιν διδότω· τοῦτον γὰρ ἐν ταῖς χερσί σου βαλών, καὶ οὐδὲ πολλὰ δεηθείς, τοῦ περὶ αὐτὸν τέλους ἐτύγχανον. Τί δαὶ τὸ δεηθὲν καὶ τί τὸ τέλος, ὅπερ ἐλάμβανον; Ἐγὼ μὲν ἔλεγον ἐπὶ τοῦ εὐθυτάτου κριτηρίου τοῦτον ἀναγαγεῖν, εὕρισκον δὲ ὑμᾶς οὐκ εἰς μακρὰν πειθομένους καὶ κατανεύοντας, ᾗ οἱ πρὶν μῦθοι τὸν Κρονίδην εἰσάγουσιν· εἰ οὖν τῶν σῶν οὐδὲν παλινάγρετον, οὐδ' ἀπατηλόν, οὐδ' ἀτελεύτητον, ὅ τί κεν

13–14 *χλούνης – μονιὸς*: cf. Ps. 79 (80).14 || 17–18 *μεταφρασόμεσθα καὶ αὖτις*: *Il.* 1.140

22: 9 *ἡ* V: corr. G || 12 *μακρὸς* nos: *μικρὸς* V || 15 *προήχθη* V: corr. G || 17 *μεταφρασώμεσθα* V || 18 *περετέρω* V: corr. G || 19 *σκόμμασιν* V

23: 9–10 *παλινάγρετον – κατανεύσῃς*: *Il.* 1.524 sqq.

23: 2 *κατολιγώρησας* V: corr. G || 7 *εὑρίσκων* V || 8 *ἢ* V || 9 *ὅττικεν* V

ond selves. A bond of this kind is also to be found, as you have learned, in the realm of numbers, for if you reduce one into its parts, you produce another in its entirety; and this although they, as you know, do not possess any affective volition since all numbers are devoid of spirit and pleasure. If, then, such a soundness of friendship were present in rational, animate beings, perchance they might even risk death for the sake of each other, and consider every painful thing to be most pleasant and every short separation as a great length of time. But now it is not so at all: every man remains in his own place and is his own friend, like some solitary wild boar, renouncing all friendship and association, and falling under the sway of wild manners.

I have ben prompted to say these things not so as to accuse you (how could I be as senseless as that?), but in being your advocate I have accused myself. As Homer says, let us consider these things hereafter. As for you, even if you wish to accuse me in your presence, you will not further delay your coming: for I take great pleasure in your gibes. But if you postpone it, I should prepare to be my own accuser.

23. To the same

As you yourself say and I believe, you have utterly neglected the office with which you are invested. Wherefore, you are little, if at all, occupied with it, as if you were already out of it. That this is so may be confirmed by the widow's supplicatory petition: for by placing it in your hands I would have obtained the resolution of the matter even without much begging. What, then, was the supplication and what the resolution that I would have obtained? For my part, I said that this ⟨petition⟩ should be referred to the most righteous tribunal and I found you being soon persuaded and assenting, just as the ancient myths represent the son of Cronus—if, then, none of your actions, whatever you nod your head to, is revocable, deceitful, and without

κεφαλῇ κατανεύσῃς, πεισθήτω σὺν ἡμῖν καὶ ⟨ἡ⟩ ἀπρομήθευτος αὕτη χήρα· τῆς γυναικείας μικροψυχίας μηδένα λόγον ποιήσασα, τὸν αὐτὸν χάρτην πρὸς ἡμᾶς ἧκεν ἐπὶ χεῖρας κομίζουσα· οὗ τὸ ἀτελὲς ἐπαισθόμενοι καὶ τὸ βαρυπενθὲς αὐτῆς κατοικτείραντες, πρὸς ὑμᾶς αὖθις πεπόμφαμεν· καὶ εἰ μὲν αὐτός ἐστι, περὶ οὗ δεδυσωπήκαμεν, μὴ παροφθείη, ἵνα μὴ λέγωμεν ἡμεῖς· εἰ δὲ ἐκεῖνος οὗτός ἐστι καὶ σὺν ἡμῖν παρώφθη, ἴσθι πρὸς σὲ καὶ τρίτην πορείαν ποιούμενον.

24. Τῷ *αὐτῷ*

Εἴπερ ὅλως ἠπιστάμην τὴν ὑμετέραν τῆς ψυχῆς τελειότητα ἐν ταῖς τῶν πραγμάτων εὐροίαις || 111 || *ἢ δυσχερείαις ἐπαιρομένην ἢ συμπίπτουσαν, ἐνουθέτουν ἂν διὰ πλατυτέρων ῥημάτων ἢ γραμμάτων· νυνὶ δὲ καὶ πρὸς τὰς εὐπραγίας καὶ δυσχερείας ἐγνωκὼς διαφυλάττουσαν αὐτὴν τὴν ἰσότητα, οὐδέτερον τούτων ποιεῖν διενοήθην, μήπως φορτικός τις εἶναι δόξω καὶ περιττός, λέγων καὶ γράφων τὰ μὴ προσήκοντα.* Τ*ίς γὰρ οὐκ οἶδε τὴν ὑμετέραν ἐν* Χ*ριστῷ σεβασμιότητα τὸ μεγαλόψυχον ἐν παντὶ προσκτωμένην καὶ μακροθύμως καὶ γενναίως τὰ προσπίπτοντα φέρουσαν; Ἀεὶ γὰρ ἔγνω ὡς οὐδὲν τῶν παρόντων μόνιμον, ἀλλὰ πάντα τὴν πρὸς τὸ ἐναντίον ἄστατον διαμείβεται κίνησιν· οἷόν τι λέγω· τὴν λύπην χαρὰ διαδέχεται καὶ τὴν εὐπραγίαν ἡ δυσπραγία, τήν τε νόσον ἡ ὑγιεία· καὶ πάντα τὰ δοκοῦντα ἐν βίῳ εἶναι τερπνὰ ἢ ἀνιαρὰ τὴν εἰς ἄλληλα μεταβολὴν ποιεῖται καὶ στάσεως οὐδεμιᾶς ἔχεται. Ὅθεν τοὺς εὐαρεστήσαντας δι᾽ ἀρετῆς τῷ θεῷ βλέπομεν μᾶλλον ταῖς θλίψεσιν εὐδοκοῦντας καὶ ταῖς δυσχερείαις συνησθημένους καὶ πᾶσαν εὐημερίαν ἀποσειομένους καὶ τὰ τῆς στενῆς ὁδοῦ ἐπισπωμένους, ὡς ἂν ἐκείνης τῆς ἀπεράντου χαρᾶς περιδράξωνται, ἣν οὐδεμία θλίψις ἢ λύπη ἢ στενοχωρία λοιπὸν διαδέχεται.* Τ*αύτης οὖν καὶ ἡμεῖς, εἴπερ θελήσαιμεν, ῥᾳδίως ἐπιτευ* || 112 || *ξαίμεθα· καί, τὴν ἀχθηδόνα τῶν περικει-*

---

10 *ἡ* suppl. G || 15 *παροφθεὶη* V

24: 11–13 *τὴν λύπην – ἔχεται*: cf. Arist. *Categ.* 8b || 16 *τὰ τῆς στενῆς ὁδοῦ*: cf. Mt. 7.14

24: 9 *ἔγνων* V || 15 *συνισθημένους* V || 17 *παραδράξωνται* V

issue—may this neglected widow receive assurance along with me. She took no account of female pusillanimity and came to me with the same document in her hands. Noting that it has received no fulfilment and pitying her profound grief, I have sent it to you once again. And if it is the same document concerning which I have made my supplication, let it not be overlooked—not to say that I ⟨should be overlooked⟩; nay, if it is the very same and has been overlooked along with me, know well that I shall come to you for a third time.

24. To the same

If I had known at all that your spiritual Perfection was uplifted or bitterly discouraged by the prosperous or unfavorable turn of events, I would be giving you more extensive admonition by word of mouth or by letter. But as it is, since I have discovered that you preserve the same equanimity in the face of both success and difficulty, I have resolved to do neither of these things, so that I may not seem boorish and intrusive by saying and writing what is out of place. For who does not know that your Christian Reverence possesses nobility of spirit in every respect, and endures the trials that beset him with long-suffering and high-mindedness? For you have always realized that nothing in this present life is stable, but that everything is changing in a restless movement toward its opposite. Let me give examples: joy succeeds grief, prosperity follows misfortune, and health takes the place of sickness. And all those things in life that seem to be delightful or troublesome are in the process of change toward each other, and never remain stable. Thus we see that those who have found favor in God's sight by their virtue tend to be content with suffering and rejoice in difficulties, that they slough off all happiness and follow the narrow way, so that they may grasp that eternal joy which will not be succeeded in the future by any suffering or grief or distress. This joy we, too, may easily achieve, if we but desire it. Casting

μένων ἡμῖν δημοσίων φροντίδων καὶ ἄκοντες ἀποβάλλοντες, κοῦφοι λοιπὸν καὶ εὐσταλεῖς πρὸς τὸ τοῦ βίου τούτου πέλαγος διανηξόμεθα ὑπὸ τῆς τοῦ κτίσαντος καὶ μόνης κυβερνώμενοι νεύσεως. Οὐκοῦν μὴ ἐπὶ τῇ συμβάσῃ τῆς ἀξίας ἀποβολῇ ἑαυτοὺς τῷ τῆς λύπης παραπέμψωμεν κλύδωνι, μηδέ, ὅτι διαδοχὴν ἐφημέρου εὐροίας ὑπέστημεν, καταπίπτωμεν, ἀλλὰ μᾶλλον τῷ διέποντι καὶ διεξάγοντι πρὸς τὸ συμφέρον τὰ καθ' ἡμᾶς θεῷ εὐαρεστήσωμεν τῷ μὴ ἐάσαντι ἡμᾶς μέχρι τέλους ἐν τοῖς ἀπαρέσκουσιν αὐτῷ καὶ ἐν οἷς οὐκ εὐδοκεῖ, † ἣ ἐφηδῦναι, † πράγμασι κελεύει, ἐγκαλινδεῖσθαι καὶ ἀναστρέφεσθαι. Ἔδειξεν οὖν ὄντως ἐν ὀφθαλμοῖς ὑμῶν ὅτι ἀγαπήσει ἠγάπησεν ἡμᾶς καὶ οὐ παρεῖδεν τὴν πρὸς αὐτὸν ὑμῶν ἐκτενῆ δέησιν, ἀλλ' ἐπιβλέπων ἐπέβλεψεν καὶ ἐρρύσατο τῆς τῶν θηρευόντων παγίδος καὶ ταύτην συνέτριψεν. Εἰ γὰρ ἑαυτῶν γενοίμεθα, καὶ τὰ ἑαυτῶν μεριμνᾶν βουλευσαίμεθα, καὶ κατὰ κόσμον εὐδοκιμήσαιμεν, καὶ τῆς ἐντολῆς καὶ κηδεμονίας τοῦ θεοῦ οὐκ ἐκπέσοιμεν. Ἰδοὺ γὰρ ἀντὶ σοῦ ἐγεννήθησάν σοι ἐπὶ θυγατράσιν υἱοί σου, οἵτινες διαναπαύσουσιν ὑμᾶς ἐκ τῶν κόπων καὶ συνεχουσῶν ὀδυνῶν καὶ ἀντιλήψονται ἡμῖν ἐν τοῖς τοῦ βίου τούτου ὀχληροῖς, μόνον ἐὰν μετὰ εὐχαριστίας τὰ συμ || 113 || πίπτοντα δεξώμεθα καὶ ὑπενέγκωμεν, καὶ λογισώμεθα τὰ συμβαίνοντα ὡς τὰ συμφέροντα. Ἐὰν γὰρ ἀναλογισώμεθα τὰς μέχρι τοῦ δεῦρο κενὰς φροντίδας, τὸν πολὺν ἐκεῖνον καὶ μάταιον τάραχον, καὶ τὴν εἰκῇ τῶν πραγμάτων παλίρροιαν, καὶ τὴν νυνὶ κατασχοῦσαν ἡμᾶς διὰ τῆς ἡσυχίας ἀκίνδυνον γαλήνην, ὄντως ἂν ἐκεῖνα βδελυκτὰ καὶ ταῦτα ἐπέραστα ἡγησώμεθα· ἐν ἐκείνοις γὰρ ὁ ἐναντίος, ἐν τούτοις δὲ ὁ θεὸς ἐπευφραίνεται.

Ἀλλὰ ταῦτα μὲν οὔτε νουθετικῶς οὔτε παραμυθητικῶς γράφειν ὡρμήθημεν· ἴσμεν γὰρ τὸ ὑμέτερον ἐν τούτοις ἀδιάπτωτον καὶ ἀκέραιον· ἀλλὰ μόνον ὑπομιμνήσκοντες ὑμᾶς ὅσον ἐστὶ τῶν δημοσίων φροντίδων ὁ ἐν γαλήνῃ καὶ ἀταραξίᾳ βίος αἱρετώτερος. Ἐλπίδα δὲ ἔχομεν ὅτι καὶ διὰ τάχους σε ὀψόμεθα καὶ τὰ τῷ γράμματι λείποντα τῷ λόγῳ προσαναπληρώσομεν, ὅπως καὶ διὰ ταύτης τῆς πείρας μάθωμεν ὅτι καὶ παραμυθίας πάσης καὶ νουθεσίας εἶ ὑψηλότερος, ἐκ τοῦ φανῆναι μηδὲν παθὼν ἐκ τῆς προσπεσούσης σοι ἀνθρωπίνης ἐπηρείας τε καὶ συμβάσεως. Τοῦτο δὲ δυσωποῦμεν· εὔχεσθαι ὑπὲρ ἡμῶν ἵνα καὶ

---

29 *ἀγαπήσει – ἡμᾶς*: cf. Ier. 38.3; Eph. 2.4 || 30 *ἐπιβλέπων ἐπέβλεψεν*: cf. 1 Reg. 1.11 || 30–31 *ἐρρύσατο – συνέτριψεν*: Ps. 123 (124).7

---

21 *εὐσαλεῖς* V: *εὔσαλοι* G || 23 *συμβάσει* V || 24 *διαδοχὴν*: *διακοπὴν* propos. Ševčenko || 27 *ἣ ἐφηδῦναι* V: fort. *μηδ' ἐφησθῆναι* vel *ἐφηδύνεσθαι* scribendum || 28 *ἐγκαλεῖν δεῖσθαι* V || 32 secundum *ἑαυτῶν* iterav. V || 33 *εὐδοκημήσαιμεν* V: corr. G || 42 *βδελλυκτὰ* V

aside, however unwillingly, the burden of the public cares that are laid upon us, we shall henceforward be light and unencumbered in swimming through the ocean of this life, guided only by the hand of the Creator. Therefore, let us not abandon ourselves to a storm of grief at the loss of office that has occurred, nor let us be thrown into despair because we have suffered a change in our everyday prosperity; rather let us find favor with God who manages our affairs and brings them to a conclusion for our advantage inasmuch as He has not allowed us to wallow and live to the very end among circumstances that do not please Him and that He bids us not to take pleasure in. Therefore He has shown clearly in your sight that "He has loved us with a great love," and has not disregarded your constant prayers to Him, but "in looking upon you He has looked upon you with favor," and "has rescued you from the snare of the fowlers, and has broken the snare." For if we should become masters of ourselves and resolve to consider our own affairs, we may both prosper in this world and not fall short of God's commandment and providence. For behold, in your place sons have been born to your daughters, who will give you rest from your labors and from the pains that beset you, and will assist you in the troubles of this life, if only you accept what happens to you with gratitude and endure it, and count as advantages the events that are occurring. For if you consider the empty concerns that have occupied you till now, that long and vain confusion, and random ebb and flow of events, and ⟨compare them⟩ with the peace, free from all danger, that now enfolds you as the result of your retirement, truly you will regard the former as abominable and the latter as desirable: for the Enemy delights in the one, but God finds pleasure in the other.

I have been impelled to write this not in a spirit of admonition nor of consolation: for I know of your unerring and unshakable spirit in these matters. My purpose was merely to remind you how preferable is a life of peace and calm to public worries. But I hope to see you soon and to supply with my words the omissions of this letter, so that I may learn from that ⟨face-to-face⟩ experience that you stand above all consolation and exhortation, from your manifest survival unscathed from the abuse and disaster that have come upon you as happens among men. This I beg of you: pray

ἡμᾶς, οἷς τρόποις ὁ θεὸς ἐξεπίσταται, τῆς τοῦ βίου τούτου ἐλευθερώσῃ βορβορώδους ἰλύος, ὡς ἂν δυνηθείημεν μιᾶς ἡμέρας χρόνον καθα || 114 || ρὰν αὐτῷ τὴν λατρείαν προσαγαγεῖν καὶ τὴν ἐν ἡμῖν ἀποκλυσώμεθα τῆς ψυχῆς σηπεδόνα, ὅτι πολλῆς καὶ πλείστης ἐπιδέεται τῆς προσοχῆς τε καὶ νήψεως. Ὑμᾶς δὲ Κύριος ὁ θεὸς ἐν τῇ κατ' αὐτὸν εὐοδώσῃ θεραπείᾳ, εἰς πλείονα τῆς ἀρετῆς ὑμῶν προκοπήν, ἣν εἰς ἀρέσκειαν αὐτοῦ καθ' ἡμέραν ἐκτελεῖτε καὶ διαπράττεσθε.

25. Νικηφόρῳ διακόνῳ καὶ χαρτοφύλακι

Ἐρομένῳ μοι φιλικῶς, ὦ φιλότης, ἀπόκριναι· οὐκ ἔσχε κόρον ἡ περὶ τὸ θεῖον ἀκόρεστός σου διάθεσις τῆς γείτονος ἰλύος καὶ συγχυτικῆς ὀχλήσεως καί, οἷον ποιητικῶς εἰπεῖν, βρομώδους κνίσης ἑλισσομένης περὶ καπνῷ, ἀλλ' ἐγκαρτερεῖ καὶ περιφῦσα τούτοις, ὡς ἡ τοῦ Διὸς γούνασι Θέτις, μᾶλλον ἐμπεριέχεται ἢ τοῖς πρὸς ὀσμὴν ἀγροῦ πλήρους παρακαλοῦσιν ἡδύσμασιν; Μὴ δῆτα, ὦ φιλόμουσε, τούτοις προσκαθῆσθαι βιάζοιο, δίδου δὲ σεαυτὸν καὶ τῆς παρ' ἡμῖν καθαρᾶς αὔρας ἀπόλαυε· οἶσθα τὰς βορέου πνοὰς ὡς ἡμᾶς ἀκράτους ἰούσας καὶ ψυχαγωγούσας καὶ φερούσας ζωάγρια. Ἢ οὐ μέμνῃ, ὅτε τῶν πιστακῶν ὑπεκλίθημεν ἔνερθε καὶ χαριέντως ἐβοριάζομεν, εἰ καὶ μὴ κατὰ τὸν προφήτην συκάμινα † ἢ οτ . . . περφεαρροῖ † τὸ διειδὲς ἀνιμῶμεν ὕδωρ ἐκεῖνο τὸ κηρίου καὶ μέλιτος γλύκιον; Εἰ οὖν ἐκείνοις || 115 || ταῦτα συγκρίναις καὶ τὴν περιστοιχοῦσαν καὶ περιγράφουσαν ὑμᾶς ἀηδίαν τοῖς ἥδουσιν ἐμπαραθήσῃ, εἴσῃ που πάντως οὐκ εἰς μακρὰν τὸ διάφορον· ὑφ' οὗ νυσσόμενος, μᾶλλον δὲ καὶ λίαν θελγόμενος, Ἀχιλλέως γενέσθαι σοι πόδας ἐξῄτηκας, ὡς ἂν τῶν ἡμετέρων ἐντὸς λειμώνων εἰσήλασας. Δεῦρο δὴ οὖν ἐς τάχος καί, ταῖς ἐπεισρεούσαις ἀνίαις, ῥευμάτων δίκην, ὁσημέραι, καὶ † ταῖς ταύταις † ὕουσι χαίρειν εἰπών, θυμηδίας ἐμπί-

---

53 ἐλευθερώσει V || 57 εὐοδώσει V || 59 ἐκτελεῖν τε καὶ διαπράττεσθαι V

25: 3–4 *κνίσης – καπνῷ*: *Il.* 1.317 || 4–5 *τοῦ Διός – Θέτις*: cf. *Il.* 1.500 || 5 *ὀσμήν – πλήρους*: Gen. 27.27 || 8–9 *τὰς βορέου – ζωάγρια*: cf. *Il.* 5.697–98 || 11 *συκάμινα*: Am. 7.14 || 12 *τὸ κηρίου – γλύκιον*: cf. Ps. 18(19).11 || 15–16 *Ἀχιλλέως – πόδας*: cf. *Od.* 11.538–539

25: 10 *ἐβοριάζομεν* V: vide comment. || 11 *ἢ ὅτ' ἐκ φρέατος* vel sim. legendum || *ἀνιῶμεν* V || 12 *ἐκείνους* V corr. G || *τοῦτο* Karlsson || 13 *περιστυχοῦσαν* V || 14 *ἐμπαραθέσω εἰσί που* V: *ἐμπαραθήσω, εἰσί που* Karlsson || 15 *νισσούμενος* V || 18 *ὡσήμεραι* V || *τ' αὐταῖς* Karlsson

for me, that God may free me, by the means He knows well, from the filthy slime of this life, so that I may be able for the space of one day to offer Him my worship in purity, and may wash from my soul the corruption that is in me, because there is need for the greatest care and the utmost sobriety. As for you, may the Lord our God lead you forward in His service, for your greater progress in virtue, which you accomplish and achieve daily for His pleasure.

25. To Nikephoros, deacon and *chartophylax*

When I inquire of you, O my friend, do answer me in a friendly manner. Has not your mind, which is insatiable in matters divine, been sated by the mire that surrounds you, by the bothersome confusion or, to say with the Poet, that evil-smelling vapor "that rolls about with the smoke," but persists in these things and clings to them, like Thetis to the knees of Zeus, ⟨wishing⟩ to be encompassed by them rather than by the charms that evoke the smell of a laden field? Do not force yourself, O friend of the Muses, to abide by those things; yield to me, and enjoy the clean air that is here. You know that the northern breezes blow upon us in all their purity, bringing gratification and renewed vigor.

Do you not remember when we lay down beneath the pistachio trees and were pleasantly refreshed . . . if not mulberries (as the prophet has it)—or when . . . we drew from a well(?) that clear water that was sweeter than wax and honey? So if you compare these things with those, and if you set these pleasures beside the unpleasantness that surrounds and encompasses you, you will surely soon perceive the difference. Goaded on by this ⟨realization⟩ and, indeed, greatly pleased, you would wish to have the feet of Achilles that you might leap into my meadows. Come quickly now, bid farewell to the troubles that pour upon you every day like streams and those(?) that rain upon you, and fill yourself with delight. For you know that none of

πλαθι· ἔγνως γὰρ ὡς τούτων οὐδὲν πρὸς διαμονὴν διαρκές τε καὶ στάσιμον· ἀλλὰ καὶ τῶν δυσχερῶν βραχὺ τὸ βιώσιμον, καὶ τῶν εἰς θυμηδίαν φερόντων ἐπίκηρον τὸ ἀξίωμα.

26. Τῷ αὐτῷ

Πότε σε τῆς ἀηδίας ἐκπλύναιμεν, ὦ λίαν εὐωδέστατε; Τίς Ξάνθος καὶ Σκάμανδρος καὶ δινήεις Ἕρμος τὰς τῆς νυκτὸς ἐκείνης ἀποσμήξειε στροφοδινίας, καὶ τὰς τῶν ἀλάλων ἐμπίδων ἰώδεις δήξεις; Δέδοικα γὰρ μήπως ταῦτα λέγων καὶ γράφων ἀναξάνω τὴν τότε συμβᾶσαν ἐπήρειαν καὶ μαλακίας ὑμῖν αἴτιος γένωμαι. Εἰ οὖν οὐδέν σοι τούτων μέλον, γενοῦ πρὸς ἡμᾶς· διψῶμεν γάρ σου τῆς θέας, ἄνερ ἐπιθυμιῶν τῶν τοῦ πνεύματος, ἢ οἱ πολλῷ φλεγόμενοι καύματι· ἡ δὲ λέξις ἡ ἁλυκὴ τὴν τοῦ παρ' ὑμῖν ὕδατος || 116 || ἐκμιμουμένη † κατὰ σὴν † ἁλυκότητα καὶ γλυκύτητα, τὸν τῆς βραχείας ἀνεμάξατο χρόνον.

27. Τῷ αὐτῷ

Εἰ τὴν τοῦ Αὐγείου κόπρον, ὡς ὁ παλαιὸς ἐκεῖνος Ἀλκμήνης ἔκγονος, καθήραμεν, ἀλλὰ μὴ τὸν τῆς κακοδοξίας συρφετὸν τῇ ἐκκλησίᾳ κακῶς προσεισφθαρέντα τῶν ταύτης περιβόλων τῷ πτύῳ τῆς ὀρθῆς ὁμολογίας ἐβάλομεν, τυχὸν ἡμῖν μισθὸς οὐχ ὁ τυχὼν ἐπωφείλετο. Ἐπεὶ δὲ ⟨οὐ⟩κ ἐκεῖνον, τοῦτον δὲ καὶ προῖκα τὸν θεῖον ὑπέδυμεν δίαυλον,

---

26: 1–2 *Ξάνθος – Ἕρμος*: cf. *Il.* 2.877; 5.479; 20.92 || 6–7 *ἄνερ – Πνεύματος*: cf. Dan. (sec. vers.) 9.23, 10.11,19; Greg. Naz. *Funebris oratio in patrem,* PG 35, 985A; idem *Oratio in Baptisma,* PG 36, 416C

26: 5 *γένομαι* V || 7 *ἢ* V || *η ἀλῦκη* V || 8 *κατασην . . . γλυκοτητα* V: an *καὶ τὴν σὴν* scribendum?

27: 1–2 *εἰ – καθήραμεν*: Appolod. II.5, ed. R. Wagner, p. 77.7–78.11

27: 1 *σύγγονος* in textu: *ἔκγονος* in marg. V || 2 *τὸν* G: *τὸ* V || 3 *τὸ πτύον* V: *τῷ πτύῳ* corr. G || 4 *ἐβάλομεν* V: an *ἐξεβάλομεν* legendum? || 5 . . . *κ ἐκείνου τοῦτο δὲ* V || *ὑπέδειμεν* V

these things is lasting or stable in the long run, and that, on the one hand, the lifespan of difficulties is short, while, on the other, the value of whatever causes pleasure is perishable.

26. To the same

When may we wash you clean of sorrow, O you who smell so sweet? What Xanthus, what Scamander, what eddying Hermus shall wipe off the confusion of that night and the poisonous sting of those speechless mosquitoes? For I fear that in saying and writing these things I may break open afresh ⟨the wound of⟩ the ill-treatment that befell you then and cause you indisposition. But if you care nought for these things, come to me: for I thirst after the sight of you, O man of spiritual desires, as those who are inflamed by much heat ⟨long for a cool breeze⟩. As for the "salty" style, imitating the saltiness and sweetness of your waters as well as yours (?), it has assumed the brevity of its vowels (?).

27. To the same

If we had cleaned out the dung of Augeias, like the famous son of Alcmene in ancient times, instead of ⟨using⟩ the shovel of Orthodoxy to cast from the precincts of the Church the sweepings of evil doctrine that had penetrated therein to our undoing, perchance no mean reward would be owed to us. But since we have undertaken not the former ⟨task⟩, but this holy race, and did so gratis, we should expect the

μήποθεν ἄλλοθέν ποτε ἢ πρὸς θεοῦ τὴν ἀνάρρησιν ἀναμένοιμεν· ἢ μᾶλλον ἡμᾶς ἀριπλούτους καὶ τὰ μέγιστα κατὰ ψυχὴν κερδησείοντας διαδείξειεν, ἢ τοὺς κακῶν λημματίας ὁ ἐκ τοιούτων πόρων δαψιλῶς συνεισφερόμενος ἔρανος, οἷς ἐφ᾽ οἷς δρῶσιν οὐκ ἐπινυστάξει τὸ τῆς δίκης ἔνδικον ὄμμα. Οὐδὲ γὰρ Αὐγείας τὸ τοῦ Ἡρακλέως διέφυγε ῥόπαλον. Στέργε οὖν σὺν ἡμῖν καὶ συγκαρτέρει ὅσον ἔστιν, εἰδὼς τὸ τῆς ὑπομονῆς ἀνταπόδομα. Εἴπερ δὲ λοιπὸν ἐσπείσω πρὸς κώνωπας καὶ τῆς ἀκηρύκτου τούτων ἐπιστασίας ἐπιεικῶς ἠμνημόνησας, πάρεσο κωνωπεῶνι θωρακισθεὶς μήπως καὶ αὖθις ἐντὸς βέλους αὐτῶν ἁλῷς καὶ πολλὰς || 117 || ἀΰπνους νύκτας ἰαύσαις, ὡς ὁ παιδαγωγὸς Πηλείδου Φοῖνιξ, φιλάρετε.

28. Τῷ *αὐτῷ*

Ὀψὲ τῆς φθασάσης ἐπὶ τῷ κατοιχομένῳ λύπης καὶ μόλις ἀνενεγκών, μικρόν τι καὶ νεκρὸν καὶ οἷον ὀδωδὸς ἀποφθέγγομαι· ἤδη γὰρ αὐτῷ μοι τῷ προλαβόντι τοῖς ἐνερτέροις συμπεριπολεῖν ἐδόκει κευθμῶσι καὶ τοῖς ἐν νεκάσι τοῦτον συμπεριάγειν καὶ τὸν ὀφθαλμὸν καθ᾽ ᾅδου ῥίπτειν ἐρευνῶντι ἆρα ποῖ τετάξεται λήξεως. Οὕτως ἡδόμην τῷ θανόντι συνεῖναι μᾶλλον, ἢ πάλαι Πυλάδαι τοῖς Ὀρέσταις ἐκείνοις μέχρις αὐτῶν τάφων συνῆφθαι προήρηντο· ἔνθεν καὶ τῆς ὑπερημερίας καὶ τῆς Ἀκεσσαίου σελήνης ὑφ᾽ ὑμῶν ἀπηνεγκάμην τὸν ὄνειδον. Νυνὶ δὲ τῆς μετὰ νεκύων, ὡς ἐδόκουν, ἀπαλλαγεὶς ὁμιλίας, εἶτα τοῖς ζῶσι συνδιαιτώμενος καὶ σὲ τὴν φίλην ἐμοὶ κεφαλὴν ἀλγυνομένην νόσῳ πυθόμενος, εὐξάμην τί παθεῖν ἑλέσθαι; Τί ἄλλο γε ἢ τὴν παντελῆ σιγὴν ὑπ-

---

14 *ἐντὸς βέλους*: cf. Diogen. Vind. II.62; Zen. III.89; Karathanasis 176 || 15 *ἀΰπνους – ἰαύσαις*: *Il.* 9.325 (sed non de Phoenice ibi agitur)

---

6 ἢ: ἢ V || 9 *οὐκ ἔστιν νυστάξει* V: corr. Ševčenko: *οὐκ ἔτι* G || 12 *εσπισω πρὸς* V: *ἐπὶ σῷ προσώπῳ* G: *ἐσπείσω* proposuit idem G || 13 *κομπεωνι* V || 14 *μέλους* V: corr. Ševčenko

---

28: 2 *νεκρὸν – ὀδωδὸς*: cf. Ioann. Chrys. *Hom. III in ep. ad Titum*, PG 62, 681 v. 8–9 || 6–7 *Πυλάδαι – συνῆφθαι*: cf. Eur. *Or.* 1091 || 8 *τῆς Ἀκεσσαίου σελήνης*: Diogen. I.57; VI.30; Apostol. I.90; XVI.44

28: 7 *συνάφθαι προήροιντο* V || 8 *ἀκεσαίου* V || 9 *νέ . . . κύων* V (rasura)

proclamation of our success from nobody other than God. May it show us rich indeed and able to win the greatest benefits for our souls in preference to the plentiful contributions from such great resources ⟨enjoyed by⟩ those graspers after evil; for with respect to them, the righteous eye of Justice shall not slumber in surveying their deeds. Indeed, not even Augeias escaped the club of Hercules.

Acquiesce, therefore, as I do, and endure as much as is needful, knowing the recompense of patience. For the rest, if you have made a pact with the mosquitoes and have almost forgotten their undeclared onset, come armed with a mosquito net, lest you be caught again within range of their sting and spend many sleepless nights, like Phoenix, the tutor of Peleas' son, O lover of virtue.

28. To the same

Having at long last and barely recovered from my sorrow for the deceased, I am uttering a faint and dead sound, one, as it were, that smells ⟨of corruption⟩. For already it seemed to me that I was accompanying the departed one in the nether world and leading him about among the dead, and casting my eye in Hades as I was searching for the place that would be assigned to him. So greatly did I enjoy the company of the deceased, more so than that famous Pylades of olden times who chose to cleave to Orestes to the very tomb; for which reason I was blamed by you for delay like Akessaios and his moon. Now, however, having, as it seemed to me, given up the company of the dead, and thereafter dwelling among men that live, I learned that you, my dear friend, were afflicted by an illness, and I wondered what I should choose to undergo. What else, but to assume complete silence before this dreadful news

ελθεῖν πρὶν ἢ τοῖς ὠσὶ τὴν ἀπαισίαν ἀκοὴν ταύτην συνεισδέξασθαι; Ἀλλὰ λύπη σαρκοτρὼξ τοῦτο κατέσπειρεν ὑμῖν τὸ ζιζάνιον. Μὴ οὖν ἐγκυμονηθήτω, ἀλλὰ δμηθήτω, καὶ αὔραις ἀπορ || 118 || ριφθήτω, μή τινα κίνδυνον ὑμῖν ἀποτέξειεν. Ἡμῖν δὲ τοῦτο διαμπὰξ ἔργον πρὸς τὸ κρεῖττον εὐκτικῶς ἐστι βλέπειν ἐρρωμένον, εὐροοῦντα καὶ τοῖς θείοις σε δεξιῶς ἰθυνόμενον οἴαξιν, ὡς ἂν τοῦ νυνὶ κυμαίνοντος κλύδωνος ὑπεράνω γένοιο καὶ τῷ τῆς εὐπαθείας ὅρμῳ πλησιάσαις καὶ εἰσελάσαις ἐντός, καὶ ἀπολαύσαις ὧν ἱμειρόμεθα.

29. Τῷ *αὐτῷ*

Καὶ δέδεγμαι ἐπιστολήν· οὐκ ἀναίνομαι· καὶ σεσίγηκα· ἀφασία γὰρ τὴν ἐμὴν ὥπλισε γλῶτταν καὶ μενεῖν κωφεύουσαν πέπεικε, καὶ χεῖρα ἐπιθεῖναι συνήνεσε στόματι· ἀλλ' οὐχὶ πρὸς σὲ τοῦτό με παθεῖν ἔδει. Σύγγνωθι λοιπόν, ὦ ἱερώτατε γνῶμον, καὶ ἔρρωσο, καὶ εὐθύμει, καὶ εὔχου ὑπὲρ τῆς ἡμετέρας ὀλιγώρου καὶ φιλαμαρτήμονος μετριότητος.

30. Τῷ *αὐτῷ*

Ἔοικας πρὸς ἡμᾶς σιγὴν ἀσκῶν ἐπί τινας ἐπωφελεῖς * ἑαυτὸν καθείς, κἂν τούτοις τοὺς τῶν θείων ὑμῖν νοημάτων μετοχετεύων κρουνούς, κατακλυσμόν τινων ἀφραινόντων δογμάτων ἐπινοεῖν, ὦ τῆς ὀρθῆς καὶ εἰλικρινοῦς ἐπίκουρε πίστεως. Οὐ γὰρ ἐλάνθανες ὡς ἐν μερίμνης μέρει πολλάκις ἐτίθεσο, εἴ τι μνήμων ἐγώ, καὶ μάλιστα τῶν λόγων τῶν σῶν, ὅπλα λογικὰ κινῆσαι κατὰ τῶν ἀλλοκότων καὶ ἀλλοφυῶν τῶν

---

15 *ἀποτέξειαν* V || 16 *ἐρρωμένων* V || 16–17 *δεξί(ως) ἰθύνομεν οἶ αξιν* V || 18 *γένοι[τ]ο καὶ τὰ* V corr. manus recentior || *πλησιάσαι⟨ς⟩ καὶ εἰσελάσαι⟨ς⟩* corr. manus recentior

---

29: 4 *γν̃μ* (ω supra) V: *ω* supra lineam scripsit manus recentior

---

30: 1 post *ἐπωφελεῖς* lacunam statuimus || 1–2 *ἑαυτων . . . κ'ἂν* V || *ὑμι* V || 3 *κατακλυσμῶν* V || post *ὦ* lacuna ca. 2 litt. || 6 *ἀλλοφυῶν* fort. in *ἀλλοφύλων* emendandum cum G

reached your ears as well? But my consuming grief has implanted in you this tare. Let it not sprout; let it rather be cut lest it cause you some danger. As for me, my perpetual task is, by my prayers to God, to see you in good health, prosperous, and being skillfully guided by the divine helm, so that you may overcome the storm that is now raging and so approach and enter the harbor of felicity, and enjoy those things we all desire.

29. To the same

I have received your letter—I do not deny it—and have kept silent. Speechlessness has armed my tongue and caused it to remain dumb; it has decided me to lay my hand upon my mouth. Yet I should not have suffered this from you. Forgive me, therefore, O most holy expert, farewell and be of good cheer. And pray for my negligent and sinful mediocrity.

30. To the same

It seems that while saying nothing to me, you have been employing yourself in certain useful ⟨works⟩ and, in channeling therein the streams of your divine concepts, you have been planning the destruction of certain foolish doctrines, O defender of the true and pure faith. For it did not escape attention—if I have a good recollection, especially of your own words—that you were often intending to take up the arms of reason against the uncouth and alien battle lines of the heretics, so that, God granting,

αἱρετικῶν παρατάξεων, ἵν', ἣν διδῷ θεός, τὴν γιγαντιαίαν ἐκείνην τοῦ δευτέρου Γολιὰθ *καὶ μεγάλαυχον κε* ‖ 119 ‖ *φαλὴν τῇ τρισσῇ τῆς ὁμοουσίου* Τριάδος *ὁμολογίᾳ καὶ ἀνολέθρῳ στερρότητι σφενδονήσας καὶ τὴν παρ' αὐτῷ φονικὴν καὶ ψυχάρπαγα μάχαιραν ἀφελόμενος, τὴν αὐτῆς ἐκτομὴν πραγματεύσαιο καὶ ἐξέλοις τὸν τῆς ἀμωμήτου λατρείας καὶ πίστεως ὄνειδον.* Καὶ *γὰρ ἔδει ὃν αὐτός, κατὰ τῆς οἰκουμενικῆς* Ἐκκλησίας, *κυκεῶνα πικρὸν συνεκέρασεν καὶ πολλοῖς προπίνων πιστοῖς αἱρέσεως προτέθεικε κάλυξι, τοῖς ἐλεγκτικοῖς καὶ στύφουσιν ὑμῶν, μᾶλλον δὲ γλυκέσι καὶ ἡδέσι κράμασιν, ὡς ἀδόκιμον ἀπερρίφθαι καὶ [εἰ] λίαν ἐξίτηλον, καὶ πόρρω τῆς ἐκκλησιαστικῆς ἀποκριθῆναι τραπέζης, εὐφραντικὴν μηδεμίαν ἐπιδεικνύμενον ὄρεξιν· ἀλλὰ δὴ καὶ τὴν σόλοικον καὶ φλήναφον τῶν ἐκείνου λόγων συνθήκην καὶ ⟨ἥν⟩, ὡς οἶσθα, πολλάκις ἡμῖν ἀνεκάλυπτεν καὶ τὴν ταύτης χολώδη σαθρότητα ταῖς τεχνικαῖς ἡμᾶς ἐπιστασίαις στηρίζειν βαρβαρικώτατα προὔτρεπεν, ὑπὸ τῆς ὑμετέρας ἐπιστημονικῆς ἐλεγχθῆναι ⟨καὶ⟩ παιδευθῆναι [καὶ] παιδεύσεως ὡς ἂν μὴ κατὰ τὸν ἀράβιον αὐλητήν, ᾗ φησιν ἡ παροιμία, βατταρίζειν ἀπέραντα κατὰ κόσμον καὶ μέτρον προφέρειν μηδὲν ἐπιστάμενον.* Ἀλλ' *εἰ ταῦτα καλῶς ὑπετύπωσα καὶ οὕτως ἔχεις καὶ πονεῖς, ὡς ἐγὼ μὴ μάτην τεκμαίρομαι, ἐξαύδα καί, σὺν θεῷ, μὴ ⟨κεῦθε καὶ⟩ κατὰ τῶν ἐναντίων δογμάτων συμφράττοιο, καὶ εἴ τινα λόγον κατὰ τῆς σεπτῆς εἰκόνος* Χριστοῦ *καὶ τῆς σεμνῆς* Θεομήτορος *καὶ τῶν ὑπὲρ* ‖ 120 ‖ *αὐτῶν καὶ δι' αὐτῶν ἀνδρισαμένων ἢ γδουπούμενον, ἢ καὶ ὑπ' ὀδόντα πως ψιθυριζόμενον εὕροις, μηδ' ὅς φύγοι, ἀλλ' ἅμα πάντες ἐξαπολοίατ' ἀκήδεστοι καὶ ἄφαντοι· ἡμῖν δὲ μὴ φθονήσῃς τῆς ὠφελείας, ἀλλὰ καὶ παρ' ἑαυτῷ ταύτην ταμιεύου καὶ μεταδίδου τοῖς πέλας· οὐδὲ γὰρ ἐλαττωθείη μηδεὶς βιωφελής ποτε λόγος ὑπὸ τοῦ θείου λόγου τρεφόμενος.*

30: 7–8 *τοῦ δευτέρου* Γολιάθ: cf. 1 Reg. 17.49–51 ‖ 22 *κατὰ τὸν ἀράβιον αὐλητήν*: Zen. II.39; Greg. Cypr. I.32 ‖ 25 *ἐξαύδα – κεῦθε*: cf. *Il.* 1.363; 16.19 ‖ 29–30 *ἅμα – ἄφαντοι*: *Il.* 6.59–60

---

7 *αἱρετικῶν* Ševčenko: *ἑταιρικ(ῶν)* V ‖ *ἢν* V ‖ 9 *σφενδονίσας* V ‖ 12–13 *τὸν οἰκουμενικὸν ἐκκλη* V ‖ 13–14 *πολλ̄ . . . πιστῆς* V ‖ 14 fort. *κύλιξι* scribendum ‖ 16 *εἰ λίαν* V: fortasse *ἰλὺν* seu *ὕλην* scribendum ‖ *εξιτιλον* V ‖ *της* ex *τω* corr. V ‖ 18 *σωλυκον* V ‖ 19 *ἡμῶν* V ‖ 20 *οβαρικωτατα* V ‖ 28 *ὑγδουπούμενον* V ‖ 29 *ἐξαπολοίατο* V ‖ 32 *μηδεισης* V: *μηδεὶς σὸς* G

you would strike, by the triple confession of the consubstantial Trinity (whose strength is invincible) as with a slingshot, that gigantic and boastful head of the second Goliath, and, taking away from him his murderous and soul-destroying dagger, you may achieve his decapitation, and so remove the reproach from our immaculate worship and faith. For that bitter potion that he has himself mixed to the detriment of the ecumenical Church and offered as a drinking present to many of the faithful in the cups of heresy, ought, by means of your reproving and astringent (or rather sweet and mild) medicine, be rejected as unseemly and altogether stale, and be removed far from the table of the Church inasmuch as it excites no pleasurable appetite. And, indeed, his illiterate and long-winded composition which, as you know, he often showed to us and urged us most barbarously to prop up its bilious inadequacy by means of our artful attention, ought to be refuted and chastised by your learned Eminence, so that he should not stutter on endlessly like the Arab piper (as the proverb has it), unable as he is to compose anything in an orderly and measured manner.

If I have outlined those things correctly, and your attitude and labor are as I have guessed not without reason, speak out, and, with God's help, do not lie concealed! Close ranks against the doctrines of the enemy, and if you hear any words, be they loud or whispered between the teeth, against the holy image of Christ and the revered Mother of God and of those who have fought valiantly on their behalf and by their help, "let none escape, but let all perish together, unmourned and unmarked." Do not, however, begrudge us the benefit, but keep it both for yourself and convey it to your friends; for a beneficial word that is nourished by the Word of God shall never suffer any diminution.

31. Θεοφυλάκτῳ καὶ Ἀθανασίῳ μοναχοῖς

Ἔδειξεν ὁ παρεληλυθὼς τῆς ὑμετέρας χρόνος εὐσεβοῦς τελειότητος, ὦ σκεῦος θείας ἐκλογῆς καὶ τῆς ἀθανασίας ἐπώνυμε, ὡς ἄκαρπον οὐδὲν ἢ φθοροποιὸν ἐν βίῳ καὶ ζημίας ἐνεπορεύσατο πρόξενον, εὔφορα δὲ πάντα καὶ γόνιμα καὶ μεγαλόκαρπα καὶ πολύχουν τὴν ὑμῶν εἰσφορὰν ἐπεισφρέοντα· τῇ γὰρ εὐπραγίᾳ τὴν δικαιοπραγίαν συνέριθον προσκτησάμενος, χιτῶνα ἐπικερδοῦς ὠφελείας σεαυτῷ περιτέθεικας οὐκ ἐκ σηρικῶν μηρυμάτων κλωσθέντα, ἐκ νημάτων δὲ τῆς θείας ἱστουργηθέντα ῥοπῆς καὶ πολυανθέσι ἀγαθοεργίας ἐξυφανθέντα ποικίλμασιν· καὶ μάρτυρες ἀπαραλόγιστοι τὰ τῶν ὑμετέρων ἀποτελέσματα πράξεων. Ἰδοὺ γὰρ τὴν τῆς ἐπιγείου χλεύης κυμαίνουσαν πολυκλύδωνα θάλασσαν, τῷ πηδαλίῳ τῆς σωστικῆς τοῦ θείου πατρὸς ἐπιπνοίας ἀποσεισάμενος, τὴν τῆς ψυχῆς ὁλκάδα, τὴν ἐκ ταραχῆς καὶ τρικυμίας καταντλουμένην ὁσημέραι λαίλαψιν, ἐνλιμενίσας ‖ 121 ‖ *ὡς ἄριστα, τῶν ἀγωγίμων τὰ κάλλιστα περιέσωσας, καὶ εἰς τὴν τῶν πραέων γῆν καὶ κληρουχίαν ἀβρόχῳ ποδὶ συνεισήλασας· καὶ διαπτύσας τῆς κοσμικῆς περιφορᾶς τὰ ἐπίπονα πώματα, ὡς τῆς* Μερρᾶς *τὰ πικρότατα νάματα, γλυκεῖαν ἑαυτῷ καὶ πότιμον τὴν πνευματικὴν πηγὴν ἐπρυτάνευσας.* Καὶ *τίς ἄρα ὁ τὴν γαλήνιον τῆς ὑμετέρας ἀταραξίας βιοτὴν καθιστορῆσαι δυνάμενος;* Ἐν *ἀστασιάστῳ γὰρ νυνὶ τελῶν καταστήματι ψυχικῶς ἐσαββάτισας καὶ εἰς τὴν τῆς ἀπαθείας κατάπαυσιν ἔφθασας, καὶ θηλάζεις ἐν γήρᾳ καλῷ τὴν ἐγκράτειαν, καὶ τῇ θείᾳ μελέτῃ τὴν πολυΰμνητον ἐξήνθησας ἐπὶ τὸ κρεῖττον ἐπίδοσιν, καὶ παννύχοις ἀγρυπνίαις τὸ ὀπτικὸν τοῦ νοῦ καθηράμενος, τοὺς τῆς διανοίας ὀφθαλμοὺς πρὸς ἐποπτείαν θείας ἐπιστασίας ἡτοίμασας, καὶ τῇ προσευχῇ καρτερῶν, καὶ ὅλον ἑαυτὸν ἀμετεώριστον ἀναστηλῶν τῷ θεῷ καὶ τῷ ἀγαθῷ προσηλωμένος ἔρωτι, πᾶσαν προσβολὴν ἀντικειμένην καὶ πλάνης ῥεμβασμὸν σβεννύεις τοῖς ἐρημικοῖς καὶ τὴν κακίαν ἀφανίζουσιν ἄνθραξιν· τῇ ταπεινώσει τὴν πρὸς οὐρανοὺς ὑψοῦσαν ἐκτήσω ἀνάβασιν καὶ τὴν ἐν αὐτοῖς κατοικίαν ᾠκοδόμησας ἀκατάλυ-*

31: 2 *σκεῦος – ἐκλογῆς*: Acta 9.15 ‖ 7–9 *οὐκ – ποικίλμασιν*: cf. Greg. Naz. *Oratio funebris ad Caesarium,* ed. Boulenger, §XVI, 2 [= PG 36, 773C–776A] ‖ 14–15 *εἰς τὴν – κληρουχίαν*: cf. Mt. 5.5 ‖ 16–17 *τῆς – νάματα*: Ex. 15.23 ‖ 27–28 *τοῖς – ἄνθραξιν*: cf. Ps. 119 (120).4

31: 5 *ἐπεισρέοντα* V ‖ 6 *προσκτισάμενος* V ‖ 10 *χλεύης* Ševčenko: *χλαίνης* V ‖ 13 *ὡσήμεραι* V ‖ 16 *πτώματα* V ‖ 17 *ἑαυτῶν* V ‖ 24 *ἐποπτίαν* V ‖ 25 *ἀμετεωριστων* V ‖ 28 *τῇ* G: *τὴν* V

31. To the monks Theophylaktos and Athanasios

The past life of your pious Perfection, O vessel of divine election who bear the name of immortality, has shown that you have not trafficked in anything that was fruitless, destructive in this life, or a cause of harm; nay, everything has been productive, fruitful, bountiful, and conducive to the copiousness of your contribution. For, having gained righteousness as a helpmate to success, you have invested yourself with a robe of gainful benefit, not one spun of silken thread but one woven from strands of divine approval and embroidered with the variegated ornaments of virtuous bahavior. To this the results of your deeds bear unerring witness. For behold, you have escaped, thanks to the rudder of the holy father's salutary inspiration, the billowy and stormy sea of earthly mockery and, having skillfully brought to harbor the ship of your soul that had been constantly flooded by the hurricanes of tumultuous tempest, you have saved the best of your wares and have entered the land and portion of the meek with dry feet. You have spat out the unpleasant draughts of worldly fare like the bitter waters of Marah and have obtained for yourself a spiritual spring that is sweet and fit to drink. Who, indeed, could describe fully your calm and undisturbed manner of life? For, enjoying now an untroubled condition, you have taken a spiritual sabbath rest and have reached the repose of impassibility. In your good old age you are nursing self-control; through the study of things divine you have bloomed with the oft-praised progress in virtue; by cleansing your mental vision in all-night vigils you have prepared your mind's eyes to behold God's dominion; by persevering in prayer, by offering yourself to God entirely free from distraction and attached to the true love, you dissipate every hostile attack and every bout of restlessness by means of the hot coals of the desert that annihilate evil. By your humility you have gained the ascent that raises you to heaven wherein you have constructed an indestructible

τον· καὶ ὡς ἔπος εἰπεῖν, θεῖος οἶκος ἀρωμάτων γενόμενος, εὐωδίας ὑγιαζούσης μεταδίδως τοῖς σοι προσπελάζειν ἐθέλουσιν· διὸ καὶ εἰς σύνθεσιν ἐχρημάτισας μυρεψικοῦ θυμιάματος. ‖ 122 ‖

Ἀλλ' ὦ πάτερ ἀγγελοειδέστατε, τὸν ἐν σαπρίᾳ με σκωλήκων καθήμενον καὶ ἁμαρτίας ἰλύϊ κυλινδούμενον εὐωδίασον. Τὴν γὰρ ἐπὶ τῇ θείᾳ μυήσει πρώτην ἠθετηκὼς εἰς Χριστὸν συνταγὴν καὶ δι' ἔργων ἀσέμνων τῷ ἀντιπάλῳ προσθέμενος, εἶτα τὸν μονήρη βίον δι' ἀποταγῆς τῶν κοσμικῶν φροντίδων ἑλόμενος, καὶ τῆς τῶν βεβήλων οὐκ ἀποσχόμενος ἐργασίας καὶ πράξεως, οὐχ ἥκιστα καὶ τοῦτον καταρρυπώσας ἐμόλυνα. Ἀλλὰ τί γένωμαι καὶ ποῖ τράπωμαι; Ἤ τινα πόρον τῆς συνεχούσης πωρώσεως καὶ βοηθὸν ἐκκαλέσωμαι, ὡς ἂν τῆς ἠπειλημένης μοι γεέννης διαδράσω τὴν παφλάζουσαν καὶ φλογίζουσαν κάμινον; Ὅθεν καὶ ἀπὼν ὡς παρὼν γονυπετῶ καὶ τῶν ἀγχιθέων ὑμῶν ἰχνῶν ἐφαπτόμενος, τὴν ἱκετείαν προβάλλομαι. Ῥανίδα μοι τῆς ἐκτικῆς ὑμῶν καὶ βιωφελοῦς ἐπιρροῆς καταστάξατε, σβεστήριον ἐσομένην τῆς ἐπηρτημένης αἰωνίας κολάσεως. Ναί, πατέρων ἄριστε, ναί, παναοίδιμε δέσποτα· ναί, θεραπευτὰ καὶ λάτρι τῆς παναμώμου καὶ ἁγνῆς Θεομήτορος· ἐνεργὴς γὰρ ὑμῶν ἡ πρὸς αὐτὴν εὑρεθήσεται ὑπὲρ ἐμοῦ προσαγομένη τοῦ τάλανος δέησις.

Τὴν δὲ θείαν ἐντολὴν καὶ πρόσταξιν τῆς ὑμετέρας παναγίας πατρότητος, ὡς ἤδη χρεῶσται καὶ δοῦλοι εὐγνώμονες, εἰ καὶ ἀναξίως καὶ ἐνδεῶς ἔχουσαν, πεπληρώκαμεν· ἣν μὴ δοίη θεὸς τοῖς ἐμοῖς ἀμβλυώττουσιν ὀφθαλμοῖς ἐπόψεσθαι, ἀλλὰ γῆ με συγκαλύψειε καὶ τάφος ‖ 123 ‖ *διασταίη καὶ φθορὰ τὴν ἐμὴν κόνιν εἰσδέξαιτο, πρὶν ἢ τῆς ἁγίας ὑμῶν ἐκδημίας πρὸς θεὸν ἐπαισθέσθαι καὶ τῆς ἀλγεινῆς ἐκείνης ἀκούσασθαι. Χαρισθείης οὖν τοῖς ποθοῦσιν ἐρρωμένος καὶ ὑπὸ τῆς ἄνω τοῦ ὑψίστου δεξιᾶς ἰθυνόμενος, ἄνερ ἐπιθυμιῶν τῶν κρειττόνων τοῦ πνεύματος, εἰς καύχημα τῆς μοναδικῆς καταστάσεως καὶ εἰς καλλωπισμὸν τῆς καθολικῆς ἐκκλησίας καὶ στήριγμα τῆς ἐμῆς γηραλέας πτωχονοίας ⟨καὶ⟩ ἀκλινέστατον ἔρεισμα.*

31–32 *εἰς – θυμιάματος*: cf. Ex. 30.35; 35.28 ‖ 33–34 *ἐν – καθήμενον*: cf. Job 2.9c ‖ 43–44 *ῥανίδα – καταστάξατε*: cf. Lc. 16.24 ‖ 50 *χρεῶσται – εὐγνώμονες*: cf. Mt. 18.23–27; Lc. 19.12–20 ‖ 56 *ἄνερ – πνεύματος*: cf. Dan. (sec. vers.) 9.23, 10.11,19; Greg. Naz. *Funebris oratio in patrem,* PG 35, 985A; idem *Oratio in Baptisma,* PG 36, 416C

---

30 *ὑγειαζούσης* V ‖ 34 *τὴν*: *τῇ* V ‖ 38 *καταρυπώσας* V ‖ 39 *τίς γένομαι . . . τράπομαι* V ‖ 40 *πορώσεως* V ‖ *ἐκκαλέσομαι* V ‖ 43 *εὐκτικῆς* proposuit Ševčenko ‖ 46 *λάτρη* V ‖ 51 *ἀμβλυόττουσιν* V ‖ 54 *ἐκείνης ⟨φωνῆς⟩* suppl. G ‖ *ἀκούσεσθαι* V ‖ 55 *χαρισθείη* V ‖ 55–56 *τῆς ὑψίστου* V ‖ 59 *καὶ* suppl. G

abode. One may say that you have become a divine house of spices and that you convey a health-giving fragrance to those who wish to approach you; wherefore you have lent yourself to the confection of aromatic incense.

But, O most angelic father, breathe your fragrance on me who am seated in the corruption of worms and wallow in the mire of sin. For, having broken the first promise made to Christ at my divine initiation and having joined the Adversary through my unholy deeds, I then chose the solitary life by renouncing worldly cares. But that life, too, I sullied and defiled by not abstaining from profane works and actions. What, then is to become of me and whither shall I turn? What help or assistance can I summon against the callousness that possesses me so as to escape the fiercely burning furnace of Hell that I am threatened with? Wherefore, though absent, I kneel before you as if I were present and, clasping your holy feet, I offer my supplication. Shed upon me from your habitual and life-supporting stream one drop that will quench the eternal punishment that hangs over me. Yea, best of fathers and renowned master; yea, servant and worshiper of the immaculate and pure Mother of God: for your request addressed to her on behalf of my wretched self will prove effective.

As for your sacred order and command, O all-holy father, I have carried it out, though unworthily and imperfectly, as though I were already your debtor and grateful slave. May God grant me not to see it with my failing eyes; rather let the earth cover me, let the grave open for me, and let corruption overtake my dust before I learn of your holy departure unto God and hear those painful tidings. May you gratify those who love you by remaining in good health and being guided by the right hand of the Highest, you who are filled with the nobler desires of the spirit, that you may be the pride of the monastic institution, the ornament of the Catholic Church, the stay and most steadfast support of my aged and feeble mind.

32. Κωνσταντίνῳ ἀσηκρῆτι

Παίζων ἀλλ' οὐ σπουδάζων, ὡς ἐγῷμαι, τὸν χωλοβάμονα καὶ σκάζοντα τῶν ἰάμβων ἐκείνων φορυτὸν ἡμᾶς ἀνακαθᾶραι προὔτρεπες· εἰ γὰρ μὴ τοῦτο ἦν, ἐσπούδακας ἂν ἤδη καλῶς μετρηθέντας καὶ τομαῖς τε καὶ βάσεσιν ἐναβρυνομένους ἀπειληφέναι, καὶ τοῖς αἰτήσασι δοῦναι, ὡς ἂν καὶ οἱ τῆς πάλαι πονησάσης διαδειχθεῖεν προαγῶνες, καὶ νῦν αἱ παρὰ τῆς τῷ στέφει προλαμπούσης ἀναφανεῖεν εὐσεβεῖς ἐπιμέλειαι· τὸ γὰρ συντηρῆσαι τὰ ὄντα τοῦ κτήσασθαι τὴν ἀρχὴν αἱρετώτερον. Ἀλλ' ὡς εἰκάζειν ἔχω, σύ τε καὶ ὁ καλῶν τῇ πάλαι μᾶλλον ἀμετρίᾳ συντίθεσθε, ἢ τῇ βασίμῳ τῶν τριμερῶν εὐρυθμίᾳ συνήδεσθε. Πάρεσο τοίνυν, εἰ οἷόν τε, πειράσων τὴν τῶν μετρηθέντων συνθήκην, ὦ τῶν ἐμῶν κριτὰ νοημάτων· οἶδα γὰρ ὡς ἔτι καὶ τρίτην ἡμῖν ἐπιφορτίσαις διόρθωσιν, ἡμαρτημένα καὶ πόρρω τοῦ σκοποῦ φερόμενα γράψασιν. ‖ 124 ‖

33. Ἰωσὴφ ἡγουμένῳ τοῦ Ἀντιδίου

Τίς δώσει τῇ κεφαλῇ μου ὕδωρ καὶ τοῖς ὀφθαλμοῖς μου πηγὴν δακρύων; Ἰδοὺ προφητικῶς προοιμιασάμενος ἀποδύρομαι. Πῶς κλαύσω ἐπὶ τῇ ἐμῇ ψυχικῇ συντριβῇ καὶ ἐπὶ τῇ τοῦ πνευματικοῦ μου παιδὸς θανατηφόρῳ φυγῇ, ὃν εἰς χεῖρας ὑμῶν τε καὶ τῆς ὑμετέρας ποίμνης παρέθηκα; Τίς τοῦ ἄλγους μου καταπαύσει τὸν πόνον καὶ τῆς κατεχούσης λύπης φαρμάκοις ἰατρικοῖς τὸ ἀνίατον θεραπεύσειεν; Καὶ γὰρ ὁλοσώματος ὁ μώλωψ καὶ ἡ πληγὴ φλεγμαίνουσα καὶ μηδεμίαν μότωσιν ἐπὶ τῷ συντριμμῷ δεχομένη τὸ σύνολον. Ἐν γὰρ τοῖς ὑμετέροις προβάτοις καὶ ἐν τῇ τῆς ποίμνης σου μάνδρᾳ ἠσφαλισμένον καὶ συν-

---

32: 1 *παίζων ἀλλ' οὐ σπουδάζων*: vide supra 10.3 ‖ 10–11 *ὦ – νοημάτων*: cf. Greg. Naz. *Funebris oratio in patrem,* PG 35, 1040B

32: 1 *χολοβόμωνα* V ‖ *σχ̆άζοντα* V: *καχλάζοντα* coniecit G ‖ 5 *πονήσασης διαδιχθ(εν)ει πρόαγῶνες* V ‖ 8 *ἄλλως . . . ὁ κᾶ τη πᾶ μαλ˜ . . . συντίθεσθαι* V ‖ 9 *τριμερῶν* V: an *τριμέτρων* scribendum? ‖ *συνήδεσθαι* ex *συνείδεσθαι* V

33: 1–2 *τίς – δακρύων*: Je. 8.23 ‖ 6–7 *ὁλοσώματος – φλεγμαίνουσα*: cf. Is. 1.6

33: 7 *μώτωσιν* V ‖ 8 *ὑμ* V

32. To Constantine *asekretis*

You were joking, I think, and not in earnest when you urged me to correct the lame and halting rubbish of those iambics, for otherwise you would have taken care to receive them when they had been properly scanned and decked out with caesuras and feet, and so hand them to those who requested them in order that both the preliminary struggles of her who toiled aforetime should become apparent and the pious concerns of her who now shines in the crown be made manifest; for it is preferable to preserve what you have to acquiring it afresh (?). But, as far as I can guess, both you and the one who bids you, prefer the former disregard of metrics to taking pleasure in the regular rhythm of the trimeter. Come then, if you can, to test the metrical composition, you who are the judge of my conceits; for I know that you will force a third correction on me if what I write is faulty and wide of the mark.

33. To Joseph, abbot of Antidion

"Who shall give my head water and my eyes a fountain of tears?" Behold, I have prefaced my lament with the prophet's words. How shall I weep over the ruin of my soul and the fatal flight of my spiritual son, whom I placed in your hands and those of your flock? Who will check the pain of my grief and heal with medicinal drugs the incurable sorrow that grips me? For my body is covered with bruises, and the inflamed wound admits of no dressing in this affliction. Indeed, secured and counted as it was among your sheep and the fold of your flock, only the sheep that I

αριθμούμενον τὸ τῆς ἐμῆς παρακαταθήκης μόνον θηριάλωτον γέγονε πρόβατον. Πῶς *τοῦτο συνηνέχθη;* Τίς *σκαιὸς δαίμων ἐπὶ ταύτην ἐμεσίτευσε τὴν ἀπώλειαν;* Τίς *ὁ φθονήσας τῷ καλῶς ἐν τῇ μονῇ ὑμῶν φυτευθέντι κλάδῳ καὶ τοῦτον πρόρριζον αὐθημερὸν ἀνασπάσας καὶ εἰς βυθὸν ἀπογνώσεως ψυχικῆς συνελάσας καὶ δείξας ὡς ἄκαρπον μόσχευμα;* Τίς *τὸν δρόμον ἀνέκοψεν τοῦ καλῶς τρέχοντος καὶ εἰς μέτρον εὐλαβοῦς ἡλικίας φθάσαντος, καὶ τῷ πονηρῷ συνελθεῖν οὐκ εὐαγῶς μεταπείσας καὶ ποιήσας αὐτὸν ἀστεφάνωτον;* Οὕτω *ἀγρυπνεῖτε ἐπὶ τῇ φυλακῇ τῶν ὑμετέρων θρεμμάτων, οὕτω ἐκτρέφετε τοὺς προσερχομένους ταῖς πνευματικαῖς νομαῖς καὶ τῷ τῆς ἀναπαύσεως ὕδατι;* Τί *οὐχὶ τῇ ῥάβδῳ τοὺς λύκους ἀποσοβεῖτε καὶ τῇ βακτηρίᾳ τὸ ἐν ὑμῖν ποι-* || 125 || *μαίνετε ποίμνιον;* Τί *μὴ τὸ ἀσθενὲς ἐνισχύετε καὶ τὸ χωλὸν ἐπιδεσμεῖτε, καὶ τὸ ἀρρωστοῦν ἐπισκέπτεσθε, ἀλλὰ θηρσὶν ἁρπακτικοῖς ὡς ἀνιάτρευτον παραπέμπετε, σπαράττουσιν σῶμα καὶ ψυχήν, καὶ βρῶσιν ποιουμένοις ὡς ἀσήμαντα καὶ εὐάλωτα καὶ ποιμένα μὴ ἔχοντα;* Τοῦτο *τὸ θηριάλωτον πρόβατον ἐκ τῆς χειρὸς ὑμῶν ἐκζητήσει* Κύριος· *τοῦτο τὸ ἀπολωλὸς πρόβατον, ὡς ὑφ' ὑμῶν προδοθέν, καταδίκης ὑμῖν γενήσεται πρόξενον· τοῦτο τὸ ἀποίμαντον πρόβατον ἐν τῇ δικαίᾳ τοῦ κριτοῦ καὶ ἀρχιποίμενος* Χριστοῦ *κελεύσει κατὰ πρόσωπον σοῦ τοῦ ποιμένος στήσεται καὶ ἀμέλειάν σου κατηγορήσει, ὅτι δυνατῶς ἔχων περισῶσαι, τῷ ᾅδῃ πρὸ θανάτου παρέπεμψας.* Διατί *μὴ ἀφῆκας τὰ ἐνενήκοντα ἐννέα καὶ ἐπὶ τὸ πλανώμενον ἔδραμες καὶ ζητήσας καὶ εὑρὼν ἐπὶ τῶν ὤμων ἀνέλαβες καὶ τοῖς σεσωσμένοις συνέταξας;* Πῶς *οἴσω τὸ πένθος;* Μετὰ *τίνος τὸν θρῆνον ὀδυνηρῶς συνεργάσομαι;* Τίς *παραμυθίας λόγος προσελθὼν τὴν ἐμὴν ἀποκουφίσει τοῦ βάρους ἀχθηδόνα καὶ τὸν στεναγμὸν λωφῆσαι ποιήσει καὶ καθημερώσει τὴν τῆς ψυχῆς ἀγριότητα;* Τί *μὴ προσῆλθες τοῖς ἴχνεσι τοῦ ἁγίου καὶ κοινοῦ πατρὸς ἡμῶν καὶ δυσωπητικῶς καθικέτευσας ὅπως τὸ εὐλογηθὲν παρ' αὐτοῦ καὶ ταλαίπωρον καὶ δύστηνον πρόβατον ταῖς ἐγγυθέοις αὐτοῦ ἀνεκαλέσατο πρὸς θεὸν ἐντεύξεσιν, καὶ τῇ ἀρχαίᾳ νομῇ καὶ ποίμνῃ τοῦτο πάλιν ἀπεκατέστησεν, ἀλλὰ τὸ κλαπὲν δι' ἀμελείας θηριάλωτον εἴασας* || 126 || *καὶ τῷ λύκῳ μᾶλλον συνέδραμες εἰς τὴν τούτου δεινὴν ἁρ-*

---

10 *θηριάλωτον γέγονε*: cf. Ex. 22.13 || 15–16 *εἰς – ἡλικίας*: cf. Eph. 4.13 || 19 *τῷ τῆς ἀναπαύσεως ὕδατι*: Ps. 22(23).2 || 24 *ἀσήμαντα καὶ εὐάλωτα*: cf. *Il.* 10.485 || 25 *ἐκ τῆς –* Κύριος: cf. Is. 1.12 || 30–32 *μὴ ἀφῆκας – ἀνέλαβες*: cf. Mt. 18.12; Lc. 15.4–5 || 41 *τῷ λύκῳ – ἁρπαγὴν*: cf. Mt. 10.16; Lc. 10.3

---

12 *τὸ* V: corr. G || 13 *πρόριζον* V || 15 *μέτρον* G: *μ*[ετ] V || 17 *οὐ ἀγρυπν* (*ῶν*) *εἶτε* V || 24 *ευᾶ* (*καὶ*) *ποιμ̊* V || 25 *τουτο το το θηριᾶ* V || 30–31 *ϛθ* V || 31 *ἐζήτησας* in *ζητήσας* corr. scriba || 35 *λοφῆσαι ποιήσοι* V || 38 *πρόβατον* nos: *πρὸς* V secl. G

entrusted to you fell prey to wild beasts. How did this happen? What sinister demon was responsible for this loss? Who was envious of the shoot, well planted in your monastery, and immediately pulled it up by the roots? Who drove him to the depth of spiritual despair and proved him to be a barren sucker? Who interrupted his course as he was running well and had reached the age of discretion, impiously persuaded him to join the Devil, and made him lose his crown? Is it thus that you watch over the safety of your flock? Is it thus that you nurture those who come to the spiritual pastures and the waters of repose? Why do you not use the rod to frighten away the wolves and herd your flock with the staff? Why do you not strengthen the weak, give support to the lame, visit the sick, but instead consign them, as if they were incurable, to rapacious beasts that tear asunder body and soul and devour them, being as they are without leader or shepherd and easy prey? The Lord shall demand from your hand this ensnared sheep. This lost sheep, abandoned by you, will be the cause of your condemnation. This untended sheep, by the righteous command of Christ, the Judge and chief Shepherd, will stand in front of you, his shepherd, and accuse you of negligence in that, while it was in your power to save him, you sent him to Hades before his death. Why did you not leave the ninety-nine and run in search of the erring one, and, having found him, bring him back on your shoulders and restore him among the saved? How will I bear the grief? Who will help me in my sorrowful lament? What words of consolation will come to lighten my grievous burden, make my groaning abate, and tame the desolation of my soul? Why did you not approach the feet of our holy and common Father and implore him with earnest supplication to recall by his God-pleasing prayers to God the unfortunate wretch who had been blessed by him and restore him to his old pasture and flock? Instead, you have allowed him, who had been stolen through negligence, to fall prey to wild beasts. Indeed, you have helped

παγήν; Ἀλλ' ὄψεται Κύριος καὶ ζητῶν ἐκζητήσει καὶ τοῖς οἰκτιρμοῖς καὶ τῷ ἐλέει αὐτοῦ σώζων σώσει, καὶ μὴ συγχωρήσει τὴν ψυχὴν τοῦ ποθήσαντος αὐτὸν εἰς παντελὲς θήραμα τοῖς ὀδοῦσι τῶν ἀπαντησάντων ἐλθεῖν, ἀλλ' ἀνελκύσει τοῦτον τοῦ πτώματος καὶ ἐπὶ πέτραν στήσει καὶ κατευθυνεῖ τὰ ἴχνη αὐτοῦ καὶ κατὰ θεὸν διαβήματα, ὅπως, τῇ ἀναλύσει καὶ πρὸς τὸν ἑαυτοῦ πατέρα παλινδρομήσει, ἀξιωθείη τῆς ἁγίας στολῆς ἐκείνης ἐπενδύσασθαι τὸ ἀξίωμα, καὶ τὸν δάκτυλον τὸν ἐπιστρεπτικὸν πρὸς τὴν ἀρχὴν τῆς μοναδικῆς ἀπολάβοι βιώσεως, καὶ τῆς μεγάλης τοῦ ἰσαγγέλου καὶ κοινοῦ πατρὸς ἡμῶν φωνῆς εἰσακούσοι, "οὗτος ὁ υἱός μου νεκρὸς ἦν καὶ ἀνέζησεν, ἀπολωλὼς ἦν καὶ εὑρέθη." Μὴ οὖν ἐπινυσταξάτω ἡ πατρικὴ ὑμῶν θεοσέβεια ἐπὶ τούτοις, ἀλλὰ πᾶσαν ἐμμέριμνον ἀγρυπνίαν, ὄκνου παντὸς δίχα, ἐπιδειξάσθω, ὅπως τὸν μῶμον τούτου ἀποσμήξηται καὶ εἰς παραμυθίαν τῆς ἐμῆς γενήσεται μετριότητος· ὅτι ἀποροῦμεν πάντοθεν, καὶ τῆς ἐμῆς ἀλογήσας σωτηρίας ἐκεῖνον φαντάζομαι.

Τῇ δὲ σὺν ὑμῖν θεοσυλλέκτῳ ποίμνῃ μὴ ἀπαξιώσῃ προσειπεῖν ἐκ τῆς ἡμετέρας πτωχονοίας, ἀλλὰ καὶ τὸ γράμμα τούτοις φανερώσει καὶ δυσωπήσει ὑπὲρ ἐμοῦ τοῦ τάλανος δεήσεις πρὸς τὸν Κύριον ποιήσασθαι· οἶδα γὰρ ὅτι καὶ αὐτοὶ ἐπὶ τῷ γεγονότι ψυχικὴν συντριβὴν ἐδέξαντο· ἀλλ' ἐλπίζουσιν ὅτι, ταῖς ὑμετέραις πρὸς θεὸν ὁσίαις ἐντεύξεσιν, τῶν ἐλπίδων κοινῶς ἐπιτύχοιμεν, πρεσβείαις τῆς κυρίως καὶ ἀληθῶς Θεο || 127 || *τόκου, τοῦ ὁσίου καὶ μεγάλου πατρὸς ἡμῶν εὐχαῖς καὶ πάντων τῶν ἁγίων.*

34. Νικηφόρῳ διακόνῳ

Ἐγὼ μὲν πρὸς τὸ λέγειν ὑπάρχων πενέστατος ἐπὶ συχνὸν χρόνον σεσίγηκα, ὡς ἂν τὴν ὑμετέραν πρὸς τὸ γράφειν ἐγκαλέσωμαι πολυκτήμονα γλῶτταν καὶ μάθω πλουτεῖν [καὶ] *ζήλῳ τῆς σῆς δαψιλοῦς τοῦ λόγου προχύσεως. Ἐπεὶ δὲ νέφος οὐδὲν ἐκ τῆς σῆς οὐρανίας φρενὸς τὸν*

---

45 *ἐπὶ πέτραν στήσει*: cf. Mt. 7.24–25; Lc. 6.48 || 46 *κατευθυνεῖ – διαβήματα*: cf. Ps. 39 (40).3 || 51 *οὗτος – εὑρέθη*: Lc. 15.24

---

43 *συγχωρήσοι* V || 54 *τούτου*: *τοῦτον* sugg. Duffy || *ἀποσμίξηται* V || 57 *ἡμῖν* V || 61 *ὑμετέρες* V

34: Tit. *διακόνου* V || 2 *πολυκτημ̊* V || 3 *ζηλω* V

the wolf to make his terrible catch. But the Lord will see this: He will search him out and, in His pity and mercy, will save him and will not permit that the soul of one who had loved Him should fall prey to the teeth of his adversaries. Nay, He will set him up from his fall, place him on a rock and guide his feet and steps in godlike fashion, so that, by his release and return to his own father, he may become worthy to assume the honor of that holy garment, acknowledge the finger that will restore him to the rule of the monastic life, and hear the great voice of our angelic and common Father, "This my son was dead, and is alive again; he was lost and is found." Let not your paternal Piety, then, slumber over these matters, but be diligent and watchful in every way, without any trace of sluggishness, that you may wipe away this stain and bring consolation to my mediocrity; for I am at a loss what to do and, disregarding my own salvation, I have him on my mind.

Please convey to your divinely assembled flock the greetings of my feeble intellect. You will show them this letter and beg them to pray to the Lord on behalf of my wretched self. For I know that they, too, have experienced affliction in their souls over what has happened and hope that through your holy supplications to God, the intercession of the real and true Theotokos, and the prayers of our holy and great Father and of all the saints, we may all attain our wishes.

34. To the deacon Nikephoros

Being as I am extremely poor in my capacity for speech, I have kept silent for a long time so as to urge your affluent tongue to write, that I may learn myself how to be rich by emulating the abundant outpouring of your words. Since, however, no

ἀερώδη καὶ ἀνεμιαῖον νοῦν ἡμῶν ὑπεκάλυπτεν, ξηρὰ δὲ πάντα καὶ ἄνικμα τὴν σὴν ἐπομβρίαν ⟨οὐκ ἦν⟩ ἡμῖν προμηνύοντα, οὐκ ἔσθενον τὴν Ταντάλειον ἐκείνην, ὡς ὁ μῦθος, ἐν μέσῳ πελάγους φέρειν δίψαν καὶ πρὸ τῆς ἐκεῖσε δίκης κολάζεσθαι. Ὅθεν τὴν ἐν ἐμοὶ μικρὰν ἀναθυμίασιν πρὸς σὲ τοῦ λόγου κεκίνηκα, εἴπως τὴν ὑμετέραν καθαρὰν σταγόνα ἐφ' ἑαυτοῦ ἐπισπάσαιμι καὶ τὸν τῆς ψυχῆς αὐχμὸν καὶ τὴν δίψαν ἐπιεικῶς ἀποκρούσαιμι. Ἐπίσταξον οὖν ἐκ τῶν ψεκάδων μοι τῆς θεοπαρόχου σου πηγῆς ῥανίδα, μήπως τῇ πολυχρονίῳ τῶν λόγων ὑμῶν ἀνομβρίᾳ ὑπὸ τριβόλοις καὶ δειναῖς ἀκάνθαις πνιγείην· ἐξ ὧν ἐστιν λιμῶξαι λόγον θεοῦ καὶ πότμον ἐπισπεῖν. Τὰ δὲ καθ' ἡμᾶς σιγὴ βαθεῖα καλύπτει ὅπη καὶ ὅπως ἀποβήσεσθαι μέλλει· ἐλπὶς δὲ ἡμῖν ἀποκρέμαται ὡς ἐπὶ τὸ κρεῖττον τοῖς θείοις οἰκτιρμοῖς ἐπιδώσειεν.

35. Τῷ *αὐτῷ*

Μή με προπετῆ εἶναι δίδασκε, ἵνα τι μικρὸν τὸ προφητικὸν ὑπαλλάξω, καὶ ὑπὲρ τὰ ἐσκαμμένα γεωργίας ἄτερ ἐφάλ || 128 || *λεσθαι. Τὴν γὰρ σιγὴν ὡς θησαυρὸν κεκρυμμένον περιέπων καὶ κωφεύειν ταύτην εἶναι μέγα τιθέμενος, καὶ μὴ τοῖς ἐρῶσι λόγου μεταδιδούς, τὸ τῆς παροιμίας, ἡλίκον εἰς ἔργον ἤγαγες ⟨τὸ⟩ κύων ἐπὶ φάτνης. Μὴ οὖν οὕτω τὴν μελίρρυτόν σου γλῶτταν καθυστερίζειν ἔθιζε καὶ πᾶσαν ἡμῖν λυσιτελοῦσαν ὠφέλειαν, ἀλλὰ καὶ πρῶτος ὡς κορυφαῖος τοῦ λόγου λέγε, καὶ τὰ δευτερεῖα ἡμῖν παραχώρει, μήπως κινδύνοις ἑαυτοὺς περιπείρωμεν προλογίζοντες· καὶ εὔχου καὶ ἔρρωσο καὶ τὸ πολὺ τῆς ἀθυμίας ἀποτίναξαι, εἰδὼς ὡς εἰς λύπης κατάποσιν τὸ δυσθυμεῖν συνελαύνει, κατὰ τὸν θεῖον καὶ μέγαν διδάσκαλον.*

34: 7 *Ταντάλειον – δίψαν*: cf. *Od.* 11.582 sqq.; Apostol. XVI.9; Mantiss. Prov. II.94 || 11–12 *ἐπίσταξον – ῥανίδα*: cf. Lc. 16.24 || 13 *τριβόλοις – ἀκάνθαις*: cf. Gen. 3.18; Hos. 10.8 || 13–14 *λιμῶξαι λόγον θεοῦ*: Am. 8.11 || 14 *πότμον ἐπισπεῖν*: cf. *Il.* 6.412; *Od.* 2.250 et al.

---

7 *ταντάλιον* V

35: 1 *μή – δίδασκε*: cf. Jb. 10.2 || 2 *ὑπὲρ τὰ ἐσκαμμένα – ἐφάλλεσθαι*: Apostol. XVII.62; Macar. VIII.67; Zen. VI.23; Greg. Cypr. III.89; Karathanasis 160 || 5 *κύων ἐπὶ φάτνης*: Macar. V.34; Karathanasis 230 || 10 *εἰς λύπην – συνελαύνει*: cf. 2 Cor. 2.7

35: 1 *προπετ(ην)* V || 5 *ἡλίκοις* V || 6 *μελίρυτον* V

cloud wafted by your heavenly spirit overshadowed my empty and windy mind, and your showers were not announced to me beforehand by the prevailing drought and desiccation, I did not have the strength to suffer, as the myth has it, the thirst of Tantalus in the midst of the sea and to be punished in advance of the trial over there. For this reason I have directed toward you the scanty exhalation of my speech in the hope of drawing upon myself your pure drops and driving off to some extent the dry thirst of my soul. Do, therefore, let fall upon me one drop from the waters of your God-given fount, lest I be choked with thistles and grievous thorns because of the protracted lack of your rainlike discourse. As a result the word of God may perish and face death.

As for my affairs, their outcome is covered by deep silence. A hope remains that, through God's mercy, they may turn out for the better.

35. To the same

Do not teach me to be rash (that I may alter slightly the prophet's saying) nor to leap without practice (?) beyond the dug-up patch. For in cherishing silence as a hidden treasure and attaching great value to its being dumb and sharing no words with those that love you, you have signally put into deeds the proverb about the dog in the manger. Do not thus accustom your honeyed tongue and every benefit that is useful to us to be tardy, but be the first to speak inasmuch as you are the pinnacle of discourse, and allow me second place lest I fall into danger by speaking earlier. Pray for me, be in good health, and shake off that great despondency, knowing as you do that bad humor causes us to be swallowed by grief according to the holy and great teacher.

36. Τῷ αὐτῷ

Ἡ τῆς πρὸς ἡμᾶς τοὺς βραχεῖς ἀπολογίας ὕφεσις πρὸς οὐράνιον ὑμῖν ἀρετὴν γέγονεν ὕψωσις· ἐκεῖθεν γὰρ Χριστὸς ὁ πλάστης τῆς φύσεως κατελθών, καὶ τὸ ταπεινὸν ὑποδύς, τῆς τοῦ οἰκείου μεγέθους οὐκ ἐξέστη περιωπῆς, ἡμῖν δὲ τὴν πρὸς οὐρανοὺς τρίβον ὑπέδειξε· καὶ τί τούτου πλέον λέγειν ἔχω; Μιμητήν σε γὰρ τοῦ κτίσαντος ἀποφήνας ὀκνῶ περαιτέρω προβῆναι, μήπως ἐλαττώσω τὸν ἔπαινον.

Τὸ δὲ πρὶν ἐπίρρημα, εἴ τι πείθει τῷ τῆς τέχνης φυτοκόμῳ, μᾶλλον δὲ φάναι γεννήτορι, τῷ τοῦ Δυσκόλου φημὶ παιδί, μὴ τῆς συστολῆς ἔξω γενέσθαι ποιήσειας. Οὐδὲ γὰρ ἀνέχεται Ἡρωδιανὸς ὁ μετὰ τοῦ φύντος ἀνέδην ἱστάμενος ἐκτάσεως κανόνι τὸ συσταλὲν ἀπευθύναι καὶ ποιῆσαι μακρὸν τὸ ἀναύξητον. Εἰ δὲ συγκαταθέσθαι || 129 || βούλει καὶ τῷ † Μηλαίῳ † γραμματικῷ τούτοις ἀκλινῶς ἑπομένῳ καὶ διεσμιλευμένως περὶ τούτου καὶ ἀκριβῶς κανονίσαντι, μὴ παρώσῃ τὸν ἄνδρα φάσκοντα: "καὶ τὰ μονοσύλλαβα ἐπιρρήματα καταλήγοντα μὲν εἰς φωνῆεν ἐκτείνεται καὶ περισπᾶται, εἰ δὲ εἰς σύμφωνον συστέλλεται· ἆ τὸ ψιλούμενον καὶ περισπώμενον· ἆ δειλοί, Δαναῶν ἡγήτορες ἠδὲ μέδοντες"· εἶτα καὶ πλεῖστα κατακενώσαντα τῶν ἐκτεινομένων ἐπειπεῖν· "τὰ δὲ εἰς σύμφωνον λήγοντα βραχέα ἐστι ἢ θέσει μακρά." Πρίν· ὅπερ φασὶν ἀπὸ τοῦ πρόσθεν, συγκοπῇ κατὰ πάθος γεγονέναι· δίς, τρὶς καὶ αὐτὰ ἐκ τοῦ δυάκις κατὰ πάθος καὶ τριάκις γέγονεν· δάξ· ἔνθεν τὸ ὀδὰξ καὶ αὐτοδάξ· καὶ τοῦτο δὲ ἐν τῷ κανόνι τὸν τεχνικὸν ἰδεῖν ἐστι λέγοντα ὡς τὰ μονοσύλλαβα ἐπιρρήματα ἢ φύσει ἐκτείνεται ἢ θέσει, εἰ μὴ ἔχοι πάθος. Μὴ δῆτα οὖν τοὺς στύλους τῆς τέχνης σοφίας κατασείειν πειρώμεθα· στοιχῶμεν δὲ τοῖς ἐκείνων κανόσιν, ὡς ἂν τὸ αἰδέσιμον τῇ τέχνῃ φυλάξαιμεν καὶ μέμψεως ἑαυτοὺς ἀπολύσωμεν. Καὶ εὔχου μου, πάτερ, συνομογνωμονῶν, καὶ τῇ ἐμῇ προπετείᾳ συγγνώμων ἔσο.

36: 14 s. Locum ipsum non invenimus || 16–17 *ἆ δειλοὶ – μέδοντες*: *Il.* 11.816

36: 4 *περιοπῆς* V || 7 *πριν ἐπιρρ* . . . *πιθει* V || *τὸ* V || *φοιτοκομω* V || 9 *ὁ*: *ὢν* V || 12 *τω μηλαιω* V || 13 *παρότι* V || 14 *καὶ* V: an *ὅτι* legendum? || 16 *δηλοὶ* V || 19 *φα* V || *συγκο* V || 21 *αὐτόδαξ* accentu gravi super *α* deleto V || 23 *τέχνης καὶ σοφίας* G || 24 *στυχῶμεν* V || 26 *συνομογνῶμ* V

36. To the same

The abasement of your apology to my exiguous self has caused your elevation to heavenly virtue: for Christ, the creator of our nature, when he descended from above and assumed a humble form, did not depart from the pinnacle of His own greatness while showing to us the path to heaven. What more need I say? Having declared you to be an imitator of the Creator, I am reluctant to go any further lest I diminish your praise.

As for the adverb *πρίν*, you should not except it from shortening if you obey the gardener of the art or, to be more precise, its creator, I mean the son of Dyskolos. For Herodian, who stands freely beside the begetter, does not allow that the short should be adjusted by the rule of lenghtening so that the unaugmented becomes long. If you also wish to agree with the grammarian of Melos (?), who follows unswervingly the above and has made subtle and exact rules on this matter, do not refuse to hear the man when he says that adverbs of one syllable, if they end in a vowel, are lenghtened and take the circumflex, and if in a consonant, are shortened. Thus, alpha with a smooth breathing and a circumflex, as in "*ἆ*, ye wretched men, leaders and rulers of the Danaäns." Then, after quoting exhaustively many other examples of lengthening he adds, "as for those that end in a consonant, they are short or else long by position." It is said that *πρίν* is a contraction, by way of modification, of *πρόσθεν*, as also *δίς* and *τρίς*, which come, by way of modification, from *δυάκις* and *τριάκις*, and *δάξ* from *ὀδάξ* and *αὐτοδάξ*. This, too, one may find the grammarian saying in the canon, namely, that adverbs of one syllable are lengthened either by nature or by position unless they suffer modification. Let us not, therefore, attempt to undermine the pillars of the wise art. Let us follow the rules of those men that we may preserve the dignity of the art and free ourselves from reproach. Pray for me, father, being as you are in agreement with me and forgive my impertinence.

37. Τῷ αὐτῷ

Ὅτι μὲν νιφάδων δίκην αἱ δυσχέρειαι τοῦ ταλαιπώρου τοῦδε βίου τὰς ἀνίας ἡμῖν κατεπύκνωσαν, κατακόρως δὲ τὴν σὴν ἄσπιλον εἰς θεὸν διάνοιαν κατεπώμβρισαν καὶ τοῖς μικρὰ εἰδόσιν κρίνειν λύπας ἥκιστα, ‖ 130 ‖ πάτερ, ἠγνόηται· ὅτι δὲ πρὸς λυπροτέραν, καὶ ἀνίας γεννήτριαν νῆσον ἐπώκειλας, ἐξ ἀθυμίας εἰς παντελῆ δυσθυμίαν ἑαυτὸν συνελαύνων, εὔδηλον· αἴθε γὰρ ἐπὶ χώρας σε μένοντα ταῖς συντρόφοις τῶν μοχθηρῶν πραγμάτων ἐπιφοραῖς προσπαλαίειν, καὶ τῆς τούτων ἀπογεύεσθαι στυφούσης καρδίαν δριμύτητος ἢ τηλικαύτης ἀηδίας, ἣν ἐξεμεῖ τὸ μηδὲ νησίδιον καλεῖσθαι δυνάμενον, ἀναπίμπλασθαι. Τί γὰρ τὴν σὴν καλλονὴν τῶν οὐ καλῶν ἐν αὐτῷ κατεκήλησεν ὡς ἐπὶ τοσοῦτον ἐξᾶραι, καὶ εὐθεσίαν αὐτῷ καὶ εὐκρασίαν ἐπιφημίσαι, ἣν οὐδ' οἱ τὰς περιηγήσεις γράψαντες καὶ τὰ πρὸς χάριν ἀφοσιούμενοι ποικίλως ἐξέφρασαν, ἢ τὴν ὀξυτενῆ καὶ τραχεῖαν καὶ ἀνάντη καὶ ὀξέσιν κατεστορεσμένην οἶμον δεδυσώπηκε κάχληξιν, ᾗ οὐχ ὑπέστη πρέμνον, οὐ χλόης φυὴ τῇ βλάστῃ μηνύουσα τὴν φυτοκόμον ὥραν τοῦ ἔαρος· φυλλοχόοι δὲ μῆνες αὐτὴν γεωργοῦντες, οὐχ ὕνι τε καὶ ἀρότρῳ καὶ δρεπάνῃ, δι' ἐμμελοῦς δ' ἀμελείας τὴν ἄπληστον ἐρημίαν αὐτῆς δεικνύουσιν ἄφυτον καὶ ἀνήροτον καὶ φθίνουσαν πάντοτε. Ἔφης δὲ βαδίζων ἐς αὐτὴν καὶ περὶ τὰ μέσα που γενόμενος ὁρᾶν πεδία λωτεῦντα καὶ κοιλάδας ἀμφιλαφεῖς καὶ καταπύκνους, καὶ κρήνας ἡδὺ γάνος ἀφιείσας· καὶ τοῦτο τοῦ φόρτου τῆς ἑρμαϊκῆς τῶν ψευσμάτων ἁμάξης οὐκ οἶδ' ὅπως ἀποκνισθεῖσ' ἐστιν ἀπορρώξ· μέσα γὰρ ποῖα, ἧς οὐκ ἀρχὴ καὶ πέρας τὴν μεσότητα διορίζει, ἑτερομήκη καὶ προμήκη τυγχάνουσαν καὶ προσεοικυῖαν ὄψει διά ‖ 131 ‖ στροφον βλεπούσῃ καὶ οἷον θερσίτειον; Ὡς ἐμαυτὸν γὰρ πείθω ὑπ' ἀληθείας ὠθούμενος, οὐκ ὠγύγιον τὴν ὕπαρξιν ἀποφέρεται, μυθικῶς δὲ μᾶλλον ἀναδεδόσθαι καιροὺς ἐσχάτους ὡς δή τι μορμολυκεῖον ὑπὸ Νηρέως τοῦ βυθίου καὶ ἐναλίου δαίμονος· οὐδὲ γὰρ

37: 15–16 *φυλλοχόοι δὲ μῆνες*: cf. Hes. fr. 333 ‖ 19 *πεδία λωτεῦντα*: *Il.* 12.283; *Etym. Gen.*, ed. Alpers (1969) 17 (e Choerobosco) ‖ 20 *κρήνας ἡδὺ γάνος*: cf. Aesch. *Pers.* 483 ‖ 21 *ἑρμαϊκῆς – ἁμάξης*: cf. *Babrii fabulae* 57 ‖ 24 *οἷον θερσίτειον*: App. prov. III.19

37: 3 *κατεπόμβρησαν* V ‖ 4 *ἠγνώηται* V ‖ 4–5 *γεννήτρειαν . . . ἐπώκιλας* V ‖ 5 *δυσφημίαν* V ‖ 10 *κατεκίλησεν* V ‖ 11 *αὐτὸ* V ‖ 12 *περιηχήσεις* V ‖ 13 *κατεστορεσεμενην* V ‖ 13–14 *ἄναντι . . . δεδυσώπησε κάχλιξιν* V ‖ 14 *ἡ* V: corr. Duffy ‖ 17 *δείκνυσιν* V ‖ 18 *ἔφῆ* V: *ἔφην* vel *ἔφης* Karlsson ‖ 20 *καταπυγους* V: fort. * *καταπύρους* a *πυρὸς* legendum ‖ 22 *ἀποκνισθὲν* V ‖ 23 *ἑτερομήκει . . . προμήκει τυγχάνουσα* V ‖ 26–27 *ὡς δὴ τη μορμολυκῖ* V

37. To the same

That the annoyances of this miserable life have caused my sorrows to accumulate like snowflakes and that they have rained down excessively on your spotlessly godly mind is by no means unknown, O father, even to those who little understand how to judge grief. It is also evident that you have landed on a wretched and sorrow-breeding island, thus reducing yourself from a state of despondency to one of complete despair. Would that you had remained at your post to fight off the attacks that are habitual to evil conditions and to partake of their pungent taste that acts like an astringent on the heart instead of being filled with the nauseousness disgorged by a place that cannot even call itself an islet. Which of her ugly traits has so charmed your beautiful mind as to extol her so greatly and to ascribe to her a goodly situation and climate, which not even the authors of travel books, who devote themselves to giving pleasure in different ways, would have expressed? What has smoothed her steep, rough, uphill road that is covered with sharp pebbles, along which there is no tree, where no grass springs up, announcing by its growth the fertile season of spring? It is the leaf-shedding months that cultivate her, not with a plowshare, plow, and reaping hook, but through suitable neglect, showing her boundless solitude barren, unplowed, and always decaying. You said that walking along her, about midway, you saw blooming plains, valleys dense and thickly grown, and wells emitting sweet water. This, too, is a piece broken off, I know not how, from the load of lies of Hermes' wagon. For what kind of middle does she have, seeing that no beginning or end defines her center, being as she is lopsided and protruding, like the distorted face of Thersites? Indeed, truth has convinced me that she cannot claim to have existed since the times of Ogyges, but was in a fabulous fashion thrown up in recent times like some monster by Nereus, the demon of the seabed. For not only might she, like

κατὰ τὴν εἰδέχθειαν μόνον Ἐμπούσης δίκην τοὺς ὁρῶντας δεδείτταιτ' ἄν, ἀλλὰ καὶ αὐτοῖς κύμασιν ὑπαγομένη καὶ συγκλυζομένη καὶ πῆξιν οὐκ ἔχουσα, τοῖς ἐν αὐτῇ νύκτωρ καὶ μεθ' ἡμέραν ἀπροόπτους σεισμοὺς ἀνατείναιτο, δεινὸν θανάτου εἶδος καὶ χαλεπώτατον.

Ἀλλά τί περὶ τὴν μικρὰν Ὀξεῖαν, πλατεῖαν ἔχουσαν κακίαν, ἐνδαπανᾶν τὸν λόγον προῄρημαι, ἐνὸν αὐτὴν ὑφ' ἑαυτῆς κακίζεσθαι ὡς ἂν πραγμάτων ἡμᾶς ἀπαλλάξῃ; Ἡμεῖς δὲ τὴν εἰς θυμηδίαν ἤκουσάν σοι νῆσον ἀείσομεν, ὦ μεγίστων ἄξιε καὶ θεωριῶν καὶ ἀπολαύσεων· πέπαυσαι Κρήτη καὶ Κύπρος, Εὔβοια, Λέσβος τε καὶ Σαρδώ, καὶ ἡ πολύφορβος καὶ πολυκτήμων Τρινάκρια, τὰ μέγιστα θαλάσσης ὡς εἰπεῖν ἀκροθίνια, οὐχ ὡς ἱκανῶς μὴ ἔχουσαι τὰς ὑπεισρεούσας ὑμῖν ἀνίας μειῶσαι καὶ τοῖς παρ' ἑαυτῶν θυμηδίας πληρῶσαι καὶ γενέσθαι σοι παραμύθιον, ἀλλὰ κινδυνεύουσαι μηκέτι χριστιανῶν εἶναι καὶ εἰς νομὴν ἐχθροῖς δι' ἁμαρτίας ἀποκριθῆναι, ἄχρις ὁ ῥυόμενος πτωχὸν ἐκ χειρὸς στερεωτέρων αὐτοῦ ⟨καὶ ἐκ χειρὸς⟩ δυνάστου οἰκτιρμοῖς ἐπινεύσοι καὶ ταῖς τῶν αὐτοῦ θεραπόντων ἐπικαμφθείη δεήσεσιν. Σὲ μακάρων, εἴπερ τινές εἰσι, νῆσοι δεξάμεναι καὶ, τῆς λύπης κενώσασαι, κεχαρμένον ⟨τε⟩ ποσῶς ἀναδείξασαι, μακαρίαν φερωνύμως τὴν κλῆσιν ἐδέξαντο, καὶ τῶν καθ' Ὅμηρον ἐπαίνων, ὡς τὸ εἰκός, ἀλογήσασαι, τὸν εἰς σὲ || 132 || πόθον εἰς ἄγαν ἐξέθρεψαν καὶ τὴν τῶν λόγων σχολὴν ὑπερεθαύμασαν, καὶ πᾶν εἴ τι καλὸν παρ' ἑαυτῶν μεθ' ἑαυτῶν λαβοῦσαι καὶ ἀλλήλων θερμῶς ἁμιλλώμεναι, τοῖς σοῖς ποσὶν ξενήϊα προὔθηκαν, ἐν αἷς εἶχες πολλῶν ὁρᾶν θαυμάτων ἀκρότητας. Διὸ εἰς ὀξὺ τὴν Ὀξεῖαν ἐλέπτυνας, καὶ νησῖδα πτερωτὴν τὴν ἄλλως ἐννηχομένην τοῖς κύμασιν ἔδειξας, καὶ ζοφερῷ πεταύρῳ τοῖς λόγοις κατέκλεισας. Σοὶ γὰρ μακάρων νῆσοι προσμειδιῶσαι ἐρωτικῶς ἂν διετέθησαν καὶ συνεῖναί σε καὶ διαιωνίζειν αὐταῖς ἄτερ ὀϊζύος καὶ ἄτερ χαλεποῖο πόνοιο προσηύξαντο. Ἐκεῖ γὰρ τὸ τῆς ἀλυπίας καὶ χαρᾶς πεφύτευται φάρμακον· ἐκεῖ τὸ τῆς ἀνίας καὶ κατηφείας ἐκτίλλεται δάκρυον· ἐκεῖ σὺν ταῖς συχναῖς σπιλάσιν τῶν συμφορῶν ἤδη γενόμενον καὶ λήθης βυθοῖς ταύτας ἐμ-

---

41–42 *ὁ ῥυόμενος – δυνάστου*: Ps. 34(35).10; cf. Jb. 29.12; Ps. 71(72).12 || 43–44 *μακάρων – νῆσοι*: Zen. III.86; Macar. V.81; Karathanasis 83 || 52 *ζοφερῷ πεταύρῳ*: cf. Prov. 9.18 || 54 *ἄτερ – πόνοιο*: cf. *Il.* 13.2; *Od.* 8.529; 14.480; Hes. *Op.* 91

---

28 *ειδεχθίαν μ. ἐμπουσαις* (vel *–ες*) V || 30 *τοὺς* V || 30–31 *ἡμέραν 6* (nota astronomica *ἡμέρα* significans) . . . *ἀνατεῖναιτο* V || 31 *θάνὰτον* V || 32 *ἐχούσῃ* V || 33 *προειρημαι* V || 37 *τρινακια* V || 39 *τοῖς* V: *τῆς* G || 40 *κινδυνεῦσαι μικρὸς* (vel *μικρὸν*) V || 44 *κενωσεσαι* V || 46 *εἰκως* || 47 *εἰσάγων* V || *τὴν τῶν λόγων σχολὴν* G: *τὸν τῶν λογικῶν* (?) *σχο*[λλ] V || *ὑπεθαύμασαν* V || 48 *παρ' ἑαυτῶν* V: an *παρ' ἑαυταῖς* legendum? || 50 an *ἐν οἷς* legendum? || 52 *Σοὶ* nos: *σε* V || 54 *ὀϊξῦον* in *ὀϊξύος* corr. scriba || 55 *τῆς*: *τὸν* V || 56–57 *τῶν συχνῶν* . . . *συμφω* V || 57 *ἐφάψαντα* V

Empousa, terrify the onlookers by her ugly appearance, but being subjected to the waves that wash over her and having no stability, she might threaten her inhabitants by day or night with unexpected earthquakes, a terrible and most grievous form of death.

But why have I chosen to waste my words on tiny Oxeia (great though her evil may be) when she can condemn herself and so rid us of trouble? Instead we shall sing of the island that brings you joy, O you who are worthy of the most splendid sights and pleasures! You are no more, Crete and Cyprus, Euboea, Lesbos, Sardinia, and bountiful Sicily, rich in possessions, the very firstfruits, so to speak, of the sea. ⟨They are no more,⟩ not because they are unable to lessen the sorrows that beset you, fill you with joy by their presents, and become a consolation to you, but because they are in danger of not belonging any more to Christians and of being set apart because of our sins, a prey to the enemy, until such time when "he who delivers the poor man from the hand of the stronger and that of the ruler" shall hearken to our lamentations and is swayed by the prayers of His servants. Had the Isles of the Blest (if such exist) received you, relieved you of grief, and made you somewhat happier, they would fittingly have received the name of Blest. Disregarding with good reason Homer's praises, they would have nurtured a deep affection for you, they would have admired greatly your literary studies and, bringing along all their beautiful possessions with eager competition, would have laid them as friendly gifts before your feet, among which you would have seen many outstanding wonders. Wherefore you would have reduced Oxeia to a sharp point, given wings to that island that floats in vain on the waves, and enclosed her by your words in a gloomy trap. For the Isles of the Blest would have treated you with a loving smile and would have wished you to remain for all time in their company without woe and grievous toil. For it is there that the herb of painlessness and joy is planted; it is there that the tears of sorrow and dejection are wiped away. Would you were there already, having drowned in the depth of forget-

βάψαντα, ἥκειν ὡς ἡμᾶς ἐρρωμένον καὶ ταῖς ἐκ θεοῦ κατεστεμμένον χάρισιν· ἀλλὰ κἀκ τῆς μικρᾶς Ὀξείας οὕτω δεχθείης παρ' ἡμῶν ὡς ἂν τῆς φθασάσης αὐτὴν ἀπολούσαιμεν καὶ ἀποπλύνωμεν μέμψεως.

38. Τῷ *αὐτῷ*

Ἐδόκει μοι τῷ προοιμίῳ τῆς ἐπιστολῆς τῆς σῆς ὁμιλοῦντι τῷ τῆς θεολογίας ἐπωνύμῳ Γρηγορίῳ *προσδιαλέγεσθαι, ἀλύοντι καὶ ἀνιωμένῳ ἐπὶ τῇ τῆς χαλάζης πληγῇ καὶ τὴν ὑφ' ἣν αὕτη αἰτίαν ἐχέθη φιλοσοφοῦντι καὶ διερευνωμένῳ τρανότατα.* Ἀλλ' *ἐκεῖνος μὲν πρὸς ποῖον καὶ τίνα τὸν λόγον ὑπέφερεν, εἰδότι σοι, λέγειν οὐ βούλομαι· ᾧ δὲ σὺ νῦν ἐπέστειλας, διακόνῳ τῇ θεολόγῳ γλώσσῃ χρησάμενος, βούλομαί σε καὶ μὴ βουλόμενον μαθεῖν.* Ἰγνάτιος *οὗτός ἐστιν ὁ μικρὸς εἰς εὐσέβειαν καὶ μέγας εἰς ἁμαρτίαν, οὗ καὶ τὸ εἶναι χριστιανὸν χριστιανοὺς* || 133 || *ἐπεβάρησεν, ὡς ἱκανῷ γε μὴ πεφυκότι, διὰ τὸ πρὸς τἀναντία παροιστρῆσαι, οὕτω κικλήσκεσθαι.* Καὶ *ἐπεὶ οὐ πρὸς ὅνπερ ἔγνως γεγράφηκας, ὅτι πρὸς ἔκτρωμα καὶ τοῦ μηδενὸς εἶναι ἄξιον, δέχου τῆς βραδυτῆτος τὸ αἴτιον· ἐδεδίειν μὴ δι' ὄχλου σοι γένωμαι θαμινώτερον γράφων καὶ προσκορὴς καὶ προφητικῶς ὀνειδισθείην, ὡς εἰς πλησμονήν σοι γενηθείς, κατὰ τὴν παροιμίαν ἀπέραντα προσαυλῶν, ὦ φιλησύχιε.*

Ἀλλὰ *τοῦτο μὲν ὡς ὑπόψυχρον καὶ ἀπαρέσκον τῇ φιλολόγῳ σου διαθέσει, μέρος πληροῦν ἀπολογίας, ἐνταῦθα μεινάτω· ἐφ' ἕτερον δὲ λοιπὸν βαδιοῦμεν τῆς ὑπερημερίας αἴτιον, καί, ὡς ἐμαυτὸν πείθω, ἐπιεικῶς δικαιότατον, ὃ καὶ σὲ καταιδέσει φιλοικτίρμονα κεκτημένον διάνοιαν.* Παῖς *μοί τις ἐπὶ κλίνης νοσερᾶς προσπαλαίων πάθει τηκεδόνος κατάκειται· ὃς ἰατροῖς ἐκτεθεὶς καὶ τῆς δεούσης τημελείας παρ' αὐτῶν ἀξιούμενος, ἐν ἐλπίσιν ἦν τῆς κλίνης καὶ τῆς νόσου, ὡς τὸ εἰκός, περιέσεσθαι· ἀλλ' ἐπειδὴ φύσεως ἀντιπραττούσης κενεὰ πάντα, κατὰ τὸν* Κῷον *ἀκεστήν, ἀπειρηκὼς ἤδη καὶ πρὸς τὴν ῥῶσιν ἀπονάρκήσας, ἐπὶ τὴν ἐξόδιον ἑαυτὸν ἐκδέδωκεν, ὅσον οὔπω παρεσομένην, ἀνάπαυλαν·*

---

60 *ἀπολαύσαιμεν* V

38: 1–4 Greg. Naz. *Or. XVI*, PG 35, 933 sqq. || 13 *ὡς εἰς – γενηθεὶς*: Is. 1.14 || 14 *ἀπέραντα προσαυλῶν*: cf. Zen. II.39; Greg. Cypr. I.32 || 22 *ἐπειδὴ – πάντα*: Hippocr. *Lex.*, 2.

38: 5 ὃ V || 6 *βάλλομαι* V: corr. G || 8 *χριστιανῶ* V || 10 *προσόπερ* V || 11 *ἔκτρωμ̄* V || 12 *ἐδεδοίην* V || 18 *κατ' αιδεσει* V || 19 *παθη* V

fulness the many reefs of your misfortunes, and so come to me, healthy and crowned with the grace of God. But even if you come to me from tiny Oxeia, may you be received by me in such a manner that we may wipe and wash her clean of the foregoing blame.

38. To the same

As I was reading the preamble of your letter, I thought I was conversing with Gregory surnamed the Theologian, who was grieved and distressed by the disastrous hailstorm and was speculating and inquiring most keenly concerning its causes. Since you know to what sort of man he was proffering his speech, I need not say it; but whom it is that you have now addressed by the instrument of your godly tongue I wish you to learn, even if you are unwilling. It is Ignatios, small in piety and great in sin, whose very profession of Christianity is a burden to other Christians, inasmuch as he is incapable of assuming that name for having furiously strayed to the opposite side. And since you have written not to the man you knew, indeed to a monster who is not worthy of anything, here is the cause of my tardiness: I was afraid that I would become troublesome and tedious to you if I wrote too often and would be reproached in the words of the prophet for being a cause of surfeit and, as the proverb says, playing my flute endlessly, O my peace-loving friend.

But no more of this excuse, which may appear frigid and displeasing to your cultivated mind. So let us proceed to another cause of my unpunctuality, one which, I am convinced, is quite legitimate and will move you who have a compassionate disposition. A servant of mine is ill in bed, struggling with a consumptive disease. As he had been examined by physicians and received from them the proper treatment, he had reasonable hope of recovery from his sickbed. But since "all is in vain when nature works against you," according to the healer of Cos, he has alraedy given up, has become indifferent concerning his recovery, and surrendered himself to the final rest, which is imminent. As he is now lying, a subject of dispute, claimed by the two

καὶ νῦν ἀμφισβητήσιμον κείμενον καὶ ὑπὸ δυοῖν τούτοιν, τοῦ τε θανάτου, φημί, καὶ τῆς ζωῆς, μεριζόμενον, ἄδηλον ὅποι πεσεῖται τὰ νικητήρια· τοῦ μὲν γὰρ πρὸς ἑαυτὸν κατεπείγοντος, ὡς ἕνα τῶν ἑαυτοῦ νεκάδων, οὐκ ἐνδίκως ἀφαρπαγέντα, τῆς δὲ ἀνθελκούσης καὶ ἀναβιῶναι τοῦτον || 134 || *πειθούσης, ὡς οὐχ εἵμαρτο νῦν τοῖς ἐνερτέροις εἰς ὁμιλίαν ἐλθεῖν, ἐλεύσεσθαι δὲ πάντως ἡνίκα τοῦ συνδέσμου λυθείη καὶ συνδεθείη αὖθις, κατὰ τὸ ἐλπιζόμενον, ὑψηλότερον.* Ταύτην *μὴ παραγάγης τὴν οἴκτιστον, ὡς ἐγῷμαι, καὶ δικαίαν αἰτίαν, ἀλλ' εἰς εὔλογον ἀπολογίαν εἰσκρίνας τῆς ἡμῶν βραδυτῆτος ἐκλάθοιο.*

Ὁ *δὲ χάρτης οὐ τοσοῦτον τῇ σπάνει ὅσον τῇ τραχύτητι κακίζεται· καὶ οὐ τοῦτο μόνον ἀλλὰ καὶ κνηπία γράμματος τοῦτον περιστοιχίζει, τῇ τοῦ καλάμου ὀξύτητι τὸν ὀφθαλμὸν δραπετεύουσα, ὡς εἰ μὴ τοῦτον ἀμβλύναις καὶ ἐπιδαψιλεύσει⟨ας⟩ τὸ γράμμα καὶ πρὸς ἡλικίαν καὶ πάχος ἐκθρέψειας,* Λυγκέως *ἐμφυτευθῆναί μοι κόρας ἐπεύξαιο, ὡς ἂν τὰ πόρρω καὶ μὴ βλεπόμενα πρὸ τῶν ἐμῶν ὄψεων κεῖσθαι, μηδενὸς ἐπιπροσθοῦντος σκώλου ἢ προσκόμματος.*

39. Κωνσταντίνῳ *βασιλικῷ σπαθαρίῳ καὶ πρωτονοταρίῳ τοῦ δρόμου*

Ἐγὼ *μὲν ὡς οὐδὲ αὐτὸς ἀναίνει τὰ προσταχθέντα μοι παρὰ τῆς σῆς βιωφελοῦς ἐντολῆς, ὑπ' εὐγνωμοσύνης καὶ ταχυτῆτος ὠθούμενος, ἀπεπλήρωσα· σὺ δ' ὅσα τῇ τιμίᾳ σου κεφαλῇ κατένευσας ὑποσχόμενος, ἵνα καθ'* Ὅμηρον *εἴπω, παλινάγρετα γέγονεν.* Μὴ *σύ γε τοιοῦτος, ὦ πανεύφημε, πρὸς τοὺς σὲ στέργοντας γένοιο, μηδὲ παράβλεπε ὅσους ἂν εὐεργετεῖν ἡ χείρ σου δεδύνηται.* Διατί *μὴ τὴν τοῦ βίου μου στένωσιν κατ' ὀφθαλμοὺς τοῦ πανυπερόχου λογοθέτου παρέστησας, εἴπως, τὸν συνέχοντα με κόρον τῆς ἐνδείας ἐπιδών, ὥς τινα*

---

38 *Λυγκέως – κόρας*: cf. App. Prov. III.71; Apostol. X.79; Karathanasis 22

---

25 *δυιν* V || 27 *ὡς εν* V || 29 *οὐκ* V || 31 *παραγάγης* dubitanter scripsimus: *παραγ̅γ̅η* V || 32 *ἀπολογίας* V || 34 *σπανη* V || 35 *νηπία* V || 36 *τοῦτον*: *τοῦτο* V || 40 *σκόλου* V

39: 3–4 *τῇ τιμίᾳ σου – γέγονεν*: cf. *Il.* 1.526–27

39: 1 *αμαινει* V || 6 *δια την* V || 8 *ἐπειδὼν* V

rivals, Death and Life, it is uncertain to whom the prize of victory will go; for Death is drawing him to herself, as one of her own dead who had been unjustly snatched away, while Life is pulling him in the opposite direction and persuading him to revive because it has not been destined that he should now join those beneath the earth, but would certainly arrive there when he is released from the fastenings of the body and is put together again, as is to be hoped, in a higher sphere. Do not disregard this most pitiful and, I think, just cause, but admit it as a reasonable apology and forget my tardiness.

The trouble with your papyrus concerns not so much its scarcity as its roughness. In addition, it suffers from the niggardliness of your handwriting which, because of your pointed pen, eludes my eye. Unless you blunt your pen and are more generous with your lettering by increasing its height and thickness, pray that the eyes of Lynceus be implanted in me that I may discern what is distant and invisible without obstacle or hindrance.

39. To Constantine, imperial *spatharios* and *protonotarios* of the Course

For my part, as you yourself do not deny, I have accomplished what was enjoined on me by your life-enhancing command, prompted as I was by gratitude and haste, but the promises you gave me with a nod of your venerable head have been, to quote Homer, revoked. You should not, O most illustrious man, treat in this fashion those who love you nor disdain those to whom you can extend a helping hand. Why have you not brought to the attention of the eminent logothete my straitened circumstances so that, on seeing the excess of poverty that besets me, he would have taken

κἀμὲ τὸν βίον ἀσώτως ἀπεμπολήσαντα, || 135 || κατῳκτείρισεν, καὶ ὡς ἕνα τῶν ἐσχάτων μισθίων αὐτοῦ διέθρεψεν; Οὐ γὰρ λανθάνει, κατὰ τὴν θύραθε παροιμίαν, ἐκεῖνος ὁ θεῷ μεμελημένος ἀνήρ, ὡς δι' ἀγαθοεργίας τῆς εἰς τοὺς δεομένους, τὸν θεὸν ἐπευφραίνοι. Οὐδὲν ἔξω τῶν ἀναγκαίων τῆς ἐφημέρου ζωῆς αἰτεῖν κατεπείγομαι· οὐ χρημάτων πλῆθος, οὐ κτημάτων ὄγκον, οὐκ ἀξίας ὑπεροχήν· ἄρτον μόνον ἐπιζητῶ τὸ τῆς ταλαίνης γαστρὸς ἀπαραίτητον φάρμακον. Μὴ οὖν παρόψει τὸν ἀττικιστὴν ἐπαίτην ἐμέ, μήπως παρορῶν ὑπ' ἐνδείας καὶ πείνης βαλλόμενον σολοικίζοντά με τῷ ᾅδῃ προπέμψειας· σοὶ δὲ Κύριος ὁ τῶν ἀναφαιρέτων θησαυρῶν παροχεὺς ὑπὲρ τῶν εἰς ἡμᾶς εὐεργεσιῶν ἑκατοντάκις παρέξει τὴν ἀμοιβήν· τοῦτο γὰρ ὑμῖν ὑπάρξει εὐπορίας ἀφορμὴ πολλαπλάσιος.

40. Νικηφόρῳ χαρτοφύλακι

Λύω τὴν πρὸς σὲ σιωπὴν ἐπειδή σε πρὸς τὰ καλῶς συνομολογηθέντα, εἶτ' ἀθετηθέντα, παλινῳδίαν ᾄσαντα ἔγνων. Εἰ γὰρ μὴ τοῦτο, ἐπέδησα τὴν γλῶσσαν μᾶλλον ἢ ἔλυσα, ὥστε ⟨εἰ⟩ εἰς τὸ ἐν ᾧ σε φρονήματι κατέλιπον ἔμεινας, οὐδ' εἰ φοίνικος, τὸ τοῦ μύθου, χρόνον ἐπέζησα, προσεῖπον ἄν σε, καὶ ταῦτα ὑπὲρ πολλούς σε καὶ στέργων καὶ φιλῶν, ὡς οὐδ' αὐτὸς ἀναίνει· ἀλλ' ἵν' ἐκ τούτου σαφῶς ἴδῃς ὡς ἀπρίξ, σὺν θεῷ, τοῦ ὀρθοῦ φρονήματος ἔχομαι καὶ τούτου μᾶλλον ἢ τῶν τόπου πραγμάτων ἀντέχομαι. Εἰ γὰρ δι' ἀμφοῖν τὸ ἀπρόσκοπον ἑαυτῷ περιποιεῖν εἰλόμην, τίς μοι παρὰ τῶν λαβὰς || 136 || ζητούντων κατάγνωσις; Ἀλλ' ἐκεῖνοι μὲν περὶ ἡμῶν ἐχόντων ὡς ἔχουσιν· οἷα γὰρ ἡμῖν ἐν τῷ προαγῶνι τῆς ὁμολογίας ἢ καὶ μετὰ τὴν ὁμολογίαν συνήραντο ἢ ἐπεκούρησαν, αὐτὸς μᾶλλον ᾔδεις· τὰς γὰρ ἑαυτῶν πάντων συνέστει-

---

9–10 *ἀσώτως – διέθρεψεν*: cf. Lc. 15.13–19 || 10–11 *οὐ γὰρ λανθάνει – ἀνήρ*: proverbium non invenimus

---

9 *κατωκτείρησεν* V || 14 *τὸ* ex *τω* corr. scriba || 17 *σωλοικίζοντα* V || *σοὶ*: *σὲ* V || 18 *ἑκατοντάκι* V

40: 2 *παλινῳδίαν ᾄσαντα*: Mantiss. Prov. II.47 || 4–5 *φοίνικος – ἐπέζησα*: cf. Apostol. XVII.87

40: 2 *εἶτ* i.e. *εἶτων* V || 4 post *τοῦ* rasura ca. 3 litt. || 6 *οὐδὲν* V || 7–8 *τὸν τόπου* V || 9 *τῶν* G: *τ* V || 11 *συνείραντο* V || 12 *εἴδει* V

pity on me who have bartered away my life in a prodigal manner and fed me as one of the last of his hired servants? For he does not remain unnoticed, according to the secular proverb, the man whom God cares for, so that he may, by his good deeds to the needy, give pleasure to God. I am not hastening to ask for anything beyond the necessities of everyday life: not a quantity of money, nor a mass of property, nor a high position. It is only bread that I beg for, the indispensable remedy for my miserable belly. Do not, therefore, disregard the Atticist beggar that I am, lest, by overlooking me when I am beset by poverty and hunger, you send me to Hades along with my solecisms. The Lord, who provides inalienable treasures, will grant you a hundredfold reward for your good deeds to me. That will be for you an abundant source of wealth.

40. To Nikephoros the *chartophylax*

I am ending my silence toward you, since I have learned that you had recited a recantation with regard to those matters that you did rightly accept and then denied. If that were not so, I would have tied my tongue rather than loosed it, so that, if you had remained in the same frame of mind in which I left you, I would not have greeted you even if I lived as long as the mythical phoenix—and this despite my affection and love for you, above that of many others, as you yourself do not deny—that you may see clearly how tenaciously, with the help of God, I hold onto Orthodoxy and cling to it rather than to matters of opportunity (?). For if I had chosen to win for myself by both means a position free of offense, who would have condemned me among those who seek a handle against me? Let them, however, remain as they are with regard to me; for you have certainly known what kind of cooperation and help they gave me both in the initial stage of my confession and after my confession.

λαν κεφαλὰς καὶ τὰ ὦτα ἔμυσαν καὶ τῷ λόγῳ χαλινὸν ἐπέθηκαν καὶ ἄλλοσε τοὺς ὀφθαλμοὺς ἀπένευσαν, ὡς ἔκτρωμά τι καὶ παραπλῆγα θεώμενοι· διὰ ταῦτα καὶ ἐσίγησα καὶ σιγήσω καὶ τὰ ἑαυτοῦ κατ' ἐμαυτὸν μελετήσω, τὴν ἐλπίδα θέμενος ἐπὶ τὸν πάντα δυνάμενον.

Περὶ *δὲ τῆς συμβάσης ὑμῖν ἐπηρείας ὡς διετέθημεν καὶ συνηλγήσαμεν, καὶ τῆς ἀνίας ὑμῖν συμμετέσχομεν, ὁ τῶν κρυφίων γνώστης ἐπιμαρτυρήσει* Κύριος· *ἀλλ' εἰ μετὰ χαρᾶς καὶ σὺν ὀρθοτομίᾳ τοῦ λόγου τοῦτο δεξαίμεθα, ἀρκέσει ἡμῖν εἰς ἐπαινέτην* Παῦλος *ὁ μέγας· μόνον ἡ πρὸς θεὸν ἐλπὶς μὴ σβεσθήτω· δύναται γὰρ πολλαπλασίω τῶν ἀφαιρεθέντων χαρίσασθαι.* Ἐπὶ *δὲ τῇ τοῦ κοινοῦ ἀδελφοῦ* Ἀναστασίου *διὰ θεὸν ἐνστάσει καὶ ἥσθημεν καὶ πνευματικῆς θυμηδίας ἐπλήσθημεν· οὗ ταῖς πρὸς* Κύριον *ἱεραῖς ἐντεύξεσι καὶ ἡμεῖς τῶν ἐλπιζομένων μὴ διαμάρτοιμεν.* Ὁ *δὲ ἵππος ἀκοστήσας τέως διὰ τὸ κριθιᾶσαι ἐμμανῶς † ποιησάμενος † τὸν δεσμὸν ἀπορρήξας, κατὰ τοῦ πεδίου ἔστη κροαίνων, ⟨εἶτα⟩ καὶ τοῖς λογικοῖς συγχλοάσας, οὕτω τοῦ καιροῦ ἐπιτρέψαντος, τὴν πολυσαρκίαν ἀφέμενος, κοῦφος καὶ εὐσταλὴς ὑμῖν ὀφθήσεται· ἡ γὰρ σπάνις τῶν ἐπιτηδείων καὶ τῶν μήπω γενομένων ἐφήψατο.* Εὔχου *δέ, πάτερ, ὑπὲρ ἡμῶν καὶ ὑπομένων* ‖ 137 ‖ *ὑπόμεινον εἰδὼς οἷα τῆς ὑπομονῆς τὰ γέρα.*

41. Τῷ *αὐτῷ*

Σὺ *μὲν οἴει διὰ σιγῆς θορυβεῖν ἡμᾶς ὡς σκολιώδεις καὶ τῆς* Ἡρακλείδου Λέσχης *ἐργάτας· ἡμεῖς δὲ λόγον εἰδότες ἔστιν ὅτε κρείττονα σιωπῆς, ὧδέ πως ἀποκρινούμεθα, ὡς εἰ μὴ φθέγξαιο συνήθως καὶ τὰς αἰσθήσεις ἡμῶν πικρανθείσας λογικῶς ἐπιγλυκάναις, ἀκήρυκτόν σοι διὰ γλώσσης πόλεμον ἐπεγεροῦμεν κατ' οὐδὲν ἀνεκτότερον τῆς βατραχείου ἐκείνης καὶ μυοκτόνου παρεμβολῆς· πρὶν ἢ οὖν ὅπλα κινῆσαι,*

---

19 *σὺν ὀρθοτομίᾳ τοῦ λόγου*: 2 Tim. 2.15 ‖ 25–26 *ὁ δὲ ἵππος – κροαίνων*: *Il.* 6.506–7; 15.263–64 ‖ 30 *ὑπομένων ὑπόμεινον*: cf. Ps. 39(40).2

---

14 *ἐπένευσαν* in *ἀπένευσαν* corr. scriba ‖ *ἐκτρώματι* V ‖ 17 *ἡμῖν* V ‖ 20 *ἐπαινετὴν* V: fort. *εἶς ἐπαινέτης* legendum ‖ 24 *οὐ* V ‖ 25 *ἀκοστῆστασεως* V

41: 5–6 *βατραχείου καὶ μυοκτόνου*: *Batr.* 159

41: 5 *ἐπεγειροῦμεν* V: corr. G ‖ *τῆς* G: *τὸν* V

Indeed, they all bowed their heads, closed their ears, put a bridle on their speech, and averted their eyes as if they were beholding some sinister monstrosity. For these reasons I have been silent and shall remain silent, minding my own affairs and entrusting my hopes to the Almighty.

Concerning the trouble that befell you, the Lord, who knows all secrets, will testify as to my disposition, my sympathy, and my share in your distress. But if we are to receive this with joy and "rightly teaching the word," the great Paul will be sufficient to commend us. Only let our faith in God not be extinguished, for He can grant us many times what has been taken away. I was pleased and filled with spiritual joy at the constancy for God's sake of our common brother Anastasios. May we, too, by his holy prayers to the Lord, not be deprived of our hopes.

The well-fed horse, driven to frenzy by overeating, broke its halter and stood stamping in the plain; then, having grazed on the grass of discourse, as circumstances allowed, it lost its fat and will appear to you light and trim. For the shortage of necessities has affected even those who have not yet been born (?).

Pray for me, Father, and stand firm patiently, knowing how great are the rewards of endurance.

41. To the same

You suppose that you are confusing me by your silence for being like the tortuous practitioners of the "Conversation" of Heraclides. But I know that sometimes speech is preferable to silence and shall reply in this vein, namely, that if you do not speak to me amicably and sweeten with your discourse my embittered feelings, I shall stir up an unheralded war of words with you, in no way more bearable than that famous battle array of mouse-killing frogs. So, before raising weapons, do close the

σύμφραξαι καὶ τὴν λογικὴν ῥομφαίαν σου στίλβωσον καὶ τὴν φαρέτραν μειλιχίων ἀλλὰ μὴ ἰοδόκων βελῶν παραπλήρωσον· τήν τε περικεφαλαίαν καὶ τὴν ἀμφήκη σπάθην καὶ τὸν ποδήρη θυρεὸν ἐπ' ὤμων πραέως ἀνάλαβε· εἰ βούλει δὲ σιγύνους καὶ σαγάρεις ἐπίθηξον, ὡς μέλλων πρὸς χαλκοκνήμιδας Ἀχαιοὺς ἀπομάχεσθαι. Εἰ δὲ τὴν γλῶτταν, ἔνθ' ἕρκος ὀδόντων, ἐγκλείσειας καὶ μὴ πρὸς παράταξιν εὐσήμῳ καὶ λογικῇ σάλπιγγι εὖ μάλα τὴν ταύτης φάλαγγα παρορμήσειας, ἴσθι τορόν τι καὶ ἐνυάλιον ἡμᾶς ᾄσοντας ἐπιδραμεῖσθαί σοι, καὶ τὸ ἑξῆς διὰ τὸ δύσφημον σιωπήσομαι. Εἴ τι δέ σοι γέγονε παρουσιάσαντι [καὶ] τῷ τῶν Ἀποστόλων διωνύμῳ σηκῷ, φανέρωσον ἵν' εἰ μὲν θυμῆρες συνησθῶμεν, εἰ δὲ πενθῆρες πρὸς ὑπομονὴν ἑαυτοὺς προσαλείψωμεν. || 138 ||

42. Νικηφόρῳ διακόνῳ καὶ χαρτοφύλακι

Ἐγγίζει μοι τὸ τέλος καὶ ὁ ἀμειδὴς καὶ ἀμείλιχος, ὡς τεκμαίρομαι, θάνατος· τοὺς γὰρ περὶ ἐμὲ κείρων καὶ τῷ γείτονι παραπέμπων ᾅδη, δῆλός ἐστιν ὡς τὴν ἐμὴν ἐκτομὴν οὐχ ἥκιστα προμαντεύεται· ὃν γὰρ ἤδη πρὸ θυρῶν εἶχεν τοῦ τάφου καὶ εἴσω τῶν κατωτάτω ταμιείων συνώθει, καὶ εἰς κατάποσιν ἑαυτῷ προευτρέπιζεν, ἐκλελοιπὼς ἡμιθνῆτα, ἐφ' ἕτερον οἰκέτην ἡμῖν ἐξιππάσατο· καὶ τοῦτον ἀπόφρακτον εὑρών, πρὶν ἢ κατὰ συστάδην αὐτὸν προσβάλῃ, πόρρωθεν ἀκροβολισάμενος πυρφόρῳ βέλει πρηνέα κατέβαλεν εἰς ἄνδρας ἄρτι τελοῦντα καὶ ἰούλοις τὴν γνάθον πυκάζοντα, ἐν νεότητί τε καὶ θάρσει ἐπιεικῶς σεμνυνόμενον, εἶδός τε, μέγεθός τε, φυήν τε τῷ παρ' Ὅμηρον Βελλεροφόντῃ μικροῦ παρισούμενον, εὐνούστατον τῷ κυρίῳ ἑαυτοῦ, πιστότατον, δραστικώτατον καὶ εἴ τι καλὸν τὸν ἄριστον χαρακτηρίζει θεράποντα κατ' οὐδενὸς ἐγῷμαι λειπόμενον. Καὶ τί δή σοι τὸν ἐν

7–8 *φαρέτραν – βελῶν*: *Il.* 15.443–44; *Od.* 21.11–12; 21.59–60 || 11 *χαλκοκνήμιδας Ἀχαιοὺς*: *Il.* 7.41 || 12 *ἕρκος ὀδόντων*: *Il.* 4.350; *Od.* 1.64 et al.

---

14 *τορων* V || 15 *σου* V || *παρουσἰάσαντι καὶ τὸ* V

42: 5 *εἰς κατάποσιν*: cf. Is. 25.8 || 9 *ἰούλοις – πυκάζοντα*: *Od.* 11.319–20 || 10 *εἶδος – Βελλεροφόντῃ*: cf. *Il.* 6.155 sqq. || 8–19 *τὸ ἀκάματον – σκώληκα*: Mk. 9.43–44

42: 2 *κηρῶν* V || 6 *ἀπέφρακτον* V || 7 *προσβάλλοι* V || *ἀκροβολησάμενος* V || 8 *τελόντα* V || 11 *μικρον* V || *πιστώτατον* V || 12 *τὸ ἄριστον* V || 13 *λιπόμενον* V

ranks, polish your sword of reasoning, and fill your quiver with mild and not poisonous darts. Put on meekly your helmet, your two-edged sword and, on your shoulders, the full-length shield. If you wish, sharpen yet more your spears and blades as if about to engage to the death the bronze-greaved Achaeans. But if you shut your tongue behind the barricade of your teeth and do not urge on right well its phalanx to the front line with a clear-voiced trumpet, know that I shall assault you with a piercing and warlike chant. As for the rest, ill-omen requires my silence.

If anything has happened to you when you presented yourself at the far-famed church of the Apostles, do reveal it, so that, if it was pleasant, we may rejoice together, but if unpleasant, we may prepare ourselves for patience.

42. To Nikephoros, deacon and *chartophylax*

My end is drawing close and, as I conjecture, unsmiling and implacable Death. For, as he is cutting down and consigning those round me to nearby Hades, he is clearly foretelling my own demise. He had me already at tomb's door, was thrusting me within the nether chambers and preparing to swallow me up, when he left me half-dead and rode against another, a servant of mine. Finding him uncorseted, without waiting to attack him at close quarters, he shot at him from afar a fiery dart and threw him to the ground—one who had barely reached manhood, whose chin was covered with down, who was fittingly adorned with youth and courage, all but comparable in aspect, size, and stature to Homer's Bellerophon, excellently disposed toward his master, most faithful and energetic and, I believe, lacking none of the qualities that mark the best servant. But why am I praising to you with my words one who

ἀμορφίᾳ κείμενον καὶ φθορᾷ συνειλούμενον στολίζω τοῖς ῥήμασιν; Ἔχει τοῦτον ὁ θάνατος, καὶ μικρῷ μετ' ἐκεῖνον ἐμέ· ἀλλ' εὔχου μὴ ὡς ἐλπίζει με περιδράξοιτο, μηδ' ὡς γέροντι ταῖς ἁμαρτίαις νεάζοντι προσβαλὼν ἐξηττήσειε καὶ τοῖς ἐκεῖ παραδῷ τὴν κακίαν κολάζουσιν καὶ τὸ ἀκάματον ἐκεῖνο πῦρ ὑποφλέγουσιν καὶ τὸν ἀκοίμητον ἐρεθίζουσιν πρὸς δαπάνην ἀδάπανον σκώληκα, καὶ τὸ ἐξώτερον σκότος μελαίνουσιν καὶ τὴν ἄϋλον ἐκκαίουσιν γέενναν, καὶ τὸν ἄληκτον κλαυθμὸν ἐπιτείνουσιν, καὶ τὸν βρυγμὸν τῶν ὀδόντων φρικτῶς ἐπιθραύουσι, καὶ τὸν κρυερὸν ὑποψύχουσι τάρταρον. Ταῦτα γὰρ τὰ δίκαια τοῦ θεοῦ μοι σταθμὰ παρὰ τῆς ἀδεκάστου δίκης, ὡς τὴν ἑαυτοῦ ψυχὴν ἀδικήσαντι, || 139 || *δαψιλῶς τεταμίευται. Τούτοις ἐγώ, κατάχρεως τούτων, ἐννηχόμενος, τότε ἀπέραντα μετακλαύσομαι· οἶκον γὰρ πονηρῶν ἔργων ἑαυτὸν κατεσκεύασα, καὶ ὕλην ἀνείκαστον ἁμαρτιῶν ἐθησαύρισα, καὶ διὰ τοῦτο μερίς μοι ταῦτα καὶ κλῆρος καὶ σχοίνισμα. Διὸ ταῖς προσευχαῖς ἐπικούρησον, καὶ ἵλεω τὸν ἐλέους θελητήν μοι κατάρτισαι, ἵν' οἰκτιρμοῖς χρηστοῖς τὸ πῦρ ἐπιμαράνοιμι, τὸν σκώληκα κοιμῆσαι, τὸν σκότον σελαγίσαι, τὸν κλαυθμὸν κατασιγάσαι, τὸν βρυγμὸν ἐπιπραΰναι, τὸν τάρταρον ἐπιχλιάναι· διὰ γὰρ πασῶν με τούτων τῶν βασάνων ἀπόκειται ⟨διελθεῖν⟩ ὅτι τῷ δίψῃ πιεζομένῳ κοτύλην οὐκ ἐπεμέτρησα ὕδατος· ὅτι τὸν σκωληκιῶντα καὶ φθινάδι κεντούμενον ἐβδελυξάμην ὡς μίασμα· ὅτι τυφλοῖς οὐκ ἐγενόμην ὄμμα· χεῖρα προσκόπτουσιν οὐκ ἐπώρεξα· ὅτι τοῖς διὰ θεὸν θρηνοῦσιν ἢ βίου δυσχέρειαν οὐ συνέκλαυσα· ὅτι γυμνοὺς τῷ κρύει πηγνυμένους οὐκ ἔθαλψα. Καὶ οὔπω ταῦτα δεινά,—δίκαια γὰρ καίπερ ὄντα δεινὰ καὶ πέρα δεινῶν—ἀλλ' ὅτι σὺν τῷ Σατὰν καὶ τοῖς αὐτοῦ ὑπασπισταῖς βουκέντροις πυριφλέκτοις ὡς δύσχρηστος ἐλαθήσομαι καὶ πρὸς τὸ πῦρ ἐκδημήσω καὶ συνέσομαι τούτοις ἀδιαδόχως καυσούμενος. Τίς οὖν ἐξελεῖταί με; Τίς μοι λύτρον παρέξει τῆς βασάνου καὶ τῶν ἀφύκτων ἐκείνων κολάσεων; Ἀβάλα μὴ μήτρας μητρικῆς προεξέκυψα, μηδ' αὐγαῖς ἡλιακαῖς συνεκύρησα. Αἴθε μὴ τόσον πόδας ἐπὶ πάτον χθονὸς ἐπερείσας ἐβάδισα. Ὤφελον μὴ γλῶσσαν πρὸς φθόγγον ἐκίνησα, ἀλλ' ἐκ νηδύος νέκυς εὐθὺς ἐχρημάτισα καὶ φθορᾷ συνεζύγην ⟨καὶ⟩ εἰς ἀφάνειαν ἤλασα καὶ γῆ με διαστᾶ*|| 140 ||*σα συνέκλεισεν καὶ κῦμα χανὸν θαλάττης ἐπέκλυσεν, πρὶν ἢ τοῖς*

18–19 *τὸ ἀκάματον – σκώληκα*: Mk. 9.43–44 || 19–21 *καὶ τὸ – ὀδόντων*: Mt. 8.12 et al. || 27 *μερὶς – κλῆρος*: cf. Acta 8.21; Col. 1.12 || 28 *τὸν ἐλέους θελητὴν*: Mi. 7.18 || 36 *γυμνοὺς – ἔθαλψα*: cf. Mt. 25.43

---

17 *προσβαλεῖν* V || 20 *ἀύλως* V || 24 *τεταμείωται* V || *κατάχρεως* V || *ἐνηχόμενος* V || 31 *ἐπιχλικᾶναι* V || 32 *διελθεῖν* suppl. G || *τὸν . . . πιεζόμενον* V || 36 *κρύι* V || 37 *ταῦτα* scripsimus: *τοῦ* V || 42 *αὐγῆς ἡλιακῆς* V || 43 *ποδος* V

lies unsightly, enfolded by corruption? Death possesses him and soon will possess me in turn. Pray that he should not grasp me as he hopes to do nor, after attacking me, an old man yet youthful in sin, overcome me and deliver me to those who punish evil over there, who kindle that ceaseless fire, who provoke the sleepless worm to a consumption that does not consume, who blacken the outer darkness, who light up the immaterial Gehenna, who intensify the endless weeping, who shatter terribly the gnashing of teeth and congeal the icy Tartarus. For those are God's just rewards that have been abundantly reserved for me by the righteous tribunal for having done injustice to my own soul. Immersed in such ⟨punishment⟩, deep in debt as I am, will I then lament without end. For I have made myself a house of evil deeds, I have stored up an immense quantity of sin, wherefore those things are my share, my portion and my allotment. Help me, then, by your prayers and move Him who wills mercy to take pity on me that I may quench the fire with kind mercies; ⟨help me⟩ to put the worm to sleep, to illuminate the darkness, to appease the weeping, to soothe the gnashing, to warm Tartarus. Indeed, it is my lot ⟨to undergo⟩ all those torments since I have not given a cup of water to him who was oppressed by thirst; since I abominated as something unclean him who was eaten by worms or was afflicted by consumption; since I did not make myself an eye for the blind, did not proffer my hand to those that stumbled, did not commiserate with those who weep either for the sake of God or because of life's difficulties, did not comfort the naked who are frozen by the cold. Yet it is not these things that are terrible (for, though terrible beyond measure, they are just), but rather that I shall be driven off with fiery goads along with Satan and his followers like the useless man I am; that I shall dwell in the fire and remain with them to be burned without pause. Who will rescue me? Who will give me deliverance from the pain and those inescapable torments? Oh, that I had not come out of my mother's womb, had I not encountered the light of the sun! Would that I had not as much as walked on the earth, pressing my feet on the ground! Would that I had not moved my tongue to utter sounds, but had remained dead from birth and been yoked to corruption and been destroyed! Would that the earth had opened up to shut me in, and a gaping wave of the sea had washed over me before I had bound myself inextri-

τῆς ἁμαρτίας λίνοις ἑαυτὸν ἀλύτως συμποδίσαι καὶ τοῖς ψυχὰς ἀγρεύουσιν εὐάλωτον θήραμα καὶ θοίνην δαιμονικῆς εἰλαπίνης χαρίσασθαι. Τοιοῦτος *ἐγὼ καὶ οὕτως ἐμαυτὸν ἐπαρῶμαι καὶ σχετλιάζων ὀδύρομαι.* Διὰ *τοῦτο σὲ καὶ τοὺς ὅσοι κατὰ σὲ συγκαλῶ προστῆναι καὶ προασπίσαι καὶ ὑπερασπίσαι τῆς ἐμῆς ἀχρειότητος, ὡς ἄν μοι τὴν λειπομένην ὥραν, οὐ γὰρ ἡμέραν θαρρήσω λέγειν, ἐν μεταμέλῳ τελέσαιμι καὶ τῶν ἀπηριθμημένων βασάνων τὴν πεῖραν ἐκφύγοιμι· πρεσβείας τῆς ἁγνῆς καὶ ὑπεραμώμου* Θεοτόκου *καὶ πάντων τῶν ἁγίων καὶ ταῖς ὑμετέραις πρὸς τὸ θεῖον ἐντεύξεσιν.*

43. Τῷ *αὐτῷ*

Εἰ*δέναι βουλόμεθα τὴν πρὸς ἡμᾶς σου τελείαν ἀγάπην, ὡς ὁ ἱερώτατος, ἰλήκοι, ἀρχιερεύς, μηδεμίαν ἡδύνουσαν πρὸς θυμηδίαν κεκακωμένης ψυχῆς εἰδὼς κεραννύειν ἀντίδοτον, στυφούσας ἡμῖν πικρίδας πρὸς εὐωχίαν παρέθετο, ἃς ἐποψόμενος ἢ καὶ ὧν γευσόμενός εἰμι, καὶ οὐχ ἑκών, ποθεινότατε· καὶ εἰ μὲν ἄκος τῆς ἐν ἐμοὶ πικρίας διὰ πικρίδων εὕροιμι, τὸν* Ἱπποκράτην *οὐκ ἀληθεύειν εἴποιμι, ὃς δι' ἐναντίων τὰς θεραπείας τῶν ἐναντίων ὑπέφαινε γίνεσθαι· εἰ δὲ τῆς κλήσεως ἡ ποιότης ἀκίνητος μείνοι καὶ μηδεμίαν ἡμῖν τέκοι γλυκύτητα, ἔστω τὰ* Πικρίδου *πικρὰ τῷ* Πικρίδῃ. Ἡ*μεῖς δὲ τὴν ἰατρείαν διὰ φυγῆς πρὸς θεοῦ λαβεῖν ἐξαιτήσαιμεν.*

44. Τῷ *αὐτῷ*

Οὐ*δὲν ἔχων τῇ μειλιχίῳ σου προσαγηοχέναι ψυχῇ, καὶ γὰρ οὔπω μοι τὰ* Πικρίδου *ἐνηδύνθη, πρασίου φυτοῦ δέσμην καὶ ταύτην βραχεῖαν*

47–48 *αγορεύουσιν . . . θοίνη* V ‖ 48 *χαρίεσσαι* V

43: 2–3 *κεκακωμένης ψυχῆς*: cf. Basilii *ep.* 6, ed. Y. Courtonne, vol. I (Paris, 1957), p. 19.3–4 [= PG 32, 241B] ‖ 3 *πικρίδας*: cf. Ex. 12.8; Greg. Nyss. *Comment. in Cant. cant.* 10, ed. Jaeger, VI, 306. ‖ 6–7 *δι' ἐναντίων – γίνεσθαι*: cf. Hippocr. *De locis hom.*, XLI.2; *De ventis,* I.4

43: 2 *κεκαμένης* V ‖ 3 *εἰδὼς* G: *ειδους* V ‖ 7 *ὑπέφαινε* V: fort. *ἀπέφαινε* legendum

---

44: 1 *προσαγιοχέναι* V

cably with the threads of sin and offered myself, an easy prey and a demonic banquet, to those that hunt after souls! Such a one am I and thus do I curse and berate myself in weeping. For this reason I call on you and your companions to champion, defend, and protect my worthless self, that I may spend the remaining hour (I dare not call it a day) in repentance and avoid experiencing the torments I have detailed; by the intercession of the pure and most spotless Theotokos and of all the saints and your prayers to the Godhead.

43. To the same

I wish you to know, my perfect friend, that the most holy archbishop (may he be gracious!), who is unable to mix any pleasant antidote for the enjoyment of a distressed soul, has served me a feast of bitter chicory which, though unwilling, I am about to look upon and even taste, dear friend. If I find in chicory a remedy for the bitterness that is within me, I would say that Hippocrates was wrong when he declared that contraries are treated by contraries. But if the name keeps its quality unchanged and brings me no sweetness, let *ta Pikridou* be bitter to Pikrides. As for me, may I beg God to find a cure through flight.

44. To the same

Not having anything else to offer to your gentle spirit—for *ta Pikridou* has not yet become sweet to me—I resolved to send you a bunch of leeks, and a small one at

πεπομφέναι διέγνωκα· ἀλλὰ μὴ τὸ δριμύ σου τοῦ δώρου καθάψηται καὶ πρὸς δάκρυα κινῆσαν κινήσῃ σε ‖ 141 ‖ καὶ πρὸς ὀξυτέρους λόγους καὶ θυμοδακεῖς, δι᾿ ὧν ἡμῖν οὐ μόνον δάκρυον, ἀλλὰ καὶ πένθος ἄωρον ἐκ καρδίας θερμῆς προσγενήσεται. Καὶ εὔχου μοι· οὐδὲ γὰρ ἐνεδίδου γράφειν ἡ γλῶττα πλείονα δεσμουμένη ἢ κεκανονισμένη σιγῇ.

45. Τῷ αὐτῷ

Ἔδειξας καὶ γαστρὸς καὶ γλώττης κρατεῖν· πείθει γάρ με τὸ τῆς νηστείας οὐχ ἥκιστα τοπάζειν οὕτω, πάτερ, σεβάσμιον· αὕτη γάρ, οἷά τις ψυχῆς οἰκουρὸς ἐπιφανεῖσα, τὴν πεντάθυρον εἴσοδον τῶν αἰσθήσεων, δι᾿ ὧν ἐστι πολλάκις πρὸς ἀμετρίαν ἐκτρέπεσθαι, κλείσασα, συνάγει καὶ πάντοθεν ἤδη συστέλλουσα μύειν ποιεῖ, καὶ κατὰ μέτρον ἐνεργεῖν ὑποτίθεται, ὡς ἂν μὴ θάνατος διὰ τούτων παρακύψας ἐπεγγελάσοι καὶ τὴν φαρέτραν αὐτοῦ τῶν ἰοδόκων βελῶν κενώσας, πληγὴν ἀναινομένην τὴν διὰ μοτώσεως ἴασιν ἀπεργάσηται. Νομοθετεῖ γὰρ τὸν ὀφθαλμὸν βλέπειν ὀρθὰ καὶ πρὸς εὐθύτητα φέρεσθαι, ὡς ἐκ δεξιῶν ἑστῶτα Κύριον προορώμενον· ἀκοῇ μοχλοὺς σιγῆς ἐκ θείων μεταλλευθέντας φωνῶν περιτίθησιν, ὡς μὴ πρὸς κίβδηλον ἠχὴν καὶ ἀσέμνως ἀποδουπούμενα τετηκέναι προσφθέγματα· ὄσφρησιν καθαίρει τῆς θολερᾶς τῶν παθῶν καὶ λοιμώδους εἰσπνεύσεως, καὶ πρὸς ὑποδοχὴν ἑτοίμην ποιεῖ τοῦ συνθέτου τῶν ἀρετῶν θυμιάματος· τὴν γλῶτταν δυοῖν νόμοιν σοφίζουσα φαίνεται· τῶν τε γὰρ πρὸς ἡδονὴν φερόντων στερίσκει ταύτην ὀρέξεων, διάστυφόν τε καὶ λεπτότατον τὸ τῆς ἐγκρατείας αὐτῇ τεκταίνει δαψιλέστατον ἥδυσμα· λόγου τε μέτρα διδάσκει, καὶ σιγὴν ἐπασκεῖν ἐκπαιδεύει, καὶ θύραν ἡνίκα δεῖ φθέγγεσθαι κατὰ καιρὸν ὑπανοίγνυσιν· ἁφὴν ῥυθμίζει μὴ τοῖς μαλακοῖς ἐφηδύνεσθαι, μηδὲ ταῖς λειότησι συ ‖ 142 ‖ νεκλύεσθαι, τῷ τραχεῖ δὲ τοῦ κατὰ θεὸν βίου,

---

44: 4–5 *λόγους καὶ θυμοδακεῖς*: cf. *Od.* 8.185

---

4 *κινήσῃ*: *κινῆσαι* V ‖ 6 *μου* V

45: 7 *φαρέτραν – βελῶν*: *Il.* 15.444; *Od.* 21.11–12; 21.59–60 ‖ 20–21 *τῷ τραχεῖ – συνήδεσθαι*: Greg. Naz. *Oratio XXXIX in Sancta Lumina,* PG 36, 332c

---

45: 8 *μωτώσεως* V ‖ 14 *δυϊν* V ‖ 16 *διαστυφων . . . λεπτοτατην* V ‖ 18 *θυρα* V

that. Let not this pungent gift affect you and, by moving you to tears, incite you to sharp and biting words which, coming from your ardent heart, will cause me not only tears, but also an untimely grief. Pray for me; for my tongue did not allow me to write at greater length, being restrained or regulated by silence.

45. To the same

You have proved yourself master of both your belly and your tongue; for the holy nature of the fast persuades me, O father, more than anything else to suppose this. She it is who, appearing like some housekeeper of the soul and having shut the five-door entrance of the senses (which often give rise to excess), brings us round, causes us to contract by enclosing us on all sides, and enjoins on us to act with moderation, so that Death should not make a mockery of us by peeping through the senses and, after emptying his quiver of poisonous darts, inflict on us a wound that refuses all cure by dressing. For she ordains to the eye to look straight and seek rectitude in the expectation of seeing the Lord standing on the right side; she places on hearing bolts of silence mined from divine instructions lest it be wasted on fraudulent sounds and words indecently shouted; she cleanses smell from the turbid and pestilential inhalation of the passions and prepares it to receive the incense composed of the virtues. She is seen to instruct the tongue by means of two ordinances: for she deprives it of pleasurable appetites while preparing for it in abundance the astringent and light relish of continence; she also teaches it the proper bounds of speech and the practice of silence, while occasionally opening the door when it is necessary to speak. She trains ⟨the sense of⟩ touch not to take pleasure in soft stuffs nor to be relaxed by smoothness, but to delight, as it is said, in the harshness of a life according to God

κατὰ τὸν εἰπόντα, συνήδεσθαι, καὶ τούτου μᾶλλον ἐφάπτεσθαι καὶ τὰ περὶ τῆς ζωῆς ψηλαφᾶν καὶ πρὸς θυσίαν αἰνέσεως ὁσημέραι θεοῦ συνεπαίρεσθαι. Τ*οιαῦτα τὰ τῆς νηστείας ἀστεῖα κυήματα· τοιαῦτα τὰ τῆς ἐγκρατείας αὐχήματα· τοιούτοις δεξιοῦται τοῖς θεραπεύουσιν, ψυχὰς καρυκεύμασι· τούτοις τὸ νηφάλιον πόμα κεράννυσιν.* Τ*αύτην συνέστιον καὶ ὁμοδίαιτον ἔχων, καὶ τούτοις τὸν ὅμιλον τῶν αἰσθήσεων στολίσας ὡς ἄριστα, ὡραῖος κάλλει κατὰ τὴν μεγάλην ἡμέραν τῆς ἀναστάσεως ὑπαντήσειας, τότε λύων τὸ τῆς σιγῆς ἐπιτίμιον καὶ λόγον ἡμῖν ὠφελείας † ἐπαμφιδέξιον. †* Τ*ὸ δὲ νῦν ἔχον, αἰδοῖ τῆς νηστείας, στιγμὴν μόνην τῆς ἁγίας ὑμῶν χειρὸς σιωπῶσαν δεξαίμεθα, ἥτις ἡμῖν ἀντὶ ποικίλης λόγων ἰδέας ἐπιεικῶς λογισθήσεται.*

46. Τ*ῷ αὐτῷ*

Φθινάς μοι νόσος ἐνέσκηψε δριμεῖα κνησμὸν ἢ τὸ χολῶδες τοῦ πάθους πρὸς τὴν ἐπιφάνειαν τῆς σαρκὸς ἐπισύρουσα. Ὅ*θεν τὰς ὠλένας καὶ τὰ σκέλη κομιδῇ καταστίξασα, οἷα βέλεσιν ὀξέσιν, τὸ δύστηνον τουτοῒ σῶμα κατακεντεῖ, καὶ ὁ πραΰνων ἢ ἀμβλύνων οὐδείς· ἀλοιφαῖς δὲ γραΐδιων, μή τινος ὑπόντος ἀμύμονος ἰητῆρος, ὑπείκειν ἀναγκαστῶς βεβιάσμεθα· ἐξ ὧν θεραπεία μικρὰ μὲν ἔρχεται, συνούλωσις δὲ μακρὰν ἐπιφαίνεται· ἧς ἵνα τύχοιμεν, καὶ ἀνέσεως ὁλοσχεροῦς ἀπολαύσαιμεν, τὴν σὴν περὶ ταύτην θεραπευτικὴν ἐκκαλούμεθα μότωσιν· ἴσμεν γὰρ ὡς πολλοῖς ἀλγυνομένοις καὶ ἀνίατα πάσχουσιν τοῖς παρ' ἑαυτῆς ἰατρικοῖς φαρμάκοις ἐπαλείψασα καὶ δεσμήσασα, ἐν ἀκαρεῖ τὸ κεχηνὸς τοῦ μώλωπος πρὸς συνέ* ‖ 143 ‖ *χειαν κατεπύκνωσε, καὶ τὴν ῥῶσιν εὐπετῶς ἀνεκτήσατο· σὺν τούτοις οὖν καὶ ἡμᾶς γαληνίοις*

---

22 *θυσίαν αἰνέσεως*: cf. Lev. 7.12 sqq.; Ps. 49 (50).14, 23 et al. ‖ 27 *ὡραῖος κάλλει*: cf. Ps. 44 (45).3

21–22 fort. *ἢ τὰ περὶ τῆς ζωῆς* legendum ‖ 22 *ψιλαφᾶν* V ‖ *ὡσημέραι* V ‖ 25 *καρυκεύουσιν* V ‖ *νηφάλαιον . . . κεράννισιν* V ‖ 26 *τὸν ὅμιλον* iteravit scriba ‖ 28 *ταῖς σιγῆς* V ‖ 29 *ὠφελείας* V ‖ *ἐπαμφιδέξιον* V: vide comment. ‖ 31 *λόγον* V

46: 1 *φθινὰς νόσος*: cf. Hippocr. *De glandulis,* XIV.1 ‖ 5 *ἀμύμονος ἰητῆρος*: *Il.* 4.194; 11.518; 11.835

46: 2–3 *τὰ ὠλένα* V ‖ 5 *γραϊδίοις* V ‖ *ὑπήκειν* V ‖ 8 *μώτωσιν* V ‖ 11 *ακαρη* V ‖ *συνένέχειαν* V ‖12 *ευπετ (ου)* V

and apply itself to it, to feel round those things that concern ⟨the true⟩ life and so be elevated day by day to offer to God a sacrifice of praise. Such are the handsome products of fasting; such are the boasts of continence; such are the soul-benefiting savories she serves, with such ingredients does she mix her sobering potion. Having her as your lodger and companion and most excellently adorning with those ⟨qualities⟩ the concourse of your senses, may you meet me in all your beauty on the great day of the Resurrection, breaking on that occasion the penance of silence and addressing to me your beneficial words. Now, however, out of deference to the fast, may I receive but a silent jot from your holy hand, which I shall fairly esteem as much as a variegated discourse.

46. To the same

A fierce consumption has fallen on me, drawing irritation or the biliousness of the disease to the surface of the flesh. Whence, having completely covered my arms and legs with spots, it pierces this wretched body with sharp darts, and there is no one to soothe or mitigate it. In the absence of a "noble physician," I have been obliged by necessity to submit to old women's unguents which cause some small comfort, while cicatrization appears far off. With a view to obtaining the latter and enjoying complete relief, I am calling for your therapeutic treatment. For I know that, in the case of many persons who were in pain and suffering incurable ills, you have smeared them with your medicinal drugs and bound them so as to close swiftly gaping wounds and readily restore health. Bind me, therefore, along with your other

καὶ προσηνέσι καταδέσμοις ἐπίδησον, καὶ στῆσον ἡμῖν τὴν καταιγίδα τοῦ ἄλγους ὡς ἂν μή, τῆς ὥρας πραϋγελώσης καὶ πάντας πνευματικῶς καὶ σωματικῶς ἐνεαρίζειν προτρεπούσης, χειμῶνι τῶν δυσχερῶν ἡμεῖς προσπαλαίοιμεν.

Ἐπειδὴ δὲ τὰ ἔσχατα τοῦ Βυζαντίου κόλπου, Γαδείρων δίκην, παροικεῖν κατεκρίθημεν (τὸ γὰρ ἐπέκεινα τοῦ λάκκου ἀπέρατον), ἰχθῦς ζωγρεῖσθαι πολλάκις ἐν αὐτῷ συμβαίνει, ἐξ ὧν μικρά τις ἀπόμοιρα καὶ μέχρις ἡμῶν διελήλακεν, ἧς, ἵνα τὴν θήραν ἡμῶν ἐπευλογήσαις, ἀπόγευσαι, καὶ ὡς τὸν Ἰακὼβ Ἰσαάκ, μὴ περιέργως ἀλλὰ προθύμως προσαγηοχότας ἡμᾶς πρωτοτόκοις εὐχαῖς πρὸς ἀρετῆς ἀνάληψιν ἐπαναγαγεῖν δυσωπήθητι. Ἀλλὰ δὴ καὶ αὖθις ἀπορίᾳ γλυκαζόντων λαχάνων ἐπὶ τὴν διὰ πράσων κεχωρήκαμεν στύφουσαν, πάτερ, ἐπίδοσιν· ἣν μὴ τῇ ἐκείνων ποιότητι, τῇ δὲ ἡμετέρᾳ προσέχων προθέσει, μεθ' ἡδονῆς πραϋνούσης ἐπίβλεψον.

47. Τῷ *αὐτῷ*

Ἐπιζητῶν τὴν αἰτίαν καὶ διερευνώμενος δι' ἣν ἡ τοσαύτη σιγὴ παρὰ σοὶ χώραν εὕρετο, ἔγνων αὐτὸν ἐμὲ ταύτης εἶναι τὸν αἴτιον καὶ γεννήτορα· ὑπὸ γὰρ ὀδύνης ὀξείας τῶν ἀναδοθέντων μοι χαλεπῶν μωλώπων νυσσόμενος ἠρευξάμην ἐξ ἐλαφρίας πρὸς σέ, τὴν ἠπίαν ἐμοὶ ψυχήν, λόγους τραχεῖς, ἀλλ' οὐδαμῶς ταύτης, ὡς ἔχω, τὴν θείαν ἐπιφροσύνην ἐτράχυνα. Δέδοικα δὲ καὶ μή τις ἄλλη || 144 || *Θέτιδος ὑμᾶς ὡς τὸν Ἀχιλλέα βουλὴ παρέπεισε πρόπαλαι, ὧδέ πως ὑποτιθεμένη τῷ παιδὶ καὶ ἐπὶ λέξεως ἔχουσα, μῆνι' Ἀχαιοῖσι, πολέμου δ' ἀποπαύεο πάμπαν. Ἀλλὰ μὴ τοῦτο γε τοῖς εὐηκόοις ὠσίν σου τὸ βούλημα τίς κἂν ὀπω-*

17–18 *Γαδείρων – ἀπέρατον*: Apostol. XVI.19; Karathanasis 82; Greg. Naz. *Hom.* 43.24, PG 36, 528c et Ps. Nonnus ad locum, ed. Nimmo Smith, 263 || 21 *ὡς τὸν Ἰακὼβ Ἰσαάκ*: Gen. 27.19 sqq.

---

17 *δὲ* scripsi: *σε* V || 18 *λάκου* V || 21 *προσαγιοχότας* V || 22 *πρωτοτόκους* V

47: 8 *μῆνι' – πάμπαν*: *Il.* 1.422 || 9 *εὐηκόοις ὠσίν σου*: cf. Prov. 25.12

47: 5 *ταύτην* in *ταύτης* corr. scriba || 9 *σὸν* V

patients with your gentle and soothing bandages and halt for me this storm of pain lest I have to struggle with a winter of troubles while the season smiles gently, inviting everyone to bloom, springlike, in spirit and in body.

Seeing that I have been condemned to dwell at the far end of the bay of Byzantium as if at Cadiz (for what lies beyond the pond is inaccessible), it often happens that fish are caught in it, of which a small share has reached me. Do taste it that you may "bless" my "game" and, as Isaac did to Jacob, be so good as to restore me by your "first-born" prayers to the acquisition of virtue since my offering was made willingly and not deceitfully. Once again, in the absence of sweeter vegetables, I have resorted, father, to making you a gift of pungent leeks. Regard it with a soothing pleasure, mindful not of their quality, but of my intention.

47. To the same

In seeking and investigating the reason why so profound a silence has fallen on you, I perceived that I myself was responsible for causing it. For, being pierced by the sharp pain of the bruises that have erupted on me, I have, out of frivolity, blurted out to you, my gentle friend, some harsh words without, I believe, in any way irritating your divine wisdom. I fear, however, lest some other design has beguiled you as Thetis did once to Achilles, when she enjoined on her son in these very words to "be wroth against the Achaeans, and desist altogether from war." Let no one breathe such

σοῦν ἐνηχήσειε. Ἐκεῖνον γὰρ αὐτόν σε γινώσκομεν, οἷον ἴσμεν πλήρη γλυκύτητος καὶ πρὸ τῆς τοῦ γράμματος, ὡς μὴ ὤφελε κεχαράχθαι, θρασύτητος.

48. Τῷ *αὐτῷ*

Ἑστῶσιν ὠσὶν τὸ δὴ λεγόμενον, καὶ κεχηνόσιν ὄμμασιν τὴν σὴν ἀκουτισθῆναι φωνὴν καὶ τῆς χειρός σου προσιδεῖν γράμμα φροντὶς ἡμῖν οὐχ ἡ τυχοῦσα προσῆν· ὧν μὴ τυχόντες, ἐνεάσαμεν καὶ ἐμύσαμεν καὶ τῇ γλώττῃ σιγὴν ἐπετρέψαμεν· ἀλλ' εἰ φθέγξαιο καὶ γράψαις, ἀκούσομεν καὶ βλέψομεν καὶ τὴν γλῶτταν εἰς τὸ λέγειν ὁπλίσομεν· καὶ εὔχου μοι, λογιώτατε πάτερ.

49. Ἰ*γνατίῳ μητροπολίτῃ* Νι*κομηδείας*

Πο*λυπλόκοις σειραῖς τῶν ἑαυτοῦ ἁμαρτιῶν, κατὰ τὸν* Πα*ροιμιαστήν, ὦ ἱερώτατε πάτερ, σφιγγόμενος, τοὺς ἄξονας τοῦ ἰδίου γεωργίου τῆς σωτηρίας πεπλάνημαι καὶ πρὸς ὀρθὰς τροχιὰς βαδίζειν οὔπω δεδύνημαι· ἔνθεν τῆς ἱερᾶς ἀγέλης καὶ νομῆς ὡς πορρωτάτω κατῴκισμαι, καὶ τοῦ ζωοποιοῦ τῆς τρυφῆς χειμάρρου ἀνάξιος πεπωκέναι διήμαρτον, καὶ δέδοικα πρὸς τοὺς ἀρχιερατείᾳ λαμπρὸν ἀποστίλβοντας ὑμᾶς προσφθέγγεσθαί τι καὶ προσομιλεῖν διὰ γράμματος.* Ο*ὐκοῦν ἀπιδὼν εἰς τὴν θεομίμητον ὑμῶν πατροσύνην καὶ περίβλεπτον συγκατάβασιν, ἀφορμῆς τινος προσπεσούσης, δυσωπεῖν προήχθην· καὶ μή με τῆς προ-* || 145 || *πετείας ἐλέγξῃς ὡς τῷ μεγίστῳ σοὶ ποιμένι μηδ' εἰς πρόβατον*

11 *ὄφελλε* V

48: 1 *ἑστῶσιν ὠσὶν*: Diogen. VIII.74; Diogen. Vind. III.97; Mantiss. Prov. III.51

48: 3 *ἐὕυσαμεν* V: *ἐνεάσαμεν* Efthymiadis || 5 *ἠστολέγειν* V

49: 2–3 *σφιγγόμενος – βαδίζειν*: cf. Prov. 5.21–22; 9.12; 4.11,26 || 5 *ζωοποιοῦ – πεπωκέναι*: Ps. 35 (36).9

49: 2 *ἄξωνας* V || 4 *πορροτάτω* V || 5 *πεποκέναι* V || 10 *ὡς το* V || *μηδεὶς* V

an intention at all into your obedient ears! For I know you to be full of sweetness as you were before that rash letter had been needlessly penned.

48. To the same

With ears pricked up, as the saying goes, and eyes wide open, I was uncommonly anxious to hear your voice and behold a letter from your hand. Having been disappointed in this, I have become dumb, closed my eyes, and imposed silence on my tongue. If you but speak and write, I shall hear and see and arm my tongue for speech. Pray for me, most learned father.

49. To Ignatios, metropolitan of Nicomedia

Being bound, most holy Father, by the tangled cords of my sins, as the author of Proverbs says, I have strayed from the paths of the husbandry of my salvation and am no longer able to walk to straight wheel tracks. Wherefore, I have been removed far away from the sacred flock and pasturage and have failed in obtaining the life-giving stream of joy, unworthy as I was to drink of it; and I fear to address anything and speak by letter to you who shine brilliantly in your high priesthood. In view, however, of your godlike fatherhood and admirable condescension, I have been led to entreat you on a matter that has chanced to arise. Do not condemn me for my rashness in that I, who am not even ranked among the sheep, have been incited to write to you, a great shepherd.

ἐγὼ τεταγμένος γράφειν παρώρμημαι. Ἡ δὲ τῆς ἀφορμῆς ἐν τούτῳ ἐστὶ περιπέτεια. Ὁ τὸ γράμμα κομίζων μοναχός, εἷς ὢν τῶν ἐν τῇ μονῇ ταύτῃ προλαμπόντων, μικρᾶς τινος, ὡς ἐξεῖπεν, τῶν παρ' ὑμῶν αἰσίως ἰθυνομένων, ἐπισκοπῆς ὀρεγόμενος κατεπείγεται, ὃν καὶ κατὰ πρόσωπον τῆς ἀλαθήτου ὑμῶν καὶ διορατικῆς δίκαιον ἔκρινα παραστῆσαι, σὺν τῷ γράμματι, τελειότητος, ἵν' εἰ μὲν ὑπὸ τῆς τιμῆς διώκηται ὡς καλοῦ ἔργου, κατὰ τὸν μέγαν Παῦλον, *ἐπιθυμῶν, μὴ διαμάρτοι τῆς αὐτὸν ἐπὶ τοῦτο φερούσης ἐφέσεως· εἰ δ' αὐτὸς ταύτην διώκοι, μηδὲν τῆς ἱερᾶς ἀξίας ἐπιφερόμενος λείψανον, παραχωροῦμεν τῇ ἀκριβεῖ σου καὶ διακριτικῇ καὶ τοῦτο πατρότητι. Οὐ γὰρ λήψει τινὶ καὶ δωροδοκίᾳ, προῖκα δὲ καὶ ἀμισθὶ καμφθείς, εἰς ταύτην ἑαυτὸν καθῆκα τὴν αἴτησιν· καὶ* Κύριος *ὁ θεός, ταῖς εὐαγγελικαῖς καὶ ἀποστολικαῖς χάρισιν τὴν ἱερὰν ὑμῶν κατακοσμήσας πατρότητα, τῇ καθολικῇ ἐκκλησίᾳ χαρίσεται ὑπερευχομένην καὶ τῆς ἡμῶν μετριότητος.*

50. Θεοφάνει ἀσηκρῆτις

Ἰδού σοι τὸ τῶν θύραθε παροιμιῶν πεπόμφαμεν βιβλιδάριον· οὐκ ἐκτὸς βίας, ὡς καὶ αὐτὸς εἰκάζειν ἔχεις, φιλόμουσε, ἐπειδὴ καὶ πολλὰς ἑτέρας παροιμιώδεις ὑποθήκας ἐν αὐτῷ παραθεῖναι βουλῆς ἐγενόμεθα, ὡς ἄν, κατὰ τὴν παροιμίαν, σκευάσωμεν κυψέλην φρονήσεως, ἀλλὰ στοργῇ τῇ πρὸς σὲ καὶ μάλα κρατούμενοι τὴν βίαν θέλησιν πεποιήμεθα, καί, ἵνα καθομηρίσω σοι τὸ τῆς ἐμῆς ἀβούλητον προαιρέσεως, δῶκα ἑκὼν ἀέκοντι γε θυμῷ. ‖ 146 ‖ *Σὺ δὲ μὴ ἀναβάλῃ τὴν ἀπόδοσιν, ἀλλὰ τὸν τρισάριθμον τῷ πέντε πολλαπλασιάσας μὴ ὑπερβαθῆναι τὸν ἐκ τούτου γενόμενον ἀριθμόν, ὡς ὑπέσχου, κατάνευσον· καὶ ἔρρωσο, καὶ τῇ λήθῃ τῆς παροράσεως ἡμᾶς ⟨μὴ⟩ ἐπὶ πλεῖον παράπεμψον.*

16–17 *ὡς καλοῦ ἔργου – ἐπιθυμῶν*: cf. 1 Tim. 3.1

---

11 *τεταγμένον* primum scripsit deinde corr. scriba ‖ 12 *εντιμ̊* V ‖ 14 *ὃ καὶ* V ‖ 19 *ἀκριβῆ* V ‖ 21 *ἀμισθεὶ* V ‖ 23 *κατακοσμίσας* V

50: 4 *κυψέλην φρονήσεως*: Comic. adesp. 703 = Kock *Comic. Attic. Fragm.*, III, p. 533: *κυψέλαι φρονημάτων – οἷον θῆκαι φρονήσεως* . . . Bekker *Anecd.* I, 47, 15. Photius corrupte *κ. φρονημάτων· ἀγγεῖα. ἢ κενοὶ παντάπασιν* . . . ‖ 7 *δῶκα – θυμῷ*: *Il.* 4.43

50: 2 *εχων* V ‖ 3 *παραθῆναι* V ‖ 4 *ἀλλᾱ* V ‖ 5 *βι<* V ‖ 6 *καθομηρήσω* V

The circumstances of the matter are these. The monk who is delivering this letter, one of the most outstanding of this monastery, is driven, as he declares, by the desire for a little bishopric, among those that are auspiciously directed by you. I have thought it right to present him, with this letter, before your infallible and discerning Perfection, so that, if he be sought for this honor in "desiring," as the great Paul has it, "a good work," he should not fail in the wish that incites him to this purpose; but if he pursue the honor himself, exhibiting no trace of holy merit, I leave that to your exact and paternal discernment. For I have made this request not because I have been suborned by a bribe or a gift, but freely and without reward. May the Lord our God, who has adorned your Paternity with evangelical and apostolic graces, grant you to the catholic Church as you pray even for my mediocrity.

50. To Theophanes *asekretis*

Behold, I have sent you the little book of secular proverbs, not without constraint, as you yourself can imagine, O friend of the Muses, since it was my intention to include in it many other proverbial precepts so as to fit out, as the proverb says, "a box of wisdom." Being, however, seized by my love of you, I have made the constraint desire, and, if I may express homerically my unintended zeal, "I have given willingly with unwilling mind." Do not, however, defer returning this, but, after multiplying 3 by 5, consent as you have undertaken, not to overstep the resultant number ⟨of days⟩. Farewell, and do not consign me further to the oblivion of oversight.

51. Νικηφόρῳ διακόνῳ

Ἅλας καὶ τράπεζαν μὴ παραβαίνειν φησὶν ἡ παροιμία. Σὺ δὲ καὶ πολλάκις ἡμῖν συναλισθεὶς λήθῃ τὴν παράβασιν ἔκλωσας, καὶ ταῦτα τῆς νοστίμου σου μεταδοὺς ἡμῖν οὐκ ὀλιγάκις φθογγῆς, ἡδυνούσης ψυχῆς αἰσθητήρια. Ἀλλ' ἔοικεν ὡς μῖσος συνέριθος γέγονεν, καὶ ἡ πρὸς σέ μου θαμινώτερον τοῦ ποδὸς εἰσαγωγὴ πλησμονὴν ἐμποιήσασα συνεξύφηνεν, καὶ φθόνου τηκεδὼν διέσπασεν, καὶ εἰς ῥακία τὴν θεοποίκιλτον ἡμῶν περιστολὴν κατ' ἐκεῖνον τὸν ὁμηρικὸν Ἶρον ἐλέπτυνεν, ὡς μόλις ἐπιγουνίδα φαίνειν καὶ τὴν αἰδῶ ἀμφικαλύπτειν κακῶς ἐπισυμβῆναι καὶ ὄφλειν πρὸς τῶν ἐπηρεάζειν ἐθελόντων θερσίτειον γέλωτα. Τί ταῦτα, καὶ μέχρι τίνος τῷ μοδίῳ τῆς σιγῆς ἐγκατακρύπτεις ἀλλ' οὐκ ἐπὶ τηλεσκόπου λυχνίας ἐπαίρῃ καὶ ἀναλάμπεις τὰ τῆς λογικῆς δᾳδουχίας πυρσεύματα; Τοιγαροῦν, εἰ καί τι τῶν ἀπηριθμημένων καὶ ὅσα τὸν τῆς ἀγάπης λύειν οἶδε θεσμὸν ἐμεσίτευσεν, δμηθήτω, καὶ τοὺς αἰτίους τῆς διαστάσεως ὁ αἰθὴς πέπλος, καθ' ἃ λέγεται, φλεξάτω καὶ πιμπράτω· νέα δὲ ἡμῖν ἠλάκατα θείας ἀγάπης στρωφάσθω καὶ ἄτρακτος καὶ ἐκ τῶν τοῦ θείου πνεύματος μηρυμάτων τῆς παλαιᾶς στοργῆς ἀναπηνιζέσθω θοἰμάτιον, ὡς ἂν θαλφθέντες ταῖς ὑμετέραις γλυκέσι προσρήσεσιν, τὴν ψυχρὰν ἀποτιναξαίμεθα τῆς ὀλιγω || 147 || *ρίας ἐπίκλυσιν.*

52. Μεθοδίῳ τῷ ἁγιωτάτῳ πατριάρχῃ

Εἰ μὴ πεπειράμην τῆς σῆς πρὸς τοὺς πενομένους, ὦ δέσποτα, δαψιλοῦς ἐπιδόσεως, ἦν ἂν ἐφ' ὑμῖν τὸ παροιμιῶδες ῥησείδιον ἐπιφθέγξασθαι, "μὴ εἴπῃς ἐπανελθὼν ἐπάνηκε καὶ αὔριον δώσω," καὶ τὴν τῆς

51: 1 *ἅλας – παραβαίνειν*: Zen. I.62; Diogen. II.11; Greg. Cypr. Mosq. II.25 || 6–7 *εἰς ῥακία – ἐλέπτυνεν*: cf. *Od.* 18.5 sqq. cf. *Il.* 9.158 || 8 *ἐπιγουνίδα φαίνειν*: *Od.* 18.74 || *τὴν αἰδῶ ἀμφικαλύπτειν*: *Il.* 2.262 || 9 *θερσίτειον γέλωτα*: cf. *Il.* 2.270 || 14 *αἰθὴς πέπλος*: Zen. I.33; Diogen. I.31; Apostol. I.81 || 15 *ἠλάκατα – στρωφάσθω*: cf. *Od.* 6.53 et al.

51: 3 post *φθογγῆς* verba *εἰς ῥακία τὴν θεοποίκιλτον ἡμῶν πε(ρι)στολὴν κατ' ἐκεῖνον τὸν ὁμηρικὸν* delevit manus recentior || 7 *ἴρον* V || 8 *φέρειν* V || 10 *ἐγκατακρύπτως* V || 11 *τηλεσκοποῦ* V || 14 *ὁ αἰθὴς* nos: *ὁ τῆς ἔφης* V || *φλεξάτο* V || 17 *ἀναπινιζέσθω θ' ὑμάτιον* V

52: 3 *μὴ εἴπῃς – δώσω*: Prov. 3.28 || 3–4 *τῆς Ἀκεσσαίου σελήνης*: Diogen. I.57; Apostol. I.90; XVI.44

51. To the deacon Nikephoros

The proverb tells us not to transgress against salt and table. Yet you who have often eaten at table with me have woven forgetfulness into your transgression, and this although you have often shared with me your succulent words that sweeten the senses of the soul. It seems, however, that hatred has become your helpmate, that my frequent visits to you have caused satiety to be produced, that wasting envy has severed and torn into rags my God-adorned garment, so that, as in the case of Homer's Irus, I am miserably reduced to exposing my thigh and barely covering my private parts so as to draw upon myself Thersitean laughter from those who wish to injure me. Why is that so, and how long will you conceal under a bushel of silence the rays of your intellectual torch instead of raising it on a conspicuous lampstand and shining forth? If, then, any of the circumstances I have enumerated such as are wont to break the law of love has caused this, let it be overcome and let the fiery veil, as the saying goes, burn and consume those responsible for our rift. Let new wool of sacred love be turned for us on distaff and spindle, and let the garment of our old affection be woven with the thread of the Holy Spirit, so that, comforted by your sweet salutations, I may escape the cold flood of neglect.

52. To the most holy patriarch Methodios

Had I not experienced, O lord, your abundant generosity to the poor, I would have addressed to you that proverbial locution, "Don't say, come back and I shall

Ἀκεσσαίου σελήνης, τὸ δὴ λεγόμενον, ἐπιφημίζειν ὑμῖν βραδυτῆτα. Ἀλλ' ἐπεὶ καὶ πεπείραμαι καὶ πολλάκις ἔπαθον, τοῦτο μὲν οὐ γράφω, καὶ εἰ γέγραφα, αἰτῶ δὲ καὶ αὖθις παθεῖν κατὰ τὸν τῆς προαιρέσεως ὑμῶν ἀμώμητον ἔλεον· ἀναγκαίη γὰρ ἐπείγει, καθ' Ὅμηρον, ὡς ἡ τῆς ἄνω ῥοπῆς ἐξεπίσταται νεῦσις· μὴ δὴ βραδύνοι ἡ πρὸς πάντας ὑμῶν ταχεῖα ἐπισκοπή, ὡς ἂν μάθοιμεν καὶ δι' ὧν προπεπόνθαμεν ἐκ τελείας ὑπάρχειν τὸ τῆς πατροσύνης ὑμῶν εἰς ἡμᾶς ἀγαθὸν προαιρέσεως.

53. Θεοφίλῳ διακόνῳ καὶ πρωτονοταρίῳ

Καὶ πρὸ τοῦ με πρὸς τὸ γράφειν ἐληλυθέναι, τὴν ὑμετέραν ἔδει τὰ καθ' ἡμᾶς ἀγαπητικὴν διάθεσιν διεξάγειν ἐπὶ τὸ βέλτιον· ἐπεὶ δὲ οὐ τοῦτο, νυσσομένην διαναστῆναι καὶ εἰς τὴν τοῦ δικαίου ἡμῖν συνάρασθαι εὐκρίνειαν. Ἤδη γὰρ σκοπὸς ἡμῖν τὸ περὶ τοῦ ἱεροῦ πτυκτίου, φημὶ δὴ τοῦ Εὐαγγελίου, ἀνακινῆσαι κεφάλαιον, ὅπερ ἔχων πεφώραται ὁ νυνὶ πρόεδρος Ἱεραπόλεως· ἐλπὶς γὰρ ἦν ἡμῖν ἀναμφίλεκτος ὡς αὐτὸς ἐπειχθήσεται εἰς τὴν τούτου ἀπόδοσιν καὶ μάλιστα ἐπιστειλάντων αὐτῷ, ἡνίκα καὶ ταῖς εἰσόδοις τοῦ τάφου ἑαυτὸν || 148 || φερόμενον ἔβλεπεν· ἀλλὰ ἐπεὶ λάθετο ἢ οὐκ ἐνόησεν, κατὰ τὴν ποίησιν, τῶν δὲ ἀλλοτρίων ἐρῶν τῶν οὐκ ἀνηκόντων ἀντέχεσθαι βούλεται, τῇ τοῦ δεσπότου καὶ κοινοῦ καθηγεμόνος ἡμῶν ὑπαχθήτω κρίσει· ἥτις, εὖ οἶδα, διεσμιλευμένως δραμεῖται μηδεμίαν ἐῶσα παρατροπὴν καὶ παρέγκλισιν λυμανεῖσθαι τὴν τοῦ δικαίου εὐθύτητα. Γράμμα τοιγαροῦν ἐχαράξαμεν πρὸς τὴν αὐτῆς ἀνυπέρβλητον ἱερότητα, ὅπερ ἐπιδοῦναι ἀξίωσον καὶ εὐμενῶς προσιδεῖν καθικέτευσον· καὶ εἴπερ τῆς ἐμῆς ἐλαχιστείας ἡ

---

7 *ἀναγκαίη – ἐπείγει*: *Il.* 6.85; *Od.* 19.73

52: 5 *πολλάκις*: *πο* with superscript ς V: *πολλὰ* G

53: 9 *λάθετο – ἐνόησεν*: *Il.* 9.537

53: 10 *ἐρῶ* V: corr. G || 11 *ὑμῶν* V: corr. G || 12 *ἔω σοῦ* V: corr. G || *παρέγκλησιν* V: correctionem proposuit G || 14 *ἀνυπόβλητον ἱερώτητα* V: corr. G || 15–16 *ἐλαχιστίας . . . φανηταί σοι* V: corr. G

give you tomorrow," and ascribed to you the slowness of the moon of Akessaios, as the saying goes. But since I have experienced it and have suffered on many occasions, I am not writing in those terms (even if I have in the past) but am asking again to be treated according to the perfect mercy of your inclination. For, to quote Homer, "constraint presses hard" on me, as the Highest knows well. Let not, therefore, your swift succor on behalf of everyone be delayed, that I may learn even by my previous experiences that your paternal goodwill toward me is of a perfect intention.

53. To Theophilos, deacon and *protonotarios*

Even before I had come to writing, your kindly self should have settled my affairs for the better; but since this has not happened, you should have bestirred yourself when pressed and helped me establish the clarity of justice. It is, indeed, my purpose now to raise the matter of the holy book, I mean, of course, the Gospel, which the present bishop of Hierapolis has been convicted of possessing. It was my undoubted hope that he himself would hasten to return it, especially in view of the fact that I wrote him when he was seeing himself being swept along toward the portals of the grave. But since "he forgot or did not notice" (as the Poet says) and, in his greed for other people's property, insists on clinging to what does not belong to him, let him be subjected to the judgment of our lord and common master—a judgment which, I am sure, will proceed meticulously and not allow the rectitude of justice to be spoiled by any diversion or deviation. And so I have penned a letter to his inimitable Holiness which, pray, you will see fit to give him and entreat him to consider favorably. If the presence of my humble self should seem necessary to you in this

παρουσία χρειώδης ἐν τούτῳ φανεῖταί σοι, παρέσομαι· εἰ δὲ καὶ ἄτερ ἡμῶν περαίνεται, καλῶς ποιεῖς ἀπαλλάσσων τῆς φευκτικῆς ἡμᾶς ἐνοχλήσεως.

54. Μεθοδίῳ *τῷ ἁγιωτάτῳ πατριάρχῃ*

Καὶ *πρὸς τίνα ἀπελεύσομαι, ἢ τὰ κατ' ἐμαυτὸν ἀναρτήσω, ἀλλ' οὐχὶ πρὸς σὲ τὸν ἰθύνοντα, τὸν τῆς δίκης ἐπίκουρον, τὸν εὐταλάντως ζυγοστατοῦντα τὴν τῶν ἱερῶν κανόνων ἀρρέπειαν, τὸν τοῦ δικαίου ἐπίσκοπον, τὸν μετὰ τῶν ἀδικουμένων γινόμενον, καὶ ἐξάγοντα τὴν ἐπιβάλλουσαν ἔνδικον ἑκάστῳ στάθμην ἀδεκάστῳ ψηφίσματι;* Ἀλλὰ *τί μοι τὸ προοιμιαζόμενον βούλεται;* Ὅτι *ὑμεῖς μὲν τοιοῦτοι· ἐγὼ δὲ τὴν ἐμήν, ὁποία τίς ἐστιν, ἀνακαλύψω τῆς δίκης ὑμῖν περιπέτειαν ἔχουσαν ὧδε.*

Βίβλος *πάλαι πεπόνηται ἐκ τῶν οἰκείων πόρων τῷ ἐμῷ γνησίῳ ὁμαίμονι τῆς ἁγιαστικῆς τετρακτύος τῶν* Εὐαγγελιστῶν, || 149 || *ἥν μοι καὶ πρὸς τὰ ἐκεῖ μεταθέμενος, οἷα δή τινα κλῆρον ἀναφαίρετον, εἴασεν· ἧς μᾶλλον εἰχόμην, ἢ* Κροῖσος *ὁ τῶν* Λυδίων *ἔστεργε χρημάτων ἀπόδεσμον· οὐδὲ γὰρ ἀργύρου μοι καὶ χρυσοῦ κρῆναι, κατὰ τὴν παροιμίαν, ταύτης ἐπίπροσθε προετέθειντο, οὐδὲ λίθων ἐκ* Σουφεὶρ *διαύγειαι προετετίμηντο, οὐδὲ παντὸς ἄλλου τοῦ τὴν ἐμὴν ψυχὴν περιβλέπτου λαμπρότης ἐφήδυνε κτήματος, τῶν ἐν ἐλπίδι μοι θησαυρῶν ἐν αὐτῇ κειμένων, οἳ πρὸς τὸ ἔσχατον ἀνάγουσιν ὀρεκτὸν καὶ εἰς ὃ πᾶσα σπουδαίου ἔφεσις ἵσταται.* Ταύτην *ὁ ἐν μεθέξει τῆς μακαρίας λήξεως* Στέφανος, *ὃς ἐν τοῖς βασιλικοῖς ὑπογραφεῦσι τὸ τηνικάδε προέλαμπε, πρὸς μεταβολὴν αἰτήσας εἴληφεν· ὁ δέ γ' ἔχρησε* Μιχαὴλ *τῷ ἀοιδίμῳ ἱεράρχῃ* Συνάδων, *καὶ εἶτα, βραδυτῆτος ἐπιταθείσης καὶ μὴ ὅπερ εἴληφεν ἀποδιδούς, θαμινώτερον ὑφ' ἡμῶν νυσσόμενος μακροθυμίας ἔνδοσιν ᾔτει, ὡς ἤδη ἐν κόλποις ἐχόντων ἡμῶν τὸ ζητούμενον.* Ἐφ'

---

17 *ἡμᾶς* (deletum) *τῆς φευτικῆς ἡμᾶς* V: *ἡμᾶς τῆς φευκτικῆς* G

54: 13 *ἀργύρου – κρῆναι*: Diogen. II.93; Diogen. Vind. I.82 || 14 *λίθων ἐκ Σουφεὶρ*: cf. Is. 13.12; To. 13.17

54: 1 *αὖτήσω* V: *ἀναθήσω* G || 4 *γιγνόμενον* G || 10 *ἁγιαστικῆς* scripsi: *αἶτιατικῆς* V || 12 *ἠα κρῦσος* V: corr. G || 14 *διαυγεῖαι* V: corr. G || 22 *ἀπεδίδου* V

matter, I shall attend; but if it can be accomplished without me, you will do well to free me from an undesirable trouble.

54. To Methodios, the most holy patriarch

To whom shall I have recourse or entrust my affairs if not to you, the director, the guardian of justice, who balance impartially the scales of the holy canons, the overseer of right, who stand beside the wronged and with an equitable vote call forth for every man the just measure that is appropriate? But what is the meaning of my preamble? That you are indeed such a man; as for me, I shall disclose to you the nature of my judicial affair, which is the following.

A book of the fourfold holy Gospels was once made at the expense of my own brother; and when he passed to the other world, he bequeathed it to me as an inalienable heritage. I clung to it more than Croesus of Lydia loved his chest of money; for I preferred to it neither streams of silver and gold (as the proverb has it) nor did I value more highly the glittering gems of Ophir, nor did the splendor of any other conspicuous possession more delight my soul, since the treasures of which I am hopeful are stored up therein—treasures that lead up to the ultimate object of desire, which every zealous man strives to attain. This book Stephen (now transported to the realm of the blessed), who at that time was conspicuous among the imperial secretaries, requested and received for the purpose of emendation; and he lent it to Michael, the celebrated bishop of Synada, who, after much delay, did not return what he had taken and, on being frequently prompted by me, asked for a measure of patience inasmuch as I already had in my grasp that which I sought. Under these circumstances I showed patience and received no benefit; for death fell on him unexpectedly

ᾧ τὸ μακρόθυμον ἐνδειξάμενοι καὶ μηδὲν ἀπωνάμενοι (θάνατος γὰρ ἀπρόοπτος ἐπιπεσών, πρὸς τὴν ἐκεῖ τῶν βεβιωμένων τοῦτον ἐκάλει διάγνωσιν) ἀπωρφανίσθημεν καὶ τοῦ ἀνδρὸς καὶ τοῦ ἡμῖν ἐπέκεινα παντὸς ὄλβου στεργομένου, δέσποτα, θησαυρίσματος. Καὶ νῦν, καθ' ἃ τοῖς ὠσὶν ἡμῶν φήμη τις λόγον διάρασα ‖ 150 ‖ οὐκ ἀπαισίως διήχησεν, ὑπὸ τοῦ ἁγιωτάτου τῆς Ἱεραπολιτῶν ἐκκλησίας προέδρου κατέχεται, καὶ οὐ μέλει αὐτῷ τῆς ἀποδόσεως, ἀλλὰ βόσκεται κεναῖς ἐλπίσι, τὸ δὴ λεγόμενον, τὸ ἀλλότριον παρακερδαίνειν οἰόμενος καὶ τὸ μὴ προσῆκον αὐτῷ κατακληροῦσθαι μὴ καλῶς ἱμειρόμενος. Ἀλλ' οὐκ ἐπιτεύξεται, αἰδοῖ τῆς ἱερᾶς τιμῆς, δόλιος θήρας. Τίς γάρ μοι κλῆρος ἢ μερὶς μετ' αὐτοῦ, ἢ ποῖον κῆδος, ὅ με τούτῳ πρὸς ἀγχιστείαν συνάψειε; Οὐ γὰρ μὴ κληρονομήσει ὁ ὑπόκλοπος καὶ νόθος μετὰ τοῦ υἱοῦ τοῦ ἀληθινοῦ καὶ ὄντως νομίμου υἱοῦ. Μὴ τοίνυν παραχωρείσθω τὸ μὴ ἴδιον τῷ ξένῳ, ἀλλ' ἡ ἀπαρέγκλιτος τῆς ὁσίας πατροσύνης ὑμῶν εὐθύτης, ἀπαρεγχείρητον τὸ τοῦ δικαίου διασῴζουσα κράτος, μὴ στερηθῆναι ἡμᾶς τοῦ οἰκείου κατανεύσειε κτήματος. Ἴσμεν γὰρ αὐτὴν τοῖς εὐαγγελικοῖς τε καὶ ἀποστολικοῖς καὶ πατρικοῖς δικαιώμασιν καὶ ἐντάλμασιν ἱερῶς καλλυνομένην, καὶ ἐν ταῖς ὁσίαις καὶ θείαις αὐτῆς ἐπικρίσεσιν τὴν τοῦ δικαίου προτιμᾶν σεβασμιότητα.

55. Τῷ αὐτῷ

Οὐδὲν εἰ μὴ τὸ προθυμεῖσθαι τοῦ μεγέθους ἀξιοῦσθαι τῆς ἱερᾶς ὑμῶν πατρότητος θυμῆρες ἡμῖν καταφαίνεται καὶ εἰ κατόπιν ἑορτῆς, κατὰ τὴν θύραθε παροιμίαν, διὰ τὴν εὐτέλειαν ἥκομεν. Τοῦτο γοῦν ἀνθ' ἱκετηρίας ἐκτενοῦς προβαλλόμεθα καὶ ὥσπερ τῶν ἰχνῶν ὑμῶν ἀπρὶξ ἐπειλήμμεθα, ὡς ἂν ‖ 151 ‖ τῆς ἁγιαστικῆς παρουσίας σου, δέσποτα,

---

30 *βόσκεται – ἐλπίσι*: Apostol. III.1[d]; cf. Append. I.8 ‖ 32–33 *οὐκ ἐπιτεύξεται – θήρας*: Prov. 12.27 ‖ 33 *κλῆρος ἢ μερὶς*: cf. Acta 8.21; Col. 1.12 ‖ 34–36 *οὐ γὰρ – νομίμου υἱοῦ*: cf. Gen. 21.10; Gal. 4.30

---

30 *μέλει* G: *μᾶλλον* V ‖ 34 *τοῦτο* V: corr. G ‖ 35 *κληρονομήση* V: corr. G ‖ 37 *ἢ ἀπαρέγκλητος* V: corr. G ‖ *ἡμῶν* V: corr. G ‖ 40 *καλλυομενην* V: corr. G

55: 2 *κατόπιν ἑορτῆς*: Diogen. V.73; Greg. Cypr. Mosq. III.89; Apostol. IX.44; XIV.6; Karathanasis 171

55: 1 *τὸ* G[2]: *τῷ* V ‖ 2 *εἰ*: *ἡ* V ‖ 3 *γ'οῦν* V: corr. G ‖ 5 *ἐπιλλήμεθα* V: corr. G

and summoned him yonder to give account of his actions in life. I was deprived both of the man and, my lord, of the treasure that I loved more than all bliss. And now, according to a rumor that gave rise to words and has sounded in my ears in no ill-omened manner, it is in the possession of the most holy bishop of Hierapolis who does not care to return it, but feeds on empty hopes (as the saying goes) in the belief that he will gain another man's property, basely desiring that what is not his should be allotted to him. But "the deceitful man will not succeed in the hunt" through the respect that is due to the holy office. For what lot or portion do I have with him or what connection that would link me to him in kinship? Indeed, the deceiver and the bastard will not inherit along with the legitimate and truly lawful son. Let not, therefore, that which is not his be surrendered to the stranger, but may the unswerving rectitude of your holy Fatherhood, in maintaining inviolate the might of justice, not permit me to be deprived of my own property. For I know that you are adorned in holy fashion with the evangelic, apostolic, and patristic ordinances and precepts and that you take heed of the honor of justice in your holy and divine decisions.

55. To the same

Nothing appears pleasanter to me than to be eager of being deemed worthy of the grandeur of your holy Fatherhood, even if, because of my poverty, I have come the day after the fair, as the secular proverb has it. So much, at least, I am proffering instead of a lengthy supplication and, as it were, I am grasping tightly your feet so as

τύχοιμεν· ἧς μὴ ζημιώσῃς τοὺς παῖδάς σου, κερδησείοντας ἐντεῦθεν ψυχικῆς ἀρετῆς μεγίστην ἐπίδοσιν.

56. Κωνσταντινακίῳ κουράτορι

Μετὰ τοῦ μυρία τάλαντα τῷ οἰκείῳ δεσπότῃ ⟨ὀφείλοντος⟩ οἰκέτου τὴν σὴν εὐσπλαγχνίαν δυσωπῆσαι προήχθημεν. Μακροθύμησον ἐφ' ἡμῖν, ἀπορίᾳ πολλῇ πιεζομένοις, καὶ πᾶν τὸ ὀφειλόμενον οὐκ εἰς μακρὰν ἀπολήψῃ· ὁ γὰρ πράκτωρ πικρὸς καὶ δριμὺς ἡμῖν ἐπιφύεται ἀπειλὴν σφοδρὰν ἐπισείων, εἰ μὴ τὴν ὀφειλὴν ἐκτίσαιμεν τάχιον· ὥστε εἰ τὸ μακρόθυμον καὶ εὐμενὲς ὑμῶν τοῦτον οὐ καταιδέσει, τὰ φυλακῆς καὶ δεσμῶν πειραθείημεν, καὶ ὅσα ἐκεῖνος ὁ πονηρὸς ὑποστησαίμεθα δοῦλος, ἕως ἀποδῶμεν τὸν ἔσχατον κοδράντην· ἀλλὰ τεθαρρήκαμεν καὶ ἐλπὶς ἡμῖν ἐστιν ἀνενδοίαστος μηδὲν ὧν οὗτος ἀπειλεῖ καὶ ἡμεῖς ἀπευχόμεθα πείσεσθαι, τυχεῖν δὲ ὧν ᾐτήκαμεν παρὰ τῆς σῆς φιλοσυμπαθοῦς καὶ ἠπίας χρηστότητος.

57. Κωνσταντίνῳ φοιτητῇ ἄρτι τῆς αἰχμαλωσίας ἀνακληθέντι

Πῶς ἡμᾶς ᾤου διατεθεῖσθαι, φίλτατε παίδων, ἡνίκα τὴν ἐπ' ἀλλοδαπεῖς καὶ ἀλλοθρόους ἄνδρας πικρὰν καὶ ἀνήμερον ἀπαγωγὴν δοριάλωτος ἤνυες; Ἆρ' ὡς ἔκ τινος ληθεδόνος πεπωκότας καὶ φρενῶν ἡμοιρηκότας τῆς σῆς ἐκλελῆσθαι φιλικῆς διαθέσεως; Ἢ λύπῃ δυσλύτῳ

---

6 ἧς nos: ἣν V ‖ ζημιῶσαι V: ζημίωσαι G

56: 1–2 *μυρία – οἰκέτου*: cf. Mt. 18.24 sqq. ‖ 8 *ἀποδῶμεν – κοδράντην*: Mt. 5.26

56: 9 *ἀνενδύαστος* V: corr. G ‖ *μηδ' ὧν* V: corr. G

57: 2 *ἀλλοθρόους ἄνδρας*: cf. *Od.* 1.183; 3.302; 14.43; 15.453

57: 1 *ἀλλοδαπ* V ‖ 2 *ἀνήμερον*: *–νη* supra lineam scripsit V ‖ *δοριάλωτον* V ‖ 3 *ληθαιδόνος πεποκότας* V

to obtain your sanctifying presence. Do not deprive your children of it, who stand to gain thereby a great increase in spiritual virtue.

56. To the curator Konstantinakios

Like that servant who owed his master ten thousand talents, I have come to implore your mercy. Have patience with me who am oppressed by great poverty, and you will soon recover my entire debt. For the bailiff pursues me with bitterness and harshness, holding out a grievous threat unless I discharge my debt speedily. If, therefore, your gentle patience does not put this man to shame, I may experience imprisonment and chains and suffer the same fate as that wicked servant until I have paid the last farthing. I am convinced, however, and have indubitable hope that I shall not undergo any of those things that he threatens me with and that I wish to avert, but, instead, shall obtain my request from your compassionate and gentle Goodness.

57. To Constantine, his pupil, lately recalled from captivity

What do you think my feelings were, dearest of children, when you endured, a captive, that bitter and harsh deportation among foreign and alien men? Had I drunk, as it were, from some Lethe and lost my wits so as to forget utterly that you were

συνδεομένους κοπετὸν σὺν ὑμῖν ἀπεργάζεσθαι καὶ θερμὸν ἀφιέντας ἐκ καρδίας δάκρυον παρειὰς λελουμένας ἐκμάττειν || 152 || *καὶ τὴν ψυχὴν ἀπολέγεσθαι, οὐκ ἀνεχομένους φέρειν ἀδακρυτὶ τὴν σὴν ἀνεπίληστον στέρησιν; Ἀλλ' εἰ τὸ δεύτερον, καλῶς ὑπολαμβάνειν εἶχες καὶ λίαν ὀρθῶς· οὕτω γὰρ εἶχεν τότε τὰ καθ' ἡμᾶς καὶ ἐν τούτοις διέκειτο· πᾶσα γὰρ αἴσθησις ἡμῶν ἐπιεικῶς κατηλγύνετο καὶ τῶν οἰκείων ἀντιλήψεων διεσφάλλετο, ἐν τριόδῳ, κατὰ τὴν παροιμίαν, ἀπορίας ὑπάρχουσα, ποίοις ἆρα* Κωνσταντῖνος *κακοῖς συνεκύρησεν· ἆρ' ὑπὸ φονικῆς μαχαίρας κατείργασται; Ἆρα δουλείᾳ βαρυπενθεῖ κακοήθους δεσπότου μεμοίραται; Ἆρα δεσμοῖς ἀϊδίοις ὑπ' ἀπειλῆς, ὡς ὁ καιρὸς ἐδίδου, πεπέδηται; Ἆρα βλέμματι βλοσυρῷ καὶ δειμαίνοντι ἀντωπεῖν ἢ καὶ ὅλως ὄμμα κινεῖν ἢ διανοίγειν τεθάρρηκεν; Ἆρα γλώσσῃ φρικτὸν βαρβαριζούσῃ τὸν ἄλογον ὑποκρίνεται;* Καὶ *ἁπαξαπλῶς ἀνεμετρεῖτό μοι καὶ ἡ τῶν κακούντων ὠμότης καὶ ἡ σὴ δριμυτάτη καὶ ἀσυμπαθὴς ἀπάνθρωπος κόλασις.* Καὶ *ἐπεὶ ταῦτα καὶ οὕτω διενεγκεῖν ἡμᾶς τῶν ὑμετέρων δυσχερειῶν ἀνέγνωκας, πῶς ἤδη τοῦ κρείττονος οἰκτιρμοῖς ἀφάτοις τὴν ἀνάκλησιν ὑμῖν ἐνεργήσαντος, καὶ τῶν ἀπηριθμημένων ἀνιαρῶν ὑπεκλύσαντος, ἄλλοι, καὶ τυχὸν μὴ πονήσαντες, τῆς ἐραστῆς ἐμοὶ θέας δαψιλῶς ἀπολαύουσιν, καίτοι τὴν ἄλλως ἡμεῖς τῷ ζόφῳ τῆς κατηφείας νυκτομαχήσαντες, ἅτε περικαθάρματα καὶ περιψήματα παρεβλέμμεθα, καὶ πάντων ἐφ' ὑμῖν ἑόρτιον κροτούντων ὑμέναιον, ἡμεῖς θρηνητικῶς ἀλαλάζομεν; Ἀλλ' ἐπὶ καιρο*|| 153 ||*ῦ τὸ τῆς θύραθε παροιμίας καλὸν ἐπειπεῖν, γόνυ κνημῖδος ἔγγιον· πάντες γὰρ ὑμῖν εἰς ἀδελφοὺς καὶ οἰκείους ἐγνησιώθησαν· ἡμεῖς δὲ ξένοι καὶ νόθοι καὶ πόρρωθεν ἥκοντες λελογίσμεθα. Ἀλλ' εὖ ἧκας· τὸ σὲ γὰρ ἀνασεσῶσθαι καὶ ὑπὲρ ἐλπίδα πᾶσαν τῆς ἐθνικῆς ἀναλελῦσθαι βίας καὶ πρὸς τὰ πάτρια ἤθη καὶ θεῷ φίλα καὶ ἡμῖν ἀναδραμεῖν οὐ τὸ τυχὸν ἡμῖν προεξένησε παρηγόρημα· ὥστε καὶ μήτε θεασάμενοί σε στέργομεν.* Καὶ *εἰ τούτου τύχοιμεν τὴν εἰς σὲ στοργὴν ἐπὶ πλεῖον αὐξήσαιμεν.*

6–7 *τὴν ψυχὴν ἀπολέγεσθαι*: cf. Jon. 4.8 || 11 *ἐν τριόδῳ*: Zen. III.78; Greg. Cypr. Mosq. III.14 || 14 *δεσμοῖς ἀϊδίοις*: Iud. 6 || 24 *περικαθάρματα καὶ περιψήματα*: 1 Cor 4.13 || 27 *γόνυ – ἔγγιον*: Zen. III.2; Diogen. III.78; Greg. Cypr. Mosq. II.50

---

5 *ἡμῖν* V || 6 *ἐκμάττει* V: corr. G || 10 *κατηλγυναιτο* V: corr. G || 12 *συνεκήρυσεν* V: corr. G || 15 *ἀντοπειν* V: corr. G || 16 *κυ(εῖν) η διανυχειν* V: corr. G || 17 *ἀναμετρεῖτο* V: *ἀναμετρείτω* G[1]: *ἀνεμετρεῖτο* proposuit G[2] || 20 *τοῦ* G: *τὰς* V || 22 *ἐραστῆς* G: *ερ(ασ)ης* V || 22–23 *θεᾶς* vel *θεασ(ων)* . . . *ἀπόλαυσιν* V: corr. G || 23 *καίτοι* Polemis: *καὶ οἱ* V || 24 *παρεβεβλέμμεθα* proposuit G || 27 *ἄγγιον* V || 28 *πόρροθ(εν)* V: corr. G || 31 *προεξένισε* V: corr. G || 32 *θεαμένοι* V: corr. G || 32 *τοῦτο* V: corr. G

57

dear? Or, shackled with indissoluble grief, was I raising a lamentation along with you and, shedding hot tears from my heart, was I wiping moist cheeks and renouncing my life since I could not suffer without weeping my unforgettable deprivation of you? If you supposed the latter, you were perfectly right and correct. For such indeed was my state and those were my feelings. Nearly all my senses were utterly bruised and lost their perception, being, as the proverb says, at the crossroads of perplexity. What misfortunes had Constantine met? Had he been slaughtered by a murderous dagger? Had he fallen to the wearisome slavery of an evil-minded master? Had he been bound under some threat with everlasting chains, as misfortune had it? Had he the courage to withstand a grim and terrible gaze, indeed to move his eyes about or even open them? Does he pretend to be dumb before a dreadful barbaric tongue? In brief, I went over both the cruelty of your oppressors and your most harsh, merciless, and inhuman torment. And since you realized that I have borne to such an extent your hardships, how is it that now, when the Highest in His ineffable compassion has accomplished your recall and freed you from the aforementioned miseries, others, who perhaps have not grieved, are enjoying freely the sight that is so dear to me, while I, who have fought vainly in the gloom of dejection, have been scorned as "filth" and "offscouring"; and whereas everyone raises a festive song for you, I am crying out in mourning? The secular proverb comes well to hand, "The knee is nearer than the shin"; for everyone else has won kinship with you as brother and friend, while I am considered a stranger, a bastard, and one come from afar. Welcome, in any case. For the fact that you have been saved, that you have been freed against all expectation from alien violence and have returned to your ancestral home that is dear to God and to me, has caused me no small consolation. And so, even though I have not seen you, I love you. And if I should be vouchsafed that also, my love for you would increase all the more.

58. Λέοντι πρωτοσπαθαρίῳ, ἀσηκρῆτις

Εἶδον πῶς τὴν λύσιν εὑρίσκουσιν αἱ πρὸς ὑμᾶς ἱκετεῖαι καὶ τῆς ἀντιληπτικῆς μεθέξεως ὑμῶν ὀξεῖαν ἀποφέρονται τὴν περαίωσιν. Οὐδὲ γὰρ εἴπερ ἐν χερσὶ τῶν δεομένων ἦν τὰ αἰτούμενα, τοιαύτης ἔτυχεν ἐπτερωμένης, ὡς εἰπεῖν, ἑτοιμότητος· νυνὶ δέ, ⟨οὐ⟩ καθ' ἃ λέγεται, ἅμα ἔπος ἅμα ἔργον τὰ καθ' ἡμᾶς ἐξανύεται· καὶ ταῦτα οὐ τῆς ὑμετέρας ἀλήπτου ψυχῆς καθαπτόμενος φθέγγομαι· μηδὲ γὰρ οὕτω μανείην, ἢ φρενῶν ἔξω πέσοιμι· οἶδα γάρ, ἐκθύμως εἰς τὴν ἐμὴν συμπάθειαν ἔδραμες εἰ καὶ μὴ κατέλαβες· ὃ δέ με πρὸς ἀφασίαν κινεῖ καὶ ὅλως ἐξίστησιν καὶ πρὸς βυθὸν ἀπορίας συγκάτεισιν, οὐ σιγῇ παραδοῦναι βεβούλημαι. Τί δὲ τοῦτό ἐστιν ἐρῶ.

Πάντες οἱ ἀπὸ ἡλίου ἐκβολῶν καὶ μέχρι Ἡρακλείων στηλῶν καὶ Γαδείρων, πράγμασιν ἀδοκήτοις καὶ συμφοραῖς πιεζόμενοι, ὑπὸ τὴν θαλπικὴν τοῦ κοινοῦ προστάτου ἡμῶν τε μετὰ θεὸν καὶ πολλῶν καὶ πάντων καταφεύγουσιν πτέρυγα, καὶ τῇ αὐτοῦ δικαιοπραγίᾳ || 154 || τοὺς ἑαυτῶν οἰκτισμοὺς ἐπιρρίπτουσιν, ὡς ἂν τῶν ἐλπιζομένων ἀπρὶξ περιδράξαιντο· οὕς, κατὰ τὴν θύραθε παροιμίαν, ἑστῶσιν ὠσὶν καὶ κεχηνόσιν ὄμμασιν προσανέχων καὶ εὐμενείᾳ βαθυτάτῃ δεχόμενος, ταῖς αὐτοῦ ἀδεκάστοις σοφαῖς ἐπικρίσεσιν, οἷα σφραγῖδι, τὰς πάντων στραγγαλιώδεις διαφορὰς εὐλύτως ἐπιδεσμεῖ καὶ χαρίεντας πρὸς τὰ ἑαυτῶν ἤθη παλινδρομεῖν ἐπαφίησιν, ὡς ἤδη τὸ ζητούμενον ἀπαράγραφον ἔχοντας· οὐδὲ εἴποτέ τινος αἰτήσεως διακούσοι καὶ ταύτης ὑπ' ἐντροπῆς καλυπτομένου προφερομένης ὡς περικάθαρμα καὶ περίψημα καὶ βδελυκτὸν ἀποτρόπαιον ἥγηται. Τῇ γὰρ πενιχρότητι καὶ εὐτελείᾳ μου προσέχων, ⟨διατί⟩ τῆς αὐτοῦ κηδεμονίας ἀλλοτριοῖ καὶ ἀνάξιον τίθεται, δέον ὡς ἠπορημένῳ διὰ θεὸν ἐπικουρεῖν, ⟨καὶ⟩ μακραῖς ἐλπίσι θαρρεῖν ἐγκελεύεται; Ἢ οὐ μέμνῃ ὅτι με τῆς ἐν ἀρχῇ μοναδικῆς ἡσυχίας αὐτοὶ κατεσπάσατε, Ὀλυμπίαθεν ἀφελκύσαντες, καὶ οὐ τοῦτο μόνον, ἀλλὰ καὶ ὑπ' ἐνδείας ἐάσαντες καταπαίζεσθαι, ὡς καὶ αὐτῶν τῶν τοῦ ἀσώτου κερατίων, ἧ φησιν ἡ κυρία ῥῆσις, ἱμειρόμενον ἀπο-

---

58: 4–5 *ἅμα ἔπος ἅμα ἔργον*: Zen. I.77; Diogen. Vind. I.36; Karathanasis 109 || 16 *ἑστῶσιν ὠσὶν*: Diogen. VIII.74; Diogen. Vind. III.97; Mantiss. Prov. III.51 || 22 *περικάθαρμα καὶ περίψημα*: 1 Cor 4.13 || 29 *τῶν τοῦ ἀσώτου κερατίων*: cf. Lc 15.16

58: 1 *εἶδ̑* V: *εἶδες* G || *ἡμᾶς* V || 1–2 an *τῇ ἀντιληπτικῇ μεθέξει* scribendum? || 5 *ἔπος* G: *ἵππος* V || *ὑμᾶς* V || 7 *ἐκθύμως ⟨ὅτι⟩* G || 9 *συγκάτεισιν*: *συγκαθίησιν* sugg. Duffy || 15 *οἰκτιρμοὺς* V || 18 *αὐτοῦ* V || 21 *ἐν ουδε* V: *⟨καὶ⟩ οὐδὲ* G || 23 *βδελλυκτον* V || 24 *μὴ* ante *προσέχων* supplevit G || 26 *ἐκκελεύεται* V

58. To Leo *protospatharios, asekretis*

I have seen how supplications addressed to you are resolved and receive a swift fulfillment by your helping participation. Nay, even if the object of the request were in the grasp of the petitioners, would it have won, if I may say so, such winged readiness. Now, however, my affairs are not being settled, according to the saying, "no sooner said than done"; and this I declare not so as to upbraid your unattainable spirit, for I would not be so insane or senseless ⟨as to do so⟩. Indeed, I know, you hastened ardently to show sympathy to me, even if you did not succeed. I do not wish, however, to pass over in silence the circumstance that moves me to speechlessness, astonishes me altogether, and plunges me into the depth of despondency. I shall explain what it is.

All men, from the rising sun to the Pillars of Hercules and Cadiz, when they are pressed hard by unexpected troubles and misfortunes, take shelter under the warm wing of the common protector (after God) of ourselves and many, indeed all others, and cast their lamentations upon his justice so as to grasp firmly what they desire. Awaiting them with ears pricked up and eyes wide open (as the secular proverb says) and receiving them with the deepest goodwill, he readily binds up everyone's tortuous differences by his impartial and wise decisions as with a seal, and lets them return happily to their own homes as if they already held what they sought without exception. Nor, if he ever hears of a petition, even one put forward by a man who covers himself up in shame, does he consider it as "filth" and "offscouring" and an ill-omened abomination. Being, therefore, aware of my poverty and indigence, why does he deprive me of his protection and regard me as unworthy (whereas he ought to help me for the sake of God as one needy) and bid me have confidence in distant hopes? Do you not, indeed, remember that you yourselves drew me away from my previous monastic quietude and dragged me down from Olympus? Not only that, but you also allowed me to be made a mockery through indigence to the extent that I longed to taste, like the prodigal, the fruit of the carob tree, as the Lord's saying has

γεύσεσθαι; Πῶς *ταῦτα, καὶ διατί, ἀνθ' ὧν ἔδει με ταῖς πολυτρόποις εὐποιΐαις ἐπιεικῶς ἐναβρύνεσθαι, πένομαι καὶ τηκεδόνι λιμῶν περισφίγγομαι;* Ἀλλ' *ἐμὲ μέν, οὕτω δόξαν, ταλαιπωρεῖσθαι χρεών· δειναῖς γὰρ ἁμαρτίαις ἑαυτὸν περιέπειρα, αἵ με καὶ τῆς ἐντεῦθεν εὐπαθείας στερήσουσι καὶ τῆς ἐκεῖθεν δυσπραγίας ἐπιδαψιλεύσονται τὴν ἀντίδοσιν· ὑμᾶς δὲ ταῖς μεγίσταις κατ' ἀξίαν ἀξίαις καὶ τιμαῖς ἐμπρέπειν εὐδοκήσοι θεὸς πολυχρονίοις μακρότησι* ‖ 155 ‖ *καὶ μετὰ τῆς αὐτῆς δόξης τε καὶ φαιδρότητος τῇ ἄνω παρεστάναι μακραίωνι καταξιώσοι λαμπρότητι.*

59. Νι*κηφόρῳ χαρτοφύλακι*

Οἶδ' *ὅτι καθάψῃ μου, καὶ δὴ σιωπῶν, ἐκεῖνο προσφυῶς ὑπειπὼν τὸ ῥησίδιον εὐριπίδειον· σίγα σίγα λεπτὸν ἴχνος ἀρβύλης, ὃ καὶ κατὰ καιρὸν ἐρεῖς τὸ προαλὲς καὶ κολοιῶδες τῆς ἐμῆς γλωσσαλγίας ἐλέγχων· ἐγὼ δέ, διακόνῳ τῷ γράμματι χρώμενος τούτῳ, καί μοι, ἐρῶ, ἐξαύδα, μὴ κεῦθε νόῳ, ἵνα σοῦ τῆς πρὸς ἡμᾶς σιωπῆς ἐπιγνῶμεν ἐπιεικῶς τὸ πολύφωνον.*

60. Νι*κηφόρῳ διακόνῳ*

Εἴπερ *ὅλως ἔγνωκας ὡς ἔχομέν τι κατὰ σοῦ καὶ πονήρως διακείμεθα, ἔδει σε, κατὰ τὴν ἐντολήν, τῷ θυσιαστηρίῳ προσαφεῖναι τὸ δῶρόν σου καὶ τὴν πρὸς τὸν ἀδελφὸν καταλλαγὴν ἐμπορεύσασθαι.* Ἀλλ'

---

31 *τηκεδονη* V: corr. G ‖ 37 *φαιδρότητος* in marg. loco *λαμπρότητος* quod in textu scriptum est ‖ *καταξιώσει* V: corr. G

59: 2 *σίγα σίγα – ἀρβύλης*: Eur. *Or.* 140 ‖ 4–5 *ἐξαύδα – νόῳ*: *Il.* 1.363

59: 1 *ἐκεῖνος* V: corr. G ‖ 2 *ρησίδειον* V: *ῥησείδιον* G ‖ 4 *διωκωνω* V: corr. G ‖ *τουτο καὶ μου* V: corr. G ‖ 5 *επιεικ(ου)* V: corr. G

60: 2–3 *τῷ θυσαστηρίῳ – ἐμπορεύσασθαι*: cf. Mt. 5.23–24

60: 2 *προσαφῆναι* V

it. How and why is it that I am poor and pressed hard by wasting hunger, whereas I ought to be enjoying pretty well all manner of benefit? But since it has been so decreed, it is needful that I should suffer hardship; for I have become entangled in terrible sins which will both deprive me of well-being down here and repay me with abundant misery over there. As for you, may God see fit that for a length of many years you remain conspicuous in the greatest dignities and honors, which you deserve, and make you worthy to attain the eternal brilliancy of heaven with the same glory and splendor.

59. To Nikephoros the *chartophylax*

I know that even as you keep silent you will upbraid me by appropriately referring to that short saying of Euripides, "Silence, silence, let the point of your boot ⟨tread softly⟩," which you will quote in season as you censure the daw-like rashness of my garrulity. I, however, shall press this letter into my service by saying, "Speak out to me, hide it not in your mind," that I may fairly recognize the loquaciousness of your silence with respect to me.

60. To the deacon Nikephoros

If you had any knowledge that I had aught against you and was badly disposed toward you, you should, according to the commandment, have left your gift before the altar and obtained your reconciliation with your brother. But, as God can see and

ὡς θεὸς ἐφορᾷ καὶ τὸ τῆς συνειδήσεως κριτήριον ἀνενδοιάστως μαρτύρεται, οὐκ ἀνέβη διαλογισμὸς ἐν τῇ καρδίᾳ ἡμῶν κατὰ τῆς σῆς ὑπολήψεως· καὶ πῶς διεκρίθης, μονιοῦ δίκην, ἐπὶ τοσοῦτον ἐξ ἡμῶν ἠπορήμεθα· καὶ γὰρ νόσῳ μοχθηρᾷ προσπαλαίσαντες, ὡς μικροῦ, κατὰ τὴν παροιμίαν, διὰ δακτυλίου ἑλκυσθῆναι, καὶ παρὰ πολλῶν τῶν τὴν κυρίαν φωνὴν πληροῦν εἰδότων πολλάκις τημεληθέντες, ἥκιστα παρὰ τῆς σῆς εὐμενοῦς ῥοπῆς ἐπεσκέμμεθα. Ἀλλὰ δὴ καί τινες ὑπὸ φήμης αἰρόμενοι, δι' ἐξοδίου ἐκφορᾶς ἡμᾶς τῷ θανάτῳ προέπεμψαν· || 156 || *καὶ οὐδὲ σὺν αὐτοῖς σε τὰ πρὸς κηδείαν ἡμῶν ἔγνωμεν ἀπεργάσασθαι· καὶ λέγομεν ὡς τοῖς μισοῦσιν ἡμᾶς προσέθου, καὶ τούτοις ἐπιβοηθῶν τῇ φιλίᾳ τῇ πρὸς ἡμᾶς ἠσυνθέτηκας, ὃ μὴ γένοιτο, μηδ' εἰς ἐχθρῶν κεφαλὰς διαβῇ τὸ βλάσφημον, εἰ καὶ λήθη ποσῶς μεσιτεύσασα τοῦτο τοπάζειν δίδωσι.* Θ*άρσει τοιγαροῦν ὡς οὐδὲ τοῖς περιστείλασιν ἡμᾶς τῷ τάφῳ συνέδραμες· ἢ γὰρ ἂν ἐπιτυμβίους ἐλέγους ἡμῶν ἐπεμέτρησας καὶ στίχον ἐπικὸν ἑξάτονον ἔτεμες ⟨καὶ⟩ ἰωνικῷ μείζονι συμπλέξας ἐμμέτρως ἐλάττονα, μέλος ᾖσας ἡμῖν ἐπιτάφιον.* Τ*ούτοις γὰρ ἀφοσιοῦσθαί σε τὴν πρὸς ἡμᾶς φιλίαν καὶ καθ' ᾅδου τελοῦντες ἠλπίζομεν.* Ἀ*λλα θεῷ τελεία χάρις τῷ καὶ ἡμᾶς ἐκ τῆς φήμης τῶν θανατούντων ἐκλύσαντι καὶ τοὺς ὑμετέρους δακτύλους μὴ πρὸς μέτρα νεκρῷ καὶ κόπους κινήσαντι.* Π*ολλὰ καὶ ἄλλα γράφειν ὁ καιρὸς ἐδίδου, ἀλλὰ τὸν λόγον μέτρον ἄριστον ὑπετέμετο ὡς ἂν μὴ τὴν ὑμετέραν κατὰ λόγον ἰοῦσαν γλῶτταν πρὸς ἀμετρίαν ὁπλίσαιμεν.*

61. Τῷ *αὐτῷ*

Ἐ*ν τοῖς καθ' ὕπνον ὀνείροις μου σήμερον ἐδόκουν ἐξ ἀμπέλου κνίζειν περκάζοντας βότρυας, οὓς σὺν ἑτέροις τραγήμασιν συλλέγων ἐν πίνακι, τραπέζῃ μεστῇ δαψιλοῦς εὐωχίας καὶ δαιτυμόσιν* || 157 || *οὐκ ἀσήμοις ὡς δή τινα ξενίζοντα παρετίθουν ξενήϊα· καὶ τοῦτο μόνος οὐκ*

---

5 *οὐκ ἀνέβη – ἡμῶν*: cf. Lc. 24.38 || 8 *διὰ δακτυλίου ἑλκυσθῆναι*: Zen. III.18; Apostol. V.86[a]; Diogen. II.8; Diogen. Vind. II.41; Karathanasis 84 || 13 *τοῖς μισοῦσιν – προσέθου*: cf. Gen. 37.8

---

4 *ἀνενδυάστως* V: corr. G || 9 *πληροῦν εἰδότων* Polemis: *πληρούντων ηδοτων* V: *πληρούντων καὶ εἰδότων* G || 11 *προέπεμψαν*: *ο* erasum in V || 12 *ἐπεργάσασθαι* V || 17–18 *ἐλέγχους . . . ἐξατ*(ον) V: *ἐλέγχους . . . καὶ στίχους ἐπικοὺς ἑξαμέτρους* G || 18 *μείζωνι* V: corr. G || 20 *κ'θᾄδου* V: corr. G

61: 4 *μόνον* V

the tribunal of my conscience witnesses unhesitatingly, no thought arose in my heart against your Honor. Indeed, I am at a loss why you have parted yourself so far from me like a wild boar. For I have struggled with a grievous illness to the point of being drawn through the ring (as the proverb has it) and was often cared for by persons who knew how to fulfill the Lord's saying, yet was in no wise visited by your kind self. Some indeed, carried off by rumor, consigned me to burial and death, and I know that you did not even join them in performing my funeral. I declare that you have sided with those that hate me and, in helping them, have transgressed against your friendship toward me. May not this happen, may not the slander pass into the heads of my enemies, even though oblivion, by its partial interposition, allows us to suppose this. So be of good cheer in that you have not even helped those who covered me with a tomb, for then you would have had to scan for me a funerary elegiac poem and fashion epic verses in hexameter, and weave the major ionic in due measure with the minor, and so sing to me a burial song. Even as I was near Hades I was hoping that you were devoting to such matters your friendship toward me. But complete thanks be to God who has both freed me from the report of those who were putting me to death and has spared your fingers from the toil of composing verses for a dead man. It would have been opportune to write many other things, but due measure has trimmed my speech that I may not lead to excess your tongue which proceeds according to reason.

61. To the same

In the dreams of my sleep today it seemed to me that I was culling ripe grapes from a vine, which I collected on a plate together with other sweetmeats and was serving as unusual offerings to distinguished guests at a table filled with abundant

ἔπραττον· σὺν ἐμοὶ δὲ καί τις ἄλλος ἀγνοούμενος ἐπίπροσθέν μου βαδίζων ἐφαίνετο, ὃν εἰς πρόσωπον οἱ συμπόται διέπτυον, καὶ τὰ πρὸς αὐτοῦ κομιζόμενα πρὸς γῆν ἐρρίπτουν, καὶ τοῦτον πόρρω τῆς εὐωχίας ἀπέκρινον· ἐμὲ δὲ καὶ ἀποδοχῆς ἠξίουν καὶ ὡς αὐτῶν ἕνα καθέδρᾳ συνέταττον. Τί ἆρα τὰ τῆς ὄψεως βούλεται, αὐτὸς ἐπικρίναις· δακρύων γὰρ ἀπεύχομαι σημαίνειν φορὰν τὰς ῥᾶγας ἐκείνας τῆς τοῦ ὑμετέρου ἀποδημίας ὁμαίμονος εἵνεκεν· λύσιν δὲ λύπης ὡς ἐκ θείου προσδέξασθαι παρ' ὑμῶν εὐαγγελίου τεθάρρηκα εἰς τὴν χαρίεσσαν ἀφορῶν εὐωχουμένων καθ' ὕπνους φαιδρότητα. Εἰς τοῦτό μοι τὴν ὄψιν ἐκβήσεσθαι δοίη θεός, ἀλλὰ μὴ θρῆνον μεσιτεῦσαι καὶ δάκρυα, δυσωπήσει τῇ πρὸς τὸν Υἱὸν καὶ θεὸν τῆς πάντα πόνον καὶ θανατηφόρον δάκρυον ἀφαιρούσης ἐκ παντὸς προσώπου προστάτιδος ἡμῶν Θεομήτορος καὶ πάντων τῶν ἁγίων. Γένοιτο. Γένοιτο.

62. Τῷ αὐτῷ *παραμυθητική*

Ἀδελφὸς ἦν μοι πάλαι πατρὸς ἐν τάξει γνησίως ‖ 158 ‖ *στεργόμενος, τῇ τε κατὰ Χριστὸν προβαθμίῳ ποσότητι, καὶ τῇ τῶν θείων λογίων εὐρύθμῳ ποιότητι. Ἐκ βρέφους γὰρ τὰ ἱερὰ γράμματα κατὰ Παῦλον, ὡς ὁ νήφων ἐν πᾶσιν ἀσκήσας* Τιμόθεος, *αἰδοῖός τε, σεμνός τε παρὰ πᾶσιν ἐκρίνετο· ὡς ἱερὸς ἱερωθείς, λειτουργὸς ἀρχιερέων τὴν ἀρετὴν οὐρανίων καὶ θεράπων ὀτρηρὸς ἐχρημάτισεν, πρᾶος, προσηνὴς τῷ πνεύματι, ταπεινός, εὐμενής, μειλίχιος, φίλιος, ξένιος, ἱκέσιος καὶ παντὶ δεξιῷ προτερήματι κατὰ πάντα κοσμούμενος. Ἀλλ' ἰλιγγιῶ τί γέγονεν εἰπεῖν· εἰ γὰρ προλογήσω ὡς θάνατος αὐτὸν συνηρπάκει, θρηνητικὸν ἀλαλαγμὸν ἐγερῶ καὶ γοερὸν ἀποκλαύσομαι καὶ πλῆρες οἴκτου καρδιακὸν ἐκκαλέσομαι δάκρυον. Τὸ γὰρ ἀπροόπτως ἐπιπεσὸν οἶδε πολλάκις ὡς ἀπό τινος καταστήματος τὴν ψυχὴν ἐφ' ἕτερον*

---

5 *ἀγνωούμενος* V ‖ 8 *αὐτον* V ‖ 9 *ἐπι κρήναις* V ‖ 10 *ἐπεύχομαι* V ‖ *ρῶγας* in *ράγας* corr. V ‖ *ἡμετέρου* V ‖ 12 *εὐαγγελί* V

62: 3–4 *ἐκ βρέφους* – *Τιμόθεος*: cf. 2 Tim. 3.15; 4.5 ‖ 6 *θεράπων ὀτρηρὸς* cf. *Il.* 1.321 ‖ 11 *ἐκκαλέσομαι δάκρυον*: cf. Aesch. *Agam.* 270

62: 3 *γράμματα* delevit manus recentior ‖ 6 *εχρημάτησεν* V ‖ 9 *τιγεγοὺ εισειν* V: *τὸ γεγονὸς οἴσειν* G ‖ 12 *ἐφ' ἕτερον* nos: *ἐφετ̀ς* (= *αιον*) V: *ἐφέστιον* G

festive provisions. This I was not doing alone; for another man, unknown to me, appeared to be walking in front of me. The fellow drinkers spat in his face, threw to the ground the dishes he was serving, and excluded him from the festivities, while they treated me as worthy of reception and placed me on a seat as if I were one of them. What this vision signifies you may judge for yourself. I pray that those grapes do not indicate the shedding of tears on account of the demise of your relative. Nay, I am confident that I shall receive from you a release from my sorrow through some divine tidings of joy, having regard to the cheerful joyousness of the guests in my dream. May God grant me that the vision should find such fulfillment and not cause weeping and tears by the intercession before her Son and God of our protectress, God's Mother, who wipes all pain and deathly tears from every face, and that of all the saints. Be it so!

62. A letter of consolation to the same

I had a brother once whom I truly loved as if he were my father by virtue of the degree of his precedence in Christ and the well-ordered quality of his divine utterances. For he had studied the holy Scriptures from his infancy like Timothy who was watchful in all things (to quote Paul) and was considered reverend and honorable by all men. Having been ordained as one holy, he served as the minister and eager attendant of pontiffs of heavenly virtue. He was gentle, kindly in spirit, humble, well-disposed, gracious, friendly, hospitable, open to supplication, and adorned in all respects with every good advantage. But I am filled with dizziness if I am to declare what has happened to him: for if I say at the outset that death has seized him, I shall raise a mournful cry, lament plaintively, and elicit from my heart tears filled with pity. Indeed, an unforeseen event is often able to move the soul from one disposition to

μετάγειν, καὶ μεστὴν ἀποδεικνύναι θάμβους καὶ δείματος· ὅθεν ἐμφιλοχωρῶν τῷ κατ' ἐμὲ πάθει τῇ ὑμετέρᾳ μονῳδίᾳ συναλγῆσαι προήρημαι, οὐκ ἐξ αὐτῆς δὲ βαλβῖδος, ᾗ λέγεται, ταύτην ἀναξᾶναι βεβούλημαι. Καὶ τοῦτο ποιῶν μιμεῖσθαι δοκῶ τὸν τοῦ Κύρου τοῦ Παρυσάτιδος ἄγγελον μηνύσαντα θάνατον, καθ' ἃ Κτησίας ἱστόρησεν. Ἐλθὼν γὰρ ἐκεῖνος ὁ θανατηφόρος ὡς τὴν Παρύσατιν ἄγγελος, οὐκ εὐθὺς ἀπεδούπησεν ὡς Κῦρος ἀπέθανεν, ἀλλ' ἤγγειλε πρῶτον ὅτι νικᾷ· ἡ δὲ ἥσθη· καὶ ἀγῶνι συμμιγείς; προσήρετο. Βασιλεὺς δὲ πῶς πράττει; Ὁ δέ, πέφευγε ‖ 159 ‖ *φησίν. Ἡ δὲ ὑπολαβοῦσα, Τισαφέρνης αὐτῷ τούτων αἴτιος· καὶ πάλιν ἐπανερώτα, Κῦρος δὲ ποῦ νῦν; Ὁ δὲ ἄγγελος ἀμείβεται· ἔνθα δεῖ τοὺς ἀγαθοὺς ἄνδρας αὐλίζεσθαι. Ὁρᾷς ὡς κατὰ μικρὸν προϊὼν τὸν θάνατον εἰπεῖν ταμιεύεται· καὶ τῇ ἀκουσιότητι δουλεύων προβιβάζει τὴν μητέρα τὸν τοῦ παιδὸς προμαντεύσασθαι θάνατον. Τοῦτο δὴ καὶ αὐτὸς δεδοκίμακα, μὴ προτέραν ἀπογυμνῶσαι τὴν ὑμετέραν τῆς λύπης ἐπήρειαν, πρὶν ἂν τῆς ἐμῆς τραγῳδίας θεατρίσω τὰ πάλαι θρηνήματα.*

Τί οὖν ἐρῶ; Ὅτι σὺ μὲν οὐδεμίας τῆς ἐξ ἡμῶν παραμυθίας δεδέησαι, καὶ εἰ τῇ ῥομφαίᾳ τῆς δυσθυμίας δεδίχασαι· ἔχεις γὰρ ἐνδομυχοῦσαν παράκλησιν τὴν τῆς θείας λογιότητος παίδευσιν, ἣ καὶ ὑπνοῦντι συγκαθεύδει σοι καὶ διανισταμένῳ φαιδρῶς συνεγρήγορε, καὶ οὐκ ἐᾷ τὴν κατήφειαν στυγνόν τι πρὸς ὑμᾶς ἰδεῖν ἢ καὶ ἀμειδὲς ἐκρῆξαι, τὸ δὴ λεγόμενον, ἀλλὰ μέτρα τῇ λύπῃ φυλάττουσα ὅλον σε δεικνύει χαρίεντα· ἔγνως γὰρ καὶ καλῶς ἀνέγνως ὡς οὐ μένομεν, οὐδὲ μονίμῳ ζωῇ συνδεδέμεθα, ἐπεὶ τῆς ὑποσχεθείσης ἀϊδιότητος ἑαυτοὺς ἐξωθήσαμεν. Ἀναλόγισαι γὰρ τὸν χειρὶ θεοῦ φυραθέντα καὶ κραθέντα γενάρχην ἡμῶν, ὡς καλός, ὡς θαυμαστός, ὡς ἄξιος τοῦ παντός· ἔργον γὰρ τῆς ἀκαμάτου χειρὸς ἐκείνης καὶ νεαρὸν ὑπῆρξε πλαστούργημα· ἀλλ' ἐπεὶ τῆς ἐντολῆς τοῦ πλάσαντος κατόπιν διὰ τῆς συμβουλίας τοῦ ὄφεως ἔδραμεν, τὸν θάνατον ‖ 160 ‖ *ὡς πατρῷον κλῆρον ἐδέξατο, καὶ παντὶ τῷ γένει τάφον βαθὺν ἐκαινούργησε καὶ τῆς ζωῆς ἐκτομήν, ὡς δι' ἀξίνης τῆς παραβά-*

---

15 *ἐξ – βαλβῖδος*: Zen. II.7; Greg. Cypr. Leid. I.56; Karathanasis 153 ‖ 16–25 *τὸν τοῦ Κύρου – θάνατον*: Ctesias, *Pers. fr.* 42, ed. Müller, ex Dem. Phal. *De eloc.* §§222–23, paucis mutatis, ubi autem peior lectio *ἡ δὲ ἥσθη καὶ ἠγωνίασε* loco *ἡ δὲ ἥσθη· καὶ ἀγῶνι συμμιγείς; προσήρετο*. Cf. Greg. Corinth. c. 8 in Walz, *Rhetores Graeci* VII, 1180 ‖ 33 *ἀμειδὲς ἐκρῆξαι*: locum non inveni ‖ 35 *ἔγνως – ἀνέγνως*: cf. Basilii *ep.* spuriam 41, ed. Y. Courtonne, vol. I (Paris, 1957), p. 98 [= PG 32, 348A] ‖ 38 *ἄξιος τοῦ παντὸς*: Zen. II.2; Greg. Cypr. Leid. I.51 ‖ 40–41 *τὸν θάνατον – ἐδέξατο*: cf. Gen. 2.17

---

14 *προείρημαι* V ‖ 15 *ἡ* V ‖ 16 *παροισατιδος* V ‖ 17 *καθὰ* V ‖ 18 *παροισατιν* V ‖ 19 *ἴσθη* V ‖ 21 *τισσαφερν(ης)* V ‖ 23 *δὴ* V ‖ 30 *δυσθυμίας* Polemis: *δυσφημίας* V ‖ *ἔχεις* nos: *εἰς* V ‖ 31 *ἢ* V ‖ *ὑπ̣ν̣τι* V: *ὕπνιόν τι* G ‖ 33 *ημας* V ‖ *εκριξαι* V ‖ 36 *ἀναλόγησαι* V

another and to instill into it terror and fear. For this reason I have chosen to share in your lament by dwelling on my own pain, instead of wishing to exacerbate it from the starting post, as the saying goes. In doing so, I am, methinks, imitating the messenger who announced the death of Cyrus, son of Parysatis, as reported by Ctesias. For when that messenger of death came to Parysatis, he did not blurt out at once that Cyrus had died, but announced first that he was being victorious. She was pleased. "Has he joined battle?" she asked, "And how is the king doing?"—"He has fled," he said. She rejoined, "Tisaphernes has caused him these things." And then she asked further, "Where is Cyrus now?" The messenger replied, "At the place where brave men ought to dwell." You see how, advancing by gradual steps, he postpones the announcement of death and, being subjected to constraint, leads the mother to divine her son's death. The same I, too, have attempted, namely, not to reveal the injury of your sorrow before representing the former tears of my own tragedy.

What, then, shall I say? That you stand in need of no condolence on my part, even if you are cut asunder by the sword of despair: for you have within yourself a hidden consolation—the culture of your divine learning which lies beside you when you are asleep and wakes up splendidly when you arise, and does not allow despondency to look sullenly in your face or to erupt gloomily, as the saying goes, but imposes a limit on your sorrow and makes you altogether cheerful. Indeed, you know and rightly acknowledge that we do not abide nor are we tied to a permanent life inasmuch as we have expelled ourselves from the promised eternity. Consider our ancestor who was kneaded and compounded by God's hand—how fair he was, how admirable, how worthy of all things; for he was the work of that untiring hand and its youthful creation. But when, through the serpent's counsel, he disregarded the Creator's command, he received death as his inheritance, he inaugurated a deep tomb for his whole race, and wrought with the adze of the transgression the severance of

σεως, ἐτεκτήνατο. Καὶ *οὐκ ἐπὶ μόνοις τοῖς πταίσασιν ὁ τῆς ἐπιτιμίας πέλεκυς στομοῦται καὶ τὴν τομὴν ἀφίησιν, ἀλλά, κατὰ τὸν εἰπόντα μέγαν διδάσκαλον, καὶ ἐπὶ τοὺς μὴ ἁμαρτήσαντας ἑτοιμάζεται καὶ στιλβοῦται καὶ τείνεται.* Ἀναζεύξεις *τῷ νοῒ καὶ ἐπὶ τὰς ἀνέκαθεν γενεάς, καὶ ὄψει τὸν μέγαν* Ἀβραὰμ *ἀργυρίου τάφον ὠνούμενον· τὴν τῆς τομῆς γὰρ ταύτης πλῆξιν ἐξεδέχετο·* Ἀβραὰμ *τὸν διὰ πίστεως γνησιωθέντα θεῷ καὶ σπέρμα δαψιλέστερον ἄμμου καὶ ἀστέρων ἀριθμοῦ κρείττους φυλὰς ἐκ τῶν ἑαυτοῦ μηρῶν ἀναβλύσαντα· εἶτα τὸν* Ἰσαάκ, *τὸν* Ἰακώβ, *τὸν ἐκ τούτου φύντα* Ἰούδαν, *ἐξ οὗ τὸ κατὰ σάρκα* Χριστὸς *ἀνατέταλκεν· τὸν* Μωϋσῆν *τὸν ὑπὸ θεοῦ μαρτυρηθέντα θεράποντα, δι' οὗ* Αἴγυπτος *ὧδε κἀκεῖ κολάζεται καὶ θάλασσα τέμνεται, καὶ* Φαραὼ *πανδημεὶ τοῖς ὕδασιν θάπτεται, καὶ νόμος προβαίνει, καὶ θεὸς τῶν ὀπισθίων ἑαυτοῦ θεωρὸν ἀναδείκνυσιν· τὸν* Ἀαρών, *τὸν* Φινεές, *τοὺς ἐν νόμῳ πάντας τὸ σεπτὸν τῆς ἱερατείας σεμνύναντας, τὸν* Σαμουήλ, *τὸν* Δαβίδ, *τὸ τῶν προφητῶν ἀκροθίνιον, τὸ τῆς καρδίας θεοῦ ἀδιάψευστον ἀπεικόνισμα.* Διάβηθι *πρὸς τὴν χάριν τῷ λόγῳ, καὶ εἴσῃ τοὺς φωστῆρας ἐκείνους ταῖς ἀρεταῖς διαλάμψαντας, μετὰ πᾶσαν τὴν εἰς θεὸν ἀσύγ* ‖ 161 ‖ *κριτον εὐαρέστησιν, γυμνοῖς τοῖς ἁγίοις ἐκείνων σώμασιν ταῖς ἱεραῖς σωροῖς που εἰσδύντας καὶ τὴν ἐσχάτην ὑπομένοντας σάλπιγγα· οἷον τὸν* Πρόδρομον, *ᾧ βροτὸς οὐδεὶς ἐν γεννητοῖς γυναικῶν παραβάλλεται· τὸν* Πέτρον, *ὃν θυρωρὸν οὐρανῶν θεὸς ἀποδείξας τὰς τούτων κλεῖς ἐνεχείρησεν· τὸν* Παῦλον, *ὃν οἱ τοῦ παραδείσου λειμῶνες μετάρσιον ὑπεδέξαντο, ᾧ καὶ θεὸς τὰ τῶν ἀρρήτων ἀκροαμάτων τρανῶς προσεθάρρησεν· τὸν ἀγγελοείκελον* Στέφανον, *ᾧ διέστησαν οὐρανοί, καὶ* Χριστὸς Ἰησοῦς *ἐφάνη τῷ* Πατρὶ *παρισούμενος.* Καὶ *τί σοι τῶν τοῦ νόμου φυλάκων καὶ τῶν τῇ χάριτι διακονησαμένων διέξειμι τὸν κατάλογον, ὅπου γε καὶ πᾶσα κτίσις τὴν τῆς μεταποιήσεως ἀλλοίωσιν ἀπεκδέχεται;* Οὐρανοὶ *γὰρ ῥιζηδὸν παρελεύσονται καὶ τακήσεται στοιχεῖα καυσούμενα, καὶ γῆ καὶ τὰ ἐν αὐτῇ ἔργα φλεγήσονται.* Καὶ *οὐ θαυμαστὸν εἰ καὶ ἡμᾶς, μέρος ὄντας τῆς κτίσεως, ὑπομεῖναι τὴν ἐκείνων δεῖ ἀφθαρσίας ἀλλοίωσιν.*

45–46 *ἐπὶ τοὺς – τείνεται*: Rom. 5.14 ‖ 47 *τὸν μέγαν – ὠνούμενον*: Gen. 23.9 sqq. ‖ 49 *σπέρμα – ἀριθμοῦ*: Gen. 13.16; 15.5 ‖ 52–53 *δι' οὗ – τέμνεται*: Ex. 14.29–31 ‖ 54–55 *καὶ θεὸς – ἀναδείκνυσιν*: Ex. 33.23 ‖ 61–62 *τὴν ἐσχάτην – σάλπιγγα*: cf. 1 Cor. 15.52 ‖ 62–63 *οὐδεὶς – παραβάλλεται*: Mt. 11.11; Lc. 7.28 ‖ 64 *τὰς – ἐνεχείρησεν*: Mt. 16.19 ‖ 65–66 *ᾧ καὶ θεὸς – προσεθάρρησεν*: 2 Cor. 12.2–4 ‖ 66–67 *Στέφανον – παρισούμενος*: Acta 7.55–56 ‖ 70–71 *οὐρανοὶ – φλεγήσονται*: Mt. 24.29, 35 etc. ‖ 73 *τὴν ἐκείνων – ἀλλοίωσιν*: cf. 1 Cor. 15.53–54

---

44 *μεγα* V ‖ 46 *τίνεται* V ‖ *ἀνάζευξις* V ‖ 47 *ἀβραὰμ* V ‖ 48 *ἀβραὰμ* V ‖ 49 *κρειττ* V ‖ 58 *ἴσι* V ‖ 60 *τὰ ἅγια* V ‖ 61 *σοροῖς* V ‖ 62 *ᾧ* G: *οὗ* V ‖ 69 *κτησις* V ‖ 70 *ρυζηδὸν* V ‖ 73 *δι'* V

life. Not only for the sinners is the axe of punishment sharpened and used for cutting, but, as the great teacher has said, it is prepared, burnished, and raised even for those who have not sinned. Turn back your mind to the first generations, and you will see the great Abraham buying a tomb for money, for he was expecting the blow of that severance—Abraham, who by his faith had become intimate with God and produced from his loins a seed more abundant than the sand and tribes greater in number than the stars. Then Isaac, Jacob, and the latter's son Judah, from whom Christ is descended according to the flesh; Moses, too, whom God confirmed as His servant, through whom Egypt was chastised in divers places, the sea was parted, Pharaoh was buried in the waters with all his host, the Law went forth, and God made him the beholder of his back parts; Aaron, Phinehas, all those who adorned the holiness of the priesthood under the Law, Samuel, David, the pinnacle of the prophets, the true likeness of God's heart. Go on in your discourse to the realm of Grace, and you will find that those luminaries who had shone by their virtues, after pleasing God in an incomparable manner, entered their sacred graves in their naked holy bodies to await the last trumpet: for example, the Forerunner, to whom no mortal man born of woman may be compared; Peter, whom God made door-keeper of heaven and to whom He entrusted its keys; Paul, whom the meadows of paradise welcomed high above this world and to whom God openly confided His secret words; the angel-like Stephen for whom the heavens opened up and Jesus Christ appeared as equal to the Father. But why am I enumerating to you the guardians of the Law and those who have served Grace, when all creation is awaiting its change through transformation? For the heavens shall utterly pass away, the stars shall melt as they burn, the earth and all the works therein shall be consumed. No wonder that we also, who are part of creation, shall needs undergo the same alteration through incorruptibility.

Ὀρφανὸς ἀπελείφθην ἀλλὰ καὶ πατὴρ πρὸ τούτου καὶ κατὰ κῆδος ἡμῖν ⟨εἴ⟩ τις ἐγγίζων ἀπῴχετο καὶ πάντες ὅσοι τὸ τῆς εὐνοίας πρὸς ἡμᾶς ἀποσώσουσιν ὄνομα, πρὸ ἡμῶν ἢ καὶ μικρῷ μεθ' ἡμᾶς τῷ τῆς πλακὸς ταύτης ὑποδύσονται πανοικτίστῳ καλύμματι, καὶ οὐδεμία παραίτησις δυσωπῆσαι δυνήσεται· οὐ κρῆναι χρυσοῦ καὶ ἀργύρου, || 162 || *καθ' ἃ λέγεται, τὴν τῆς ταφῆς ὁδὸν ἐξωνήσαιντο· οὐ πατρὸς σπλάγχνα τὸν υἱὸν ἐξαιρήσεται· οὐ στοργὴ μητρὸς τὸν ἑαυτῆς τοκετὸν καθέξειν ἰσχύσειεν. Μία δὲ μόνη και ταύτην οἶδε ῥᾴστην ποιεῖν τὴν μετάβασιν, ἡ πρὸς τὰ θεῖα καὶ θεὸν ἐπιστροφὴ καὶ εἰλικρινὴς ἐπιμέλεια καὶ τῆς ἀρετῆς μελέτη καὶ πρὸς τὰ κρείττω προκοπὴ καὶ ἐπαύξησις· τούτοις ἑαυτοὺς βελτιώσωμεν· τούτοις, ἀναγκαίοις οὖσιν πρὸ τῆς ὥρας ἐκείνης, τὴν ψυχὴν ἑαυτῶν καθοπλίσωμεν, μὴ δακρύοις ἐπιτυμβίοις τοὺς ἀποιχομένους προπέμποντες, ἑαυτοὺς δέ, κατὰ τὴν κυρίαν ῥῆσιν, θερμῶς ἀποκλαίοντες. Οὕτω γὰρ καὶ τὸν ἐκεῖ κριτὴν καὶ τὴν κρίσιν εὕροιμεν ἵλεω, καὶ χωρήσωμεν εἰς τὰς ἀκαταλύτους μονάς, ἀλλὰ μὴ δεθείημεν χεῖρας καὶ πόδας κατ' ἐκεῖνον τὸν ὀκνηρὸν οἰκέτην καὶ πονηρόν, ᾧ πρῶτος ἐγὼ τοῖς πρακτέοις παρασυμβληθεὶς ἀπέραντα μετακλαύσομαι καὶ ἀπορριφήσομαι πρὸς τὰ τοῦ σκότους τοῦ ἐξωτέρου μετ' ὀργῆς ἀφεγγῆ καταγώγια. Ὧν ὑμᾶς μὴ πειραθῆναι δῴη θεὸς ταῖς αὐτῷ φίλαις ἑαυτοὺς ἀρεταῖς ὡραιώσαντας, ἀλλὰ ταῖς ἐκεῖσε καλλοναῖς καὶ ἀπολαύσεσιν ἐντρυφῶντας διαιωνίζειν ταῖς τῶν ἁγίων χοροστασίαις. Γένοιτο. Γένοιτο.*

63. Τῷ *αὐτῷ*

Τὸ χαραχθὲν νυνὶ πρὸς μὲ γράμμα τῆς σῆς μὲν ὑπῆρχε || 163 || *χειρός, οὐ μὴν δὲ τοῦ σοῦ κύημα νοός· οὐ γὰρ ἐγνώρισά τι τῶν ἐν αὐτῷ σεσημειωμένων μέμψεων, ὅ μοι κηλῖδα καὶ μολυσμὸν ἐπιτρίψειεν,*

---

74 *ὀρφανὸς ἀπελείφθην*: cf. To. 1.8 || 78 *κρῆναι χρυσοῦ καὶ ἀργύρου*: Diogen. II.93; Diogen. Vind. I.82 || 86–87 *ἑαυτοὺς – ἀποκλαίοντες*: Lc. 23.28 || 89 *τὸν ὀκνηρὸν – πονηρὸν*: Mt. 25.26 sqq. || 89–90 *ᾧ – παρασυμβληθεὶς*: cf. Ps. 48 (49).13, 21

---

74 *ὀρφανὸς ἀπελείφθην* nos: *ὀφθαλμὸς ἀπελήφθη* V || 76 *ἀποσώσ(ιν)* vel *–ειν* V || *ἢ* G: *εἰ* V || *τῷ* nos: *τὸ* V || 78 *κρῖναι* V || 79 *καθὰ* V || *ἀφῆς* V || 85 *ἑαυτῶ* V || *ἐντυχομεν(ους)* V: *οἰχομένους* G || 87 an *ἀποκλαύσωμεν* legendum? || 90 an *πράξεσι* legendum? || 92 *ἡμᾶς* V || 93 *ὡραιώσαντες ἀλλὰ ταῖ* V

63: 1 *ὑπεῖρχε* V || 2 *τῶν* G: *τὴν* V

I have remained an orphan, but, earlier, my father and all my kinsmen had departed, and all those who are well-disposed toward me shall be covered by that most lamentable slab either before me or soon after me, and no entreaty shall have the power to prevail over it; no founts of gold and silver, as the saying goes, can buy off the road to the tomb; a father's affection will not deliver his son, nor will a mother's love be able to withhold her offspring. One thing only can make this journey easy, I mean our conversion to things sacred and to God, sincere attention, the study of virtue, progress and increase toward the higher state. Let us improve ourselves by such acts; let us fortify our souls by such acts, necessary as they are before the hour, lest in escorting the departed with funereal tears, we weep ardently over ourselves, as the Lord's saying has it. In this manner may we find the Judge and the judgment merciful over there and so enter the everlasting mansions. Let us not be bound hand and foot like that slothful and wicked servant, to whom I, more than anyone else, shall be compared with regard to the things that I should have done and regret them endlessly as I am angrily cast in the gloomy lodgings of the outer darkness. May God grant that you, who have adorned yourself with the virtues that are dear to Him, do not experience that fate, but rather enjoy eternally the beauties and delights over there among the choirs of the saints. Be it so! Be it so!

63. To the same

The letter you have now penned to me is indeed by your hand, but is not a product of your mind; for I did not recognize ⟨in myself⟩ any of the censures noted therein such as would impute to me a stain and a pollution, but which rather hold out

ἑτέροις δέ τισιν, οὐ καλῶς, ἀγνωμονήσασιν ἐπισεῖον παροράσεως ἔγκλημα· οὕς, ὡς ἐγῷμαι, τῷ γραφεῖ καλάμῳ πικρὰν ἀπήνειαν καὶ δριμεῖαν τῷ μέλανι συγκεραννὺς ἐπωνείδιζες· ἀλλὰ τούτοις οὐκ οἶδ' ὅπως ἀφείς, ἐμοῦ δὲ τοῦτο μνησθεὶς καὶ τραχὺ προσιδὼν ἄκρατόν μοι τὸν θυμὸν διὰ τοῦ γράμματος ἀπεκένωσας. Διατί; Ὅτι ⟨οὐ⟩ συνήλγησα, ὅτι ἐπὶ τῷ συμβάντι πάθει οὐ συνέπαθον; Μαρτυρήσει ἡ ἔφορος δίκη, ὅτι καὶ τοῦ ἄλγους ἐπῃσθόμην καὶ τῷ πάθει συνέπαθον. Ἀλλ' ὅτι τὸ μὴ παρουσιάσαι με κατὰ πρόσωπον φλεγμονὴν ἀνίας ὑμῖν ἀπεγέννησε; Καὶ τοῦτο τῆς διακρίσεως ὑμῶν πέλαγος, ὃ πάντα μετρεῖν οἶδε καὶ κατὰ δύναμιν ἀπαιτεῖν; Γῆρας γὰρ καὶ νόσος καὶ καιρός, ἐπίτασιν φέρων χειμέριον, οὐ πόρρω συγγνώμης τετάχαται. Τί γὰρ καὶ καθυστερήσαμεν; Οὐ διὰ γράμματος τὸν ὀφθέντα προσηγγείλαμεν ὄνειρον; Οὐ διαφόροις ἐπισκέψεσι διὰ τῶν ὑπηρετεῖν ἡμῖν εἰωθότων ἐπυθόμεθα εἰ ἄρα κομψότερον ὁ πάσχων ἔσχεν; Ἀλλ' εἰς ὕδωρ κατὰ σὲ σπείρομεν, ᾗ φησιν ἡ παροιμία, καὶ χάρις οὐδεμία μετόπισθεν εὐεργέων. Εἰ δὲ κατὰ πρόσωπον ὑμῶν σταίημεν, ‖ 164 ‖ ἑαυτοὺς ξένους ἐπὶ πλεῖον ἐκείνου τοῦ γράμματος δείξαιμεν.

64. Νικηφόρου Ἰγνατίῳ

Εἰ σαφῶς ᾔδεις, φίλος ἐμοὶ καὶ πατέρων αἰδεσιμώτατε, ὡς ἀεὶ κατὰ νοῦν τὴν σὴν τριπόθητον ἀρετὴν περιφέροντες διὰ παντὸς ἐνοπτριζόμεθα ταύτην καί, ὥσπερ κατ' ὀφθαλμοὺς βλέπομεν, οὕτω τὰ τῆς ὑμῶν ἐπιεικείας ἰνδάλματα φαντάζεται παρ' ἡμῖν, οὐκ ἂν ὡς ἀγνοήσαντας καὶ λήθῃ τὴν σὴν ἀνεπίληπτον παραπέμψαντας σύνεσιν ἐλογίζου τε καὶ ἐτίθεσο· ἀλλ' ἔοικας, εἰ μὴ τοῦ ἀληθοῦς πόρρω τοπάζομεν, ⟨τὸ⟩ σφοδρὸν τῆς ἡμῶν πρὸς σὲ διαθέσεως, ἢ ἕξεως μᾶλλον εἰπεῖν (δυσκινήτως γὰρ καὶ οὐκ εὐκινήτως ἔχομεν πρὸς τὴν σὴν ἀμετάβλητον μεταβάλλεσθαι ἢ ἀλλοιοῦσθαι φιλίαν, οὕτως ἐρατεινὴ καὶ πᾶσι περί-

---

4 εγ deletum deinde *εὐγνωμόνησα σ(ιν)* V: corr. G ‖ 5 *ἀπήνειαν καὶ δριμεῖαν* nos: *ἐπὶ πήνης καὶ δριμὺν* V ‖ 8 *συνήλγησας* V ‖ 14 *τεταχατε* V ‖ 16 *εἰωθότω* V ‖ 17 *σπέρομεν* V

63: 16–17 *ἐπυθόμεθα – ἔσχεν*: cf. Jo. 4.52 ‖ 17 *εἰς ὕδωρ – σπείρομεν*: Zen. III.55; Diogen. VII.67 ‖ 18 *καὶ χάρις – εὐεργέων*: *Od.* 22.319; cf. 4.695

64: Tit. Νικηφο V ‖ 1 *ἴδης* V ‖ 7 *σφόδρα* V

against others, who have improperly shown ingratitude, the accusation of neglecting you. It was them, I believe, you were upbraiding by your writing pen as you mixed with your ink a bitter and harsh cruelty. But having, I know not how, forgiven them, you bethought yourself of me and, with a savage look, poured upon me through your letter your intemperate anger. Why? Because I did not share in your suffering, because I did not sympathize with your grief? All-seeing Justice will testify that I was both conscious of the pain and did sympathize with your grief. Was your distress inflamed by the fact that I did not visit you in person? Is such the ocean of your discernment that is able to measure everything and make demands according to one's ability? Indeed, old age, illness, and the season, which brings a wintry onset, are well nigh considered as valid excuses. Have I also been tardy? Have I not announced by letter the dream I had had? Have I not inquired through my servants who visited you on several occasions whether the patient was feeling better? But, in your case, I was sowing in water, as the proverb says, and no gratitude followed my good deeds. If I were to stand in front of you, I would show you all the more how undeserving I am of that letter.

64. Nikephoros to Ignatios

If you had known clearly, O my friend and most reverend of fathers, that I always carry in my mind your thrice longed-for Virtue, that I constantly see it in a mirror—for, just as I behold you in front of my eyes, so I imagine the image of your kindness—you would not have thought and considered that I had ignored and consigned to oblivion your unforgettable Prudence. You seem, however, unless I am far from the truth, to be unaware of the strength of my disposition or rather attraction toward you (for I am slow and not fast in being altered with regard to your unalterable

πυστος) οὐκ εἰδέναι, ὥστε εἰ μὴ προβλῆτος ἀκτῆς πυκνὰ τοῖς ῥεύμασι βαλλομένης τῶν ἀνέμων ὀρινομένων, οὐχ ἥκιστα, αἱ συνεχεῖς τε καὶ ἀλλεπάλληλοι καταιγίδες τῶν τοῦ βίου φροντίδων τὴν ἐμὴν ἀθλίαν καὶ τληπαθῆ ψυχὴν ἔβαλλον, οὔποτε ἀνιεῖσαι ἢ ἐνδιδοῦσαι, πάντα καιρὸν καὶ πᾶσαν ὥραν ἔργον τοῦ πρὸς σὲ στέλλειν καὶ τὰ κατὰ σὲ πυνθάνεσθαι ἐποιούμην, φιλαίτατε.

Ἀμέλει δι' οὐδὲν ἕτερον ἢ τούτου γε ἕνεκα μέχρι τοῦ δεῦρο τὰ τῆς περιστερᾶς καὶ τοῦ κόρακος ἡμῖν τεταμίευται· οὔτε δὲ κατὰ τὸ πυκνόν, ὥσπερ ἔφης, τῶν περιόδων, ἐν αἷς οὐ καθ' ἡμᾶς || 165 || *ἀλλὰ καθ' ὑμᾶς πεφώραται, κολάζεται τὰ τοῦ κόρακος· οὔτε γὰρ πυκνότητα περιόδων τὸ σταλὲν ἐμπεριεῖχε γράμμα· δύο γὰρ ἢ τρεῖς ἀλλ' οὐ πλείους, ὡς ἐγὼ νομίζω, ἐν αἷς οὐκ ἐμέλλομεν ἀκούοντες ναυτιᾶν· οὐ διὰ τὸ ἀπίθανον· ἔστι γὰρ καὶ ἐν πυκνότητι περιόδων συνεχεῖ ἐνθυμημάτων εὑρεῖν πιθανότητα· ἀλλ' ἦν διὰ τὸ πιθανὸν μᾶλλον ἀγαπᾶν· καὶ γὰρ ἦν πληρεστάτως τὸ σταλέν· ὥστε γραφῇ κατηγορίας ἥλως, τοῖς μὴ παθοῦσιν πάθος τι προσαγγείλας, ἢ ἐπικαλέσας· ἐπεὶ οὐδὲ κατά τινα σύνθεσιν τῶν περιόδων ἡμάρτηται, ἢ καθ' ἕτερον ἧστινος τρόπον παρατηρήσεως ἰδέας λόγου, ἵνα τὸ σὸν περὶ τὴν μέθοδον δεινὸν καὶ ἄλλως πολυμαθές, ὃ καὶ λίαν τεθαυμάκαμεν καὶ ἐν θάμβει πολλῷ πεποιήκαμεν, παραδράμωμεν. Ἑρμογένης γάρ τις ἄλλος ἡμῖν, οὐκ ἐν παισὶ γέρων, ἐν δὲ γέρουσιν παῖς, κατὰ τὸ ᾀδόμενον καὶ φερόμενον, ἀλλ' ἐν γεραιτέροις εἶ γεραίτατος, ἢ γεραιότατος καὶ συνετώτατος ἀναπέφηνας, ἄλλην τινα συνθεὶς ἰδέαν λόγου βελτίω πολὺ καὶ ἐξοχωτάτην, ὡς ἐγᾦμαι, καὶ Ἀριστείδου ἐπέκεινα.* Τί *δαὶ καὶ τὸ κωμικὸν ἡμῖν εἰς μέσον παρήγαγες, πιστούμενος ἡμᾶς πάντως διὰ τούτου ὡς τὸ γράφειν ἀφελῶς καὶ δοκεῖν οὐκ ἐν συντάξει λέγειν, τοῖς ψέγουσιν μᾶλλον, οὐ τοῖς εὐφημοῦσιν* || 166 || *ἁρμόδιον;* Καὶ *οὕτω γε τῷ πρέποντι καὶ τῇ ἀληθείᾳ δοκεῖ ὡς ἂν τὸ τῆς ὀργῆς καὶ τῆς ἀπεχθείας τῆς πρὸς τοὺς δι' ἔχθρας ὄντας τῇ περισκελίᾳ καὶ συμπλοκῇ τῶν λόγων ἐμφαίνοιτο τοῖς μεμφομένοις καὶ μετ' ὀργῆς ὅτι πλείστης ἐπιτιμῶσι διὰ τοῦ γράμματος.* Πῶς *γὰρ ἂν καὶ πρέπῃ λόγων εὐθύτης τε καὶ ὀρθότης καμπύλῳ νοήματι καὶ στρεβλῷ;* Τὸ *ὅμοιον γὰρ ἐπακολουθεῖ τῷ ὁμοίῳ καὶ ὡσαύτως τὸ συγγενὲς τῷ*

64: 10 *προβλῆτος ἀκτῆς*: cf. *Od.* 5.405; 10.89; 13.97–98 || 11 *τῶν ἀνέμων ὀρινομένων*: cf. *Il.* 9.4 || 21 *οὐκ ἐμέλλομεν – ναυτιᾶν*: cf. Demetrium, 15 || 29–30 *οὐκ ἐν – παῖς*: Fl. Philostrati *Vitae Sophistarum* II 250, ed. C. L. Kayser, II, p. 83.15–16; *Suda* E 3046 || 41 *τὸ ὅμοιον – τῷ ὁμοίῳ*: Apostol. XII.68

---

10 *προβλητος ἀκτὶς* V || 14 *ωρ<* V || 15 *φιλέτατε* V: corr. G || 23 *ἀλλ' ἢ* V || *πληρεστατου* V || 26 *ἢ τιν(ος)* V: *ἤ τινα* G || 27 *ἠδέας* V || 30 *γερετέροις ἢ* V || 33 *ἀριστίδου* V || 36 *τῷ πρέποντι* nos: *τὸ τρεπτόν τι* V

friendship, so lovely it is and widely celebrated). For if, just like a jutting shore that is repeatedly struck by the waves as the winds are roused, the constant and repeated squalls of life's troubles did not strike my wretched and miserable soul without let or respite, I would have used every season and every hour to write to you and inquire of your news, O dearest friend.

It was for that and no other reason that I have kept in reserve until now ⟨the story⟩ of the dove and the crow. Not that ⟨the words⟩ of the crow, as you have said, are to be reproved on account of the frequency of their periods, whereof you—not I—have found them at fault. Indeed, the letter I sent you did not contain frequent periods—two or three and no more—not enough to cause nausea as we listened. Nor for being implausible, since it is possible to find plausibility of invention even in a continuous frequency of periods. On the contrary, ⟨my missive⟩ should have been appreciated for its plausibility which it had in full measure. Hence you stand convicted of making an accusation, namely, for having denounced or invoked a fault where no fault existed, since ⟨my letter⟩ was not deficient in the composition of its periods or according to any other manner of observance of whatever style—if I may set aside your technical skill and deep learning which I greatly admire and am astonished by. Indeed, you appear among us like another Hermogenes—not, as they say, an old man among boys and a boy among old men, but you are the oldest among the older, or rather the most respected and wisest in having invented some other concept of style, a far superior and most excellent one, well above that of Aristides, I should say. Why, indeed, did you also introduce that quotation from comedy, thereby confirming that I was writing carelessly and, it seems, without regard to composition—⟨a quotation⟩ more suitable for blame than for praise? For it appears, in truth, fitting that the anger and hatred toward one's enemies should be manifested in the harshness and intertwining of diction in the case of those who are expressing censure and excessively angry condemnation by letter. How, indeed, can a straightforward and correct diction be suitable for a bent and crooked notion? Surely, like follows like and

64

συγγενεῖ. Τίς *δὲ καὶ μῶμον ἐπάγοι τῇ ὑμῶν ἀμεμφεῖ τελειότητι περὶ πάντα, εἰ μὴ μώμου λοιπὸν ἢ μανίας μᾶλλον εἰπεῖν πλήρης εἴη;* Γράφε *τοίνυν αὐτὸς καὶ διορθοῦ μᾶλλον ἡμᾶς· τὸ γὰρ σόλοικον τὸ σὸν σώους ἄλλους καὶ ἀσολοίκους περὶ τὸ λέγειν καθίστησιν, καὶ τὸ βάρβαρον ὡσαύτως μὴ βαρβαρίζειν τοὺς δοκοῦντας ὀρθολεκτεῖν παρασκευάζει.* Ἱ*μειρόμεθα δὲ σὲ θεάσασθαι, ποθεινότατε, ἢ τὰς ἡλιακὰς ἀκτῖνας ὁ τὰς κόρας ἐστερημένος.*

---

42 *μῶμον* nos: *μόνον* V || 44 *διορθου* V || *σολυκον* V || *σοους* V || 45 *ἀσολάκους* V

kin follows kin. Who, however, would reproach your Perfection that is blameless in all respects, unless he were himself filled with reproach or rather with folly? So 'tis better that you write yourself and correct me, for your solecisms make others healthy and free from solecism and your barbarisms cause those who appear to speak correctly not to speak like barbarians. I desire to see you, my longed-for friend, more than the blind man wishes to see the rays of the sun.

COMMENTARY

1–3.

These three letters concern the same sequence of events and appear to have been written at fairly short intervals, one after the other. The events in question were, more or less, as follows: the Church of Nicaea, already burdened by the imposition of the *συνωνή*, had to face a departure of some of her *πάροικοι*, who demanded for themselves a fair share of the produce they had raised. The *οἰκονόμος* of the Church, who may have defrauded the *πάροικοι*, was arrested by the authorities. Ignatios laid him under a penance, but was nevertheless anxious to see him reinstated in his office. In his absence he sent to Gregory the keys of the Church's granary so as to enable the imperial official to take the amount necessary for feeding the troops. A *kourator* (perhaps in charge of the domain in which the disturbance had taken place) was also drawn into the affair. In short, the thematic administration was putting considerable pressure on the Church for the delivery of foodstuffs. This may (but need not) have been caused by an extraordinary military situation.

1.

Gregory the *spatharokandidatos:* A person of the same name and rank is also the addressee of Photios' letter 30, which concerns a theological point and is, unfortunately, impossible to date on internal evidence (ed. Laourdas and Westerink, 80–81). The rank of *spatharokandidatos* came ninth in descending order in the scale of eighteen palatine dignities, immediately below that of *protospatharios* and above those of *dishypatos* and *spatharios:* see table in Oikonomidès, *Listes,* 292. It is first attested as a single word in the early ninth century: ibid., 297. In view of seals no. 2921 and 2935 (Zacos-Veglery, vol. I.3, 1656 and 1662), dating from the seventh and eighth century respectively, J. Haldon suggests that the title may have occasionally been employed earlier; see *Byzantine Praetorians,* Ποικίλα Βυζαντινά (Bonn, 1984), 186–87. Judging by the context, Gregory appears to have been *protonotarios* of the theme of Opsikion, like Nicholas, the addressee of letters 7–8, that is, the officer responsible for the civil administration of the province. On this office see Bury, *System,* 94; Oikonomidès, *Listes,* 315. The *protonotarios* often held the rank of *spatharokandidatos;* G. Schlumberger, *La sigillographie de l'Empire byzantin* (Paris, 1884), 103; id., *Mélanges d'archéologie byzantine* (Paris, 1895), 223; V. Laurent, *BZ* 33 (1933), 344, etc. It was he who was responsible for supplying the army with provisions. On his ability to oppress provincials, see Theoph. Cont., 443.15.

2 *ἀνεμιαίας φρενός*: cf. VN 139.13: *τῆς κουφώδους καὶ ἀνεμιαίας ἀπι-*

στίας κατάπαυσις, ibid., 166.25: *τοῖς ἀνεμιαίοις καὶ ἀστάτοις . . . ληρήμασι.* The word is also attested in the *Life of St. Thomais of Lesbos* = *BHG*[3] 2455; cf. Th. Detorakis, Ἀθηνᾶ 80 (1985–89), 226.

7 *πάροικοι*: tenant farmers, on whom see, most recently, M. Kaplan, *Les hommes et la terre à Byzance* (Paris, 1992), 264 ff. Cf. also A. Kazhdan's comment on our text, *BSl* 53 (1992), 198. As here, Theoph., 486.29–487.5, in a well-known passage describing the "vexations" imposed by Emperor Nikephoros I (801–811), specifically connects the *paroikoi* with "pious foundations," that is, orphanages, hostels, poorhouses, churches, and imperial monasteries. What is not clear to us is whether, as Kazhdan believes, Ignatios draws a distinction between *paroikoi* and *μισθοφόροι* (paid laborers). In other words, was the complaint of the malcontents that they had been treated "as if" they were paid laborers (*μισθοφόρων δίκην*), that is, by receiving a smaller share of the produce in kind or cash? On the other hand, the terms *πάροικος* and *μισθωτός/μισθωτής* are sometimes used interchangeably (see Lemerle, *Agr. Hist.*, 180), and it is equally possible to translate *μισθοφόρων δίκην* as "like the paid laborers they were." Ignatios' rebuttal of the complaint does not appear to us to favor either interpretation.

10 ff Note the statement that the Church did not own any farm animals or agricultural implements. It acted simply as landlord.

14 *γεωργικὸς νόμος*: There is a difficulty here. The Farmer's Law (ed. W. Ashburner, *Journal of Hellenic Studies* 30 [1910], 85 ff), as we know it, makes no mention of *πάροικοι* and is concerned instead with owner farmers living in a village commune. It recognizes only two kinds of contract: the *μορτή* and the *ἡμισεῖα*. The former (*Farmer's Law,* cc. 9–10) lays down that the owner will receive 1/10 of the produce and the tenant (*μορτίτης*) 9/10; the latter (cc. 11–15) concerns a division into two of the produce and appears to have applied mostly, if not exclusively, in the case of an indigent landlord who was unable to exploit his own fields: see Kaplan, *Les hommes et la terre,* 259 ff. While the *ἡμισεῖα* cannot be relevant to our case, one may wonder whether Ignatios is referring to the *μορτή*. A share of 1/10 is certainly extremely low, so Lemerle (*Agr. Hist.*, 38) may be right in supposing that this kind of contract also included other clauses, in particular that the tenant would be liable to the property tax. Theoph., loc. cit., does say that the *πάροικοι* paid the *καπνικὸν* (poll tax), but is rather vague concerning the property rates. He implies, if we understand him correctly, that the *πάροικοι* were liable for part of the latter. For, after stating that Nikephoros I transferred to the imperial demesne the best estates of the said charitable foundations, he adds: "As to the rates (*τέλη*) upon them, they were to be imposed on the domains and *πάροικοι* that remained to the said charitable foundations, so that their *τέλη* were doubled." If the Church received only 1/10 of the revenue in kind from its landed properties and was, in addition, liable to part of the property tax, its condition would indeed have been precarious. On the other hand,

Ignatios may be referring to some customary, unwritten law that laid down different arrangements.

19 *σιταρχία*: Ignatios uses this classical term in the sense of *συνωνή*. See below, letter 7.14.

20 *πλατύνεται*: cf. VT 395.27: "It would take an experienced orator to compose a biography of Tarasios, *μὴ ὅτι γε ἡμῖν εὐτελείᾳ λόγου πλατυνομένοις πρὸς τοσοῦτον ὄγκον εὐγενείας ἀναδραμεῖν*, . . ." etc.

2.

1 ⟨*ἐν*⟩ *μέρει πληροφορίας*: cf. letter 30.4–5 and VT 409.27: *εἰ γὰρ δῶμεν ἐν μέρει πίστεως εἶναι τὰ πρὸς αὐτοῦ προτεινόμενα*, that is, "If we grant that these allegations are credible." This usage may be a borrowing from Demosthenes, 21.165, 166 (*ἐν χάριτος μέρει . . . τοῦτ' ἐν εὐεργεσίας ἀριθμήσει μέρει*).

3 ⟨*ἐν*⟩ *λήθῃ*: The addition appears necessary and may be justified by a parallel in letter 11.7–8: *ἐν λήθῃ γέγονεν*; but cf. VT 395.16: *ὅσα πεπείραμαι καὶ τῇ εὐτελεῖ καὶ πενιχρᾷ μου μνήμῃ μένειν ἐπίσταμαι*. Heikel supplies ⟨*ἐν*⟩ . . . *μνήμῃ*, whereas Nikitin would emend *καὶ* to *κἄν*.

9 *οἰκονόμος*: On this office from the fifth to the tenth century, see Darrouzès, *Offikia,* 16 ff. The *οἰκονόμος*, who had charge of church estates and revenue, was normally a cleric, either priest or deacon. Canon 11 of Nicaea II stresses the obligation of bishoprics and monasteries to have an *οἰκονόμος*.

22 *λαοῦ* = "army," as often in Byzantine texts.

3.

1 Ἰδού σοι: a common epistolary incipit. Cf. St. Basil's letter 337 *ad Libanium,* ed. Y. Courtonne (Paris, 1966), 204 [= PG 32, 1081B]: Ἰδού σοι καὶ ἕτερος ἥκει Καππαδόκης.

κουράτωρ: This must have been an ecclesiastical, not a civil or imperial *kourator,* otherwise Ignatios would not have been responsible for him. We assume that he was the administrator of an estate (perhaps situated at some distance from Nicaea) subject to the *oikonomos.* Cf. V. Laurent in *BZ* 33 (1933), 353 note 3; Darrouzès, *Offikia,* 81 note 304. The sixth-century inscription from Colophon, *διὰ Κυριακοῦ τοῦ εὐλαβεστάτου πρεσβυτέρου καὶ κουράτορος*, may also refer to an ecclesiastical *kourator* (H. Grégoire, *Recueil des inscriptions chrétiennes d'Asie Mineure* [Paris, 1922], no. 94), though this cannot be regarded as certain since, in spite of canonical prohibitions, clergymen did on occasion assume secular *kouratoriai.* This may also be the case of Euprepianos, disciple of Theodore the Studite, who, pretending to be a layman, was *more procuratoris* in charge of buying and loading beasts of burden for an abbess in the mountains of Prusa: . . . *μόνον τε ὄντα καὶ μειζοτερικῶς ἤγουν κουρατορικῶς τῇ ἡγουμένῃ δουλεύοντα ζῷά τε ἐπαγοράζοντα καὶ*

φορτοκομεῖν ἐκ τῶν ἔσω ἔξω . . . (letter 329.9–11, ed. Fatouros, 470). On the office of *kourator* in general, see I. Ševčenko, *Byz* 35 (1965), 568–72.

3 *ἀμφοτέραις ταῖς ἰγνύαις ὀκλάζων*: cf. VT 406.9: *ἀμφοτέραις ἰγνύαις ὀκλάζουσιν* and *Scholia in Lucianum,* ed. H. Rabe (Leipzig, 1906), 20.18.

4 *ἀποικία*: probably to be understood literally as "settlement away from home."

8–9 *τοιαύτη . . . ἀντιλήψεως*: ironic.

10ff *εἰ μὴ γὰρ ⟨οὐκ⟩ ᾔδει*, etc.: a difficult passage. The required meaning seems to be: "Unless you were ignorant of the sorry state of the Church, one would be tempted to accuse you of acting foolishly. The Church is in need of persons who can administer her affairs properly, but you have arrested those very persons and forced them to act in the interests of the government." The third person *ᾔδει* (itself an emendation) instead of *ᾔδεις* may be due to attraction by *ὑπεροχή*, but *παρ' αὐτοῦ ἀπαχθέντων καὶ κατ' ὀφθαλμοὺς αὐτοῦ ὁσημέραι παρεστώτων* is difficult to explain. Should one correct to *αὐτῆς . . . αὐτῆς* . . . , or does *αὐτοῦ* refer to another person, for example, the *comes* of Opsikion?

21–22 *σκῶλον . . . ἐκβάλλων, λείαν*: cf. VN 153.16–17: *τὰ ἐν μέσῳ σκῶλα καὶ σκάνδαλον . . . ὑφελόμενος* . . . ; VGD 68.3: *ἅπαν πρόσκομμα καὶ σκῶλον ἐξέβαλε τῆς ἐπὶ τὴν ἀρετὴν ἀγούσης ὁδοῦ, καὶ λείαν ἑαυτῷ ταύτην κατασκευάσας* . . . ; VT 406.30: *καὶ πᾶν σκῶλον* (*σκολιὸν* perperam Heikel) *ἐκβάλλων εὐθείας ποιεῖ τὰς τρίβους τῆς πίστεως* . . . ; Greg. Naz., *Orat. in laudem Basilii,* PG 36, 540B: *λύει τὰ ἐν μέσῳ σκῶλα καὶ προσκόμματα*. Further examples in Lampe, s.v. See also Nikitin's comment, "O nekotoryh," 11.

4.

A letter of courtesy, accompanied by a gift of olive oil, probably written not long after Ignatios had been appointed to the see of Nicaea.

Nikephoros (cf. no. 19): otherwise unknown, possibly a little older than Ignatios (line 16). He cannot be the same as the *chartophylax* Nikephoros who took part in the Council of 787 (Mansi, XII, 1051D) both because the difference in time is too great and because another *chartophylax,* Constantine, is recorded in 798 (Dölger, *Regesten,* no. 351). Another *chartophylax* Nikephoros, known as a canonist, flourished at the end of the eleventh century; see P. Gautier, "Le chartophylax Nicéphore," *REB* 27 (1969), 159–95.

Chartophylax: On the history of this office, see Darrouzès, *Offikia,* 19ff, 334ff. He was the archivist of the patriarchate and, according to Anastasius Bibliothecarius (Mansi, XVI, 38D), received all letters addressed to the patriarch of Constantinople, except those sent by other patriarchs; introduced to the patriarch all prelates and clerics; and drafted letters of recommendation for candidates to holy orders and abbots. He was not, however, in the ninth century the chief of the patriarchal chancellery, a position he was to attain later. See also below, letter 53.

5.

A courtesy letter largely devoid of content. If it dates from Ignatios' episcopate, it indicates that the author, as might have been expected, paid periodic visits to Constantinople. He does not, unfortunately, describe the nature of the misfortunes that befell him. Note that all the allusions are biblical, suggesting that John was not a person of much culture.

Kouboukleisios: member of the patriarch's *cubiculum.* On this honorific office, attested mostly in the tenth and eleventh centuries, see Darrouzès, *Offikia,* 39 ff. Constant. Porph., *De Cerimoniis,* II.39, 637 informs us that before his time the patriarch used to have a *praepositus* at the head of his *kouboukleisioi* and quotes to that effect a document of Heraclius addressed to Patriarch Sergios. It seems that the emperor had some control over the composition of the patriarchal *cubiculum.* See Nicholas I, letter 155.9: Εἰ γὰρ καὶ γέγονε βασιλικὴ πρόσταξις τοῦ ἐξωσθῆναί τινας τῶν κουβουκλειςίων, etc. (ed. R. Jenkins and L. Westerink [Washington, D.C. 1973], 474).

6.

Constantine *hypatos:* probably the same person who appears in the *Vita Ioannicii* (by Sabas; absent from the Life by Peter), *AASS,* Nov. III, 365C–366A, where he is described as ὕπατος or ὑπατικός. He was a frequent visitor of the saint, by whom he was once reprimanded for having struck his servant. His son Nikephoros was healed by Ioannikios of a stutter. These incidents, if related in correct sequence, pertain to the reign of Theophilos. On the chronology of the *Vita Ioannicii,* see Mango, "Two Lives," 396 ff.

The rank of *hypatos* (consul) stood in the ninth century fairly low in the hierarchy—twelfth out of eighteen, below that of *spatharios* and above that of *strator.* It disappeared in the tenth century, or, to be more exact, it was revalued and conferred on a single individual who had a judicial function. Philotheos (Oikonomidès, *Listes,* 155) distinguishes between ὕπατοι βασιλικοὶ and ὕπατοι παγανοὶ (without function) τῆς συγκλήτου. Constantine must have belonged to the former class since he held a post, which appears to have been judicial. Cf. R. Guilland, "Le consul," *Byz* 24 (1954), 548–78 = *Recherches sur les institutions byzantines,* II (Amsterdam, 1967), 44 ff; Oikonomidès, *Listes,* 296, 325.

To a Constantine *hypatos* belonged the following seals of the Zacos-Veglery collection: vol. I.1, nos. 780–81; vol. I.2, nos. 1441–42, 1808–9; and vol. I.3, no. 3092.

The interpretation of this letter must start with the garbled name of the bishop in line 9. Gedeon's emendation Ἰκονίου is clearly impossible since the bishop of Iconium could claim no jurisdiction over monasteries situated in Bithynia. We opt for the correction Νικομηδείας (which is not too violent, if one assumes the accidental erasure of the initial letter in the model and considering the near identity of ν

and μ in early minuscule) because the district of Pylai was situated within the diocese of Nicomedia and none of the suffragan bishoprics of either Nicomedia or Nicaea, which might have been involved, had a name at all resembling the reading of the MS (ἦκο$\overset{\eta}{\upsilon}$). That, however, does not completely solve the problem, for it may be asked why the metropolitan of Nicomedia addressed himself to Ignatios over the improper activities of the *kourator* of Pylai and why it was Ignatios who took the matter up with the central government. Not knowing whether Ignatios was himself a bishop at the time, we must leave the matter in suspense.

5 *ἐκκλησιαστικοῦ . . . κεφαλαίου*: We fail to understand why Kazhdan, *BSl* 53 (1992), 199, takes the word *κεφάλαιον*, frequently used by Ignatios, to mean "tax."

8 *ἀποδιδοὺς τὸ γραμμάτιον*: Note that the message was delivered by the bearer and was not contained in the letter.

8–9 *ἐπισκόπου* Νικομηδείας: If our emendation is correct, the unnamed prelate may have been the predecessor of Ignatios, the addressee of letter 49.

10–11 *ὁ τοῦ ξενοδόχου* Πυλῶν *κουράτωρ*: This reading (rather than Gedeon's emendation *ξενοδοχείου*) is defensible in the sense of "the *kourator* on the staff of the *xenodochos* of Pylai." Pylai, the situation of which has long been in dispute, is probably to be identified with the Byzantine site at Çiftlik köyü, 4.5 km east of Yalova, rather than with Yalova itself, which is a modern settlement. It was a small harbor town which, from the seventh century onwards, served as the terminal of the main military road leading to Nicaea and, across Asia Minor, to the eastern frontier. First mentioned in the fourth century (Peutinger Table and Sozomen, IV.26.1, ed. J. Bidez–G. C. Hansen [Berlin, 1960], 182, concerning the death of the patriarch Macedonius in 360), it is frequently alluded to in Byzantine sources down to the thirteenth century. Some of the pertinent material has been collected by X. A. Siderides, ΚΕΦΣ 28 (1904), 105 ff, who incorrectly placed Pylai at Hersek. See also E. Honigman, *Byz* 14 (1939), 625 ff, and especially L. Robert, "Un voyage d'Antiphilos de Byzance," *Journal des Savants* (1979), 269 ff. On the Byzantine remains at Çiftlik köyü (which include harbor installations, a standing baptistery, a cistern and an aqueduct), see, in part, S. Eyice, *CahArch* 10 (1959), 256–58, and Mango, *TM* 12 (1994), 150 ff; on inscriptions found there, both antique and Byzantine, see L. Robert, *Hellenica* 8, 30 ff; idem, "Noms de métiers dans des documents byzantins," Χαριστήριον 'Αν. Κ. 'Ορλάνδου, I (Athens, 1964), 328 ff = *Opera minora sel.*, II (Amsterdam, 1969), 919 ff; S. Şahin, *Bithynische Studien* (Bonn, 1978), 30 ff; and Th. Corsten, *Die Inschriften von Apameia* (*Bithynien*) *und Pylae = Inschriften griechischer Städte aus Kleinasien* 32 (Bonn, 1987), 108 ff.

The *xenodocheion* of Pylai is first attested on a boundary stone of the reign of Constantine VI and Irene (780–797), found at either Çiftlik köyü or Yalova in 1974 and now in the Istanbul Archaeological Museum (inv. no. 74.74): Şahin, op. cit., 37 ff

and pl. VII, who mistakenly believes that *xenodocheion* was a place name. In the *Kletorologion* of Philotheos (899), the *ξενοδόχος Πυλῶν*, along with those of Sangaros and Nicomedia, is listed as being subject to the Great Curator (Oikonomidès, *Listes,* 123). In the tenth century, Theodore Daphnopates addresses a letter to Nikephoros *ξενοδόχος Πυλῶν* and gives an idyllic description of the rural pleasures available to his correspondent: letter 37, ed. J. Darrouzès and L. G. Westerink (Paris, 1978), 207 ff. Seals of *xenodochoi* of Pylai: ΚΕΦΣ 31 (1907–8), 51; Zacos, II, 163; N. Zikos in N. Oikonomides, ed., *Studies in Byzantine Sigillography,* II (Washington, D.C., 1990), 173–74.

10 *μοναστήρια*: Several monasteries are known to have been in the general area of Pylai: Janin, *Grands centres,* 100 f, among them, that of Asekretis (ibid., 86) and perhaps that of the Kathara (*τὰ Καθαρά*) (ibid., 158 ff). It is not clear why they should have paid dues to the neighboring *xenodocheion.*

28 *ἐπισκήψεως*: cf. VGA 21.11.

7.

Nicholas must have been *protonotarios* of the theme of Opsikion. On the office see above, no. 1; Bury, *System,* 94; Oikonomidès, *Listes,* 315. In Philotheos (Oikonomidès, ibid., 121), the *πρωτονοτάριοι τῶν θεμάτων* are subject to the *χαρτ. τοῦ σακελλίου*. They are not mentioned in *Taktikon Uspenskij.*

13 *περιφορᾶς*: in the sense of a meal carried round the table, as in Xen. *Cyr.* 2.2.4. Cf. Pollux 6.55; Athen. 3.120c; 7.275b.

14 *συνωνή* (*coemptio*): originally the obligatory purchase of produce by the state at a fixed (usually low) price. See E. Stein, *Histoire du Bas-Empire,* II (Paris-Brussels-Amsterdam, 1949), 199. It is believed, following G. Ostrogorsky, "Die ländliche Steuergemeinde des byz. Reiches," *Vierteljahrschrift für Sozial- und Wirtschaftsgeschichte* 20 (1928), 49 f; idem, *BSl* 9 (1947–48) 296 note 272, that by the tenth century the *synone* had been commuted to a land tax payable in cash, but that is not its meaning here. It should be noted that in this and the following letter Ignatios is concerned not with impositions on the Church of Nicaea as landowner, but on the members of its clergy. He speaks of the *synone* not as a regular tax, but as an extraordinary imposition in kind, coupled with *ἀγγαρεία* and *ἐπήρεια*, terms that are often found in combination; cf. Lemerle, *Agr. Hist.,* 168, 174. It can hardly be supposed that clergymen were exempt from the land tax. In commenting on letters 7–8, Kazhdan, *BSl* 53 (1992), 200, is, we believe, mistaken in taking *συνωνή* and *σιταρχία* to be two different taxes.

18 *πρὸ τῶν ἰχνῶν*: On this formula of humility, see Karlsson, *Idéologie*², 36.

20 *ἐκδήμου*: probably in the sense that this imposition was "alien."

σκοτόμαινα: cf. VT 399.16; VGD 67.5–6; VN 205.16.

22 *ἰουλίου μηνός*: time of harvest?

27 *μοδίους ἕξ*: This was a second imposition, clearly levied in kind and probably caused by some extraordinary circumstances. On the *modius* see E. Schilbach, *Byzantinische Metrologie* (Munich, 1970), 95ff. The cash price of 6 modii would normally have been about half a solidus. See Ostrogorsky, *BZ* 32 (1932), 320ff.

28 *ὠμογέροντος*: applied to men in their forties: Eusebius, *Historia ecclesiastica* 7.21.9, quoting Dionysius of Alexandria. Cf. E. Miller, *Mélanges de littérature grecque* (Paris, 1868), 429: *ὑποπόλιος, ὃν καὶ ὠμογέροντα καλοῦσιν*. Applied more specifically to persons aged forty-five to fifty-five or forty-nine to fifty-six: A. Delatte, *Études sur la littérature pythagoricienne* (Paris, 1915), 183–84.

8.

Adds little to no. 7, except that the exemptions enjoyed by the clergy of Nicaea are said to have been based on an imperial decree and ancient custom. Such a decree does not appear to have survived, although we hear of special privileges granted to the Churches of Thessalonica (*Cod. Just.,* I.2.8, X.16.12), Constantinople (*Nov. Just.,* 43.1; 59 praef.) and Alexandria (*Cod. Theod.,* XI.24.6).

14 *πρωτογέροντος*: a *hapax.*

9.

Nikephoros, bishop of Caria (Aphrodisias), appears to be unknown. For the episcopal list see R. Janin, art. "Carie," *DHGE* 11 (1949), 1036–37. Seals of metropolitans: Laurent, *Corpus* V.1, nos. 514–19. That of Sergios (Laurent, no. 514) is dated to 787–815 by Zacos-Veglery, I.3, no. 2982.

Nikephoros was on his way to Constantinople, no doubt to take part in the festivities of Easter week, when metropolitans attended on the emperor and a number of them were invited to dinner at the imperial table: Oikonomidès, *Listes,* 205.12 (Easter Monday); *De Cerimoniis,* Bonn ed., 92.24, 93.5, 96.5 (Thursday of Easter week). If Nikephoros had brought his letter himself (lines 1–2), it is not entirely clear how it was that he did not stop at Nicaea (lines 15–16). Did he leave it at some neighboring spot to be delivered to Ignatios?

16 *ἐνοπτρίζεσθαι*: on the letter as mirror, see Karlsson, *Idéologie*[2], 96.

17 *ἡμέρᾳ τῆς καθιδρύσεως*: on the day of his actual appointment or its anniversary? In either case, this letter appears to have been written not long after his ordination as bishop.

19 *δημοσίου*: This probably refers to the fisc rather than to a crowd of people; perhaps "Treasury officials."

19–20 Note that Ignatios feels no obligation to celebrate Easter in his own cathedral.

COMMENTARY

10.

It follows from this letter that the bishopric of Taion had been reestablished a short time previously by Ignatios' predecessor, whom he does not name (see also no. 17). This must have followed an urban upgrading as laid down in canon 38 of the Trullan Council [P. Joannou, *Discipline générale antique,* I (Rome, 1962), 172–73]. In the *Notitiae,* Taion first appears in No. 4 (ascribed to Basil of Ialimbana), ed. J. Darrouzès, 254.198. As regards the date of *Not.* 4, Grumel has argued in *REB* 19 (1961), 198–207, that its archetype was drawn up between 848 and 858, but Darrouzès, ibid., 42–45, is content to place it fairly close to the Council of 869. Grumel's argument is certainly invalid, but needs to be briefly considered because of its bearing on our Ignatios. Older *Notitiae* and conciliar lists assign to Nicaea only three suffragans (Modrine/Melina, Linoe, Gordouserba). To these, three more are added in *Not.* 4 (Noumerika, Taion, Maximianai). With regard to the last, MS H (Vat. gr. 1167) notes that it had been set up by the metropolitan (scil. of Nicaea) Nikephoros and confirmed by the metropolitan Alexander (first half of the 10th century). As for Nikephoros, he was ordained either by Methodios or Ignatios and was ousted by Photios in 858: see V. Laurent, *EO* 34 (1935), 467 ff. Believing (erroneously) that our Ignatios succeeded Theophanes Graptos (d. 11 Oct. 845), Grumel argued that our letter 9 was written in the fall of 845, that is, after October (but why the fall when it speaks of Easter?) and that letter 20 referred to the winter of 847–848 or later. He concluded that Nikephoros was ordained in 848 at the earliest. The only valid point that may be deduced from Grumel's study is that the bishopric of Maximianai was probably created shortly after ca. 850.

Taion lay to the east of Nicaea in the area of Geyve, but its exact site has not been established. It is the same as the Tottaium or *ῥεγεὼν* Τ*ατάϊον* of earlier sources, mentioned along with Doris as belonging to the territory of Nicaea. See *Cod. Theod.,* XII.1.119: Tottai et Doridis oppidorum sive mansionum; *ACO,* II.1, 3 (1935), 59.16 [418]: Τ*αττάϊος καὶ* Δ*ωρὶς ῥεγεῶνές εἰσιν ὑπὸ τὴν* Ν*ίκαιαν*. Hierokles, 694, 1–2, also has *ῥεγεὼν* Τ*ατάϊον* and *ῥεγεὼν* Δ*ωρίς*. Instead of Doris we find Dablis in Ptol. *Geogr.,* V.1, Müller 804; *Tab. Peut.,* IX.2–3; *Itin. Ant.,* 141; *Itin. Burd.,* 573–74. We need not concern ourselves with the problem whether Doris was the same as Dablis (so Ramsay, *Hist. Geogr.,* 181–82); or different from it (so E. Honigmann, *Le Synekdèmos d'Hieroklès* [Brussels, 1939], ad loc.). See also Ruge, *RE* 4.2, 1947, s.v. Dablae and IV.A, 2462, s.v. Tataion. It may be worth pointing out, however, that Dablis was known in the seventh century for its hot springs (*Vita Theod. Syceot.,* ed. A. J. Festugière (Brussels, 1970), c. 146.38), a circumstance that may facilitate its identification.

For the eastward extension of the territory of Nicaea, see C.W.M. Cox and A. Cameron, *Monumenta Asiae Minoris antiqua* 5 (1937), 33, no. 60; and A.H.M.

Jones, *Cities of the Eastern Roman Provinces*[2] (Oxford, 1971), 423 note 28; for the diocese, see Janin, *Grands centres,* 106ff.

The bishopric of Taion (spelled Ταττᾶΐου, Ταΐου, Ταείου) regularly appears in *Notitiae* subsequent to the ninth century, usually in fifth place among the six suffragans of Nicaea. Seal of a bishop (11th century): Laurent, *Corpus,* V.1, no. 398.

5ff Sacred vessels: These appear to have been borrowed temporarily because the new bishopric did not possess any.

14 *δέδοται αὐτῇ*: It follows that Ignatios' correspondent was the first incumbent at Taion.

21 Inalienability of church plate (and other property): See, e.g., *Ioannis scholastici synagoge L titulorum,* ed. V. N. Beneševič, I, Abh. Bayer. Akad. d. Wiss., Philos.-hist. Abt., N.F., Heft 14 (1937), 142, tit. 46 (with references to earlier canons); Hiereia, Mansi, XIII, 329ff; Canon of Germanos, Grumel, *Regestes,* I.2, N. 342 (text in Pitra, *Iur. eccl.,* II, 299); Photios, *Nomokanon,* X.4, ed. G. A. Rhalles and M. Potlis, *Σύνταγμα . . . ,* I (Athens, 1852), 239.

26 *χρυσίου ποσότητα ἀποτιννύτω*: payment of gold; not regarded as simony, the practice of such an offering was encouraged by the Church. See *Coll. 93 capp.* in V. N. Beneševič, *Syntagma XIV titulorum,* I (St. Petersburg, 1906), 775, c. 49. In the early tenth century the *συνήθης παροχὴ* for the bishopric of Sebaste was 100 solidi: Life of St. Luke the Stylite, ed. H. Delehaye, in *Les saints stylites* (Brussels, 1923), 202.28–31.

11.

Noumerika (a name that would appear to be of military origin) is first mentioned in the Life of St. Theodore of Sykeon. On the accession of Heraclius (610), Comentiolus, the brother of Phocas, revolted and seized Ancyra. Heraclius sent an emissary, the priest Philippicus, to treat with him. Afraid to proceed any further, Philippicus waited at Noumerika (*ἐπὶ τὰ μέρη Νουμερικῶν τῆς Βιθυνίας*) and was apprehended there by some soldiers friendly to Comentiolus, who marched him off to Ancyra. On his way he was able to see the saint at Sykeon, who assured him that he was not in any danger (c. 152.38; Festugière did not understand that Noumerika was a proper name). It follows that Noumerika was a post on the road leading to Ancyra and that it lay some distance west of Sykeon. For the historical circumstances see W. E. Kaegi, Jr., *BZ* 66 (1973), 314–15. Ramsay (*Hist. Geogr.,* 181) identifies Noumerika with Doris/Dablis.

The bishopric of Noumerika, like that of Taion, first appears in *Notitia* 4. A bishop Constantine attended the Council of 869: Mansi, XVI, 144D. Cf. Lequien, *OrChr,* I, 661–62; Fedalto, *Hierarchia,* I, 112. Laurent, *Corpus,* V.1, nos. 395–96, publishes two seals of bishops, one of Christopher (9th century), the other anonymous (10th century). The former is attributed to the years 787–815 by Zacos-

Veglery, I.2, no. 1330, who do not realize the implications of their dating. There is also an extant seal of Bishop Theodore: Zacos, II, no. 726. Noumerika appears to have possessed a highly revered church (or icon?) of the Virgin: see Zacos-Veglery, no. 934C, seal of Menas *Stratelates* (7th century?) with an invocation to the Theotokos of Noumerika. See also ibid., no. 1330; no. 377 in V. Laurent, *La collection C. Orghidan* (Paris, 1952), 192–93; and the late eleventh-century seal no. 261 in the Henri Seyrig collection (J.-C. Cheynet, C. Morisson, and W. Seibt, *Les sceaux byzantins de la collection Henri Seyrig* [Paris, 1991], 177–78). Finally, an unnamed bishop is mentioned in a letter of Psellos, ed. K. N. Sathas, *Μεσαιωνικὴ Βιβλιοθήκη*, V (Paris-Venice, 1876), 257.

4 ff *τῷ θεῷ πάλαι καθιερῶσθαι* . . . etc.: It is not immediately apparent whether the three circumstances singled out by Ignatios (having been in the clergy for a long time, being learned in holy Scripture, and occupying the highest post in the Church of Constantinople, i.e., that of bishop) apply to himself or to the bishop of Noumerika. The logic of the argument requires the former interpretation. If so, we may draw the conclusion that Ignatios had been in the clergy for many years before being ordained to the see of Nicaea.

9 ff It is not clear why the bishop of Noumerika was unwilling to meet Ignatios, but some financial difficulty may be suspected.

12.

A routine expression of sympathy and thanks for gifts received.

11 *ὁλκῆς ἀργυρίου*: cf. VT 407.7.

13.

Date: Probably from the time of Ignatios' episcopacy.

Heleno(u)polis, modern Hersek, near the mouth of the stream Drakon (Yelkendere, formerly Kırkgeçit suyu), founded by Constantine in 327 and named after his mother, the empress Helena (*Chron. Pasch.*, 527; Jerome, *Chron.*, 01.276, Helm, 231; Philost., *Historia ecclesiastica* ii.12, Bidez, 24). It had previously been a village called Drepanon or Souga (so Malalas, 323) and was the burial place of St. Lucian of Antioch (martyred 7 Jan. 312). The late tradition that Helena was born there is in all probability false. See C. Mango, *TM* 12 (1994), 143 ff.

Helenopolis served as a point of (dis)embarkation on the important route from Constantinople to Nicaea, but its harbor was subject to silting due to the alluvium carried down by the Drakon. For the important works initiated there by Justinian, see Procopius, *De aed.*, 5.2; also cf. *Anecd.*, 30.8. By the eleventh century Helenopolis had greatly declined (Attaliates, 144), and today no ancient remains are to be seen. See D. Stiernon, "Hélénopolis," *DHGE*, fasc. 135, 877–84.

The bishop of Helenopolis was subject to the metropolitan of Nicomedia: Dar-

rouzès, *Notitiae,* 2.194, 3.229, etc. For its omission in the *Notitia* of Epiphanius, ibid., 8, 17, 40. Episcopal list: Lequien, *OrChr,* I, 621–24 and Fedalto, *Hierarchia,* I, 102–3. Cf. Laurent, *Corpus,* V.1, no. 386 (seal of bishop Synetos, probably of first half of 9th century); and Stiernon, "Hélénopolis," 882.

1 Prainetos, named, it seems, after a local divinity Preietos, corresponds to modern Karamürsel. See F. K. Dörner, "Praietos," *RE* 44 (1954), 1832–34. Although destroyed by earthquake in 740 (Theoph., 412.14), it continues to be mentioned down to the eleventh century. Shortly before his death (959), Constantine VII landed there on his way to Nicaea and Bithynian Olympus (Theoph. Cont., 464). An epigram, *Anth. Pal.,* XVI.281, concerns the restoration of an abandoned bath there by the "priest" Alexander of Nicaea, who has been identified with Bishop Alexander of Nicaea, fl. ca. 925–945; cf. P. Maas, *Kleine Schriften* (Munich, 1973), 469; L. Robert, *Hellenica* 4, 131; A. Cameron, *The Greek Anthology from Meleager to Planudes* (Oxford, 1993), 316ff. The latter was an addressee of the tenth-century anonymous professor of the London MS. See R. Browning, *Byz* 24 (1954), 445–46; J. Darrouzès, *REB* 14 (1956), 91–96; idem, *REB* 18 (1960), 113–14; and A. Markopoulos, *JÖB* 44 (1994), 313–26.

For the bishopric, also subject to Nicomedia, see Lequien, *OrChr,* I, 621–22; Fedalto, *Hierarchia,* I, 105; and Laurent, *Corpus,* V.1, no. 385. Assuming he was traveling from Nicaea, Ignatios probably followed the pass of the Draco, which would have led him both to Prainetos and Helenopolis.

1–2 *τὴν πορείαν . . . ἐστειλάμεθα*: cf. VT 407.26.

5ff Salt production at Helenopolis is not, to our knowledge, otherwise attested. The flat and marshy coast would have been suitable for that purpose. In the Ottoman period, salt was produced both at Tuzla (Cape Akritas) and at the far end of the gulf of Nicomedia: *Narrative of Travels . . . ,* by Evliya Efendi, trans. J. von Hammer, II (London, 1850), 32.

11ff The nature of the transaction is not entirely clear because of the ambiguity of the words *εἰς γὰρ δωδεκάτην αὐξήσει χρυσίου ποσότητα*. We have understood them to mean, as does Kazhdan, *BSl* 53 (1992), 199, that the full price would be 12 nomismata. It is also possible, however, to interpret *δωδεκάτη* as one-twelfth (presumably interest), in which case the total price would remain unspecified. In either case the quantity of salt must have been considerable and may have been intended to supply the needs of the bishopric of Nicaea for a fairly long period. It is plausible to suppose that in Nicaea salted fish was produced in large quantities (cf. letter 14).

In Diocletian's Edict (3.8–9, ed. S. Lauffer, 104–5 and comm. 220, 1 modius castrensis (17.5 l.) of salt is worth 100 den. Cf. Tarif of Anazarbus in G. Dagron and D. Feissel, *Inscriptions de Cilicie* (Paris, 1987), 179. H. Cadell, "Problèmes relatifs au sel dans la documentation papyrologique," *Atti dell'XI congresso internazionale*

di Papirologia (Milan, 1966), 272–85. In the sixth-century P. Cairo Masp. 67.141/I, verso/19, one artaba of salt costs 1/3 carat. No prices appear to be recorded for the ninth century.

14.

Date: episcopal period.

A humorously erudite note to accompany a gift of fish, presumably the notoriously bad *kordakia* of Lake Ascanius, which have been discussed exhaustively by L. Robert, *Journal des Savants* (July–Dec. 1961), 97–166 and (Jan.–June 1962), 5–74. Fish was a common gift sent by epistolographers; see H. Hunger, *Die hochsprachliche profane Literatur der Byzantiner,* I (Munich, 1978), 231 and note 166. On the Byzantine custom of sending gifts with letters in general, see A. Karpozilos, "Realia in Byzantine Epistolography X–XII c.," *BZ* 77 (1984), 20–37.

The train of thought is somewhat deficient in logic: You serve the rarest delicacies at your table.—No, actually you live quite frugally—If I have exaggerated the daintiness of your cuisine, that was merely to excuse my poor gift.

15.

Perhaps on the same matter as no. 14.

16.

Date: episcopal period. This letter forms the basis of Grumel, *Regestes,* I.2–3, ed. J. Darrouzès (1989), no. 428, misdated to after 11 Oct. 845 on the false assumption that Ignatios acceded to the bishopric of Nicaea after the death of Theophanes Graptos.

In letter 495.30 ff Theodore the Studite refers to an abbot of Komai (*ὅ τε τῶν Κωμῶν ἡγούμενος καὶ ὁ τοῦ Γουλαίου*) who had been dispossessed of his post by the Iconoclasts (approximate date 822–826), ed. Fatouros, 730. Janin (*Grands centres,* 115, 143) believes that the reading *Κωμῶν* is a mistake for *Βωμῶν* (the well-known monastery *τῶν* Ἡλίου *Βωμῶν* at Elegmoi, modern Kurşunlu), but apart from the fact that *Κωμῶν* is independently attested in two texts, it must have lain in the diocese of Nicaea, whereas Elegmoi was situated in that of Nicomedia.

7–8 By taking asylum in a church, the murderer placed himself under ecclesiastical jurisdiction. Legal sources about the right of asylum: *Cod. Theod.,* IX.45.4; *Cod. Just.,* I.12.3; *Nov. Just.,* 17.7; *Nov. Just.,* 38, and *Ecloga* 17.1, ed. L. Burgmann (Frankfurt am Main, 1983), 226–27. See also A. Dain and G. Rouillard, "Une inscription relative au droit d'asile," *Byz* 5 (1929–30), 315–26. In VT 407.1–408.18 Ignatios refers to a *spatharios* who, accused of having taken public revenues, sought asylum at the church of St. Sophia. A similar event is recorded in the Funeral Oration of St. Basil by Gregory of Nazianzos, ed. Boulenger, §LVI; Theodore the Studite alludes

to asylum in letter 537, "Μαρίᾳ σπαθαρέᾳ" (ed. Fatouros, 810), as does Photios in letter 4, addressed to the future Caesar Bardas (ed. Laourdas and Westerink, I, 57).

9 *οἰκουμενικοῦ πατριάρχου*: The meaning of the title *oikoumenikos,* applied from the sixth century onwards to the archbishop of Constantinople, must have still been no other than that of "superior"; see S. Vailhé, *EO* 11 (1908), 65–69 and 161–71; H. Grégoire, *Byz* 8 (1933), 570–71; V. Grumel, *Revue des études grecques* 58 (1945), 212–18; V. Laurent, *Miscellanea G. Mercati* 3 = Studi e Testi 123 (1946), 373–96; and idem, *REB* 6 (1948), 5–26.

13–14 *πρακτικαῖς . . . διατάξεσι*: probably with reference to penitentials, which laid down a tariff of penalties for specific offenses.

14 *τὸ σπίλος*: The noun recurs in its neuter form in the Life of St. Nikephoros of Medikion (*BHG*[3] 2297), ed. F. Halkin, *AnalBoll* 78 (1960), 422.23.

19 *τοῦ χρόνου οἰκονομία*: The canon uses this same term (*τὰ δὲ εἴκοσι ἔτη οὕτως οἰκονομηθήσεται*) with regard to the *division* of the twenty-year period: four years standing outside the door of the church, five years in the station of a catechumen, seven years as a penitent, four years attending service with the faithful without taking communion. Ignatios, however, appears to take *οἰκονομία* as a possible reduction of the length of sentence in that he makes the latter dependent on the penitent's progress. He must have trusted the man sufficiently to have dispatched him without guard as bearer of his own letter.

17.

Date: episcopal period.

The *dioiketai* were tax collectors on the staff of both the logothete of the Genikon (Oikonomidès, *Listes,* 115.1 and comm. 313) and of the logothete of the herds, the latter in areas of horse breeding (ibid., 117.29, 338); that is, they were responsible to the central administration. The districts (*διοικήσεις*) assigned to them were of variable extent: N. Svoronos, "Cadastre," *Bulletin de correspondance hellénique* 83 (1959), 56 ff, with further references. In this case, it is clear that the region of Taion formed a separate *dioikesis,* and the tax collector appears to have been a local man, seeing that his father had illegally acquired church property, presumably before the bishopric of Taion had been reestablished.

For Taion see above, no. 10.

37 *ἐγγραφῆναι κυρίαν*: The verb suggests that the church property would have been registered in taxation records as proof of ownership.

18.

Date: episcopal period.

Gangra (modern Çankırı), metropolis of Paphlagonia. See R. Janin and D. Stiernon, "Gangres," *DHGE* 19 (1981), 1091–1103; for episcopal list see ibid., 1100–1101; for its churches, J. Darrouzès, *REB* 50 (1992), 98–101.

COMMENTARY

In the list there is a blank between Constantine, who attended the Council of 787, and Basil, who attended that of 879/880. Could this have been the same Constantine? If so, it would be an argument for placing Ignatios' episcopate at a relatively early date. At any rate, from several expressions (lines 25–26, 39–40) it can be deduced that Ignatios is feeling guilty for having perpetrated sinful (iconoclastic?) acts.

12 *ἐπερειδομένους*: In letter 17.25 the same expression is used of the bishop leaning on his staff rather than the flock leaning on the bishop. There may be, therefore, some grounds for emending *ἐπερειδομένους* to *ἐπερειδόμενοι* or *ἐπερειδομένη*.

19–20 *ἀμαληκίτης . . . πόλεμος*: We fail to understand why Kazhdan, *JÖB* 44 (1994), 238, sees here a reference to an Arab invasion.

33ff Note this case of informal instruction given to another bishop's protégé or young relative.

19.

Date: The letter appears to have been written from Constantinople when Ignatios was on the patriarchal staff. Note the reference to "our spiritual brother the *chartophylax*" (presumably Nikephoros).

On Nikephoros of Caria, see above, no. 9.

The letter concerns a property settlement whose precise details are far from clear. Nikephoros of Caria had been named sole trustee or guarantor of what we take to have been a dowry agreement connected with the marriage of an unnamed imperial *strator.* Upon the death of his co-parent (*σύντεκνος*) Nikephoros now wishes to undo the agreement made previously by bestowing part of the property of the deceased upon a former son-in-law (or conceivably brother-in-law), who was not even a "genuine" in-law (*γαμβρός*). Ignatios urges his correspondent not to interfere and leave the matter to the discretion of the widow, especially in view of the fact that the *strator* was threatening to lay a complaint before the patriarch. The exact relationship of the persons involved is difficult to determine because of the ambiguity of the term *γαμβρός*. We take it that only one estate was contested and that therefore the deceased *σύντεκνος* was the woman's husband. The *strator,* who stood to lose by the proposed arrangement, may have been married to the widow's daughter, but we are not sure how the "spurious" *γαμβρός* was related to the family.

10 Unless *ἡ γαμική* (scil. *συγγραφή*) can be understood as a substantive, like *τὸ γαμικόν* (see F. Preisigke, *Wörterbuch d. griechischen Papyrusurkunden* [Heidelberg, 1924–], s.v. = Ehevertrag) or a similar phrasing in letter 31.54 (*τῆς ἀλγεινῆς ἐκείνης*), a lacuna must be assumed. For a similar use of the feminine adjective *ἡ εἰδική* as a substantive, see letter 38.1 of Leo, metropolitan of Synada (937–ca. 1003), ed. M. P. Vinson (Washington, D.C., 1985), 62–63 and 123. We accept *συνάλγημα* as a deliberate pun on *συνάλλαγμα*.

12 *Strator:* honorific title, sixth from the bottom of the palatine hierarchy, above *candidatus* (fifth) and below *hypatos* (seventh): Bury, *System,* 22; Oikonomidès, *Listes,* 298. On its specific function in the course of the eighth and ninth centuries, see also Haldon, *Byzantine Praetorians,* 159–60 and 186–87. In the eighth century, Theophanes Confessor, a rich and aristocratic young man, was given the rank of *strator* to lure him into imperial service. In the ninth century, Basil, the founder of the Macedonian dynasty, was appointed *strator* by Michael III; see Theoph. Cont., 231.15ff.

23–24 *κριτῇ . . . ἔξω κριτηρίων*: presumably a civil rather than an ecclesiastical tribunal.

20.

At the end of letter 19, Ignatios refers to a courtesy letter of his that had gone unanswered. We may imagine that Nikephoros eventually wrote back and that letter 20 is a polite response to the bishop's letter. If so, the cryptic reference to certain business matters in 19ff has to do with the same affair as letter 19.

15–17 *ἡ γὰρ τῆς ὥρας . . . κρύους*: The letter, it seems, was penned in wintertime. Note the difficulty of winter travel.

25 *ἡ τοῦ κεφαλαίου περιπέτεια*: the same expression used in letter 19.9.

21–24.

These four letters, addressed to the same person, appear to be in chronological sequence and are all to be dated before 826. Democharis was in office as logothete of the Genikon early in 821, when Theodore the Studite, who did not know him personally, pressed him to influence Michael II in favor of icons (letter 426, ed. Fatouros, 596–97). He calls Democharis "an ornament of diverse learning," compliments him for having "refuted John, the leader of impiety" (i.e., John the Grammarian), and states that he had held a number of government posts before attaining "the topmost one" (a slight exaggeration). Theodore's letter 454 is a letter of consolation to the widow of Democharis, to be dated between 821 and 826 (Fatouros, 421*). The deceased is described as educated, pious, and a champion of orthodoxy. We also learn that the pair had children and owned an *οἰκία μεγαλοφυής*, which we take to mean "a house of a distinguished family" (cf. letters 420.19 and 521.23–24). Rather more problematic is the reference to "the death of the blessed *strategos*" (Fatouros, 643). Does that mean that the last post held by Democharis was that of provincial governor, as F. Winkelmann has surmised (*Quellenstudien zur herrschenden Klasse von Byzanz im 8. und 9. Jahrhundert* [Berlin, 1987], 137–38)? Or that he had been a *strategos* before assuming civil duties in the capital? At any rate, the logothete of the Genikon was classed among the *sekretikoi* (Oikonomidès, *Listes,* 107) and could hardly have been designated as a *strategos.*

Photios' letter 49 (ed. Laourdas and Westerink, I, 94) is addressed *Ἰωάννῃ πατρικίῳ καὶ σακελλαρίῳ τῷ κατὰ τὸν Δημόχαριν*. In the early Byzantine period the preposition *κατά* meant "in the service of" (see A. Cameron, *Glotta* 56 [1978], 92–93), but its precise connotation in the ninth century is unclear. It may have meant "belonging to the household or family of X."

It may be presumed that all four of Ignatios' letters were written in Constantinople, but it is difficult to determine what position the author occupied at the time. If he was an official in the patriarchal establishment, why did a group of punished shipmasters have recourse to him and why did he persist in presenting a petition on the part of an injured widow? In a later period we encounter a patriarchal *ἐπὶ τῶν δεήσεων* (on whom see Darrouzès, *Offikia,* 378 ff), who transmitted appeals either to the emperor or the patriarch, but there is no trace of such an office in the ninth century.

It may be noted that Ignatios addresses Democharis in a tone of familiarity.

21.

Tit. *Λογοθέτης τοῦ γενικοῦ*: Next to the *sakellarios,* the logothete of the Genikon was in the ninth century the most important financial minister of the empire, who surveyed and collected all taxes. He is defined by Ignatios himself as *τῶν δημοσίων φόρων προεστὼς* in VGA 53.3. See Bury, *System,* 90; Oikonomidès, *Listes,* 313 ff; for prosopography, R. Guilland, "Les logothètes," *REB* 29 (1971), esp. 11 ff. In 810 the logothete was a patrician Niketas: Dölger, *Regesten,* no. 370.

14 *μήπως . . . συνεκύρησα*: cf. VGD 52.5.

16 *κρηδέμνοις*: a Homeric synonym for the word *σουδάριον* used in VGD 58.4. Cf. also the description of unjustly condemned merchants of Amastris in VGA 42.10 ff: *ὄψεις ἠλλοιωμένας καὶ πρόσωπα συμπεπτωκότα*, etc.

20–21 Scourging and tonsure were a standard punishment for relatively minor offenses. Cf. *Ecloga,* 17.15 and 17.29, ed. Burgmann, 230 and 236; *Book of the Prefect,* 1.12 (*διὰ δαρμοῦ καὶ κουρᾶς*); 2.11 (*τυπτόμενοι καὶ κουρευόμενοι*); 3.3, 3.5, 3.6, etc., ed. J. Koder, 80, 88, 90. Several officials suffered the same punishment, followed by exile, in the reigns of Irene and Nikephoros I (Theoph., 465.3,7; 466.27; 467.26; 483.27).

24 *Ἀνδρωτή* (*Ἀνδροτή* cod.): This island, described as small, waterless, treeless, and situated close to the mainland, appears to be unknown, nor is it entirely clear why Ignatios says that its name had been given to it *οὐκ εὐαγῶς*. Perhaps a sexual double-entendre is meant. Cf. Photios' *Lexicon,* ed. C. Theodoridis, 1774 *ἀνδρωθεῖσα*; *ἀνδρὶ συνοικήσασα, διακορηθεῖσα* and 1775 *ἀνδρώσασθαι· συγγενέσθαι*. Gedeon, *Νέα βιβλ.*, 23 note 2, suggests it was Koutali(s), a small island of the Prokonnesos group, whose Byzantine name is unknown, because, he says, all the other islands close to Constantinople had kept their ancient names. He repeats the

same argument in his preface to E. K. Balsames and N. S. Lampadarides, *Προκοννησιακὰ ἱστορικά* (Athens, 1940), 12–14. There is, however, no reason to suppose that Androtê was close to Constantinople or even in the Propontis.

The following considerations may be relevant. First, one may wonder why a small, waterless, and treeless offshore island should have been inhabited at all. A possible explanation is that a number of families migrated to it at a time of danger, as happened in the Dark Ages in a number of cases (e.g., Monemvasia, Dubrovnik, Venice). If so, Androtê must have been in a region subject to enemy attack. Second, it lay on a route of grain traffic directed to Constantinople. Unfortunately, we know very little about such traffic in the ninth century: it seems that sources of supply lay both to the east and to the west of the capital. See J. L. Teall, *DOP* 13 (1959), 117ff; M. F. Hendy, *Studies in the Byzantine Monetary Economy* (Cambridge, 1985), 46ff. Third, we may note the statement that Ignatios had seen the island himself. As far as we know, he had not traveled widely, which may suggest that Androtê lay in his country of origin or between that country and Constantinople. Now, VGA, which we consider to be a work of Ignatios, was clearly written for local consumption. Note in particular the final prayer (p. 71.3–4): *τὴν πόλιν σου ταύτην φρούρησον, τὴν ποίμνην σου ταύτην φύλαξον*, etc. It is possible, of course, that Ignatios was merely commissioned to compose this Life without being himself a native of Amastris, but if he was a Paphlagonian, it may well be that Androtê was known to him because it was a small island off the Black Sea coast. In VGA 54.10ff he shows familiarity with the sea route from Constantinople to Amastris and the turbulent waters at the mouth of the Sangarios. At Amastris itself there are two offshore islands, one (called Boztepe) now joined to the mainland and fortified on the landward side, the other (Büyükada) quite deserted. See S. Eyice, *Küçük Amasra tarihi* (Ankara, 1965), 8f, who notes the existence of remains, possibly of a monastery, on the latter island. The Byzantine name of these islands is unknown. Theoph., 375.14, speaks of *ἡ νῆσος Ἀμάστρης* with reference to the future patriarch Kyros who had been a hermit on it. There are also a couple of little islands to the west of Daphnousia (Kefken): see map in W. von Diest, *Von Pergamon über den Dindymos zum Pontus,* Petermans Mitt., Ergänzungsheft 94 (1889). Further islands are at the mouth of the Artanas River (modern Şile) and east of Amastris, near Kerasous, the latter being known in antiquity as Aristias, Ardous, or Arkonesos. See Arrian's *Periplus,* ed. A. Diller, *The Tradition of the Minor Greek Geographers* (Oxford, 1952), 118, 124f.

The north coast of Asia Minor, including Paphlagonia, was a grain-exporting area in the Middle Ages: *De Administrando Imperio,* §53.533–35, ed. G. Moravscik and R. Jenkins (Washington, D.C., 1967), 286.

27 *τῷ δημοσίῳ λόγῳ*: possibly intended for the military units (*tagmata*) stationed at Constantinople. There is no clear evidence, after the cessation of the *annona*

in the seventh century, for the provision by the state of grain or bread for the population at large. According to the *Book of the Prefect,* 18.1.4, ed. J. Koder (Vienna, 1991), 128–30, bakers bought wheat, whose price was apt to fluctuate. The state intervened only to regulate weights and profits. On the other hand, there is some evidence for the maintenance of bread distribution to army units. See *Hypnomnesticon* of Theodore Spoudaios (mid-7th century), ed. R. Devreesse, *AnalBoll* 53 (1935), 70–71, concerning an "imperial baker," *ἤτοι ἐπάνω τῶν τοῦ δημοσίου μαγκίπων τῶν τὰς ἀνώνας πασῶν τῶν σχολῶν ἀπολυόντων, ὃ ἐπιλέγεται* Τετράνσιτον.

32 *χαρᾶς φερωνύμῳ*: a pun on the name of Democharis.

41 *ἠπειρόθεν*: one would expect *ἠπειρόσε*, seeing that the women would have crossed *to* the mainland to obtain combustibles and water, unless Ignatios saw them as they were returning to the island. For another incorrect form in *–θεν*, cf. letter 58.27.

46 *ἰατρὸς γαληνότατος*: a pun on the name of Galen; cf. letter 46.12.

47 We were inclined to emend the poorly attested *στορεστής* to *στορεύς τις*, but cf. *Anth. Pal.,* I.118 (anon.):

> Ἀλλ' *ὦ γαλήνη καὶ στορεστὰ τῆς ζάλης*
> *σύ,* Χριστέ, *δείξαις ἀβρόχους ἁμαρτίας*
> *τῷ σῷ πρὸς ὅρμῳ προσφόρως προσορμίσας*, etc.

May this poem be by Ignatios? The only other attestation of *στορεστής* is in the *argumentum* to the Cyclops of Theocritus: *Scholia in Theocritum vetera,* ed. C. Wendel (Leipzig, 1914), 240.

22.

5–7 According to Pythagorean numerology, two numbers were said to be "friendly" when each was the sum of all the aliquot parts of the other. See T. Heath, *A History of Greek Mathematics,* I (Oxford, 1921), 75. The source of our passage may be Iamblichus, *In Nicomachi arithmeticam,* ed. Pistelli and Klein, 34–35: *ἄλλους γάρ τινας ἄντικρυς φίλους ἀριθμοὺς καλοῦσιν ἐν τῷ προσοικειοῦν τάς τε ἀρετὰς καὶ τὰς ἀστείας ἕξεις τοῖς ἀριθμοῖς, οἷον τὸν σπδ' καὶ τὸν σκ'. γεννητικὰ γὰρ ἀλλήλων τὰ ἑκατέρου αὐτῶν μέρη κατὰ τὸν τῆς φιλίας λόγον, ὡς* Πυθαγόρας *ἀπεφήνατο· ἐρομένου γάρ τινος "τί ἐστι φίλος" εἶπεν "ἕτερος ἐγώ,"—ὅπερ ἐπὶ τούτων τῶν ἀριθμῶν δείκνυται.* This shows, incidentally, that the reading *μέρη* is sound. The *Arithmetica introductio* of Nicomachus of Gerasa was known at Constantinople in the ninth century: see Photios, *Bibliotheca,* cod. 187; it must have been one of the standard textbooks of Byzantine litterati: see W. Treadgold, *The Nature of the Bibliotheca of Photius* (Washington, D.C., 1980), 6–7. Nicomachus and Diophantus are mentioned in VT 402.22.

23.

The widow's petition appears to have been of a financial nature. Unfortunately, the identity of the "righteous tribunal" is not specified. Was it the court of the prefect of the city or some special court, like the one instituted by Nikephoros I at the Magnaura (Theoph., 478.31–479.1), which appears to have been concerned precisely with matters of taxation?

The wording of this letter is somewhat lacking in clarity. It would seem that Democharis readily agreed to Ignatios' request, but did not take the trouble to make sure that his decision was implemented.

24.

A letter of consolation, peppered with biblical quotations, on the addressee's losing his office, which, as we learn from letter 23, he had himself begun to neglect.

21 *πρὸς τὸ τοῦ βίου τούτου πέλαγος διανηξόμεθα*: Properly, *διανήχομαι* takes a direct accusative without a preposition, but Ignatios construes it with a dative; see the opening words of VT 395.3: *μέλλων ἀπείρῳ μεγέθει* (so codd.) *πελάγους ἀρετῶν διανήξασθαι.*

24 *διαδοχήν* is defensible in the sense, not of "succession," but of "being succeeded," that is deprived (usually of an office). Thus Theoph., 265.5: *ὁ δὲ αὐτοκράτωρ πάλιν τῆς στρατηγίας τὸν Φιλιππικὸν διαδεξάμενος*, means "having dismissed from his military command," not "received him back into office," as incorrectly given in Lampe, s.v. *διαδέχομαι*, 3. So also Theoph., 239.6–7: *διεδέχθη Προκόπιος, ὁ ἔπαρχος τῆς πόλεως* and elsewhere. Further examples in Ducange, *Gloss. graec.*, App., s.v. *διαδέχεσθαι* ("magistratum alicui abrogare"). Treadgold (*Revival,* 427 note 341) postulates that Democharis' office was taken over by the logothete Pantoleon, also a correspondent of Theodore the Studite (letters 425 and 523).

34 We learn here that the children of Democharis mentioned by Theodore the Studite (above, *ad* 21–24) were daughters. John Duffy calls our attention to a similar passage in the Life of Nicholas the Studite, PG 105, 917B: *πολύπαιδες τῇ εὐτεκνίᾳ* [wrongly printed as *ἀτεκνίᾳ*] *τῆς παιδὸς οἱ ἄπαιδες ἐχρημάτιζον.*

54–55 Probably a veiled reference to the author's inability to worship with icons.

25.

Perhaps no more than an elaborate invitation to Nikephoros to put aside his cares of office and join the author in the country, but difficult to understand because of the corrupt state of the text.

9ff A *locus desperatus.* The difficulty starts with *συκάμινα*. The only "prophet's" passage (setting aside Ps. 77:47 and Is. 9:10, which are both inapplicable) that

is at all appropriate is Amos 7:14: *οὐκ ἤμην προφήτης ἐγὼ οὐδὲ υἱὸς προφήτου, ἀλλ' ἢ αἰπόλος ἤμην καὶ κνίζων συκάμινα*, which is understood to mean "scratching figs" (to make them ripen): cf. below, comm. on 61.1–2. If Ignatios intends to say that he and his friend were eating, not the prophet's figs or mulberries, but pistachio nuts, one could emend the problematic *ἐβοριάζομεν* to *ἐβοράζομεν*. The verb *βοράζω* or *βορᾴζω* = *τρέφω* (hence "to feed" rather than "to eat") is found, however, only in *Etym. magn.*, Gaisford 205.6, 737.21. It is more likely that the reference is not to eating but to resting, which suggests Mic. 4:4, *ἀναπαύσεται . . . ἕκαστος ὑποκάτω συκῆς αὐτοῦ*, in which case one could either emend the text to *εἰ καὶ μὴ . . . συκέαι ἦν* or suppose that Ignatios confused fig trees with mulberry trees. We are still left with the *hapax ἐβοριάζομεν*. Karlsson, *Idéologie*,[2] 128 ff, translates it as "être rafraîchi par le vent du nord" and cites *βορειάζει ἢ βορίζει* = "tira la tramontana" in the *Tesoro* of Somavera (1709) as well as the analogy with *ἡλιάζω* = "to bask in the sun." There is also *ἀερίζω* in Hesychius, s.v. *ἀναψῦξαι*. I. D. Polemis has suggested *εὐωριάζομεν*, which phonetically would have been indistinguishable from *ἐβοριάζομεν*. The extremely rare *εὐωριάζω* (found in Hesychius and Photios' *Lexicon*) is said, however, to mean "to be negligent" (*ὀλιγωρεῖν, μὴ ἔχειν φροντίδα, παρακούειν*). Ignatios might have connected it with *εὐωρία* (fineness of season or freedom from care). Hesychius also has *εὐωρεῖ· παίζει*.

26.

2 It is not clear what unpleasant experiences Ignatios is referring to. The "mosquitoes" reappear in the next letter.

3 *τὰς τῶν ἀλάλων ἐμπίδων ἰώδεις δήξεις*: The patrician Nicetas, a saint of the Second Iconoclasm, suffered from mosquitoes in Bithynia; see his *Vita*, ed. D. Papachryssanthou, *TM* 3 (1968), 331.

7–9 An obscure passage where, as indicated in the manuscript, Ignatios is punning on the brevity of the vowels *α* and *υ* in the word *ἁλυκή*. We take *λέξις* to mean "diction, style": cf. *γλυκύτης τῆς λέξεως* in Dionysius of Halicarnassus, *De compositione verborum*, 11.2. The meaning of the sentence is, however, unclear to us.

27.

Ignatios is referring to some endeavor (a written work?) undertaken by himself and Nikephoros so as to free the Church from heresy. For this they have received no reward, whereas the evildoers (Iconoclasts?) enjoyed considerable resources. Ignatios advises patience. Even if his correspondent had made peace with his assailants, he should remain on his guard. Letter 30 refers more explicitly to an anti-iconoclastic treatise by Nikephoros, but one in which, it seems, Ignatios had no part.

8 *λημματίας* appears to be a neologism meaning "profiteer," from *λῆμμα* = "gain, profit" rather than a mistake for *λημματίας* = "high-spirited."

28.

Ignatios had not written earlier because of his grief over the death of a friend. Knowing, furthermore, that Nikephoros was ill, he thought it wiser to keep silent about the bad news, but in the end made it known. Now that Nikephoros had been informed, he should do his best to eradicate all dejection.

2 *νεκρὸν καὶ οἷον ὀδωδὸς*: cf. Photios' letter 15.5, ed. Laourdas and Westerink, I, 66.

6 *Πυλάδαι τοῖς Ὀρέσταις* . . . : an epistolographic allusion to designate friendship; cf. Symeon mag. et logoth., letter 95.5–7, in Darrouzès, *Épistoliers,* 155; and Theodore, metropolitan of Cyzicus, letter 27, Νέος Ἑλλ. 19 (1925), 292.15–16.

8 Akessaios (or Akesios) is said to have been the steersman of Neleus. He would delay sailing until the moon was full: E. Miller, *Mélanges de littérature grecque* (Paris, 1868), 353.

11 *εὐξάμην τί παθεῖν ἑλέσθαι* is decidedly awkward. One would expect instead "I wondered what I should choose to do" (rather than choose to suffer). Were it not for the circumstances that the first *τί* is picked up by the second *τί*, one might have been tempted to correct *τί παθεῖν* to *τλη παθεῖν* ("I vowed to observe patience").

29.

5 *μετριότητος* need not imply that Ignatios was a bishop at the time. Cf. letters 33.55 and 49.24.

30.

Date: after 821, possibly 821–828.

It is at last made clear here (cf. letter 27) that Nikephoros was engaged in composing a refutation of the iconoclastic position. Who is hinted at by the name of Goliath remains unclear. It is worthy of notice that he should have approached Ignatios and Nikephoros with the request of improving his composition from a "technical" point of view. That suggests that the ideological position of the two friends was sufficiently ambiguous at the time to have given the impression that they went along with the party in power.

A reference to a new Goliath occurs in the peroration of the Encomium to St. Pancratios of Taormina (*BHG*[3] 1411) by Gregory the Pagurite: *τοὺς πιστῶς σε γεραίροντας καὶ ἐπιτελοῦντας τὴν μνήμην σου ἐξ ἐπιδρομῆς ἀλλοφύλων λύτρωσαι. τοὺς πόθῳ σοι προστρέχοντας ἐξ ἐμφυλίου πολέμου διατήρησον. τὰς αἱρέσεις σφενδόνισον· τὸν νέον Γολιὰθ κατάβαλε* . . . , ed. C. J. Stallman-Pacitti, *Byz* 60 (1990), 364.20–23. According to the editor, the raiders here referred

to are the Arabs attacking Sicily, the civil strife that of Thomas the Slav (821–823) and Goliath either Leo V, Michael II, or Theophilos, the last two being the most likely (ibid., 336–38). In view of the mention of a civil war, which cannot be regarded as accidental, Goliath's identity would better accord with Michael II than Theophilos. Old Testament names often served to designate such influential and detested Iconoclasts as the emperors Constantine V (styled Tabeel) and Leo V (Amalek, son of Tabeel) or John Grammatikos (Iannes). Michael II is, however, represented in all our sources as an uncultivated man, and there is no evidence that he engaged in literary composition.

1 The incipit *ἔοικας* occurs no fewer than twenty-one times in the letters of Isidore of Pelusium.

8 ff Although in the accepted text of 1 Kings 17:40 David arms himself with five stones, their number was often reduced to three for trinitarian reasons—indeed, some manuscripts of the Septuagint read three instead of five. Cf. Life of St. David of Thessalonica (*BHG*[3] 493), ed. V. Rose (Berlin, 1887), 5: *λαβὼν μεθ' ἑαυτοῦ τρεῖς λίθους, προτύπωμα τῆς ἁγίας τριάδος*. I. Ševčenko points out to us the Slavonic Life of St. Constantine (Cyril), c. 6: "May he reveal you as a second, new David, set against Goliath, whom he vanquished with three stones": text in P. A. Lavrov, *Materialy po istorii vozniknovenija drevnejšej slavjanskoj pis'mennosti* (Leningrad, 1930), 7–8; French translation in F. Dvornik, *Les Légendes de Constantin et de Méthode vues de Byzance* (Prague, 1933), 355. Also the Slavonic Laudation of Cyril and Methodius: "As David once dashed the pride of the foreigner to the ground and destroyed him and prefigured the Trinity by means of three stones": Lavrov, 84, 90. One may also mention the custom, recorded by Antoninus of Piacenza (ca. 570), namely that those who passed by Goliath's alleged grave on Mount Gilboa would throw three stones on it: "ternas lapides portantes et super ipsum tumulum iactantes," ed. Geyer, CSEL 39, 179.9. Cf. I. Opelt, "Das Grab des Riesen Goliath," *Jahrbuch für Antike und Christentum* 3 (1960), 17–23. On the Cyprus silver plate of David and Goliath (date ca. 630), now in the Metropolitan Museum, David's sling and three stones are represented in the exergue.

31.

Although the title names two recipients, this letter seems to be addressed to a single person, namely, the monk Athanasios. The same pattern is followed in letter 238 of Theodore the Studite, addressed *Εὐοδίῳ καὶ Ἰωάννῃ τέκνοις* (ed. Fatouros, 371–72). The initial metaphors, if they are not purely conventional, suggest that Athanasios may at first have followed a commercial career, which he renounced at the instigation of an unnamed holy father. In the correspondence of Theodore the Studite we meet two monks named Athanasios: the abbot of the monastery of Paulopetrion (near Cape Akritas), who died in 826 (Fatouros, 261*, n. 407) and can hardly, therefore, have been the person that concerns us here; and the Studite proto-

presbyter Athanasios (many mentions, see Fatouros, indices). The latter is referred to, in uncomplimentary terms, in the *Life of Ioannikios* by Peter (422A and 431A) and was still alive in 843. A monk Athanasios is also the recipient of five letters of Photios (nos. 20, 26, 27, 93, 212); although this Athanasios also resided on Mount Olympus, the letters addressed to him date from as late as the first patriarchate of Photios (858–867); see Laourdas and Westerink, I, 71. A monk Theophylaktos is mentioned as one of the oldest companions of St. Ioannikios (*Vita* by Peter, 389B–390A; by Sabas, 345A) and, probably a different one, in the posthumous miracles of St. Peter of Atroa (*La Vita retractata et les miracles posthumes de saint Pierre d'Atroa,* ed. V. Laurent [Brussels, 1958], 169–71), but it is doubtful if any of the above can be identified with Ignatios' addressees.

This letter was written when Ignatios was old (line 58), so probably in the 840s. Though ornate in style, it avoids classical allusions as befits the status of the addressee.

2 For the almost obligatory pun on the name Athanasios, cf. Theod. Stud., letter 231.25 (ed. Fatouros, 365).

8–9 *πολυανθέσι . . . ποικίλμασιν*: referring to silken garments with floral decoration; cf. VT 402.2–7.

11 *θείου πατρός*: Is Ioannikios meant here as in letter 33? Or is it the Theophylaktos named in the title?

15 *ἀβρόχῳ ποδί*: cf. *Phaedo* 243D, but too common to count as a classical allusion.

16 *περιφορᾶς*: As in letter 7.13, the primary meaning is that of serving a meal or drink (hence *πώματα*), but probably combined with the "Christian" sense of "distraction, turbulence." For examples of the latter see Lampe, s.v.

18 ff Note the catalogue of monastic achievements (*ἀταραξία*, *ἀπάθεια*, *ἐγκράτεια*, *ταπείνωσις*, etc.), thanks to which, as in John Climacus, Athanasios wins his *ἀνάβασις* to heaven.

34 ff For the autobiographical details see Introduction, p. 19 f.

46–47 Athanasios must have been attached to a monastery dedicated to the Theotokos; one such monastery was founded by Ioannikios (*Vita* by Peter, 397A; by Sabas, 351BC and 378B); see also Janin, *Grands centres,* 154 (no. 1).

49 ff The "command" or request on the part of Athanasios appears to have concerned his death and/or burial.

54 *ἀλγεινῆς ἐκείνης*: cf. letter 19.10.

32.

Date: after 842.

A Constantine *spatharios* and *asekretis* was the recipient of Photios' letter 211 (ed. Laourdas and Westerink, II, 111–15), which gives no clues for attempting any dating; in the opening words Constantine is reckoned among the friends of learning

(τοῖς φιλομαθοῦσιν), a feature also characteristic of Ignatios' addressee. To a Constantine *asekretis* belonged three seals dating from the ninth century, according to Laurent, *Corpus,* II, 22–23. On the reverse of the second of them Constantine is designated as *βασιλικὸς σπαθάριος* and *ἀσηκρῆτις*, whom Laurent is inclined to identify with both Photios' and Ignatios' addressees (ibid., 22).

Ignatios, as a literary expert, is being requested for the second time (cf. line 11) to correct an iambic poem celebrating both the pious concerns of the reigning empress (surely Theodora) and the preliminary struggles *τῆς πάλαι πονησάσης*, whom we take to have been Empress Irene, that is, a poem of iconophile propaganda. Constantine is acting as an intermediary on behalf of another person (*τοῖς αἰτήσασι, ὁ καλῶν*), presumably higher placed than himself: in other words, the composition of the poem is being overseen by a government committee. It would appear that Ignatios' first version, which had been metrically correct (*ἤδη καλῶς μετρηθέντας*), had been disregarded in favor of another that did not observe the rules of prosody. Fearing that his second version may be equally unacceptable, Ignatios invites Constantine to come in person so they can agree on the final text.

4 *βάσεσιν*: probably in the sense of "metrical units." Cf. George Choiroboskos, *Commentarius in Hephaestionem,* ed. M. Consbruch (Leipzig, 1906), 211.17–212.1.

7 *τὸ γὰρ συντηρῆσαι . . . αἱρετώτερον*: The meaning of this clause is not completely clear to us. We take *τὴν ἀρχὴν* to be adverbial ("to begin with," "at all"), since *κτήσασθαι τὴν ἀρχὴν* can hardly mean here "to acquire power." Cf., for example, *Basilii scholia in Greg. Naz.,* PG 36, 705C: *μέγα μὲν τὸ μηδὲ τὴν ἀρχὴν τυχεῖν ἁμαρτάνοντας* (*omnino peccasse*). The meaning may be: Better to have kept what was there (i.e., Ignatios' first version) than seeking something new.

8 *τῇ πάλαι ἀμετρίᾳ*: Note the awareness of a cultural revival by comparison with the immediately preceding period.

33.

Date: before 846.

A forceful letter of remonstrance concerning the flight of a novice whom Ignatios had placed in the monastery of Antidion. The imperious tone suggests that Ignatios was in a position of some authority at the time. The use of the epithet *μετριότης* (line 55), which he applies to himself, does not, however, imply that he was a bishop at the time. Cf. letters 29.5 and 49.24.

The "common father" (line 36), who is "equal to the angels" (line 50) is surely St. Ioannikios. It was he who had blessed the novice and who might have been able, had the abbot Joseph chosen to appeal to him, to bring the novice back by his prayers. That implies: (1) that Ioannikios was still alive (he died on 3 Nov. 846); and (2) that he was at the time resident at Antidion or its immediate vicinity. According to the *Vita* by Peter, Ioannikios spent two years of his own novitiate at Antidion (ca. 792/3)

and returned to it at an indeterminate date toward the end of his life (413 and 425AB), in any case before 843. The *Vita* by Sabas gives a somewhat different chronology (first residence at Antidion 796/7–797/8; return to it some time between 825 and 837), which, as we have tried to show elsewhere, has been deliberately doctored: see Mango, "Two Lives," 393–404.

Joseph was abbot of Antidion when Ioannikios died and was buried at the monastery (*Vita* by Sabas, 383A) and it was he who commissioned Sabas to compose the saint's revised Life, probably some time in the mid-850s (ibid., 333A).

Taken in conjunction, the above data suggest that our letter could not have been written much before 846.

Antidion (see Janin, *Grands centres,* 135 ff) was located on the slopes of the Bithynian Olympus, below a peak called Crow's Head (Κόρακος κεφαλή): *Vita* by Sabas, 340B. It was a considerable distance from the monastery of the Agauroi (Eunuchs): *Vita* by Peter, 388AB; note the expression *τὸ τῆς ὁδοῦ μῆκος ἐγκόπως διοδεύσας*. On his way from Agauroi to Antidion Ioannikios passed by a village called Kastoulos *πρὸς* Ἀ*τρώαν* and spent a few days in a nearby monastery called *τῶν* Τ*ελάου*. Finding it less than peaceful, he went up the mountain to Antidion (*Vita* by Sabas, 340A). Two other localities on the way from Agauroi to Antidion were Meriloukome and Trapeza (*Vita* by Peter, 423BC = *Vita* by Sabas, 362C–363A).

Agauroi was situated 15 stadia (ca. 3 km) from "the little town of Prousa," at the foot of a hill called Mount Trichalix or Mount Agaurinon: *Vita Eustratii* (*BHG*[3] 645), ed. Papadopoulos-Kerameus, 370. It seems to have been to the west of Prousa, because the dead body of Eustratios was carried thither from Constantinople by way of the hot baths of Prousa (Çekirge): ibid., 397.

As for Atroa, it is described as a plain lying next to Mount Olympus: Leo Diaconus, ed. C. B. Hase (Bonn, 1828), 177 (*κατὰ τὴν τῷ* Ὀ*λύμπῳ παρακειμένην τῆς* Ἀ*τρώας πεδιάδα*). John Tzimiskes, returning from Syria (975), stopped there at the house of the patrician Romanos and was poisoned by a eunuch. This would indicate that Atroa was not too far from the main highway leading, by way of Nicaea, to the eastern front. The same conclusion is suggested by the notice that the thematic armies gathered *ἐν τῇ* Ἀ*τρώᾳ* to proclaim Constantine VI emperor (790): Theoph., 466. That would argue for Atroa being to the north or, possibly, east of Mount Olympus. Ramsay, *Hist. Geogr.,* 189, has already suggested it was the same as ancient Otroia, described by Strabo (12.7) as being a short distance from the Ascanian lake and placed on the *Classical Map of Asia Minor* by Calder and Bean some 10 km south of Nicaea, that is, at modern Yenişehir. Whether that is so or not, one may wonder whether Antidion belonged to the diocese of Nicaea rather than that of Nicomedia (which included Prousa).

The Byzantine topography of the Olympus area has been more confused than elucidated by the arbitrary ideas of B. Menthon, which have been to a large extent

accepted by V. Laurent and R. Janin. B. Menthon, *L'Olympe de Bithynie* (Paris, 1935), 49–50, places Atroa southwest of Prousa on the grounds, it seems, that a village known in his days as Misi reminded him of the Byzantine Mesôn, described as being at Atroa in the *Vita Constantini Iudaei* (*BHG*³ 370), *AASS,* Nov. IV, 641D. So also Laurent, *La Vie merveilleuse,* 37–38 and Janin's map in *Grands centres,* 130. The solution of this and other problems will have to wait for a more systematic survey of the terrain.

47–48 *τῆς ἁγίας στολῆς*: probably with reference to the so-called *μικρὸν σχῆμα*.

34.

The only point of interest in this extremely convoluted appeal for a letter on the part of Nikephoros is the reference to the word of God being in danger of perishing. This may concern the theological endeavor mentioned in letter 30.

35.

1 ff The rashness in question stems from speaking or rather writing first, that is, before Nikephoros, who is so great an expert in the art of discourse. The first sentence, if it is not corrupt, is unclear to us. In particular, the sporting proverb *ὑπὲρ τὰ ἐσκαμμένα ἅλλεσθαι* (to leap beyond the area that has been dug up for a soft landing in the long jump) does not accord well with *γεωργίας ἄτερ*, whatever may be the exact meaning of *γεωργία* (cultivation of literature?).

36.

7 ff What follows is presumably in answer to a query from Nikephoros, unless Ignatios is correcting a mistake made by his friend (cf. mention of "impertinence" at the end).

7 *τέχνης* in the sense of grammatical rules. Cf. *τὸν τεχνικὸν* in line 21.

8 *Δυσκόλου . . . παιδί*: Herodian was the son of Apollonios Dyskolos of Alexandria according to the biographical notice in *Herodiani technici reliquiae,* ed. A. Lentz, I (Leipzig, 1867), vi. It seems that in the eyes of Ignatios, Herodian, rather than his father, was the creator of systematic grammar. The reference, as K. Alpers kindly informs us, appears to be to Herodian's treatise *περὶ παθῶν*, fragments of which, drawn from lexica, are edited by Lentz, II (Leipzig, 1868), 166–388 (irrespective of the question whether they are all correctly attributed). Cf. H. Schultz, "Herodianus," *RE* 8.1 (1912), 966f. Ignatios may have been acquainted with the complete text of this work, which was cannibalized by lexicographers in the ninth to tenth centuries. Herodian returns to the same matter in his *Περὶ καθολικῆς προσῳδίας*, c. XIX, Lentz, I, 491.7–9: *πᾶν μονοσύλλαβον ἐπίρρημα, εἰ μὲν ἔχει φύσει βραχεῖαν, δῆλον ὡς ὀξύνεται, πάξ . . . δὰξ παρὰ τοῦ δήκω, ὅπερ*

καὶ ὀδὰξ λέγεται, and 492.6: *τὰ ἔχοντα δίχρονον ἐκτεταμένον περισπᾶται, "ἆ δειλὲ πάντων,"* etc.

12 Μηλαίῳ γραμματικῷ: a crux. The manuscript gives *μηλαιω*, which could be read either as Μηλαίῳ or *μὴ λαιῷ*. The form Μηλαῖος is unknown. The ethnikon of Melos is Μήλιος and of Melis (Malis) Μηλιεύς: Stephanus Byzantius, *Ethnica,* ed. A. Meineke (Berlin, 1849), 450. Besides, no famous grammarian is recorded as a native of either Melos or Malis. If we accept *μὴ λαιῷ* as the correct reading, the only possible interpretation is as a negative equivalent to *δεξιῷ*, that is, "dexterous, skillful." I. Ševčenko calls to our attention the study by E. Follieri, "Ciriaco *ὁ μελαῖος*," in *Zetesis. Album amicorum . . . aangeboden aan Prof. Dr. E. de Strycker* (Antwerp-Utrecht, 1973), 502–28. Previously interpreted as "native of Mili" (near Messina), *μελαῖος* is an alternative spelling of *μέλεος* ("idle, miserable"). The "miserable grammarian" (if we adopt the reading *μελαίῳ*) would presumably refer to Ignatios himself. In that case we would have to credit him with the composition of a grammatical handbook that does not appear to have survived. Cf. Introduction, p. 14.

19 *δίς, τρίς*: cf. Apollonius, *De adverbiis, Grammatici graeci,* I.1, ed. R. Schneider (Leipzig, 1878), 174.18–19: *καὶ κατὰ τοῦτο οὖν τις σημειώσαιτο τὸ διχῶς καὶ τριχῶς, ὅτι πλεονοσυλλαβεῖ τοῦ δὶς καὶ τρίς. Ἀλλ' ἴσως ἐπεὶ οὐδὲ ὁλόκληρα αὐτὰ τὰ ἐπιρρήματα, ἐν δὲ συγκοπῇ, καὶ τὰ παρακείμενα οὐ τῇ συγκοπῇ ἠκολούθει, τῇ δὲ ὁλοκλήρῳ προφορᾷ.*

21 *κανόνι* should perhaps be capitalized. Theodosius wrote a textbook called Κανόνες (*Gramm. gr.,* IV.1, 3–99) and Choiroboskos a set of scholia on it (*Gramm. gr.,* IV.1–2).

37.

Date: After ca. 830, perhaps by several years.

German translation and short commentary by G. Karlsson, *Orientalia Suecana* 33–35 (1984–86), 212–14.

Nikephoros, driven by despondency, withdrew to the island of Oxeia and seems to have written from there a (jocular?) letter extolling the beauties of that barren spot.

On Oxeia, the most westerly of the Princes' islands, see Janin, *Grands centres,* 65–67. In the ninth century it appears as a place of detention: Platon, the uncle of Theodore the Studite, was held there from 809 until 811 (*Laud. in Platonem* [*BHG*^{3} 1553], PG 99, 841C), and a certain Gebon, a pretender to the throne, in 856 (*Vita Ignatii* [*BHG*^{3} 817], PG 105, 505B). One may surmise that there was at the time a monastic establishment on the island to which Nikephoros would have withdrawn, but it is not specifically recorded. In the late eleventh/early twelfth century Gregory Taronites spent some time on Oxeia, where he found a single monk in residence: see synaxarion notice published by Mango in *JÖB* 42 (1992), 222–23.

32 Ὀξεῖαν, *πλατεῖαν*: a double pun. The island nearest Oxeia was called Platê.

COMMENTARY

36 Crete: The date of the Arab invasion, of which widely divergent accounts are given in Byzantine and Arab sources, has been much discussed. The best evidence suggests that the Andalusian Arabs landed on Crete in 827 or 828 and that the conquest of the island took many years to complete. See especially E. W. Brooks, "The Arab Occupation of Crete," *English Historical Review* 28 (1913), 431–33; A. A. Vasiliev, *Byzance et les Arabes,* I (Brussels, 1935), 52ff; G. C. Miles, "Byzantium and the Arabs," *DOP* 18 (1964), 10; D. Tsougarakis, *Byzantine Crete* (Athens, 1988), 30ff. Repeated Byzantine attempts to expel the Arabs, undertaken under the leadership of Photeinos and Damianos (date uncertain), Krateros (in the reign of Theophilos), and the logothete Theoktistos (843), all ended in failure.

Cyprus had been since 688 a neutral zone, which paid taxes to both Byzantium and the Caliphate, but belonged to neither power. See R.J.H. Jenkins, "Cyprus between Byzantium and Islam, AD 688–965," in *Studies Presented to D. M. Robinson,* II (St. Louis, 1953) (= *Studies on Byzantine History of the 9th and 10th Centuries* [London, 1970], XXII).

Euboea: The only recorded Arab attack on Euboea took place in ca. 880, when the emir of Tarsus unsuccessfully laid siege to Chalcis: Theoph. Cont., 298.1–299.12; Cedrenus, II, 225.9–226.24; and Skylitzes, 151.27ff. Cf. H. Grégoire, "La carrière du premier Nicéphore Phocas," *Προσφορὰ εἰς Σ. Π. Κυριακίδην* (Thessaloniki, 1953), 247–48; and Miles, *DOP* 18 (1964), 7, who also notes (ibid., 18, and fig. 13) a Koranic inscription in the Museum of Chalcis. Ignatios must be referring to an earlier raid, which may possibly be connected with a story told in the *Vita Theoctistae Lesbiae, AASS,* Nov. IV, 227, cc. 8–9, according to which a certain Nisiris, commander of the Cretan fleet, suffered shipwreck off Cape Xylophagos (Kavodoro) of Euboea. Cf. V. Christides, *Byz* 51 (1981), 93; Tsougarakis, *Byzantine Crete,* 45 note 89. On the unreliability of the Life of Theoktiste, see L. G. Westerink, *Nicétas Magistros, Lettres d'un exilé* (Paris, 1973), 44–45. We may also note the statement in Theoph. Cont., 137, that, following the defeat of the Byzantine navy by the Arabs off Thasos (Oct. 829), *κατὰ τὸ ἑξῆς δὲ* (i.e., not necessarily in the same year) *τὰς Κυκλάδας νήσους, ἀλλὰ μὴν καὶ τὰς ἄλλας ἁπάσας, ὁ τῶν Ἰσμαηλιτῶν κατασύρων στρατὸς οὐκ ἐπαύετο.* Cf. Vasiliev, *Byzance et les Arabes,* I, 90. In a different context this is also recorded in the *Life of the Empress Theodora,* ed. A. Markopoulos, *Σύμμεικτα* 5 (1985), 263 (§7.9–11): *Ὡσαύτως καὶ πλήθη πλοίων αὐτῶν ἐξελθόντα τὰς Κυκλάδας νήσους ἠρήμωσαν καὶ τὴν Κρήτην καὶ Σικελίαν παρέλαβον.*

Lesbos: The Life of Theoktiste, 229, refers to an Arab plundering expedition at an indeterminate date after ca. 830. Cf. Miles, *DOP* 18 (1964), 8 and note 28, who records an Idrisid dirham of H 232/A.D. 846–847 found on the island. K. M. Setton, "On the Raids of the Moslems in the Aegean in the 9th and 10th Centuries and Their Alleged Occupation of Athens," *AJA* 58 (1954), 313 and note 8, without sufficient justification, places this raid in 826–827.

Sardinia, after enjoying a century of relative peace, suffered repeated Arab raids from 806 onwards, particularly in 821–822. M. Amari, *Storia dei Musulmani di Sicilia,* 2nd ed. (Catania, 1933), I, 350–65; E. Besta, *La Sardegna medioevale. Le vicende politiche del 450 al 1326* (Palermo, 1908), I, 34–44; C. Bellieni, *La Sardegna e i Sardi nella civilità dell'alto medioevo* (Cagliari, 1973), II, 539 ff, 621 ff, 641 ff; A. Boscolo, *La Sardegna bizantina e alto-giudicale* (Sassari, 1978), 64–67, who mentions Muslim attacks in 807, 810, 813, 821 and concludes with the words "a partire dall' 822 la Sardegna rimaneva immune da aggressioni musulmane per più di un secolo." For the sigillographic evidence relating to the Byzantine presence see Laurent, *Corpus,* V.1 721 ff; and *Catalogue of the Byzantine Seals at Dumbarton Oaks,* ed. J. Nesbitt and N. Oikonomides, I (Washington, D.C., 1991), 36–37.

37 Sicily: The Arab invasion began in 827. See, among others, Vasiliev, *Byzance et les Arabes,* I, 61 ff; P. J. Alexander, "Les débuts des conquêtes arabes en Sicile," *Bollettino del Centro di Studi filologichi e linguistichi siciliani* 12 (1973), 1–35 (= *Religious and Political History and Thought in the Byzantine Empire* [London, 1978], XIV).

40 *κινδυνεύουσαι μηκέτι*: Our correction is somewhat drastic, but the meaning is sufficiently clear. "Christians" is equivalent to "Romans."

42 It is possible to understand *δυνάστου* in the sense of "emperor," especially if the emperor of the day was heretical, and translate "shall hearken to the lamentations of the ruler." We have preferred to postulate a small lacuna in view of the biblical sources; on the one hand Ps. 34:10 (*ῥυόμενος πτωχὸν ἐκ χειρὸς στερεωτέρων αὐτοῦ*), on the other, Ps. 71:12 (*ὅτι ἐρρύσατο πτωχὸν ἐκ χειρὸς δυνάστου*) and Job 29:12 (*διέσωσα γὰρ πτωχὸν ἐκ χειρὸς δυνάστου*).

38.

4 *πρὸς ποῖον*: Gregory's oration (PG 35, cols. 933 ff) is entitled *Εἰς τὸν πατέρα σιωπῶντα διὰ τὴν πληγὴν τῆς χαλάζης*, although, strictly speaking, he was not addressing his father.

7–10 A clear admission of past involvement with the Iconoclasts.

34 We have translated *χάρτης* by "papyrus," but this passage should not be taken as evidence for the continuing use of papyrus at Constantinople.

35 *κνηπία*: Our correction appears certain. Cf. Lampe, s.v. *κνιπεία* and *σκνιπία*. The spelling varies: in Theoph., 296.5, the MSS give *σκνιπία*, *κνιπία* and *κνηπία*. Cf. *Vita Andreae sali,* PG 111, col. 656B: *κνιπὸς* (stingy) *δαίμων ὡς μικρὸν πιθήκιον ἐπὶ τὸν ὦμόν σου κάθηται τὸν δεξιόν*, and *Scholia in Lucianum,* 62: *μικρολογία* = *κνιπότης*.

39.

A *protonotarios* of the Course with the same name happens to be known; he appears in the sources as competing with Michael III in the hippodrome. Being in-

formed about the raids of the Arabs in the Thrakesion theme, he tried in vain to call the attention of the emperor to this important matter; see Theoph. Cont., 198–99; Skylitzes, 124; Glycas, 542. Since this occurred after Photios' first ascension to the patriarchal throne (858), he must have outlived Ignatios. We are also informed by the same sources that he was a patrician and father of the logothete Thomas. The fact that he is also designated as *βασιλικὸς σπαθάριος* supports his identity with the addressee of letter 32.

Tit. *πρωτονοτάριος τοῦ δρόμου*: most senior subordinate of the logothete of the Course, the minister responsible for the public post and foreign relations. Usually of spathar rank: Bury, *System,* 92; Oikonomidès, *Listes,* 311; R. Guilland, "Les logothètes," *REB* 29 (1971), 38–40; D. A. Miller, "The Logothete of the Drome in the Middle Byzantine Period," *Byz* 36 (1966), 446.

7 *λογοθέτου*: probably Theoktistos, who was already in office under Theophilos and served as Theodora's chief minister until his murder in 856.

40.

1 ff We are given here a tantalizing, but, unfortunately, very vague reference to some kind of doctrinal formula that had been accepted, then revoked. Both Nikephoros and Ignatios were involved in this procedure and both ended up on the orthodox side, although Ignatios' confession appears to have met with a hostile reception. The date is probably after the death of Theophilos (842).

8 We have kept *τόπου*, which is not necessarily wrong (whatever exactly it may mean), although it is tempting to correct it either to *τύπου* (formulation) or *τόμου*.

δι' ἀμφοῖν: both on account of my correct doctrine and the accepted formulation (?).

17 *συμβάσης ὑμῖν ἐπηρείας*: This may mean that Nikephoros was as badly treated as Ignatios with reference to his recantation.

22 *'Αναστάσιος*: A monk Anastasios appears in VGD 62.16 ff. He must have been one of Ignatios' informants when composing this *vita.*

25 Ignatios is quoting here a famous Homeric simile that is applied to Paris (*Il.* 6.506) and, once again, to Hector (15.263):

> *ὡς δ' ὅτε τις στατὸς ἵππος, ἀκοστήσας ἐπὶ φάτνῃ,*
> *δεσμὸν ἀπορρήξας θείῃ πεδίοιο κροαίνων*, etc.

The occurrence of the verb *κριθιᾶσαι* proves that he was acquainted with a commentary, but the question remains how he understood the passage. Scholiasts disagreed about the meaning of the *hapax ἀκοστήσας*, interpreting it as *ἄκος τῆς στάσεως λαβών, τουτέστιν ἴαμα καὶ κριθιάσας* or *δυσχεράνας ἐπὶ τῆς φάτνης στάσει* or as *ἀγοστήσας* (*ἀγοστός* = filth): *Scholia in Iliadem,* Erbse, II, 215–17. Eustathios (658.40) gives the alternatives: *πολυκριθῆσαι* according to the

ancients; *σχεῖν ἄχος ἐν τῷ ἵστασθαι* (being tired of standing); *ἀκολάστως διατεθῆναι* (*ἀκοστήσας* being shortened from *ἀκολαστήσας*); *ἀγοστήσας* = *ῥυπανθείς*, hence desiring its habitual pasture and bathing. The Homeric simile is often quoted, for example, by Demetrius, *Eloc.* 89; Greg. Naz., *Or.* 43.24, PG 36, 528c (of his eagerness to rejoin Basil), and the comment of Ps.-Nonnus ad loc., ed. Nimmo Smith, 263–64.

The drift of our passage, which is unfortunately corrupt, seems to be that the stallion, after becoming overfed, broke its bonds and lost weight by grazing in a "literary" pasture. Several difficulties remain: (1) The meaningless *ποιησάμενος* may conceal *ποίης*, the stallion being desirous of grass rather than barley. Cf. the scholiast's *οὕτω γὰρ ποθεῖ τὴν συνήθη δίαιταν* (Erbse, II, 216). Something like *ποίης ἱμειρόμενος* or *ὀρεγόμενος* would give a satisfactory sense. (2) *τοῖς λογικοῖς συγχλοάσας* (a *hapax?*) probably means "having fed on grass in the company of men of letters," although *χλοάζω* (act.) = to be green or budding. The middle *συγχλοασάμενος* would be more correct.

The stallion presumably represents a person who, after a period of inactivity (comparable to that of Paris in the *Iliad*), has entered the fray of literary or theological endeavor. His identity is unknown to us.

29 *ἡ σπάνις . . . μήπω γενομένων ἐφήψατο*: a hyperbole; cf. Lysias, *Or.* 7.1: *δοκεῖ μοι δεῖν καὶ τοὺς μὴ γεγονότας ἤδη δεδιέναι περὶ τῶν μελλόντων ἔσεσθαι.*

41.

1 *σκολιώδεις*: The only attestation of this word given in LSJ and Stephanus is in *Apollonii sophistae lexicon homericum,* ed. I. Bekker (Berlin, 1833), 126, s.v. *παιπαλόεντος*: *τραχέος καὶ σκολιώδους*. Cf., however, VN 202.9: *συμφορήσας σκολιώδη* [*σκολοιώδη* cod.; *κολοιώδη* de Boor] *λέσχην* of the iconoclastic committee organized by Patriarch Theodotos.

1–2 *Ἡρακλείδου Λέσχης*: Heraclides of Pontus was the author of a poem in three books, famous for its obscurity, in the form of a conversation between learned men: A. Meineke, *Analecta alexandrina* (Berlin, 1843), 377–81; *RE* 8 (1913), 487–88, s.v. Herakleides 49; E. Heitsch, *Die griechischen Dichterfragmente der römischen Kaiserzeit,* II (Göttingen, 1964), 41. According to the *Suda* (463), he wrote *βιβλία γ' δυσερμήνευτα καὶ πολλὴν τὴν ἀπορίαν ἔχοντα προβαλλομένων ζητήσεων ἅτινα Λέσχας ἐκάλεσεν*. According to Artemidorus, *Oneir.* 4.63, they contained *ἱστορίαι ξέναι καὶ ἄτριπτοι* (unusual). A commentary on the *Λέσχη* is mentioned in *Etym. gud.,* 247.49.

The first sentence of the letter is unclear and may require emendation. As it stands, it ought to mean, "You think you are troubling me by your silence for my being tortuous and obscure." That is not very satisfactory. We could consider emend-

ing *ὡς σκολιώδης ⟨τις⟩ καί . . . ἐργάτης*, that is, "Being tortuous and a practitioner of Heraclides, you think," etc. The question remains, however, whether Ignatios is making a specific reference to the *Leschê,* which may have mentioned some tortuous or crooked-looking worker who confused his interlocutors by his silence, in which case one may read *ὡς ⟨ὁ⟩ σκολιώδης [καὶ] . . . ἐργάτης*. Even if Ignatios was not acquainted with the original text, he may have known the above-mentioned commentary.

3–4 *τὰς αἰσθήσεις ἡμῶν πικρανθείσας*: possible allusion to the monastery of Pikridion, Ignatios' place of involuntary reclusion in his later days.

5–6 *βατραχείου . . . μυοκτόνου παρεμβολῆς*: See H. Wölke, *Untersuchungen zur Batrachomyomachia* (Meisenheim am Glan, 1978), 33.249 (edition of our letter based on Karlsson's collation). The *Batr.* was known in ninth-century Byzantium. It is cited by Choiroboskos, *Scholia in Theod. Canones, Gramm. gr.* IV.1, 139.1, with regard to the quantity of the word *μῦς*, and the epithet *λιμνοχαρής* (*Batr.* 12.212) occurs in the Life of Theophanes by Methodius (*BHG*[3] 1787z), ed. Latyšev, 22.32.

14 *τορόν τι καὶ ἐνυάλιον*: VN 147.9.

15–16 *παρουσιάσαντι . . . διωνύμῳ σηκῷ*: *παρουσιάζω* (cf. letter 63.10) is unclassical. LSJ quotes only *Anonymi Scholia in Ethica Nicomachea,* ed. G. Heylbut (Berlin, 1892), 438.6. Lampe gives only Gregorius magnus (translated by Zacharias), *Dial.* 4.36, Patrologia latina 77, 383B. Further examples in Stephanus, s.v. (all Byzantine). Nikephoros may have been summoned to present himself for an interview. The epithet *διωνύμῳ* is ambiguous, since it can mean either "far-famed" or "having two names" (e.g., Sts. Peter and Paul). We have chosen the former alternative in the light of VT 400.28: *ἐν τῷ τῆς* Μαγναύρας *διωνύμῳ παλατίῳ*; and VN 192.14–15: *τὸ τοῦ θείου λόγου διώνυμον τέμενος*. The reference must be to the famous church of the Holy Apostles on the fourth hill.

17 *προσαλείψωμεν*: literally, "smear ourselves as with an ointment." Cf. *Od.* 10.392.

42.

Date: presumably late in Ignatios' life.

6ff Possibly refers to the death of the same servant whose illness is mentioned in letter 38.

43–47.

Date: 843 or a little later.

Probably written in that sequence at short intervals. In no. 43, Ignatios had not yet been relegated to Pikridion; in no. 44, he had been there a short time; no. 45 was

written during Lent, and no. 46 in the spring or early summer. We assume that the *ἀρχιερεύς* in no. 43 is Methodios.

Pikridion and its monastery: see Janin, *CP,* 465–66; *Églises,* 403–4; A. Berger, *Untersuchungen zu den Patria Konstantinoupoleos,* *Ποικίλα Βυζαντινά* 8 (Bonn, 1988), 688. The monastery was built by Pikridios, chamberlain (*κοιτωνίτης*) under Empress Irene (*Patria,* ed. Th. Preger [Leipzig, 1901], 265), probably the same as John Pikridios, *protospatharios* and *βάγυλος* (preceptor), whom Irene exiled in 790, along with others, *ἐπὶ τὰ κατωτικὰ μέρη* (Greece?) and "as far as Sicily" (Theoph., 465.3–5). When the army refused to recognize Irene, Pikridios returned soon after October of the same year, and was sent on a mission to the Armeniac theme (ibid., 466.22–25). The monastery is recorded in 817, when its abbot Theodosios signed, along with Theodore the Studite and three other abbots, two letters to Pope Pascal (nos. 271.5 and 272.5; ed. Fatouros, 400 and 402). The fact that Theodosios took a resolute stand against Iconoclasm (no. 267.30; ibid., 395) may have been a reason why Ignatios was relegated to his monastery.

In 902 the patrician Constantine Karamalos, judged responsible for the capture of Taormina by the Arabs, was interned in the monastery: Leo Gramm., 275.3; Georgios mon. Continuatus, 861. In the tenth/eleventh century, the scholar John Sikeliotes delivered an imperial oration *ἐν τοῖς Πικριδίου*: cf. C. M. Mazzucchi, "Longino in Giovanni di Sicilia," *Aevum* 64 (1990), 183 note 1.

The monastery is known to have been *πέραν*, that is, on the north side of the Golden Horn, near a church of St. Anthimos (*Synaxarium CP,* 9.25), presumably the one built by Justinian (Procop., *De aed.* 1.6.9–14). The latter was on the water's edge, across the bay from the church of Sts. Cosmas and Damian. Traditionally, *ta Pikridiou* has been placed at modern Hasköy, which appears to be not far from the truth, seeing that the church of Sts. Cosmas and Damian was probably just outside the Blachernae walls (as Mango argues in *Θυμίαμα στη μνήμη της Λασκαρίνας Μπούρα* [Athens, 1994], 189 ff) rather than at Turkish Eyüp, as commonly asserted. By the time of Gyllius (1544–50), the area of Hasköy was known as Hagia Paraskeve: *De Bosporo thracio,* ii.2 (1561 ed.), 57. On the Greek church of that name, attested as a *hagiasma* since 1539, see M. I. Gedeon, *Ἔγγραφοι λίθοι καὶ κεράμια* (Constantinople, 1892), *ρλδ'* ff.

43.

3 *κεραννύειν ἀντίδοτον*: On the possible allusion to the monastery of Antidion, see Introduction, p. 19.

44.

9 *κεκανονισμένη σιγῇ*: cf. letter 45.28. During Lent, or was Ignatios placed under a special penance?

45.

3ff *πεντάθυρον*: The classic statement of this theme is by John Chrysostom, *De inani gloria,* ed. A. M. Malingrey, SC 188 (Paris, 1972), c. 23ff.

7 *ἰοδόκων*: In Homer *φαρέτρη ἰοδόκος* is a quiver holding arrows. By adding *βελῶν*, Ignatios changes the meaning of *ἰοδόκων* to "poisonous" (as in Nicander, *Theriaca,* 184).

28 *σιγῆς ἐπιτίμιον*: perhaps to be understood metaphorically. The meaningless *ἐπαμφιδέξιον* is difficult to explain as a simple misreading. The sense requires a participle meaning "offering," "addressing," or the like. The ending *–δεξιον* suggests *δεξιούμενος*, which has the right meaning and proparoxytone ending, but that would call for *λόγῳ ἡμᾶς*. It may be, therefore, that Ignatios started by writing another participle, say *ἐπαφιείς*, then added *δεξιούμενος* (abbreviated) as an improvement without bothering to adjust the construction. D. I. Polemis proposes *ἐπαναφανεὶς διεξιών*.

46.

1 *φθινὰς νόσος*: also in *Vita S. Theophylacti Nicomediae,* (*BHG*³ 2451), ed. F. Halkin, *Hagiologie byzantine* (Brussels, 1986), 181.3.

8ff It appears that Nikephoros did have medical skills and that the appeal to them should not be understood metaphorically; cf. some relevant expressions in letters 4.17–18 and 43.2–7.

12 *γαληνίοις*: a pun on the name of Galen as in letter 21.46.

14 *πραϋγελώσης*: *πραΰγελως* is attested as a single word, notably in *Anth. Pal.,* IX.229, X.4, etc.

17 *τὰ ἔσχατα*: an exaggeration if *ta Pikridiou* was at or near modern Hasköy. Ignatios must have been forbidden to cross the Golden Horn to Constantinople.

47.

1 *διερευνώμενος*: cf. letter 38.4.

5 The harsh letter can hardly be the same as no. 46.

49.

Date: 843–846.

Probably written from the monastery of Pikridion, if not from another monastery (if *μονῇ* in line 12 is right) to which Ignatios had been relegated. He appears to have been under sentence of excommunication: *τρυφή* is applied to the eucharist in the Liturgy of St. Basil, ed. Brightman, 344.27, while Cyril of Alexandria uses *τρυφῆς χείμαρρος* of Christ: *Comm. in Isaiam,* 3.3, PG 70, 749c. It is worth noting that, in spite of his disgrace, Ignatios carried some weight with the orthodox establishment; otherwise the unnamed monk would not have sought his support.

Ignatios of Nicomedia is known to have offered a bishopric to Paul, brother of St. Peter of Atroa. Paul died on 26 August 844; ed. Laurent, 152–53 (§103.7). Ignatios of Nicomedia must have been ordained in 843 and appears to have been deposed before November 846, if he was the same as the Monomachos (Christian name not given), whose company Patriarch Methodios was urged to avoid by St. Ioannikios: *τοῦ τε σὺν αὐτοῖς* (the Studites) *Κακοσάμβα καὶ τῆς Νικομηδείας ἐπισκοπῆς ἐκπεπτωκότος τοῦ Μονομάχου ἤτοι θεομάχου* (*Life* of Ioannikios by Peter, *AASS,* Nov. II, 432B). It follows that Ignatios belonged to the Studite party, condemned in 845/6 (Grumel, *Regestes,* nos. 433–34). A Studite monk Ignatios often appears in Theodore's correspondence: see on him Fatouros, 242*, n. 342. The name Monomachos was also borne by the patrician Nicetas: D. Papachryssanthou, *TM* 3 (1968), 316–17. This Ignatios may also have been the owner of seal no. 377; cf. Laurent, *Corpus,* V.1, 271.

5 *τῆς τρυφῆς χειμάρρου*: cf. Canonem Ignatii in XLII Mart. Amor., *Analecta hymnica graeca,* VII (Rome, 1971), 88.

13–14 *μικρᾶς . . . ἐπισκοπῆς*: The metropolitan of Nicomedia had in the ninth century eleven suffragan bishoprics, some of them quite minor: Darrouzès, *Notitiae,* 4, 253–54. Among them Prousa is listed first and Eriste last.

50.

This letter is of significance for the tradition of Greek paroemiographers. It seems that Ignatios, who frequently quotes proverbs, had made his own compilation from "secular," that is, ancient texts and was intending to augment it. This does not appear to have survived, although it may have left a trace in other anthologies. On the subject see K. Rupprecht, "Paroimiographi," *RE* 36.3 (1949), 1747ff. The collections that circulated in the Byzantine period were mostly epitomes of ancient ones, such as those that go under the names of Zenobius (2nd century A.D.), who himself boiled down earlier compilations by Didymus and Lucillus, and Diogenianus, represented, *inter alia,* in the *Suda.* A conflated *vulgata* is believed to have emerged by ca. A.D. 900. The term *ὑποθῆκαι* (line 3) suggests a didactic element and may imply that Ignatios' personal compilation, in addition to proverbial locutions, which normally carry no moral message, also contained *γνῶμαι*, as conjectured by P. Odorico, *Il prato e l'ape* (Vienna, 1986), 7ff. See also ibid., 18ff, for the argument that a gnomologion may have been compiled at Constantinople in the circle of John the Grammarian. For a relevant use of *ὑποθῆκαι*, see VN 160.27: *γραφικαῖς ὑπο-θήκαις*.

51.

3 *νοστίμου*: cf. letter 13.9.

14 *αἴθης πέπλος*: the robe, smeared with blood, of Nessus.

17 *ἀναπηνιζέσθω*: strictly speaking, *ἀναπηνίζομαι* means "to unravel" rather than its opposite, as here.

52.

Date: 843–847.

One in a series of begging letters, as appears from line 6. The classical allusions are meant to appeal to Methodios' learning.

1 *πεπειράμην*: pluperfect with no augment, as in VN 163.6 (*συγκεκρότητο*); 173.29 (*τετύπωτο . . . μεμόρφωτο*); 177.13 (*νενέκρωντο*), etc.

9–10 *ἐκ τελείας . . . προαιρέσεως*: For a similar wording see the letter of Theodore metropolitan of Cyzicus (10th century), ed. S. Lampros, Νέος Ἑλλ. 19 (1925), 186.15–16: *ὡς ἐκ γλυκείας σοι καὶ οὐ πικρᾶς προσδεχθείησαν προαιρέσεως*.

53–54.

Date: 843–847.

These two letters were written simultaneously and concern the same matter. Ignatios had inherited from his elder brother (on whom see letter 62) a manuscript of the four Gospels, which he lent to Stephen *asekretis.* The latter passed it on to Michael of Synada, who kept it until his death. It then came into the hands of the bishop of Hierapolis, who had been refusing to return it. Ignatios is now appealing to the *protonotarios* (as chief of the patriarchal bureau) and, through him, to the patriarch for the return of his property.

Stephen *asekretis* was probably in office in 796, when Theodore the Studite had a discussion with him on certain theological and canonical questions (letter 5; cf. Fatouros, 148*), and was apparently still in the same post in 821, when Theodore wrote him his letter 419, urging him to intervene in favor of images with Michael II, who had recently ascended the throne. A Stephen occupying the same post in the reign of Theophilos is mentioned in the *Life* of St. Michael the Synkellos; after he had been denounced to the emperor for his orthodox beliefs, he suffered persecution and fell into heresy. Michael's encouraging letters made him confess that Christ should be venerated in icons. Along with the *spatharios* Kallonas, he was condemned to banishment, and his property was confiscated; see ed. M. Cunningham (Belfast, 1991), 74.25–78.22. Finally, a Stephen *asekretis,* surnamed Kapetolites, is recorded as a poet at the court of Theophilos in ca. 838, but, in view of what is stated in the *Life* of St. Michael, he does not seem to have been identical to the one in question. See Theoph. Cont., 143, and Introduction, p. 15.

Michael of Synada, one of the most prominent members of the iconophile party, was ordained by Tarasios between 784 and 787, served on several diplomatic

missions, and, after speaking up against Leo V at the famous meeting of December 814, was banished soon thereafter to Eudokias in Phrygia. He was moved to Constantinople by 817–818 (Theodore Studite, letter 364) and probably remained in confinement until the accession of Michael II. He died on 23 May 826. See especially J. Pargoire, "Saints iconophiles," *EO* 4 (1900–1901), 347 ff; Fatouros, 362*, n. 712. It follows, in any case, that Ignatios had not seen his book for a good twenty-five years.

The bishop of Hierapolis (probably the metropolis of Phrygia Pacatiana, modern Pamukkale, rather than the suffragan of Synada in Phrygia Salutaris) cannot be identified. The only known ninth-century incumbents appear to be Ignatios, appointed after 862–863 (cf. Grumel, *Regestes,* no. 474), who was present at the Councils of 869 and 879, and Nikon, transferred by Photios from either Laodicea or Nicaea (Grumel, *Regestes,* no. 546). See W. M. Ramsay, *The Cities and Bishoprics of Phrygia,* I (Oxford, 1895), 120; Laurent, *Corpus,* V.1, no. 730; R. Aubert, in *DHGE* 24, 1446; and K. Belke and N. Mersich, *Phrygien und Pisidien, Tabula Imperii Byzantini* 7 (Vienna, 1990), 268–72.

53.

A Theophilos, deacon, *kouboukleisios,* and *protonotarios,* owned seal no. 120, which, according to Laurent, *Corpus,* V.1, 98–99, dates from the second half of the ninth century.

On the office of *protonotarios,* see Darrouzès, *Offikia,* 355 ff.

4 *πτυκτίου*: On this term see B. Atsalos, *La terminologie du livre-manuscrit à l'époque byzantine,* I (Thessaloniki, 1971), 95 ff.

11 *διεσμιλευμένως*: in the sense not of *perpolite, subtiliter,* but of *ἠκριβωμένως* as in Hesych.

14 *ἀνυπόβλητον*: The MS reading appears impossible. Lampe, s.v., cites this word from Ps.-Justin, *Quaest. et resp.* 114, PG 6, 1364A, with the meaning "not subject to."

54.

2 *εὐταλάντως*: Lampe quotes *εὐτάλαντος* from George Pisides' *Hex.,* 208 (PG 92, 1449A).

10 *αἰτιατικῆς* (so V) *τετρακτύος*: *αἰτιατικῆς* (= causal, accusatory) appears inappropriate. *Τετρακτύς*, the Pythagorean term for the sum of the first four numbers, that is, 10, had been applied to the four Gospels since Eusebius (references in Lampe, s.v.).

14 *Σουφείρ*: same spelling in *Hesych.* and *Suda.* It varies in the Septuagint.

19 *ὑπογραφεύς*: *asekretis.*

20 *πρὸς μεταβολὴν*: We understand this to mean that Stephen borrowed Ignatios' Gospel in order to correct or collate a copy of his own. The normal term for collation was *ἀντιβολή*.

56.

On the office of *kourator* see the commentary on letter 3 above and, most recently, M. Kaplan, "Maisons impériales et fondations pieuses," *Byz* 61 (1991), 355–56; idem, *Les hommes et la terre,* 313 ff, who points out that a *μέγας κουράτωρ* first appears in the Life of St. Ioannikios by Sabas (c. 45, p. 371) "vers 830" ("vers 840" would be more accurate) and connects the creation of that office with the setting up of imperial *oikoi* (ta Eleutheriou, Mangana). There is still, however, no *μέγας κουράτωρ* in the *Taktikon Uspenskij* of 842–843. Konstantinakios appears to have been an imperial curator, either of a particular estate (or *oikos*) or the *μέγας κουράτωρ*. A curator Constantine, who was of iconophile persuasion, is the addressee of letter 233 of Theodore the Studite (date 815–818) and is probably also meant in letter 493.3 ff (*ἡγουμένῳ*); see Fatouros, 294*, n. 520.

On the *πράκτορες* who collected the tax, see Bury, *System,* 89.

The question naturally arises why Ignatios should have owed money to a *kourator.* Was it a personal loan or tax liability? If the latter, Ignatios was either subject to a hearth tax (*kapnikon*) or he owned land, but it is not clear why such land would have fallen within the competence of a *kourator,* who had charge of imperial, not private, property. A possible key to this problem may be provided by the enigmatic *ὁ τῆς κουρατωρίας* (*Taktikon Uspenskij* in Oikonomidès, *Listes,* 61.10), who, in the *Kletorologion* of Philotheos (ibid., 113.34), figures as a subordinate of the logothete of the Genikon, hence the official responsible for the collection of general taxes.

57.

Constantine was probably taken prisoner by the Arabs. The invasion of Asia Minor in 838, which culminated in the capture of Amorium, naturally comes to mind.

58.

The recipient of this letter may be identified with one of several officials by the same name occurring in the sources: a Leo imperial *protospatharios* and *protoasekretis* was the owner of seals nos. 3 and 4 and an imperial *protospatharios* and *asekretis* the owner of no. 64, whom Laurent, *Corpus,* V, 5–6, identifies with the official who read out the edict of Basil I during the last session of the Council of 869/870 (cf. Mansi, XVI, 186c) and the addressee of Ignatios. A Leo *protospatharios* also owned seals 2136, 2140, 2141, and 3139 in Zacos-Veglery, vol. I.2, 1181–84 and vol. I.3, 1756, dating from the ninth century.

A Leo *protospatharios* was also the addressee of Photios' letter 209 (ed. Laourdas and Westerink, II, 109), and seems to have been well versed in classical learning. Moreover, a Leo *asekretis* was, together with his brother Galaton, the recipient of letters 106, 219, and 232 in the same correspondence (ibid., I, 146; II, 126–30 and 148–49).

In 802 a Leo *spatharios,* hailing from Sicily, was sent to Charlemagne with an embassy aiming to reconcile the East and the West and came back with a marriage proposal of the Frankish ruler to Empress Irene; see Treadgold, *Revival,* 118–19 and note 157 (with references to the sources). In 811 he escorted a western embassy to the court of Nikephoros I; see *Annales regni Francorum,* ed. F. Kurze, MGH *SS. rerum Germanicarum* (1895), 133–34.

13 *θαλπικήν*: cf. VT 402.34.

The identity of the "common protector," clearly a person of considerable importance, is, unfortunately, left in the dark. One may think of the logothete Theoktistos. If, however, the addressee was the same as the aforementioned Sicilian Leo *spatharios,* one may also think of Patriarch Methodios.

26ff For the autobiographical statement, see Introduction, p. 20.

27 *'Ολυμπίαθεν*: surely not from Olympia, but from the Bithynian Olympus. The same incorrect form in VGD 63.18: *ἐκχωρήσας οὖν 'Ολυμπίαθεν* (*'Ολυμπόθεν* E), as pointed out by Ševčenko, "Hagiography," 123 and note 71.

60.

14–15 *ὃ μὴ γένοιτο*, etc.: We take this to mean "let not the slander, that is, the report of your transgression, be picked up by my enemies, although that may have happened as things come to be forgotten."

17–19 The enumeration of three types of meter (elegiac, hexameter, ionic) is merely for effect, and the third, in any case, was hardly ever used in the Byzantine period, except in the refrain of anacreontics. For the ionic *a maiore* (– – ∪ ∪) and *a minore* (∪ ∪ – –), see, for example, Hephaestion, *Encheiridion,* ed. Consbruch, 11–12, 35–39, and G. Choiroboskos' *Scholia,* ibid., 242–46.

61–63.

These three letters concern the same event, namely, the death of a relative of Nikephoros.

61.

1 *κνίζειν*: The context requires the meaning "to pick" rather than "to scratch." There is a long history of confusion about this rare verb, connected with its only occurrence in the Bible, Amos 7:14 (*κνίζειν συκάμινα*): cf. above, *ad* 25.9ff. The scratching applies not to mulberries (*συκάμινα*) but to Egyptian figs (*συκόμορα*),

as explained by Athenaeus, II.51b. These last the natives, *ἐπὶ βραχὺ κνίσαντες σιδηρίῳ*, leave on the plant and they ripen in three days. In commenting on Amos, Theodoret (PG 81, 1700 BC) notes that Aquila had misunderstood *κνίζων* as *ἐρευνῶν συκομόρους*, Theodotion as *χαρακῶν* (read *χαράσσων*), and Symmachus as *ἔχων συκομόρους*. The Septuagint, he concludes, must have meant *χαρακῶν* (read *χαράσσων*) or *συλλέγων*. Theodoret's explanation passed into the *Suda*, s.v.: Κνίζων· Ἀκύλας ἐρευνῶν, Θεόδοτος χαράσσων, Σύμμαχος ἔχων ἢ συλλέγων. Cf. also *Scholia in Greg. Naz.*, PG 36, 913C: *τὸ κατατέμνεσθαι κνίζεσθαι λαμβάνεται· Ὑπερείδης ἐχρήσατο τῇ λέξει.*

9ff Ignatios seems to have regarded grapes as a bad omen, whereas in Artemidorus, *Oneir.*, 1.73, they are a good sign even out of season, and betoken success with women (*τὰς διὰ γυναικῶν ἢ ἀπὸ γυναικῶν ὠφελείας σημαίνει· φανερὰς μὲν ἡ λευκή, λαθραίας δὲ ἡ μέλαινα*). Ignatios may have been familiar with one of the alphabetical dream books, for example, that of the "Patriarch Nikephoros," ed. F. Drexl, *Festgabe A. Ehrhard* (Bonn, 1922), 103.49, *βότρυας ἔσθειν ὀμβρικὴν δηλοῖ βλύσιν*; 114.276, *ῥᾶγας ἐσθίειν ὑετοῦ βλύσιν δόκα* (rain = tears). So also the dream book of the "Patriarch Germanos," ed. F. Drexl, Λαογραφία 7 (1923), 434.23. For other interpretations see "Patriarch Nikephoros," 109.159 (*κλῆμα κρατήσας ἐγκαλεῖσθαι προσδόκα*); "Patriarch Germanos," 440.118 (same); 443.169 (*ὄμφακες ὀπῶραί τε νόσον σημαίνει*); F. Drexl, "Das anonyme Traumbuch des cod. *Paris. gr.* 2511," Λαογραφία 8 (1925), 372.390 (*σταφυλὴν μέλαναν φαγεῖν θόρυβον καὶ μάχην βαρεῖαν σημαίνει*). For the alphabetical dream books, whose dating is rather uncertain, see S. M. Oberhelman, "Prolegomena to the Byzantine *Oneirokritika*," *Byz* 50 (1980), 487–503.

62.

1 Ἀδελφός: presumably the same who owned the Gospel book that is the subject of letters 53–54. He appears to have been a priest serving on the establishment of an unnamed bishop. If the text is sound, as its careful balance and the coupling of *ποσότης, ποιότης* suggest, *τῶν θείων λογίων* would seem to refer not to holy scripture (its normal meaning), but to the brother's holy utterances or teaching (sermons?).

9 Note that Ignatios, instead of *προλογίζω* as in letter 35.9, here uses *προλογέω*.

16ff Although the full text of the *Persica* was available at Constantinople in the ninth century (Photios, *Bibl.*, cod. 72), there can be no doubt that the passage given here has been borrowed from Demetrius, whose comment (§216) Ignatios paraphrases: <u>*Κατὰ μικρὸν*</u> *καὶ κατὰ βραχὺ* <u>*προϊὼν*</u> *μόλις, τὸ δὴ λεγόμενον, ἀπέρρηξεν αὐτό, μάλα ἠθικῶς καὶ ἐναργῶς τόν τε ἄγγελον ἐμφήνας* <u>*ἀκουσίως*</u> *ἀγγελοῦντα τὴν συμφορὰν καὶ τὴν μητέρα εἰς ἀγωνίαν ἐμβαλὼν καὶ τὸν*

ἀκούοντα. Demetrius uses this passage as an example of suspense in narrative rather than of delicacy, that is, in postponing the announcement of the bad news. Our text of Demetrius is to all intents and purposes based on Paris. gr. 1741 of the mid-tenth century: see stemma in P. Chiron's ed. (Paris, 1993), CXXXIV. We can now establish its existence at Constantinople a hundred years earlier. Cf. also letter 64.

90ff Note the characteristic admission of past sins.

63.

10 *παρουσιάσαι*: cf. letter 41.15.

15 *διὰ γράμματος* with reference to letter 62.

16 *τῶν ὑπηρετεῖν . . . εἰωθότων*: Note that, in spite of his alleged poverty, Ignatios had a number of servants.

64.

The subject of this unusually convoluted letter is not easy to determine. Nikephoros had sent his friend a composition or, perhaps, the draft of a composition (twice called *γράμμα*), which Ignatios proceeded to criticize on stylistic grounds and, in particular, for its excessive use of periods. Nikephoros defends himself against the charge: he had not introduced too many periods; besides, the frequency of periods does not detract from the plausibility or appropriateness of the ideas expressed. He goes on to state that a contorted style best suited the anger and hostility he felt. In other words, the *γράμμα* must have been a denunciation. But what of the crow and the dove, a title that suggests a fable? In the Aesopic corpus there exists a fable entitled *Περιστερὰ καὶ κορώνη*, which goes as follows: A dove, reared in a pigeon house, was boasting of having many chicks. A crow said to her: "The more children you have, the more servitude you will endure [or the more sorrows you are accumulating]." Moral: The most unfortunate among slaves are those who produce children during their servitude (*Corpus fabularum aesopicarum,* ed. A. Hausrath and H. Hunger, I.2 [Leipzig, 1959], no. 218). It is hard to see, however, what this has to do with the subject of the present letter. A more appropriate analogy may perhaps be found in *ep.* 381. 126 (ed. Fatouros, 525) of Theodore the Studite: *οὐ μίγει ὁ θεὸς κορώνην καὶ περιστεράν, ἀλλὰ τὰ ὅμοια τοῖς ὁμοίοις*, "God does not mate a crow with a dove, but like with like." This appears to have been a proverb (otherwise unattested) expressing incompatibility. We take the title, therefore, as a code name for a composition that pitted a metaphorical crow against a metaphorical dove. Using such a code name would have been particularly appropriate if Ignatios was indeed the author of the *tetrasticha* on themes borrowed from Babrius (above, p. 14). We may wonder whether the *γράμμα* had anything to do with the anti-iconoclastic tract referred to in letter 30, in which case the crow would have been the spokesman for Iconoclasm. The crow was seen not only as greedy, loquacious, and repulsive, but

also as impious: in Babr. 78 (cf. 152) it is represented as robbing the altars of the gods of their offerings. In dreams, crows denoted demons (*κόρακας ἰδὼν δαίμονας τούτους νόει*): F. Drexl, "Das Traumbuch des Patriarchen Nikephoros," *Festgabe A. Ehrhard,* 109.164.

19 *κολάζεται*: The reading is defensible, although one may envisage changing it to *κωλίζεται*, that is, divided into clauses, themselves the constituent parts of periods.

20f. Cf. Demetrius, 15: *τῶν τε τὰς πυκνὰς περιόδους λεγόντων οὐδ' αἱ κεφαλαὶ ῥᾳδίως ἑστῶσιν . . . οἵ τε ἀκούοντες ναυτιῶσι διὰ τὸ ἀπίθανον*. Note the succession of technical terms, *ἐνθύμημα* (on which see Demetrius, 30–33), *πιθανότης*, *ἰδέα λόγου* (quality, of which there were seven according to Hermogenes).

33 Aristides: Aelius Aristides, considered a model rhetorician.

44–46 For the distinction between *σολοικίζειν* and *βαρβαρίζειν*, see Prolegomena *τῶν Θεοδώρου ὀνοματικῶν κανόνων ἀπὸ φωνῆς* Γεωργίου Χοιροβοσκοῦ, *Gramm. gr.* IV.1, 103–4.

POSTSCRIPT

After we had completed the foregoing work I received an article by A. Kazhdan entitled "Letters of Ignatios the Deacon Once More: Some Doubts about Authorship," *JÖB* 44 (1994), 233–44.

Professor Kazhdan's "doubts," aimed at an article I published in 1981 (*TU* 125, 403–10) and based on Gedeon's faulty edition, may be summarized under the following headings:

1. He tentatively suggests that the collection of sixty-four letters may not be by the same author and that it falls into two separate groups, nos. 1–24 and 25–64, respectively, distinguished by subject matter, the status of the addressees, and the relative frequency of proverbs and classical quotations.

2. He is not convinced that the author (of Group 2) identifies himself as Ignatios in letter 38 or that he is named in the intitulation of no. 64.

3. He questions the view that the author of Group 1 was ever metropolitan of Nicaea. Had he been metropolitan, he would have had more exalted correspondents.

4. He is not satisfied that the author of Group 2 was confined to the monastery of Pikridion.

5. He doubts that the "sin" which the author repeatedly confesses was adherence to Iconoclasm and believes that it was instead his escape from a monastery.

Finally, setting aside his own misgivings about unitary authorship, Kazhdan sketches the single author's career as follows: "Possibly (but no more than that) he was a monk on Mt. Olympos at the beginning of his career, held a high administrative post in the church hierarchy (in Constantinople or Nicaea) in the 820s, left monastic ranks and became a scholar, and in the 840s compiled a book of proverbs."

Without going into undue detail, I would make the following rejoinder:

1. I see no reason to break up the collection into two groups, much less to suppose that they are by two different authors. It so happens that the episcopal letters, which deal with practical matters (taxation, discipline, etc.) are placed at the beginning of the collection, whereas the private letters are mostly, though not exclusively, in the latter two-thirds. Not surprisingly, Ignatios varies his style and his use of classical quotations and proverbs depending on the occasion and the cultural level of his correspondents. Even so, the most frequent correspondent of "Group 2," the chartophylax Nikephoros, appears three times in "Group 1" (letters 4, 14, 15) and nos. 14 and 15 are couched in exactly the same pedantically playful tone as the letters to him in "Group 2." Significant verbal parallels with the attested hagiographic works of Ignatios (confining ourselves to "Group 1") may be found in letters 1, 2, 3, 21,

and 24. The pun on the name of Galen in 21.46 recurs in 46.12. The same quotation from *Iliad* 1.524ff featuring the adjective *παλινάγρετος* appears at 23.9f and 39.4. *Νόστιμος δεξιά* in 13.9 is echoed by *νόστιμος φθογγή* in 51.3.

2. Kazhdan's interpretation of no. 38—that the Ignatios who is named in the text is a third person, to whom the author was supposed to deliver Nikephoros' letter—strikes me as impossible. The line of thought is as follows: "As I was reading your letter (to me), I had the impression of reading the Oration of Gregory Nazianzen addressed to his father. Gregory knew what kind of person he was addressing, but you, it seems, did not. You were writing to Ignatios, a dreadful sinner. That is the cause of my lateness in replying to you, viz. that, sinful as I was, I did not wish to importune you." The argument is far-fetched and "frigid," as the author himself admits. But what sense would it make if Ignatios was a third person? As for the expressions of self-abasement which Kazhdan finds excessively offensive (*ἔκτρωμα*, "unworthy of being called a Christian," "worthless"), they are quite characteristic of our author and can easily be paralleled elsewhere. To take one example at random, the author of the *Protokanonarion* calls himself *ἐκτρωμάτων ἔκτρωμα καὶ κύων οὐκ εὔχρηστος* (M. Arranz, *I penitenziali bizantini,* 44).

For the intitulation of no. 64, see above, p. 156.

3. It is abundantly clear to me that the author was for a time metropolitan of Nicaea (see esp. letters 8, 9, 10, 11, and 17). This point hardly requires demonstration.

4. The question of Pikridion is extraneous to that of authorship. Even so, I maintain my interpretation, which is based on direct allusions (*ta Pikridou,* Pikrides in letters 43–44) and repeated puns on the name of the monastery. Its situation at the far end of the Golden Horn accords with the expression *τὰ ἔσχατα τοῦ Βυζαντίου κόλπου* (46.17), which refers neither to the open sea nor to the gulf of Nicomedia. The comparison with Cadiz is a humorous exaggeration typical of our author. He was not in that monastery of his own free will, but had been placed there by Patriarch Methodios (no. 43), no doubt so as to purge his past misdemeanors. See our Introduction, p. 11f.

5. There is no evidence that the author ever absconded from a monastery or that he felt chronically guilty for having committed such an act. He did spend some time in a monastery on Olympus (quite possibly Antidion), but was lured away from it by an offer (of a teaching post?), made by some highly placed officials in the capital. However, he makes it plain (letter 31.34ff) that his "pact with the Devil"—the iconoclasts in my opinion—had occurred *earlier,* when he had first been ordained.

In sum, none of Kazhdan's objections carries conviction. The author of the Letters was a single person called Ignatios, who was active in the first half of the ninth century. He served as metropolitan of Nicaea. He was a teacher, a man of letters, and a classical scholar of some distinction. He had seriously compromised him-

self by serving the wrong party, surely the Iconoclasts. He could only have been the same as Ignatios the deacon of the *Suda* notice. I shall not elaborate here on a number of striking philological arguments that speak in the same sense.

Ignatios lived in a period of many tergiversations and compromises when one state-enforced ideology was replaced by another. His career, which we have not been able to elucidate entirely, was affected by changes "at the top." That is a situation to which Kazhdan ought to be sensitive *εἴπερ τις ἄλλος*.

ADDENDUM

A possible solution of the crux at **25.**10–11 might be: *εἰ καὶ μή . . . συκάμινα ὑπεραιωρούντων*, ⟨*καὶ*⟩ *τὸ διειδές*, etc. ("even if they were not laden with mulberries"). Cf. Libanius, *Or.* 1.53: *ἐγὼ δὲ ἐῴκειν ἀνδρὶ κατακεκλιμένῳ πρὸς πηγαῖς τε διαφανῶν ὑδάτων καὶ ὑπὸ δένδρων παντοίας ὑπεραιωρούντων χάριτας.*

C.M.

INDICES

I. INDEX NOMINUM

II. INDEX VERBORUM

* = hapax legomena
e coni. = vox e coniectura

III. FONTES

Bible

Other

INDEX

IV. INCIPITS